FEMALE PROSE WRITERS.

FEMALE PROSE WRITERS

E. F. Ellet

OF AMERICA

PHILADELPHIA

PUBLISHED BY E. H. BUTLER & CO.

THE

FEMALE PROSE WRITERS

OF

AMERICA.

WITH PORTRAITS, BIOGRAPHICAL NOTICES, AND
SPECIMENS OF THEIR WRITINGS.

BY JOHN S. HART, LL. D

FIFTH EDITION.

PHILADELPHIA:
PUBLISHED BY E. H. BUTLER & CO.
1866.

PREFACE.

THE unwonted favour extended to "Read's Female Poets of America," led to the belief that a work on the Female Prose Writers, constructed on a similar plan, would be not unacceptable to the public.

In the preparation of the biographies, much difficulty has been experienced. Few things are more intangible and elusive, than the biography of persons still living, and yet, in the case of those who have pleased us by their writings, few things are more interesting. It seems to be an instinctive desire of the human heart, on becoming acquainted with any work of genius, to know something of its author. Nor is this mere idle curiosity. It is a part of that homage, which every mind rightly constituted, spontaneously offers to whatever is great or good. This feeling of personal interest in an author who has moved us, is greatly increased where, as in the case of most female writers, the subjects of which they write, are chiefly of an emotional nature, carrying with them on every page the unmistakeable impress of personal sympathy, if not experience. Women, far more than men, write from the heart. Their own likes and dislikes, their feelings, opinions, tastes, and sympathies are so mixed up with those of their subject, that the interest of the reader is often enlisted quite as much for the writer, as for the hero, of a tale.

Knowing, therefore, how general is this desire to become acquainted with the personal history of authors, I have taken special pains, in preparing a work on the Female Prose Writers of the country, to make the biographical sketches as full and minute as circumstances would justify, or the writers themselves would allow. The work contains two charming pieces of autobiography, now appearing for the first time, from two long-established favourites with the public, Miss Leslie and Mrs. Gilman. In almost all cases the information has been obtained directly by correspondence with the authors, or their friends. Where this has failed, recourse has been had to the best printed authorities. The work, it is believed, will be found to contain an unusual amount of authentic information, and on subjects where authentic information is equally desirable and difficult to obtain.

The task of making selections has not been easy. I have studied, as far as possible, to select passages characteristic of the different styles of each writer, and at the same time to present the reader with an agreeable variety.

Those who have not been led professionally, or otherwise, to examine the subject particularly, will probably be surprised at the evidences of the rapid growth of literature, among American women, during the present generation. When Hannah Adams first published her "View of all Religions," so rare was the example of a woman who could write a book, that she was looked upon as one of the wonders of the Western world. Learned men of Europe sought her acquaintance, and entered into correspondence with her. Yet now, less than twenty years since the death of Hannah Adams, a ponderous volume of nearly five hundred pages is hardly sufficient to enrol the names of those of our female writers, who have already adorned the annals of literature by their prose writings, to say nothing of the numerous and not less distinguished sisterhood, who have limited themselves to poetry.

A word in regard to the portraits. These have been made, wherever it was practicable from original paintings or drawings.

NOTE TO THE REVISED EDITION.

In preparing this work for a new edition the biographies, in the case of authors still living, have been carefully revised and brought up to the present time, and a considerable number of new names has been introduced, increasing materially the size of the work.

September, 1854.

CONTENTS.

CONTENTS.

Emily C. Judson,

(FANNY FORRESTER)

PORTRAITS

EXECUTED IN THE FIRST STYLE OF ART.

C M Sedgwick

CATHERINE M. SEDGWICK.

Miss Sedgwick holds about the same position among our female prose writers that Cooper holds among American novelists. She was the first of her class whose writings became generally known, and the eminence universally conceded to her on account of priority, has been almost as generally granted on other grounds. Amid the throng of new competitors for public favour, who have entered the arena within the last few years, there is not one, probably, whose admirers would care to disturb the well-earned laurels of the author of "Redwood" and "Hope Leslie."

Miss Sedgwick is a native, and has been much of her life, a resident of Stockbridge, Massachusetts. Her father was the Hon. Theodore Sedgwick, of Stockbridge, who served his country with distinguished reputation in various stations, and particularly in the Congress of the United States, as Speaker of the House of Representatives, and afterwards as Senator, and who, at the time of his death, was one of the Judges of the Supreme Court of his own State. Her brothers, Henry and Theodore, have both been distinguished as lawyers and as political writers. On the mother's side, she is connected with the Dwight family, of whom her grandfather, Joseph Dwight, was a Brigadier-General in the Massachusetts Provincial forces, and actively engaged in the old French war of 1756.

Judge Sedgwick died in 1813, before his daughter had given any public demonstration of her abilities as a writer. Her talents seem to have been from the first justly appreciated by her brothers, whose judicious encouragement is very gracefully acknowledged in the preface to the new edition of her works, commenced by Mr. Putnam, in 1849.

Miss Sedgwick's first publication was "The New England Tale." The author informs us in the preface, that the story was commenced as a religious tract, and that it gradually grew in her hands, beyond the proper limits of such a work. Finding this to be the case, she abandoned all design of publication, but finished the tale for her own amusement. Once finished, however, the opinions and solicitations of her friends prevailed over her own earnest wishes, and the volume was given to the world in 1822. The original intention of this book led the author to give special prominence to topics of a questionable character for a professed novel, and the unfavourable portraiture which she gives, both here and elsewhere, of New England Puritanism, has naturally brought upon her some censure. The limited plan of the story did not give opportunity for the display of that extent and variety of power which appear in some of her later productions. Still it contains passages of stirring eloquence, as well as of deep tenderness, that will compare favourably with anything she has written. Perhaps the chief value of "The New England Tale" was its effect upon the author herself. Its publication broke the ice of diffidence and indifference, and launched her, under a strong wind, upon the broad sea of letters.

"Redwood" accordingly followed in 1824. It was received at once with a degree of favour that caused the author's name to be associated, and on equal terms, with that of Cooper, who was then at the height of his popularity; and, indeed, in a French translation of the book, which then appeared, Cooper is given on the title-page as the author. "Redwood" was also translated into the Italian, besides being reprinted in England.

The reputation of the author was confirmed and extended by the appearance, in 1827, of "Hope Leslie," the most decided favourite of all her novels. She has written other things since, that in the opinion of some of the critics are superior to either "Redwood" or "Hope Leslie." But, these later writings have had to jostle their way among a crowd of competitors, both domestic and foreign. Her earlier works stood alone, and "Hope Leslie," especially, became firmly associated in the public mind with the rising glories of a native literature. It was not only read with lively satisfaction, but familiarly quoted and applauded as a source of national pride.

Her subsequent novels followed at about uniform intervals; "Clarence, a Tale of our Own Times," in 1830; "Le Bossu," one of the Tales of the "Glauber Spa," in 1832; and "The Linwoods, or Sixty Years Since in America," in 1835.

In 1836, she commenced writing in quite a new vein, giving a series of illustrations of common life, called "The Poor Rich Man, and the Rich Poor Man." These were followed, in 1837, by "Live and Let Live," and afterwards by "Means and Ends," a "Love Token for Children," and "Stories for Young Persons."

In 1839, Miss Sedgwick went to Europe, and while there, wrote "Letters from Abroad to Kindred at Home." These were collected after her return, and published in two volumes.

She has written also a "Life of Lucretia M. Davidson," and has contributed numerous articles to the Annuals and the Magazines. Some of her recent publications have been prepared expressly for children and young persons. "The Boy of Mount Rhigi," published in 1848, is one of a series of tales projected for the purpose of diffusing sentiments of goodness among the young. The titles of some of her other small volumes are "Facts and Fancies," "Beatitudes and Pleasant Sundays," "Morals of Manners," "Wilton Harvey," "Home," "Louisa and her Cousins," "Lessons without Books," &c.

The quality of mind which is most apparent in Miss Sedgwick's writings is that of strength. The reader feels at every step that he has to do with a vigorous and active intellect. Another quality, resulting from this possession of power, is the entire absence of affectation of every kind. There is no straining for effect, no mere verbal prettinesses. The discourse proceeds with the utmost simplicity and directness, as though the author were more intent upon what she is saying than how she says it. And yet, the mountain springs of her own Housatonick do not send up a more limpid stream, than is the apparently spontaneous flow of her pure English. As a novelist, Miss Sedgwick has for the most part wisely chosen American subjects. The local traditions, scenery, manners, and costume, being thus entirely familiar, she has had greater freedom in the exercise of the creative faculty, on which, after all, real eminence in the art mainly depends. Her characters are conceived with distinctness, and are minutely individual and consistent, while her plot always shows a mind fertile in resources and a happy adaptation of means to ends.

MAGNETISM AMONG THE SHAKERS.

One of the brethren from a Shaker settlement in our neighbourhood, called on us the other day. I was staying with a friend, in whose atmosphere there is a moral power, analogous to some chemical test, which elicits from every form of humanity whatever of sweet and genial is in it. Our visiter was an old acquaintance, and an old member of his order, having joined it more than forty years ago with his wife and two children. I have known marked individuals among these people, and yet it surprises me when I see an original stamp of character, surviving the extinguishing monotony of life, or rather suspended animation among them. What God has impressed man cannot efface. To a child's eye, each leaf of a tree is like the other; to a philosopher's each has its distinctive mark. Our friend W.'s individuality might have struck a careless observer. He has nothing of the angular, crusty, silent aspect of most of his yea and nay brethren, who have a perfect conviction that they have dived to the bottom of the well and found the pearl truth, while all the rest of the world look upon them as at the bottom of a well indeed; but without the pearl, and with only so much light as may come in through the little aperture that communicates with the outward world. Neither are quite right; the Shaker has no monopoly of truth or holiness, but we believe he has enough of both to light a dusky path to heaven.

Friend Wilcox is a man of no pretension whatever; but content in conscious mediocrity. We were at dinner when he came in; but friend Wilcox is too childlike or too simple, to be disturbed by any observances of conventional politeness. He declined an invitation to dine, saying he had eaten and was not hungry, and seated himself in the corner, after depositing some apples on the table, of rare size and beauty. "I have brought some notions, too," he said, "for you, B——," and he took from his ample pocket his handkerchief, in which he had tied up a parcel of sugar plums and peppermints. B—— accepted them most affably, and without any apparent recoiling, shifted them from the old man's handkerchief to an empty plate beside her. "Half of them," he said, "remember, B——, are for ——. You both played and sung to me last summer—I don't forget it. She is a likely woman, and makes the music sound almost as good as when I was young!"

This was enthusiasm in the old Shaker; but to us it sounded strangely, who knew that she who had so kindly condescended to call back brother Wilcox's youth, had held crowds entranced by her genius. Brother Wilcox is a genial old man, and fifty years of abstinence from the world's pleasures has not made him forget or contemn them. He resembles the jolly friars in conventual life, who never resist, and are therefore allowed to go without bits or reins, and in a very easy harness. There is no galling in restraint where there is no desire for freedom. It is the "immortal longings" that make the friction in life. After dinner, B——, at brother Wilcox's request, sate down to the piano, and played for him the various tunes that were the favourites in rustic inland life forty years ago. First the Highland reel, then "Money Musk."

"I remember who I danced that with," he said, "Sophy Drury. The ball was held in the school room at Feeding fields. She is tight built, and cheeks as red as a rose (past and present were confounded in brother Wilcox's imagination). I went home with Sophy—it was as light as day, and near upon day—them was pleasant times!" concluded the old man, but without one sigh of regret, and with a gleam of light from his twinkling gray eye.

"There have been no such pleasant times since, brother Wilcox, has there?" asked B——, with assumed or real sympathy.

"I can't say that, it has been all along pleasant. I have had what others call crosses, but I don't look at them that way—what's the use?"

The old man's philosophy struck me. There was no record of a cross in his round jolly face. "Were you married," I asked, "when you joined the Shakers?"

"Oh, yes; I married at twenty—it's never too soon nor too late to do right, you know, and it was right for me to marry according to the light I had then. May be you think it was a cross to part from my wife—all men don't take it so—but I own I should; I liked Eunice. She is a peaceable woman, and we lived in unity, but it was rather hard times, and we felt a call to join the brethren, and so we walked out of the world together, and took our two children with us. In the society she was the first woman handy in all cases."

"And she is still with you?"

"No. Our girl took a notion and went off, and got married, and my wife went after her—that's natural for mothers, you know. I went after Eunice, and tried to persuade her to come back, and she felt so; but it's hard rooting out mother-love; it's planted deep, and spreads wide; so I left her to nature, and troubled myself no more about it, for what was the use? My son, too, took a liking to a young English girl that was one of our sisters—may be you have seen her?" We had all seen her and admired her fresh English beauty, and deplored her fate. "Well, she was a picture, and speaking after the manner of men, as good as she was handsome. They went off together; I could not much blame them, and I took no steps after them—for what was the use? But come, strike up again; play 'Haste to the wedding.'"

B——. obeyed, and our old friend sang or chanted a low accompaniment; in which the dancing tune and the Shaker nasal chant were ludicrously mingled. B—— played all his favourite airs, and then said, "You do love dancing, brother Wilcox?"

"Yes, to be sure—'praise him in the cymbals and dances!'"

"Oh, but I mean such dances as we have here. Would not you like, brother Wilcox, to come over and see us dance?"

"Why, may be I should."

"And would not you like to dance with one of our pretty young ladies, brother Wilcox?"

"May be I should;" the old man's face lit up joyously—but he smiled and shook his head, "they would not let me, they would not let me." Perhaps the old Shaker's imagination wandered for a moment from the very straight path of the brotherhood, but it was but a moment. His face reverted to its placid passiveness, and he said, "I am perfectly content. I have enough to eat and drink—everything good after its kind, too—good clothes to wear, a warm bed to sleep in, and just as much work as I like, and no more." "All this, and heaven too,"—of which the old man felt perfectly sure—was quite enough to fill the measure of a Shaker's desires.

"Now," said he, "you think so much of your dances, I wish you could see one of our young sisters dance, when we go up to Mount Holy. She has the whirling gift; she will spin round like a top, on one foot, for half an hour, all the while seeing visions, and receiving revelations."

This whirling is a recent gift of the Shakers. The few "world's folk" who have been permitted to see its exhibition, compare its subjects to the whirling Dervishes.

"Have you any other new inspiration?" I asked.

"Gifts, you mean? Oh, yes; we have *visionists*. It's a wonderful mystery to me. I never was much for looking into mysteries—they rather scare me!" Naturally enough, poor childlike old man!

"What, brother Wilcox," I asked, "do you mean by a visionist?"

"I can't exactly explain," he replied. "They see things that the natural eye can't see, and hear, and touch, and taste, with inward senses. As for me, I never had any kind of gifts, but a contented mind, and submission to those in authority, and I don't see at all into this new mystery. It makes me of a tremble when I think of it. I'll tell you how it acts. Last summer I was among our brethren in York State, and when I was coming away, I went down into the garden to take leave of a young brother there. He asked me if I would carry something for him to Vesta. Vesta is a young sister, famous for her spiritual gifts, whirling, &c." I could have added, for I had seen Vesta—for other less questionable gifts in the world's estimation—a light graceful figure, graceful even in the Shaker straight jacket, and a face like a young Sibyl's. "Well," continued brother Wilcox, "he put his hand in his pocket, as if to take out something, and then stretching it to me, he said, 'I want you to give this white pear to Vesta.' I felt to take something, though I saw nothing, and a sort of trickling heat ran through me; and even now, when I think of it, I have the same feeling, fainter, but the same. When I got home, I asked Vesta if she knew that young brother. 'Yea,' she said. I put my hand in my pocket and took it out again, to all earthly seeming as empty as it went in, and stretched it out to her. 'Oh, a white pear!' she said. As I hope for salvation, every word that I tell you is true," concluded the old man.

It was evident he believed every word of it to be true. The incredulous may imagine that there was some clandestine intercourse between the "young brother" and "young sister," and that simple old brother Wilcox was merely made the medium of a fact or sentiment, symbolized by the white pear. However that may be, it is certain that animal magnetism has penetrated into the cold and dark recesses of the Shakers.

THE SABBATH IN NEW ENGLAND.

The observance of the Sabbath began with the Puritans, as it still does with a great portion of their descendants, on Saturday night. At the going down of the sun on Saturday, all temporal affairs were suspended; and so zealously did our fathers maintain the letter, as well as the spirit of the law, that, according to a vulgar tradition in Connecticut, no beer was brewed in the latter part of the week, lest it should presume to *work* on Sunday.

It must be confessed, that the tendency of the age is to laxity; and so rapidly is the wholesome strictness of primitive times abating, that, should some antiquary, fifty years hence, in exploring his garret rubbish, chance to cast his eye on our humble pages, he may be surprised to learn, that, even now, the Sabbath is observed, in the interior of New England, with an almost Judaical severity.

On Saturday afternoon an uncommon bustle is apparent. The great class of procrastinators are hurrying to and fro to complete the lagging business of the week. The good mothers, like Burns's matron, are plying their needles, making "auld claes look amaist as weel's the new;" while the domestics, or help (we prefer the national descriptive term), are wielding, with might and main, their brooms and mops, to make all tidy for the Sabbath.

As the day declines, the hum of labour dies away, and, after the sun is set, perfect stillness reigns in every well-ordered household, and not a foot-fall is heard in the village street. It cannot be denied, that even the most scriptural, missing the excitement of their ordinary occupations, anticipate their usual bed-time. The obvious inference from this fact is skilfully avoided by certain ingenious reasoners, who allege, that the constitution was originally so organized as to require an extra quantity of sleep on every seventh night. We recommend it to the curious to inquire, how this peculiarity was adjusted, when the first day of the week was changed from Saturday to Sunday.

The Sabbath morning is as peaceful as the first hallowed day. Not a human sound is heard without the dwellings, and, but for the lowing of the herds, the crowing of the cocks, and the gossipping of the birds, animal life would seem to be extinct, till, at the bidding of the church-going bell, the old and young issue from their habitations, and, with solemn demeanour, bend their measured steps to the meeting-house;—the families of the minister, the squire, the doctor, the merchant, the modest gentry of the village, and the mechanic and labourer, all arrayed in their best, all meeting on even ground, and all with that consciousness of independence and equality, which breaks down the pride of the rich, and rescues the poor from servility, envy, and discontent. If a morning salutation is reciprocated, it is in a suppressed voice; and if, perchance, nature, in some reckless urchin, burst forth in laughter—"My dear, you forget it's Sunday," is the ever ready reproof.

Though every face wears a solemn aspect, yet we once chanced to see even a deacon's muscles relaxed by the wit of a neighbour, and heard him allege, in a half-deprecating, half-laughing voice, "The squire is so droll, that a body must laugh, though it be Sabbath-day."

Towards the close of the day (or to borrow a phrase descriptive of his feelings, who first used it), "when the Sabbath begins to abate," the children cluster about the windows. Their eyes wander from their catechism to the western sky, and, though it seems to them as if the sun would never disappear, his broad disk does slowly sink behind the mountain; and, while his last ray still lingers on the eastern summits, merry voices break forth, and the ground resounds with bounding footsteps. The village belle arrays herself for her twilight walk; the boys gather on "the green;" the lads and girls throng to the "singing-school;" while some coy maiden lingers at home, awaiting her expected suitor; and all enter upon the pleasures of the evening with as keen a relish as if the day had been a preparatory penance.

ELIZA LESLIE.

We have room but for a brief preface to the charming autobiography of Miss Leslie, furnished to our pages by her friend Mrs. Neal, for whom it was recently written. All that is of interest in the personal history of this gifted lady, she has herself supplied. It only remains for us to point out the characteristics of her style, and the great popularity of her writings, to which she so modestly alludes.

Her tales are perfect daguerreotypes of real life; their actors think, act, and speak for themselves; with a keen eye for the ludicrous, the failings of human nature are never portrayed but to warn the young and the thoughtless. Her writings are distinguished for vivacity and ease of expression, strong common sense, and right principle. In her juvenile tales the children are neither "good little girls, or bad little boys"—but *real* little boys and girls, who act and speak with all the genuineness and *naiveté* of childhood. No writer of fiction in our country has ever had a wider, or more interested circle of readers; and this is clearly proved by the increased circulation of all those publications in which her name has appeared as a regular contributor.

It will be noticed that the autobiography is dated from the United States Hotel, of this city, where Miss Leslie then resided—a charm to its social circle, and sought out by distinguished travellers of many nations, as well as those of our own land. Her conversation is quite equal to her writings, a circumstance by no means common with authors; her remarkable memory furnishing an inexhaustible store of anecdote, mingled with sprightly and original opinions. Her early life will be learned from the following sketch.

LETTER TO MRS. ALICE B. NEAL.

My Dear Friend:

I was born in Philadelphia, at the corner of Market and Second streets, on the 15th of November, 1787, and was baptized in Christ Church by Bishop White.

Both my parents were natives of Cecil county, Maryland, also the birth-place of my grandfathers and grandmothers on each side. My great-grandfather, Robert Leslie, was a Scotchman. He came to settle in America about the year 1745 or '46, and bought a farm on North-East River, nearly opposite to the insulated hill called Malden's Mountain. I have been at the place. My maternal great-grandfather was a Swede named Jansen. So I have no *English* blood in me.

My father was a man of considerable natural genius, and much self-taught knowledge; particularly in Natural Philosophy and in mechanics. He was also a good draughtsman, and a ready writer on scientific subjects; and in his familiar letters, and in his conversation, there was evidence of a most entertaining vein of humour, with extraordinary powers of description. He had an excellent ear for music; and, without any regular instruction, he played well on the flute and violin. I remember, at this day, many fine Scottish airs that I have never seen in print, and which my father had learned in his boyhood from his Scottish grandsire, who was a good singer. My mother was a handsome woman, of excellent sense, very amusing, and a first-rate housewife.

Soon after their marriage, my parents removed from Elkton to Philadelphia, where my father commenced business as a watchmaker. He had great success. Philadelphia was then the seat of the Federal Government; and he soon obtained the custom of the principal people in the place, including that of Washington, Franklin, and Jefferson, the two last becoming his warm personal friends. There is a free-masonry in men of genius which makes them find out each other immediately. It was by Mr. Jefferson's recommendation that my father was elected a member of the American Philosophical Society. To Dr. Franklin he suggested an improvement in lightning rods,—gilding the points to prevent their rusting,—that was immediately, and afterwards universally adopted.

Among my father's familiar visiters were Robert Patterson, long Professor of Mathematics at the University of Pennsylvania, and afterwards President of the Mint; Charles Wilson Peale, who painted the men of the revolution, and founded the noble museum called by his name; John Vaughan, and Matthew Carey.

When I was about five years old, my father went to England with the intention of engaging in the exportation of clocks and watches to Philadelphia, having recently taken into partnership Isaac Price, of this city. We arrived in London in June, 1793, after an old-fashioned voyage of six weeks. We lived in England about six years and a half, when the death of my father's partner in Philadelphia, obliged us to return home. An extraordinary circumstance compelled our ship to go into Lisbon, and detained us there from November till March; and we did not finish our voyage and arrive in Philadelphia till May. The winter we spent in our Lisbon lodgings was very uncomfortable, but very amusing.

After we came home, my father's health, which had long been precarious, declined rapidly; but he lived till 1803. My mother and her five children (of whom I was the eldest) were left in circumstances which rendered it necessary that she and myself should make immediate exertions for the support of those who were yet too young to assist themselves, as they did afterwards. Our difficulties we kept uncomplainingly to ourselves. We asked no assistance of our friends, we incurred no debts, and we lived on cheerfully, and with such moderate enjoyments as our means afforded; believing in the proverb, that "All work and no play make Jack a dull boy."

My two brothers were then, and still are, sources of happiness to the family. But they both left home at the age of sixteen. Charles, with an extraordinary genius for painting, went to London to cultivate it. He rapidly rose to the front rank of his profession, and maintains a high place among the great artists of Europe. He married in England, and still lives there.

My youngest brother, Thomas Jefferson Leslie, having passed

through the usual course of military education, in the West Point Academy, was commissioned in the Engineers, and, with the rank of Major, is still attached to the army. My sister, Anna Leslie, resides in New York. She has several times visited London, where she was instructed in painting by her brother Charles, and has been very successful in copying pictures. My youngest sister, Patty, became the wife of Henry C. Carey, and never in married life was happiness more perfect than theirs.

To return now to myself. Fortunate in being gifted with an extraordinary memory, I was never in childhood much troubled with long lessons to learn, or long exercises to write. My father thought I could acquire sufficient knowledge for a child by simply reading "*in* book," without making any great effort to learn things by heart. And as this is not the plan usually pursued at schools, I got nearly all my education at home. I had a French master, and a music master (both coming to give lessons at the house); my father himself taught me to write, and overlooked my drawing; and my mother was fully competent to instruct me in every sort of useful sewing. I went three months to school, merely to learn ornamental needle-work. All this was in London. We had a governess in the house for the younger children.

My chief delight was in reading and drawing. My first attempts at the latter were on my slate, and I was very happy when my father brought me one day a box of colours and a drawing-book, and showed me how to use them.

There was no restriction on my reading, except to prevent me from "reading my eyes out." And indeed they have never been very strong. At that time there were very few books written purposely for children. I believe I obtained all that were then to be found. But this catalogue being soon exhausted, and my appetite for reading being continually on the increase, I was fain to supply it with works that were considered beyond the capacity of early youth—a capacity which is too generally underrated. Children are often kept on bread and milk long after they are able to eat meat and potatoes. I could read at four years old, and before twelve I was familiar, among a multitude of other books, with Goldsmith's admirable Letters on England, and his histories of Rome and Greece (Robinson Crusoe and the Arabian Nights, of course), and I had gone through the six octavo volumes of the first edition of Cook's Voyages. I talked much of Tupia and Omiah, and Otoo and Terreoboo — Captain Cook I almost adored. Among our visiters in London, was a naval officer who had sailed with Cook on his last voyage, and had seen him killed at Owhyhee—I am sorry the name of that island has been changed to the unspellable and unpronounceable Hawaii. I was delighted when my father took me to the British Museum, to see the numerous curiosities brought from the South Sea by the great circumnavigator.

The "Elegant Extracts" made me acquainted with the best passages in the works of all the British writers who had flourished before the present century. From this book I first learned the beauties of Shakspeare. My chief novels were Miss Burney's, Mrs. Radcliffe's, and the Children of the Abbey.

Like most authors, I made my first attempts in *verse*. They were always songs, adapted to the popular airs of that time, the close of the last century. The subjects were chiefly soldiers, sailors, hunters, and nuns. I scribbled two or three in the pastoral line, but my father once pointing out to me a *real* shepherd, in a field somewhere in Kent, I made no farther attempt at Damons and Strephons, playing on lutes and wreathing their brows with roses. My songs were, of course, foolish enough; but in justice to myself I will say, that having a good ear, I was never guilty of a false quantity in any of my poetry—my lines never had a syllable too much or too little, and my rhymes always *did* rhyme. At thirteen or fourteen, I began to despise my own poetry, and destroyed all I had. I then, for many years, abandoned the dream of my childhood, the hope of one day seeing my name in print.

It was not till 1827 that I first ventured "to put out a book," and a most unparnassian one it was—"Seventy-five receipts for pastry, cakes, and sweetmeats." Truth was, I had a tolerable collection of receipts, taken by myself while a pupil of Mrs. Goodfellow's cooking school, in Philadelphia. I had so many applications from my friends for copies of these directions, that my brother suggested my getting rid of the inconvenience by giving them to the public in print. An offer was immediately made to me by Munroe & Francis, of Boston, to publish them on fair terms. The little volume had much success, and has gone through many editions. Mr. Francis being urgent that I should try my hand at a work of imagination, I wrote a series of juvenile stories, which I called the Mirror. It was well received, and was followed by several other story-books for youth—"The Young Americans," "Stories for Emma," "Stories for Adelaide," "Atlantic Tales," "Stories for Helen," "Birth-day Stories." Also, I compiled a little book called "The Wonderful Traveller," being an abridgment (with essential alterations) of Munchausen, Gulliver, and Sindbad. In 1831 Munroe and Francis published my "American Girls' Book," of which an edition is still printed every year. Many juvenile tales, written by me, are to be found in the annuals called the Pearl and the Violet.

I had but recently summoned courage to write fictions for grown people, when my story of Mrs. Washington Potts obtained a prize from Mr. Godey, of the Lady's Book. Subsequently I was allotted three other prizes successively, from different periodicals. I then withdrew from this sort of competition.

For several years I wrote an article every month for the Lady's Book, and for a short time I was a contributor to Graham's Magazine; and occasionally, I sent, by invitation, a contribution to the weekly papers. I was also editor of the Gift, an annual published by Carey & Hart; and of the Violet, a juvenile souvenir.

My only attempt at anything in the form of a novel, was "Amelia, or a Young Lady's Vicissitudes," first printed in the Lady's Book, and then in a small volume by itself. Could I begin anew my literary career, I would always write novels instead of short stories.

Three volumes of my tales were published by Carey & Lea, under the title of Pencil Sketches. Of these, there will soon be a new edition. In 1838 Lea & Blanchard printed a volume containing "Althea Vernon, or the Embroidered Handkerchief," and "Henrietta Harrison, or the Blue Cotton Umbrella." Several books of my fugitive stories have been published in pamphlet form, —the titles being "Kitty's Relations," "Leonilla Lynmore," "The Maid of Canal Street" (the *Maid* is a refined and accomplished young lady), and "The Dennings' and their Beaux." All my stories are of familiar life, and I have endeavoured to render their illustrations of character and manners, as entertaining and instructive as I could; trying always "to point a moral," as well as to "adorn a tale."

The works from which I have, as yet, derived the greatest pecuniary advantage, are my three books on domestic economy. The "Domestic Cookery Book," published in 1837, is now in the forty-first edition, no edition having been less than a thousand copies; and the sale increases every year. "The House Book" came out in 1840, and the "Lady's Receipt Book" in 1846. All have been successful, and profitable.

My two last stories are "Jernigan's Pa," published in the Saturday Gazette, and "The Baymounts," in the Saturday Evening Post.

I am now engaged on a life of John Fitch, for which I have been several years collecting information, from authentic sources. I hope soon to finish a work (undertaken by particular desire) for the benefit of young ladies, and to which I purpose giving the plain, simple title of "The Behaviour Book."*

U. S. Hotel, Phila., Aug. 1, 1851.

ELIZA LESLIE.

MRS. DERRINGTON'S RECEPTION DAY.

MAJOR FAYLAND had departed on his return home, and Sophia's tears had flowed fast and long on taking leave of her father. Mrs. Derrington reminded her, by way of consolation, that to-morrow was "reception day," and that she would then most probably see many of the ladies, who, having heard of Miss Fayland's arrival, had already left cards for her.

"And what, dear aunt, is exactly meant by a reception day?" inquired Sophia.

* The "Behaviour Book" has since been published.

"It is a convenient way of getting through our morning visiters," replied Mrs. Derrington. "We send round cards at the beginning of the season to notify our friends that we are at home on a certain morning, once a week. My day is Thursday. I sit in the drawing-room during several hours in a handsome demi-toilette. Full dress is not admissible, of course, at morning receptions. Any of my friends that wish to see me, take this opportunity; understanding that I receive calls at no other time. They are served with chocolate and other refreshments, brought in and handed to them soon after their arrival. They talk awhile, and then depart. There are some coming in, and some going out all the time, and no one staying long. The guests are chiefly ladies; few gentlemen of this city having leisure for morning visits. Still every gentleman manages to honour a lady's reception day with at least one call during the season. I suppose you had no such things as morning receptions at the fort?"

"No, indeed," replied Sophia; "our mornings were always fully occupied in attending to household affairs, and doing the sewing of the family. Afternoon was the time for walking or reading. But in the evening we all visited our neighbours, very much according to the fashion of Spanish tertulias."

Next morning, when dressed for the reception, and seated in the drawing-room to wait for the first arrivals, Mrs. Derrington said to Sophia—"We shall now hear all about Mrs. Cotterell's great party which came off last night. I have some curiosity to know what it was like, being her first since she came to live in this part of the town."

"Do you visit her?" asked Sophia.

"Oh, no—not yet—and probably I never may. I am waiting to see if the Cotterells succeed in getting into society."

"What society, dear aunt?" inquired Sophia.

"I see, Sophy, that I shall be much amused with your simplicity," replied Mrs. Derrington; "or rather with your extreme newness. In using the word *society*, we allude only to one class, and that of course is the very best."

"By that I understand a select circle of intellectual, refined,

5

agreeable, and every way excellent people," said Sophia; "men on whose integrity, and women on whose propriety there is not the slightest blemish, and who are admired for their talents, loved for their goodness, and esteemed for the truth and honour of their whole conduct."

"Stop—stop," interrupted Mrs. Derrington, "you are going quite too far. Can you suppose all this is required to get people into society, or to keep them there? The upper circles would be very small if nothing short of perfection could be admitted."

"What then, dear aunt, *are* the requisites?" asked Sophia. "Is genius one?"

"Genius? Oh, no, indeed. It is not that sort of thing that brings people into society. It is mostly considered rather a drawback. Mrs. Goldsworth actually shuns people of genius. Indeed, most of my friends rather avoid them. I have no acquaintance whatever with any man or woman of genius."

"I am sorry to hear it," said Sophia. "I had hoped while in New York to meet many of those gifted persons whose fame has spread throughout our country, whom I already know by reputation, and whom I have long been desirous of seeing or hearing."

"Oh, I suppose you mean lions," said Mrs. Derrington. "I can assure you that *I* patronize none of them; neither do any of my friends."

"I thought the lions were the patronizers," said Sophia, "and that their position gave them the exclusive power of selecting their associates, and deciding on whom to confer the honour of their acquaintance."

"Sophy—Sophy, you really make me laugh!" exclaimed her aunt. "What strange notions you have picked up, with your garrison education. Do not you know that people of genius seldom live in any sort of style, or keep carriages, or give balls? And they never make fortunes; unless they are foreign musicians or dancers, and I am not sure that the singing and dancing people *are* classed as geniuses. They are regarded as something much better."

"Is society composed entirely of people of fortune?"

"Oh, no; there are persons in the first circle who are not half so rich as many in the second, or even in the third, or fourth."

"Then, if society is not distinguished for pre-eminence in talent or wealth, the distinction must depend upon the transcendent goodness, and perfect respectability of those that belong to it."

"Why, not exactly. I confess that some of the persons in society have done very bad things; which after the first few days it is best to hush up, for the honour of our class. But then in certain respects society is most exemplary. We always subscribe to public charities. Charity is very fashionable, and so is church."

"And now," continued Sophia, "to return to the lady who gave the party last night. Is not she a good and respectable woman?"

"I never heard anything against her goodness, or her respectability."

"She must surely be a woman of education."

"Oh, yes; I went to school with her myself. But at all schools there is somewhat of a mixture. To give you Mrs. Cotterell's history—her father kept a large store in Broadway, and afterwards he got into the wholesale line, and went into Pearl street. Now, *my* father was a shipping merchant, and owned vessels, and my dear late husband was his junior partner. Mr. Cotterell made his money in some sort of manufacturing business, across the river. He died two years ago, and is said to have left his family very rich. Her daughter being now grown, Mrs. Cotterell has bought a house up here, in the best part of the town, and has come out quite in style, and been tolerably called on. Some went to see her out of curiosity, and some because they have an insatiable desire for enlarging their circle; some because they have a passion for new people; and some because they like to go to houses where everything is profuse and costly, as is generally the case with *parvenus*."

"And some, I hope," said Sophia, "because they really like Mrs. Cotterell for herself."

"She certainly is visited by a few very genteel people," continued Mrs. Derrington, "and that has encouraged her to attempt a party last night. But the Goldsworths, the Highburys, the Featherstones, and myself, are waiting to hear if she is well taken up; and, above all, if the Pelham Prideauxs have called on her. And besides, it may be well for *us* not to begin till she has gradually gotten rid of the people with whom she associated in her husband's time."

"Surely," said Sophia, "she cannot be expected to throw off her old friends?"

"Then she need not expect to gain new ones up here. We cannot mix with people from the unfashionable districts. Mrs. Cotterell may do as she pleases—but she must be select in her circle, if she wants the countenance of the Pelham Prideauxs."

"And who, dear aunt, are the Pelham Prideauxs?" inquired Sophia.

"Is it possible you never heard of them?" ejaculated Mrs. Derrington. "To know Mrs. Pelham Prideaux, to be seen at her house, or to have her seen at yours, is sufficient. It gives the stamp of high fashion at once."

"And for what reason?" persisted Sophia.

"Because she is Mrs. Pelham Prideaux," was the reply.

"What is her husband?" said Sophia.

"He is a gentleman who has always lived upon the fortune left him by his father, who inherited property from his father, and he from his. None of the Prideauxs have done anything for a hundred years. The great-grandfather was from England, and came over a gentleman."

"Surprising!" said Sophia, mischievously. "And whom have they to inherit all this glory?"

"An only daughter," replied Mrs. Derrington, "Maria Matilda Pelham Prideaux."

At this moment a carriage stopped at the door, and presently Mrs. Middleby was announced; and immediately after, two young ladies came in who were presented to Sophia as Miss Telford and Miss Ellen Telford. The conversation soon turned on Mrs. Cotterell's party. Mrs. Middleby had been there—the Miss Telfords had *not*, and were therefore anxious to "hear all about it."

"Really," said Mrs. Middleby, "it was just like all other parties, and like all others, it went off tolerably well. The company was such as one meets everywhere. The rooms were decorated in the usual style. Some of the people looked better than others, and some worse than others. The dressing was just as it always is at parties. The hostess and her daughter behaved as people generally do in their own houses; the company as guests usually behave in other people's houses. There was some conversation and some music. The supper was like all other suppers, and everybody went away about the usual hour."

Mrs. Derrington was dubious about taking up the Cotterells.

"I knew we should not get much information out of Mrs. Middleby," said Miss Telford to Sophia, after the lady had departed. "She always deals in generals, whatever may be the topic of conversation."

"Because her capacity of observation is so shallow that it cannot take in particulars," said Ellen Telford. "But here comes Mrs. Honeywood—we will stay to hear what she says."

Mrs. Honeywood was introduced, and on being applied to for her account of Mrs. Cotterell's party, she pronounced it every way charming; and told of some delightful people that were there. "Among them," said Mrs. Honeywood, "was the dashing widow, Mrs. Crandon, as elegant and as much admired as ever. She was certainly the belle of the room, and looked even more captivating than usual, with her blooming cheeks, and her magnificent dark eyes, and her rich and graceful ringlets, and her fine tall figure set off by her superb dress, giving her the air of a duchess, or a countess at least."

"What was her dress?" inquired Sophia.

"Oh, a beautiful glossy cherry-coloured velvet, trimmed with a profusion of rich black lace. On her head was an exquisite dress-hat of white satin and blond, with a splendid ostrich plume. She was surrounded by beaux all the evening. The gentlemen almost neglected the young ladies to crowd round the enchanting widow, particularly when she played on the harp and sung. They would scarcely allow her to quit the instrument; and, indeed, her music was truly divine. There was quite a scramble as to who should have the honour of leading Mrs. Crandon to the supper-table."

After some further encomiums on the widow Crandon, and on everything connected with the party, Mrs. Honeywood took her leave, first offering seats in her carriage to the Miss Telfords, which offer they accepted.

Mrs. Derrington rather thought she *would* take up the Cotterells.

The next of the guests who had been at Mrs. Cotterell's party was Miss Rodwell; and she also gave an account of it.

"Mrs. Cotterell and her daughter are rather presentable, and they *are* visited to a certain degree," said Miss Rodwell; "and I understand that Mrs. Pelham Prideaux *does* think of calling on them. I knew that I should meet many of my friends, or of course, I could not have risked being there myself. But, under any circumstances, the company was too large to be select. A party cannot be perfectly *comme il faut*, if it numbers more than fifty. Mrs. De Manchester says, that to have the very cream and flower of New York society, you must not go beyond thirty. And, though an Englishwoman, I think, in this respect, she is right."

"The Vanbombels, to be completely select, invite none but their own relations," observed Mrs. Derrington.

"And for the same reason," rejoined Miss Rodwell, "the Jenkses invite none of their relations at all. But who do you think I saw last evening? Poor Crandon, absolutely! I wonder where Mrs. Cotterell found her? She must have been invited out of compassion; it certainly could not have been for the purpose of ornamenting the rooms. Most likely Mrs. Cotterell did not know that poor Crandon is so entirely *passé*, nobody minds cutting her in the least. There she was rigged out in that old dingy red velvet that everybody was long ago tired of seeing. It is now quite too narrow for the fashion, and looks faded and threadbare. She had taken off the white satin trimming that graced it in its high and palmy days, and decorated it scantily with some coarse brownish, blackish lace. And then her head, with its forlorn ringlets, streaming down with the curl all out, and a queer yellowish-white hat, and a meagre old feather to match! Such an object! I wish you could have seen her! But, poor thing, I could not help pitying her, for she looked forlorn, and sat neglected, and was left to herself nearly all the time ; except when the Cotterells talked to her from a sense of duty. She played something on the harp, but nobody seemed to listen. I know that *I* was talking and laughing all the time, and so was every one else. People that are ill-dressed should never play on harps. It shows them too plainly."

"And they should never go to parties either," said Mrs. Derrington. "Poor Mrs. Crandon, has she no friend to tell her so? But I never heard before that she had fallen off in her costume. The report may be true that her husband's executors have defrauded her of a considerable portion of her property. However, I have lost sight of her for some years."

"And then," said Miss Rodwell, "it was not to be expected that Crandon could sustain herself permanently in society, considering how she first got into it."

"I own," resumed Mrs. Derrington, "I was rather surprised when I first saw Mrs. Crandon among us. It was, I believe, at Mrs. Hautonberg's famous thousand dollar party, the winter that it was fashionable to report the cost of those things; so that, before the end of the season, parties had mounted up to twice that sum. How did she happen to get there, for it was certainly the cause of her having a run all that season? I never exactly understood the circumstances."

"Oh, I can tell you all about it," replied Miss Rodwell; "for I was in the secret. Mr. Crandon was a jobber, and had realized a great deal of money, and they lived in a fine house, and made a show, but nobody in society ever thought of noticing them. After a while he took her to Europe, and they spent several months in Paris, and Mrs. Crandon (who, to do her justice, was then a very handsome woman) fitted herself out with a variety of elegant French dresses, made by an exquisite *artiste*, and with millinery equally *recherché*. When she came home, the fame of all these beautiful things spread beyond the limits of her own circle, and we were all dying to see them (particularly the evening costumes), and to borrow them as patterns for our own mantuamakers and milliners. But while she continued meandering about among her own set, we had no chance of seeing much more than the divine bonnet and pelisse she wore in Broadway, and they only whetted our appetite for the rest. So at one of Mrs. Hautonberg's *soirées*, a coterie of us got together and settled the plan. Mrs. Hautonberg at first made some difficulty, but finally came into it, and agreed to commence operations by calling on Mrs. Crandon next day, and afterwards sending her a note for her great thousand dollar party, which was then in agitation. So she called, and Mr. Hautonberg was prevailed on to leave his card for Mr. Crandon. They came to the party, thinking themselves highly honoured, and we all made a point of being introduced to the lady, and of showing her all possible civility, and of being delighted with her harp-playing. You may be sure, we took especial note of all the minutiæ of her dress, which I must say far excelled in taste and elegance every other in the room. And no wonder, when it was fresh from France. Well, to be brief, she was visited and invited, and well treated, and her beautiful things were borrowed for patterns; and by the time she had shown them all round at different parties, imitations of them were to be seen everywhere throughout our circle. The cherry-coloured velvet and the white hat and feathers were among them. She gave a grand party herself, and as it was at the close of the season, we all honoured her with our presence. Poor woman, she really thought all this was to last. Next winter we let her gently down; some dropping her entirely, and a few compassionately dragging on with her a while longer. Indeed, I still meet her at two or three houses."

"I am very sure she was never seen at Mrs. Pelham Prideaux," observed Mrs. Derrington, "even in the winter of her glory. Her French costumes would have been no inducement to Mrs. Prideaux, whose station has placed her far above dress."

"Mrs. Prideaux is rather too exclusive," said Miss Rodwell, somewhat piqued.

"What an enviable station!" remarked Sophia, "to be above dress."

"Well," continued Mrs. Derrington, to Miss Rodwell, "what did you think of Mrs. Cotterell's party arrangements? How were the decorations, the supper, and all things thereunto belonging?"

"Oh! just such as we always see in the best houses. All in scrupulous accordance with the usual routine. Yet somehow it seemed to me there was a sort of *parvenu* air throughout."

"What were the deficiencies?" asked Mrs. Derrington.

"Oh! no particular deficiencies, except a want of that indescribable something which can only be found in the mansions of people of birth."

Sophia could not forbear asking what in republican America could be meant by people of birth. To this Miss Rodwell vouchsafed no reply, but looking at her watch, said it was time to call for Mrs. De Manchester, whom she had promised to accompany to Stewart's. She then departed, leaving Mrs. Derrington impressed with a determination *not* to take up the Cotterells.

The stopping of a carriage was followed by the entrance of Mrs. and Miss Brockendale. The mother was a lady with an ever-varying countenance, and a restless eye. She was expensively dressed, but with her hair disordered, her bonnet crushed, her collar crooked, her gown rumpled, one end of her shawl trailing on the ground, and the other end scarcely reaching to her elbow. Her daughter's very handsome habiliments were arranged with the most scrupulous nicety; and the young lady had a steadfast eye, and a resolute and determined expression of face. All her features were regular, but the *tout ensemble* was not agreeable.

After some very desultory conversation, Mrs. Derrington recurred to the subject that was uppermost in her mind, Mrs. Cotterell's party; and on finding that the Brockendale ladies had been there, she again inquired about it; observing that much as she had heard of it in the course of the morning, she had still obtained no satisfactory account. "How did it really go off?" said she, addressing Miss Brockendale; but the mother eagerly answered, and the daughter finding herself anticipated, closed her lips firmly, and drew back her head.

"Oh! delightfully," exclaimed Mrs. Brockendale. "Everything was so elegant, and in such good taste, and on such a liberal scale."

"How were the rooms decorated?" asked Mrs. Derrington.

"Oh! superbly, with flowers wreathed around the columns."

"Mrs. Cotterell's rooms have no pillars," said Miss Brockendale, speaking very audibly and distinctly, and addressing herself to Sophia, near whom she was seated.

"Well, then," continued Mrs. Brockendale, "there were wreaths festooned along the walls. You cannot say there were no walls."

"There were no wreaths except those that ornamented the lamps and chandeliers," said Miss Brockendale, always addressing Sophia.

"Oh! yes, the flowers were all about the lights. That was what made them look so pretty. One thing I am certain of, the rooms were as light as day. There must have been five hundred candles."

"There was not one," said Miss Brockendale to Sophia. "The rooms were lighted entirely with gas."

"Well, it might have been a sort of gas. I declare my head is always so filled with things of importance, that I have no memory for trifles. This I know, that the furniture was all crimson velvet trimmed with gold-colour."

"It was blue satin damask trimmed with a rich dark brown," said her daughter to Miss Fayland.

"Well, the crimson might have had a bluish cast. I have certainly seen crimson velvet somewhere. The truth is, almost as soon as we entered, I saw my friend Mr. Weston, the member of Congress (either from Greenbay or Georgetown, I forget which), and so we got to talking about Texas and things; and that may be the reason I did not particularly notice the rooms. I almost got into a quarrel with this same Congress-man about the President, who, in spite of all I could say, Mr. Weston persisted in declaring has never threatened to go to war with Germany."

"Neither he has," said Miss Brockendale, this time directing her looks to her mother.

"Then he has set himself against railroads, or injured the crops, or invited over five hundred thousand millions of Irish."

"He has done none of these things."

"He has done something, I am very sure. Or, if he has not, some other President has. I never can remember how the Presidents go, and perhaps I am apt to mix them up, my head being always full of more important objects."

"I hear there was a very elegant supper," said Mrs. Derrington.

"I believe there was. But all supper-time I was talking about the tariff, and the theatre, and the army and navy, and I did not notice the things on the table. I rather think there was ice-cream, and I am almost positive there was jelly."

"Had you fine music?" inquired Mrs. Derrington.

"It seems to me that I heard music. But I was talking then to Mr. Van Valkenburgh, who has travelled over half the world; mostly pedestrian, poor fellow!"

"He is not a poor fellow," explained her daughter to Sophia. "He is a rich bachelor, and a great botanist, and entomologist; and when he rambles on foot, it is always from his own choice."

"Augustina," said her mother, "do not you recollect we met Mr. Van Valkenburgh somewhere in Europe, when we were travelling with the Tirealls?"

"I never was in Europe," said Augustina to Sophia. "When mamma went over, she took my sister Isabella, but left me a little girl at boarding-school."

"So you *were* a little girl at boarding-school; I remember all about it," continued Mrs. Brockendale, "and I did take Isabella, because she was grown up. She is married now, poor thing, to a man that never crossed the Atlantic, and never will, and so her going to Europe was of no manner of use. What a strange girl she was. When we were at Venice she *would* make me go everywhere in a boat—even to church."

"You could not well go in anything else," remarked Augustina.

"And then at Venice, she highly offended the showman by ringing the great bell of St. Mark's."

"She could not get at it."

"Then it must have been at St. Peter's, or St. Paul's, or else Notre Dame. Any how, she rung a bell."

"My sister has told me," said Augustina, turning to Sophia, "that coming out of a village church in England, she took a fancy to pull the bell-rope, as it hung invitingly down just within the entrance; and she greatly scandalized the beadle by doing so, still she pacified him with a shilling."

"But now about Mr. Van Valkenburgh," proceeded Mrs. Brockendale, "this I am certain of, that we met him on the Alps, and we were joined up there by old General Offenham and his son, who was much taken with Isabella. It might have been a match, for the young man will be a half-millionaire one of these days; but he has fits, and rolls down mountains. So that rather discouraged us, and we thought that nobody would ever marry him. Yet, afterwards, at Paris, or Portsmouth, or some of those places, the widow Sweeting snapped up young Offenham, for her third husband. So Isabella might as well have taken him."

"My sister," said Augustina, turning to Sophia, "is happily married to a man of sense, as well as of large fortune, and high respectability."

"Mr. Van Valkenburgh," pursued Mrs. Brockendale, "was telling how delightful he found the literary society of England. I wish I had been in it, when I was there. He became acquainted with them all. He even knew Shakspeare."

"His plays, of course," said Sophia.

"Oh! no, the man himself. Shakspeare called on him at the hotel, and left his card for Mr. Van Valkenburgh."

"Excuse me," said Sophia, "Shakspeare has been dead considerably more than two hundred years."

"Ah! my dear young lady," observed Mrs. Brockendale, "you know we must not believe all we hear."

"Mamma, we had best go home," said her daughter, who had sat for some moments looking as if too angry to speak, leaving to Sophia the explanation concerning Shakspeare.

Mrs. Brockendale rose to depart. "If it was not Shakspeare that called on him, it must have been Dr. Johnson," said she. "Any how, it was some great author."

They then took their leave, Miss Brockendale expressing a desire to be intimately acquainted with Miss Fayland.

"Poor Mrs. Brockendale," said Sophia, "her head reminds me

of a lumber room, where all sorts of things are stowed away in confusion. My father thinks that a defective memory is generally the result of careless or inattentive observation. But perhaps this lady was never gifted with the capacity of seeing or hearing things understandingly."

"I do not wonder that the daughter has no patience with the mother," said Mrs. Derrington. "However, they are persons of birth, and live handsomely, and are visited. We cannot expect everybody in society to be alike. Unfortunately, Mr. Brockendale, who was a most excellent man, and doated on his queer wife, and tried hard to improve her, died ten years ago, and since losing his guidance, she has talked more like a fool than ever. And worse than all, every article of her dress seems to be continually getting into disorder. As soon as her things are put right, they somehow get wrong again."

The next visiters were two rather insipid ladies, and soon after came in a remarkably handsome young man, dressed in the most perfect taste, but without the slightest approach to what is called dandyism. He had the *air distingué* which foreigners say is so rarely to be found among the citizens of America. He was introduced to Sophia as Mr. Percival Grafton, and she thought he looked exactly like a young nobleman, or rather as a young nobleman ought to look; and she was still more delighted with his conversation. After some very pleasant interchange of ideas with Miss Fayland, he inquired of Mrs. Derrington if she had yet become acquainted with Mrs. Cotterell and her charming daughter.

"Not yet," was the reply.

"Then let me advise you by all means not to delay what I am sure will afford much pleasure to yourself and Miss Fayland. The Cotterells are delightful people; polished, intelligent, natural, and having *l'air comme il faut*, as if it had been born with them. Miss Cotterell is one of the loveliest girls I have ever seen; and does infinite honour to the system on which her mother has educated her."

"Does she dress well?" inquired Mrs. Derrington.

"Charmingly," replied Grafton, "and she could not do otherwise, her good taste is so apparent in everything. She dresses well, talks well, moves well, and plays and sings delightfully. I heard her speaking French to Madame St. Ange, with the utmost fluency and elegance. She is really a most enchanting girl."

"You seem to be quite smitten!" remarked Miss Waterly, one of the insipid young ladies.

"Not to admire such a woman as Amelia Cotterell would evince the most pitiable insensibility to the united attractions of beauty, grace, and talent. But in the usual acceptation of the phrase, I am yet heart-whole. How long I may remain so is another question."

Mr. Grafton then turned the conversation to another subject, and he soon after took his leave.

"Do you know, Mrs. Derrington," said Miss Milkby, the other insipid young lady, "it's all over town already, that Percival Grafton is dying in love with Amelia Cotterell. So you must not believe exactly all he says about her and her mother."

"He really seems delirious," said Miss Waterly.

Mrs. Derrington became again dubious about taking up the Cotterells. But her doubts grew fainter as she reflected that Percival Grafton was a young gentleman of acknowledged taste in all that was refined and elegant; being himself a person of birth, and "to the manner born" of the best society. Even his grandfather was an eminent lawyer, and Percival himself had been inducted into that high profession.

While Mrs. Derrington sat, "pondering in her mind," Sophia was endeavouring to entertain the Misses Waterly and Milkby, when her aunt suddenly started from her reverie, and, her face beaming with ecstatic joy, advanced in eager *empressement* to receive a lady, whom the servant, throwing wide the door, announced as Mrs. Pelham Prideaux. When Mrs. Derrington had a little recovered the first excitement of this supreme felicity, and placed her high and mighty guest in the easiest fauteuil, and seen her well served with refreshments, she recollected to introduce her niece, Miss Sophia Fayland. The two other misses had long been within the pale of Mrs. Prideaux's notice, and they timidly hoped she was well.

This arbitress of fashion, this dictatress to society, was a woman of no particular face, no particular figure, no particular dress, and no particular conversation. But she was well aware of her position, and made use of it accordingly.

Mrs. Derrington, whose whole morning had been one long thought of the Cotterells (whenever she had a new thought she always pursued it *à l'outrance*), said something about the party of last night.

"Were you there?" asked Mrs. Prideaux.

"Oh! no. Mrs. Cotterell has come among us so lately, I know not exactly in what circle she will be."

"You might have gone," said Mrs. Prideaux, "I intend calling on her."

"Do you, indeed?" exclaimed Mrs. Derrington, with glad surprise. And Sophia's face brightened also; for she longed to know the Cotterells, and she saw that all doubt was now over.

Miss Waterly and Miss Milkby now acknowledged that they had both been at the party, and that they had liked it.

"When do you make this call, my dear Mrs. Prideaux?" asked Mrs. Derrington.

"I have not exactly determined on the day," was the reply.

"I hope Sophia and I may have the pleasure of meeting you there," said Mrs. Derrington. "When you have fixed on the exact time, will you let us know?"

"Certainly, I can have no objection," answered Mrs. Prideaux, graciously, "provided I know it myself.

"How kind you always are! It will be so delightful for us to be at Mrs. Cotterell's together. Will it not, Sophy?"

"On consideration, I cannot make this call before next week," said Mrs. Prideaux.

"Oh! never mind. Consult your own convenience. We will wait for you."

"Where does Mrs. Cotterell live?" inquired the great lady.

Miss Waterly and Miss Milkby now both spoke together, and designated the place. Mrs. Prideaux condescendingly thanked them for the information.

"Then," said she to Mrs. Derrington, "as I must pass your

door in going there, I may as well call for you in my carriage, whenever I *do* go."

Mrs. Derrington was too happy at this unexpected glory; and Miss Waterly and Miss Milkby too envious. All these young ladies could do was to accompany Mrs. Prideaux when she departed, and be seen leaving the door at the same time with her. She honoured them with a bow as they lingered on the door-step, when her no-particular-sort-of-carriage drove away. Unluckily, there chanced to be no spectators but a small party of German emigrants, and two schoolboys. Perhaps some of the neighbours might have been at their windows.

The following Monday and Tuesday, Mrs. Derrington and Miss Fayland stayed at home all the morning ready-dressed, waiting in vain for Mrs. Prideaux to call for them in her carriage.

"Surely," said Sophia, "she will apprise us in time?"

"She may probably not think of doing so," replied Mrs. Derrington.

At last on Wednesday the joyful moment arrived when the vehicle of Mrs. Pelham Prideaux, with that lady in it, drew up to the door of Mrs. Derrington, who ran down stairs, followed by her niece; and in a very short time they arrived at the mansion of the Cotterells.

CAROLINE GILMAN.

Of our living authoresses, no one has been so long before the public, and at the same time retained her place so entirely in its affections, as Mrs. Caroline Gilman.

Her first publications, which were poems, commenced as early as 1810. Among these, "Jephthah's Rash Vow," and "Jairus' Daughter," attracted particular attention. Her importance as a prose writer begins with the "Southern Rose Bud," a weekly juvenile paper, which she began in 1832, and continued for seven years. This miscellany contains a large amount of valuable literature, and is especially rich in contributions from Mrs. Gilman's own pen. Her other publications have been as follows: "Recollections of a New England Housekeeper," "Recollections of a Southern Matron" (both running through a large number of editions), "Ruth Raymond; or Love's Progress," "Poetry of Travelling," "Tales and Ballads," "Letters of Eliza Wilkinson" (written during the invasion of Charleston by the British), "Verses of a Lifetime," "The Oracles from the Poets," "The Sibyl," and several juvenile books now collected under the general title of "Mrs. Gilman's Gift."

The following graceful piece of autobiography will serve the double purpose of a specimen of her style, and a narrative of her life.

MY AUTOBIOGRAPHY.

I am asked for some "particulars of my literary and domestic life." It seems to me, and I suppose at first thought, it seems to all, a vain and awkward egotism to sit down and inform the world who you are. But if I, like the Petrarchs, and Byrons, and Hemanses, greater or less, have opened my heart to the public for a series of years, with all the pulses of love and hatred and sorrow so transparently unveiled, that the throbs may be almost counted, why should I or they feel embarrassed in responding to this request? Is there not some inconsistency in this shyness about autobiography?

I find myself, then, at nearly sixty years of age, somewhat of a patriarch in the line of American female authors—a kind of Past Master in the order.

The only interesting point connected with my birth, which took place October 8th, 1794, in Boston, Mass., is that I first saw the light where the Mariners' Church now stands, in the North Square. My father, Samuel Howard, was a shipwright, and to my fancy it seems fitting, that seamen should assemble on the former homestead of one who spent his manhood in planning and perfecting the noble fabrics which bear them over the waves. All the record I have of him is, that on every State thanksgiving day he spread a liberal table for the poor, and for this I honour his memory.

My mother descended from the family of the Brecks, a branch of which is located in Philadelphia as well as in Boston, and which, by those who love to look into such matters, is traced, as far as I have heard, to 1703 in America.

The families of 1794 in the North Square, have changed their abode. Our pastor, the good Dr. Lathrop, minister of the "Old North," then resided at the head of the Square—the Mays, Reveres, and others, being his neighbours.

It appears to me, that I remember my baptism on a cold November morning, in the aisle of the old North, and how my minister bent over me with one of the last bush-wigs of that century, and touched his finger to my befrilled little forehead: but being only five weeks old, and not a very precocious babe, I suppose I must have learned it from oral tradition.

I presume, also, I am under the same hallucination, when I see myself, at two years of age, sitting on a little elevated triangular seat, in the corner of the pew, with red morocco shoes, clasped with silver buckles, turning the movable balusters, which modern architects have so unkindly taken away from children in churches.

My father died before I was three years old, and was buried at Copp's Hill. A few years since, I made a pilgrimage to that most ancient and interesting cemetery, but its grass-covered vaults revealed to me nothing of him.

My mother, who was an enthusiastic lover of nature, retired into the country with her six children, and placing her boys at an academy at Woburn, resided with her girls in turn at Concord, Dedham, Watertown, and Cambridge, changing her residence, almost annually, until I was nearly ten years old, when she passed away, and I followed her to her resting-place, in the burial-ground at North Andrews.

Either childhood is not the thoughtless period for which it is famed, or my susceptibility to suffering was peculiar. I remember much physical pain. I recollect, and I think Bunyan, the author of Pilgrim's Progress, describes the same, a deep horror at darkness, a suffocation, a despair, a sense of injury when left alone at night, that has since made me tender to this mysterious trial of youth. I recollect also my indignation after a chastisement for breaking some china, and in consequence I have always been careful never to express anger at children or servants for a similar misfortune.

In contrast to this, come the memories of chasing butterflies, launching chips for boats on sunny rills, dressing dolls, embroidering the glowing sampler, and the soft maternal mesmerism of my mother's hand, when, with my head reclined on her knee, she smoothed my hair, and sang the fine old song

"In the downhill of life."

As Wordsworth says in his almost garrulous enthusiasm,

"Fair seed-time had my soul, and I grew up
Fostered alike by beauty and by fear;
Much favoured in my birth-place."

I say birth-place, for true life is not stamped on the spot where our eyes first open, but our mind-birth comes from the varied associations of childhood, and therefore may I trace to the wild influences of nature, particularly to those of sweet Auburn, now the Cambridge Cemetery, the formation of whatever I may possess of the poetical temperament. Residing just at its entrance, I passed long summer mornings making thrones and couches of moss, and listening to the robins and blackbirds.

The love of the beautiful then was quite undeveloped in social life; the dead reposed by roadside burial-grounds, the broken stone walls of which scarcely sheltered the sod which covered them. Now all is changed in those haunts of my childhood, and perchance costly monuments in Mount Auburn have risen on the sites of my moss-covered thrones.

Our residence was nearly opposite Governor Gerry's, and we were frequent visiters there. One evening I saw a small book on the recessed window-seat of their parlour. It was Gesner's Death of Abel; I opened it, spelt out its contents, and soon tears began to flow. Eager to finish it, and ashamed of emotions so novel, I screened my little self so as to allow the light to fall only on the book, and, while forgotten by the group, I also forgetting the music and mirth that surrounded me, I shed, at eight years, the first preluding tears over fictitious sorrow.

It was formerly the custom for countrypeople in Massachusetts to visit Boston in throngs on election day, and see the Governor sit in his chair on the Common. This pleasure was promised me, and a neighbouring farmer was good enough to offer to take me to my uncle Phillips's. Therefore, soon after sunrise, I was dressed in my best frock, and red shoes, and with a large peony called *a 'lection posey*, in one hand, and a quarter of a dollar in the other, I sprang with a merry heart into the chaise, my imagination teeming with soldiers, and sights, and sugar-plums, and a vague thought of something like a huge giant sitting in a big chair, overtopping everybody.

I was an incessant talker when travelling, therefore the time seemed short when I was landed, as I supposed, at my uncle Phillips's door, and the farmer drove away. But what was my distress at finding myself among strangers! Entirely ignorant of my uncle's direction, I knew not what to say. In vain a cluster of kind ladies tried to soothe and amuse me with promises of playmates and toys; a sense of utter loneliness and intrusion kept me in tears. At sunset, the good farmer returned for me, and I burst into a new agony of grief. I have never forgotten that long, long day with the kind and hospitable, but *wrong Phillipses.* If this statement should chance to be read and remembered by them, at this far interval, I beg them to receive the thanks which the timid child neglected to give to her stranger-friends.

I had seen scarcely any children's books except the Primer, and at the age of ten, no poetry adapted to my age; therefore, without presumption, I may claim some originality for an attempt at an acrostic on an infant, by the name of Howard, beginning—

How sweet is the half opened rose!
Oh, how sweet is the violet to view!
Who receives more pleasure from them,

Here it seems I broke down in the acrostic department, and went on—

Than the one who thinks them like you?
Yes, yes, you're a sweet little rose,
That will bloom like one awhile;
And then you will be like one still,
For I hope you will die without guile.

The Davidsons, at the same age, would, I suppose, have smiled at this poor rhyming, but in vindication of my ten-year-old-ship I must remark, that they were surrounded by the educational light of the present era, while I was in the dark age of 1805.

My education was exceedingly irregular, a perpetual passing from school to school, from my earliest memory. I drew a very little, and worked the "Babes in the Woods" on white satin, in floss silk; my teacher and my grandmother being the only persons who recognised in the remarkable individuals that issued from my hands a likeness to those innocent sufferers.

I taught myself the English guitar at the age of fifteen from hearing a schoolmate take lessons, and ambitiously made a tune, which I doubt if posterity will care to hear. By depriving myself of some luxuries, I purchased an instrument, over which my whole soul was poured in joy and sorrow for many years. A dear friend, who shared my desk at school, was kind enough to work out all my sums for me (there were no black-boards then), while I wrote a novel in a series of letters, under the euphonious name of Eugenia Fitz Allen. The consequence is that, so far as arithmetic is concerned, I have been subject to perpetual mortifications ever since, and shudder to this day when any one asks me how much is seven times nine.

I never could remember the multiplication table, and, to heap coals of fire on its head in revenge, set it to rhyme. I wrote my school themes in rhyme, and instead of following "Beauty soon decays," and "Cherish no ill designs," in B and C, I surprised my teacher with—

"Beauties in vain their pretty eyes may roll,
Charms strike the sight, but merit wins the soul."

My teacher, who at that period was more ambitious for me than I was for myself, initiated me into Latin, a great step for that period.

The desire to gratify a friend induced me to study Watts's Logic. I did commit it to memory conscientiously, but on what an ungenial soil it fell! I think, to this day, that science is the dryest of intellectual chips, and for sorry quibblings, and self-evident propositions, syllogisms are only equalled by legal instruments, for which, by the way, I have lately seen a call for reform. Spirits of Locke, and Brown, and Whewell, forgive me!

About this period I walked four miles a week to Boston to join a private class in French.

The religious feeling was always powerful within me. I remember, in girlhood, a passionate joy in lonely prayer, and a delicious elevation, when with upraised look, I trod my chamber floor, reciting or singing Watts's Sacred Lyrics. At sixteen I joined the Communion at the Episcopal Church in Cambridge.

At the age of eighteen I made another sacrifice in dress to purchase a Bible with a margin sufficiently large to enable me to insert a commentary. To this object I devoted several months of study, transferring to its pages my deliberate convictions.

I am glad to class myself with the few who first established the

Sabbath School and Benevolent Society at Watertown, and to say that I have endeavoured, under all circumstances, wherever my lot has fallen, to carry on the work of social love.

* * * *

At the age of sixteen I wrote "Jephthah's Rash Vow." I was gratified by the request of an introduction from Miss Hannah Adams, the erudite, the simple-minded, and gentle-mannered author of the History of Religions. After her warm expressions of praise for my verses, I said to her,

"Oh, Miss Adams, how strange to hear a lady, who knows so much, admire me!"

"My dear," replied she, with her little lisp, "my writings are merely compilations, Jephthah is your own."

This incident is a specimen of her habitual humility.

To show the change from that period, I will remark, that when I learned that my verses had been surreptitiously printed in a newspaper, I wept bitterly, and was as alarmed as if I had been detected in man's apparel.

The next effusion of mine was "Jairus's Daughter," which I inserted, by request, in the North American Review, then a miscellany.

A few years later I passed four winters at Savannah, and remember still vividly, the love and sympathy of that genial community.

In 1819 I married Samuel Gilman, and came to Charleston, S. C., where he was ordained pastor of the Unitarian Church

In 1832, I commenced editing the "Rose Bud," a hebdomadal, the first juvenile newspaper, if I mistake not, in the Union. Mrs. Child had led the way in her monthly miscellany, to my apprehension the most perfect work that has ever appeared for youth. The "Rose Bud" gradually unfolded through seven volumes, taking the title of the "Southern Rose," and being the vehicle of some rich literature and valuable criticism.

From this periodical I have reprinted, at various times, the following volumes:

"Recollections of a New England Housekeeper;" "Recollections of a Southern Matron;" "Ruth Raymond, or Love's Progress;" "Poetry of Travelling in the United States;" "Tales and Ballads;" "Verses of a Lifetime;" "Letters of Eliza Wilkinson, during the invasion of Charleston;" also, several volumes for youth, now collected in one, and recently republished, as "Mrs. Gilman's Gift Book." The "Poetry of Travelling," "Tales and Ballads," and "Eliza Wilkinson," are out of print. The "Oracles from the Poets," and "The Sibyl," which occupied me two years, are of later date.

On the publication of the "Recollections of a New England Housekeeper," I received thanks and congratulations from every quarter, and I attribute its popularity to the fact that it was the first attempt, in that particular mode, to enter into the recesses of American homes and hearths, the first unveiling of what I may call the altar of the Lares in our *cuisine*.

I feel proud to say that a chapter in that work was among the first heralds of the temperance movement, a cause to which I shall cheerfully give my later as well as earlier powers.

My ambition has never been to write a novel; in the "Matron" and "Clarissa Packard" it will be seen that the story is a mere hinge for facts.

After the publication of the "Poetry of Travelling," I opened to a notice in a review, and was greeted with, "This affectation will never do." It has amused me since to notice how "this affectation" has spread, until we have now the "Poetry of Teaching," and the "Poetry of Science."

My only pride is in my books for children. I have never thought myself a poet, only a versifier; but I know that I have learned the way to youthful hearts, and I think I have originated several styles of writing for them.

While dwelling on the above sketch, I have discovered the difficulty of autobiography, in the impossibility of referring to one's faults. Perchance were I to detail the personal mistakes and deficiencies of this long era, I might lose the sympathy which may have followed me thus far.

I have purposely confined myself to my earlier recollections, believing that my writings will be the best exponents of my views and experience. It would be wrong, however, for me not to allude, in passing, to one subject which has had a potent influence on my life, I refer to mesmerism or magnetic psychology. This seemingly mysterious agency, has given me relief when other human aid was hopeless, and I believe it is destined, when calmly investigated, to be, under Providence, a great remedial agent for mankind.

My Heavenly Father has called me to varied trials of joy and sorrow. I trust they have all drawn me nearer to him. I have resided in Charleston thirty-one years, and shall probably make my final resting-place in the beautiful cemetery adjoining my husband's church—the church of my faith and my love.

8

SARAH HALL.

Mrs. Sarah Hall was born at Philadelphia, on the 30th of October, 1761. She was the daughter of the Rev. John Ewing, D. D., who was, for many years, Provost of the University of Pennsylvania, and Pastor of the First Presbyterian Church at Philadelphia.

At the close of the revolutionary war, in the year 1782, she was married to Mr. John Hall, the son of a wealthy planter in Maryland, to which State they removed. Here she spent about eight years, upon a beautiful farm on the shores of the Susquehanna.

After their residence in Maryland, they settled in Philadelphia, where Mr. Hall filled successively the offices of Secretary of the Land Office, and Marshal of the United States, for the district of Pennsylvania.

Endowed by nature with an ardent and lively imagination, she early imbibed a keen relish for the beauties of polite literature, and devoted much time to such pursuits. When the Port Folio was established by Mr. Dennie in 1800, she was one of the literary circle with which he associated, and to whose pens that work was indebted for its celebrity. Elegant literature was at that time more successfully cultivated in Philadelphia than in any other part of the Union. To write for the Port Folio was considered no small honour; and to be among the favoured correspondents of Mr. Dennie was a distinction of some value, where the competitors were so numerous, and so highly gifted; for among the writers for that work were a number of gentlemen, who have since filled the most exalted stations in the Federal government, both in the cabinet and on the bench, and who have, in various ways, reaped the highest rewards of patriotism and genius. Some of the most sprightly essays and pointed criticisms which appeared in this paper, at the time of its greatest popularity, were from the pen of Mrs. Hall.

When the Port Folio came under the direction of her son, the late

John E. Hall, who was its editor for more than ten years, she continually aided him in his labours; and her contributions may readily be distinguished, as well by their vivacity as the classic purity of their diction. She survived but a few months that son, her eldest, whom she had encouraged and assisted in his various literary labours for about twenty years.

She studied the Scriptures with diligence, and with prayer—with all the humility of Christian zeal, and with all the scholar's thirst for acquisition. By such means, and with the aid of the best libraries of Philadelphia, Mrs. Hall became as eminent for scholarship in this department of learning, as she was for wit, vivacity, and genius. Her "Conversations on the Bible," a practical and useful book, which is now extensively known, affords ample testimony that her memory is entitled to this praise. This work is written with that ease and simplicity which belongs to true genius; and contains a fund of information which could only have been collected by diligent research and mature thought. While engaged in this undertaking, she began the study of the Hebrew language, to enable herself to make the necessary critical researches, and is supposed to have made a considerable proficiency in the attainment of that dialect. When it is stated that she commenced the authorship of this work after she had passed the age of fifty, she being then the mother of eleven children, and that during her whole life she was eminently distinguished for her industry, economy, and exact attention to all the duties belonging to her station, as the head of a numerous family, it will be seen that she was no ordinary woman.

In a letter to a literary lady in Scotland, written in 1821, Mrs. Hall makes the following remarks, which will be read with interest, as showing the change that has taken place in the last thirty years:—

"Your flattering inquiry about my 'literary career' may be answered in a word—literature has no career in America. It is like wine, which, we are told, must cross the ocean to make it good. We are a business-doing, money-making people. And as for us poor females, the blessed tree of liberty has produced such an exuberant crop of bad servants, that we have no eye nor ear for anything but work. We are the most devoted wives, and mothers, and housekeepers, but every moment given to a book is stolen. The first edition of the 'Conversations' astonished me by its rapid sale; for I declare to you, truly, that I promised myself nothing. Should the second do tolerably, I may perhaps be tempted to accede to the intimations of good-natured people, by continuing the history to the end of the Acts of the Apostles. Yet I found so much difficulty in the performance of the first part, having never written one hour without the interruption of company, or business, that I sent off my last sheet as peevishly as Johnson sent the *Finis* of his Dictionary to Miller, almost vowing that I would never again touch a pen. In fact it is, as your friend says, 'She that would be a notable housewife, must be that thing only.'"

Mrs. Hall died at Philadelphia, on the 8th of April, 1830, aged 69. A small volume containing selections from her miscellaneous writings, was published in Philadelphia, in 1833. This volume contains also an interesting sketch of her life, from which the present notice has been compiled.

ON FASHION.*

Most of you writers have leaped into the censor's throne without leave or license; where you were no sooner seated, than, with the impudence one might expect from such conduct, you have railed, with all the severity of satire and indecency of invective, against our folly, frivolity, forwardness, fondness of dress, and so forth. You can't conceive what a latitude is assumed by the witlings of the day, from the encouragement of such pens as yours. Those well dressed young gentlemen who will lay awake whole nights in carving the fashion of a new doublet, and who will criticise Cooper without knowing whether Shakspeare wrote dramas or epic poems, these wiseacres, I say, saunter along Chestnut street, when the sun shines, and amuse themselves with sneers against our sex: and in nothing are we so much the object of their ridicule as in our devotion to fashion, on whose shrine, according to these modern peripatetics, we sacrifice our time, our understanding, and our health. We have freedom of the press, and freedom of religion, and why should we not enjoy a freedom of fashions?

What do these sapient gentlemen wish? Would they have a dress for females established by an act of the Assembly, as doctors of medicine have been created in Maryland? "Which dress aforesaid of the aforegoing figure, colour, materials, fashion, cut, make, &c., &c., all the good spinsters of Pennsylvania shall wear on all highdays and holydays, under pain, &c., &c." Horrible idea!—What! tie us down to the dull routine of the same looks, the same bonnets, the same cloaks?—take from us that charming diversity, that delightful variety, which blooms in endless succession from

* Addressed to the editor of the Port Folio.

week to week, with the changes of the season—make us tedious to ourselves, and as unalterable and unattractable as an old family picture—or, what is equally out of the way and insipid, an old bachelor?

But some of you talk of simplicity of nature; of the gewgaw display of artificial charms; of deforming nature's works by the cumbrous and fantastical embellishments of art, and so forth. Now, sir, if you will pin the argument to this point, I shall have you in my power. Pray, is nature simple, barren, tedious, dull, uniform, and unadorned, as you old bachelors would have us to be, so that we might resemble your comfortless selves? Look at the trees—are they all of the same colour? Are they not so infinitely diversified in their shades and figures, that, to an observing eye, no two are alike? Observe the flowers of the garden: do they exhibit the same sombre or pale hue? Do they present that dull simplicity which you recommend to us, whom your gravest philosophers allow to be the handsomest beings in creation? Do you prefer the dull uniformity of a trench of upright celery to the variegated bed of tulips? What would you say of a project to reform nature by robbing the rose of its blushing red, the lily of its silver lustre, the tulip of its gorgeous streaks, the violet of its regal purple, and allowing the vale to be no longer embroidered with their various beauties? or, of blotting from the clouds their golden streaks and dazzling silver, and banishing the gay rainbow from the heavens, because they are not of a uniform colour, but for ever present more varieties and combinations of beauties than our imagination can paint? And shall not we, who, at least, pretended to have the use of reason, imitate nature? Nature has given for our use the varied dyes of the mineral and vegetable world, which enables us almost to vie with her own splendid gilding. Nature made us to be various, changeable, inconstant, many-coloured, whimsical, fickle, and fond of show, if you please, and we follow nature with the greatest fidelity when, like her, we use her beauties to delight the eye, gratify the taste, and employ the mind in the harmonious varieties of colour and figure to which fashion resorts, and to which we devote so much time and thought.

Attend to these hints, and if you properly digest them, I have no doubt so sensible a head as you possess must nod assent to my doctrine, that to study fashion and be in the fashion is the most delightful and harmless employment upon earth, and the most conformable to our nature. But if you should be so perverse as to think erroneously on this subject, I advise you to keep your observations to yourselves, or to have your heads well wigged the next time you come amongst us.

MARIA J. McINTOSH.

THE Clan McIntosh is noted in the earliest Scottish history, as the leader in that powerful confederation known as the "Clan Chattan." This family sided with the House of Stuart in its last bold struggle for power, and the whole Highland force fought under its chief, Brigadier-General McIntosh. With the defeat of the Royal family came the fall of their faithful adherents and the confiscation of their property, and with one hundred and thirty Highlanders John Moore McIntosh accompanied Oglethorpe's party, and settled on the Altamaha, in the district now called Georgia.

The refugees carried with them their love for the fatherland, even to the names of its hills. They styled their frontier settlement New Inverness (since changed to Darien), and the county received, and still bears, the family title of McIntosh.

Colonel William McIntosh, the son of the first settler of the new colony, fought as an officer in the French and Indian wars, and died leaving a son, Major Lachlan McIntosh, who was the father of Miss Maria J. McIntosh, the subject of the present sketch.

By profession Major McIntosh was a lawyer, but with the readiness that warlike times engender, at the first summons of danger he stepped from the legal arena to the higher joust of arms, and fought, with the enthusiastic bravery of a Georgian, through all our revolutionary war.

After the establishment of peace, he married a lady of the name of Maxwell, and settled in the practice of his original profession at Sunbury, Liberty county, in Georgia, where our author was born, and where she has spent the greater portion of her life. This place is a small village, beautifully situated at the head of a bay or long arm of the sea. The house of Major McIntosh, a stately old mansion, commanded a full view of the water, and was, for years, a general gathering place for the gentry of the State. The remembrance of the generous hospitality, the faithful adherents, the graceful society, and the luxuriant beauty of nature, that displayed itself in and around the family mansion, is still vivid in the mind of our author, and shows itself in the fervour and enthusiasm of her language whenever she writes of the land of her childhood.

But the day-dreams of youth were doomed to a sad awakening. Miss McIntosh, in 1835, after the death of both her parents, left her native place, to reside in New York, with her brother, James M. McIntosh, of the U. S. Navy. With the change of residence came a change in the investment of her property. The whole of her ample fortune was vested in New York securities just previous to the commercial crisis of 1837, and the lady awoke from her life-dream of prosperity, in a strange city, totally bankrupt.

By an almost universal dispensation of Providence, which ordains means of defence and support to the frailest formations of animal life, with the new station was granted a power of protection, of pleasure, and maintenance, unknown to the old. New feelings and powers came into life. Thoughts that before were scarcely formed, emotions that had never shaped themselves into expression, and ideas of the high and holy in life that had been hitherto unshapen dreams, suddenly attained a new growth. Hundreds of seeds that hung to the tree when all was sunshine, were shaken to the earth by the blast, watered by the storm, and sprung to a vigorous life,—until, at length, the very subject of misfortune blessed the evil that had been changed to a good.

Two years after the loss of her property, Miss McIntosh had completed her first work. It was a small volume, bearing the marks of a feeling, religious mind, and written in a pleasant, easy style, suitable for children, and bore the name of "Blind Alice." Few understand how sensitive is the anxiety of an author for his first work; how he watches and criticises his dearest feelings when they are about to be made public property, and issued to the world. But how much greater must be this sensitive dread when the author is a woman, and a woman whose whole life and support are cast upon that one venture? Miss McIntosh had all these feelings to struggle with in their fullest strength, and, in addition, the delays and difficulty of obtaining the publication of a work by a new writer.

For two years the manuscript of this little volume lay alternately on the table of the author and the desk of the publishers. At last, in January, 1841, it was issued anonymously. Its success was complete; and with renewed energy the author resumed her pen, and finished and published in the summer of the same year "Jessie Graham," a work of similar size and character. "Florence Arnott," "Grace and Clara," and "Ellen Leslie," all of the same class and style, appeared successively, and at short intervals, the last being published in 1843.

These works are generally known as "Aunt Kitty's Tales." They were received with constantly increasing favour, as the series proceeded, and, after its completion, were republished in England with equal success. They are simple tales of American life, told in graceful and easy language, and conveying a moral of beauty and truthfulness that wins love at once for the fictitious character and the earnest writer. And many a girl, as she read of the charities of Harriet Armand, of Florence Arnott, and O'Donnel's cabin, and the nameless Aunt Kitty, who wove a moral with every pleasure, a lesson with every pain, and yet so secretly that the moral could never be discerned until the tale was finished, has laid down the book and wondered involuntarily who Aunt Kitty was.

In the year 1844, she published "Conquest and Self-Conquest." This work is a fiction of a more ambitious character than any of the preceding. The hero of the tale is a midshipman. One portion of the plot is laid in the city of Washington, another at sea. It is then changed to New Orleans, and again to the piratical island of Barrataria, on the Mexican coast. Frederick Stanley, the hero of the story, is made to feel that constant self-restraint will win self-command, and that self-command will rule his own happiness and the minds of others.

In the same year appeared another work, entitled "Woman an Enigma." It is an attempt to delineate, not moral principles that are well defined—not religious duties, that are more easily depicted,—but the ideal, impalpable, varied substance of woman's love. This seems to be a natural ground for a woman to walk upon, when she has passed the days of girlhood, and arrived at such a distance from the scenes of passion as to look back with a calm eye on the rush of early thoughts.

The first scene in the book opens in a convent in France, where young Louise waits upon a dying friend, and the friend leaves her ward as an affianced bride to her brother the Marquis de Montrevel.

The vow is duly made between the noble courtier and the trusting girl. Louise is then taken to Paris by her parents and introduced to fashionable life, with its gayeties and seductions, while the Marquis is absent on his estate. The new world of pleasure has no effect on the novice, save so far as it stimulates her to excel, that she may the more be worthy of her husband's love. She mingles in the dance to acquire grace, in the soirée to learn the styles of fashionable life, and all for the sole purpose of being the better fitted to be the companion and wife of the high-born noble. But the absent lover hears of the brilliant life of his so lately timid girl, and, ignorant of the mighty power that impels her to the exertion, scorns the supposed fickleness that will give to the many that regard which he had hoped to have won exclusively for himself.

Then follows the portion of the work which most perfectly pictures the author's ideas of womanly love. The earnest toil of the poor girl for the pittance of a smile that is rewarded by jealousy with a sneer; the pas sionate pride of the wounded woman; the stern sorrow of the man; and the final separation, are all true to the instincts of that master feeling.

In 1845 appeared "Praise and Principle," a fiction of the same size as the others just named.

The hero of the story, Frank Derwent, is an American boy, and is introduced to the reader while at school. Having opposed the only relative from whom he could hope for assistance, he is thrown wholly on his own resources, yet by the practice of great self-denial, by energy and a steadfast adherence to truth and principle, he attains a high position as a lawyer, and wins the hand of a fair client. The foil to this character is Charles Ellersby, a school companion of Frank, and a competitor in the world for the praise that Frank discards for the love of the dearer right. Frank wins an honourable name and a happy home, while Charles receives, as a bitter punishment, that curse of manhood, a fashionable wife,—and in a year is ruined.

The whole work illustrates the character of the author, and her constant endeavour to write not so much for the entertaining powers of the tale, which is for a day, but for the inner life of the story, that is for all time.

"The Cousins, a Tale for Children," appeared in the latter part of the same year. This is a small volume, originally written for the series of Aunt Kitty's Tales, and is the last work she has published anonymously.

In 1847 was published "Two Lives, or To Seem and To Be," and with it the name of the author, who had heretofore been unknown. The success that it won may be estimated by the fact that it reached a seventh edition in less than four years from its publication.

In 1848 appeared "Charms and Counter Charms," a work of greater size and power, and on the most complex plan of any yet written by our author, and received with so great favour that it is already in its sixth edition.

Miss McIntosh here treats of a subject that woman seldom attempts, and the bearing of the tale is mainly on this one point; namely, the necessity of the marriage rite not only for the morality of the world, but for the morality, happiness, fidelity, and religion of any individual couple.

Euston Hastings, the hero of the story, a man somewhat on the Byronic order, whom having seen you turn to watch, scarcely knowing why, wins and marries a young girl, Evelyn Beresford. But before the marriage, and after the engagement, he declares to the lady of his choice his so-called liberal views on the subject of religion.

Not long after, Evelyn asks his views in regard to marriage. The man of the world replies—

"I answer you with confidence, because I know such is your affinity with purity and truth that you will discover them though they appear in forms which conventionalism condemns; and I tell you, without disguise, that I think marriage unnecessary to secure fidelity where there is love, and insufficient where there is not."

The revelation of these foreign views does not, however, alienate the woman's heart, and Evelyn is soon bound to her husband by the same holy tie that he considers a conventional form.

But Evelyn loves with an engrossing passion. With a strength of feeling that demands a constant return, and forgetting the hundred busy things that are calling a man's attention, she desires the whole time and the whole regard of her husband. This selfish, exclusive love, that engrosses the object when it submits, and is thrown into tears when it does not, produces the natural consequence on a man to whom perfect liberty is an accustomed right. He seeks for the regard from other persons, that he cannot receive from his wife without a corresponding degree of personal restraint. This course produces another result on Evelyn. She feels wounded and becomes reproachful. Instead of winning him by her charms, she calls him to her society by her rights, until at last Hastings leaves secretly for Europe, and is supposed to have fled with another lady.

The blow falls fearfully heavy on one who had centred all her hopes on the dearly loved husband. Everything is forgotten but her mighty love, and she follows him abroad. A valet accompanying leads her to Rome, and she meets her husband. He is struck by her devotion and the wrongs he has inflicted. He provides her a house and every attention, and they reside together happy in the love which is at last acknowledged above every consideration. But it is on this express agreement, that Evelyn is not to be known as his wife, and that they are free to part whenever either of them may choose

Hastings has the liberty that he so dearly prizes, and Evelyn the lover that she regards more than all the world besides.

It is in this curious relation that the power of the writer is shown. The most ultra case is taken upon which to build the argument for the holiness of the marriage vow. A couple are duly married, and the marriage is made public to all the world. They live together for a time as man and wife. They are then separated, and again come together, not on the strength of the marriage rite, but only on their mutual love.

But does this new connexion produce the happiness to Evelyn that she desired? On the contrary, there is a sense of wrong in every pleasure. She looks at her own servants with shame; and between her and every flower she touches, every kiss she receives, there seems springing up a consciousness of guilt.

At length Hastings is taken ill, and lies unconscious and near to death. Evelyn watches by his side with tearful fidelity, and in agony unutterable attends him through the dark valley, and at length sees him recovering with feelings of joy and childlike happiness

But during the course of this weary illness she is made to see the right way, even amid the darkness by which she had been surrounded; and, when Euston has entirely recovered his health, the young wife (though not bearing the name) flees from the land of beauty and the arms of her lover, in an agony of grief, leaving behind her a letter explaining her change of views and the cause of her departure.

At last, in the heart of the sensualist, the crust of worldliness is broken up, and Euston Hastings, roused from the guilty selfishness of his life, leaves Rome to seek the wife who has become his all in the world. He finds her in Paris, and they are again united, not by any wavering passion, but by holy love and marriage, which gains a higher beauty from the bright faith and exquisite description of its able defender.

This work, though a high-wrought tale of fiction, is really an exposition of a theory, and the reader frequently finds himself laying aside the book to think, Is that theory really so? and finds that, after the work is read, there is within the fabric of the tale, an inner temple of right and wrong; where are engraven principles that are pervading his memory equally, if not more constantly than the plot of the fiction.

"Woman in America; Her Work, and Her Reward," the next succeeding work in the order of publication, was issued in 1850.

In this work, the author, apparently tired of teaching only through the medium of fiction, addresses herself to reasoning and argument. We read here the ideas of a religious woman, well acquainted with all grades of American society, in an earnest tone denouncing the servility of her sex to the rules of fashion and opinion, modelled not by the good and virtuous, but by the dissolute societies of Europe, and forms and customs made not after the model of a naturally honest, or even commonly virtuous ideal, but copied after the ever-changing, never true, leader of some dissolute or fastidious circle—it may be, of Paris, it may be of Saratoga. The only rule that seems never to have changed among this class of people until it is embodied in their social confession of faith, is "Money makes the man." Mahogany doors are closed to the gentleman-labourer, that are flung wide open to him when he becomes a millionaire. White arms are outstretched to the banker, that are folded in scorn to his approach when a bankrupt.

"Evenings at Donaldson Manor," was published as a Christmas Guest, for the year 1850. It was a collection of tales that had appeared at different times in periodicals.

"The Lofty and the Lowly" is a work depicting the peculiar social characteristics of the North and South. It has had a large sale both in this country and in England.

It will be obvious to every one familiar with Miss McIntosh's writings, that she is a delineator entirely of mental life. The physical in man, in animals, and nature, is never used, except so far as is necessary to bring forward the mind and its virtues, desires, and principles. She has apparently excluded from her attention everything that did not absolutely belong to the moral life.

Evelyn and Euston live for a summer on the Tiber, but not the faintest tinge of the golden light, or the lowest breath of Roman air enters within their villa.

Hubert Falconer builds a frontier cottage, but he never listens to the sighing pines, or treads the forest aisles.

Mind, with its wayward creeds, can alone be seen in the Imperial City. Feelings right and wrong, and promises faithfully performed are more to Hubert than earth, air, and water, and the glorious gifts of Nature.

Miss McIntosh still further restricts herself in the characters of her story, and selects only the common ones of practical life, as though anxious for the principle alone, and the fiction that would draw the reader off from the moral is discarded. In her quiet pages there never occurs the extreme either of character or passion. It is only the system of conscience—the rule of right—the law of God that is portrayed, and the more marked characters, or the more easily delineated beauties and feelings of life and nature are left with a rigid indifference to those whose design is to please more than to instruct.

Yet the reader, when the book is closed, and he has gone to his daily labour, or mingles in social life, finds lingering in his brain, and warming in his heart, a true principle of honour and love that is constantly contrasting itself with the hollow forms by which he is surrounded, and if he fails to bear himself up to that high ideal of principle which he feels to be true, he still walks a little nearer to his conscience and his God, and long after the volume is returned to the shelf and forgotten, a kindly benediction is given to the noble influence it incited.

And thus will it be with the author that lives in the hearts and not in the fancy of her readers. And long after she is returned to the great library of the unforgotten dead, a blessing wide as her language, and fervent as devotion, will descend on the delineator of those lofty principles that showed the nobleness of simplicity, and the holiness of truth.

The extract which follows is from "Woman in America."

TWO PORTRAITS.

PERMIT us, in illustration of our subject, to place before you a sketch of an American woman of fashion as she is and as she might be—as she *must* be to accomplish the task we would appoint her. Examine with a careful eye "the counterfeit presentment" of these two widely differing characters, and choose the model on which you will form yourselves. And first, by a few strokes of this magic wand—the pen—we will conjure within the charmed circle of your vision, the woman of fashion as she is.

Flirtilla,—for so noted a character must not want a name,—may well be pronounced a favourite of nature and of fortune. To the first she owed a pleasing person and a mind which offered no unapt soil for cultivation; by favour of the last, she was born the heiress to wealth and to those advantages which wealth unquestionably confers. Her childhood was carefully sequestered from all *vulgar* influences, and she was early taught, that to be a *little lady* was her highest possible attainment. At six years old she astonished the *élite* assembled in her father's halls, and even dazzled the larger assemblages of Saratoga by her grace in dancing and by the ease with which she conversed in French, which, as it was the language of her nursery attendants, had been a second mother-tongue to her. At the fashionable boarding-school, at which her education was, in common parlance, *completed*, she distanced all competitors for the prizes in modern languages, dancing, and music; and acquired so much acquaintance with geography and history as would secure her from mistaking Prussia for Persia, or imagining that Lord Wellington had conquered Julius Cæsar—in other words, so much knowledge of them as would guard her from betraying her ignorance. To these acquirements she added a slight smattering of various natural sciences. All these accomplishments had nearly been lost to the world, by her forming an attachment for one of fine qualities, personal and mental, who was entirely destitute of fortune. From the fatal mistake of yielding to such an attachment she was preserved by a judicious mother, who placed before her in vivid contrast the commanding position in which she would be placed as the wife of Mr. A—, with his houses and lands, his bank stock and magnificent equipage; and the *médiocre* station she would occupy as Mrs. B—, a station to which one of her aspiring mind could not readily succumb, even though she found herself there in company with one of the most interesting and agreeable of men. Relinquishing with a sigh the gratification of the last sentiment that bound her to nature and to rational life, she magnanimously sacrificed her inclinations to her sense of duty, and became Mrs. A—. From this time her course has been undisturbed by one faltering feeling, one wavering thought. She has visited London and Paris, only that she might assure herself that her house possessed all which was considered essential to a *genteel* establishment in the first, and that her toilette was the most *recherché* that could be obtained in the last. She laughs at the very idea of wearing anything made in America, and is exceedingly merry over the portraitures of Yankee character and Yankee life occasionally to be met in the pages of foreign tourists, or to be seen personated in foreign theatres. She complains much of the promiscuous character of American society, dances in no set but her own, and, in order to secure her exclusiveness from contact with the common herd, moves about from one point of fashionable life to another. attended by the same satellites, to whom she is the great centre of attraction. Her manners, like her dresses, are imported from Paris. She talks and laughs very loudly at all public places, lectures, concerts, and the like; and has sometimes, even in the house of God, expressed audibly her assent with or dissent from the preacher, that she may prove herself entirely free from that shockingly American *mauvaise honte*, which she supposes to be all that keeps other women silent. Any gentleman desiring admission to her circle must produce authentic credentials that he has been abroad, must wear his mustaches after the latest Parisian cut, must interlard his bad English with worse French, and must be familiar with the names and histories of the latest ballet-dancers and opera-singers who have created a fever of excitement abroad. To foreigners she is particularly gracious, and nothing throws her into such a fervour of activity as the arrival in the country of an English Lord, a German Baron, or a French or Italian Count. To draw such a character within her circle she thinks no effort too great, no sacrifice of feeling too humiliating.

It may be objected that all our descriptions of the fashionable woman as she is, relates to externals; that of the essential character, the inner life, we have, in truth, said nothing. But what can we do? So far as we have yet been able to discover, this class is destitute of any inner life. Those who compose it live for the world and in the world. Home is with them only the place in which they receive visits. We acknowledge that few in our country have yet attained to so perfect a development of fashionable character as we have here described; but to some it is already an attainment; to many—we fear to *most*, young women of what are called the higher classes in our large cities—it is an aim.

Nobler spirits there are, indeed, among us, of every age and every class, and from these we must choose our example of a woman of fashion as she should be. On her, too, we will bestow a name—a name associated with all gentle and benignant influences—the name of her who in her shaded retreats received of old the ruler of earth's proudest empire, that she might "breathe off with the holy air" of her pure affection, "that dust o' the heart" caught from contact with coarser spirits. So have we dreamed of EGERIA, and Egeria shall be the name of our heroine. Heroine indeed, for heroic must be her life. With eyes uplifted to a protecting Heaven, she must walk the narrow path of right,—a precipice on either hand,—never submitting, in her lowliness of soul, to the encroachments of the selfish, and eager, and clamorous crowd,—never bowing her own native nobility to the dictation of those whom the world styles great. "Resisting the proud, but giving grace unto the humble," if we may without irreverence appropriate to a mortal, words descriptive of Him whose unapproachable and glorious holiness we are exhorted to imitate.

In society, Egeria is more desirous to please than to shine. Her associates are selected mainly for their personal qualities, and if she is peculiarly attentive and deferential to any class, it is to those unfortunates whom poverty, the accidents of birth, or the false arrangements of society, have divorced from a sphere for which their refinement of taste and manner and their intellectual cultivation had fitted them. Admission to her society is sought as a distinction, because it is known that it must be purchased by something more than a graceful address, a well-curled mustache, or the reputation of a travelled man. At her entertainments, you will often meet some whom you will meet nowhere else; some promising young artist, yet unknown to fame,—some who, once standing in the sunshine of fortune, were well known to many whose vision is too imperfect for the recognition of features over which adversity has thrown its shadow. The influence of Egeria is felt through the whole circle of her acquaintance;—she encourages the young to high aims and persevering efforts,—she brightens the fading light of the aged, but above all is she a blessing and a glory within her own home. Her husband cannot look on her—to borrow Longfellow's beautiful thought—without "reading in the serene expression of her face, the Divine beatitude, 'Blessed are the pure in heart.'" Her children revere her as the earthly type of perfect love. They learn, even more from her example than her precept, that they are to live not to themselves, but to their fellow-creatures, and to God in them. She has so cultivated their taste for all which is beautiful and noble, that they cannot but desire to conform themselves to such models. She has taught them to love their country and devote themselves to its advancement—not because it excels all others, but because it is that to which God in his providence united them, and whose advancement and true interest they are bound to seek by all just and Christian methods. In a word, she has never forgotten that they are immortal and responsible beings, and this thought has reappeared in every impression she has stamped upon their minds.

But it is her conduct towards those in a social position inferior to her own, which individualizes most strongly the character of Egeria. Remembering that there are none who may not, under our free institutions, attain to positions of influence and responsibility, she endeavours, in all her intercourse with them, to awaken their self-respect and desire for improvement, and she is ever ready to aid them in the attainment of that desire, and thus to fit them for the performance of those duties that may devolve on them.

"Are you not afraid that Bridget will leave you, if, by your lessons, you fit her for some higher position?" asked a lady, on finding her teaching embroidery to a servant who had shown much aptitude for it.

"If Bridget can advance her interest by leaving me, she shall have my cheerful consent to go. God forbid that I should stand in the way of good to any fellow-creature—above all, to one whom, by placing her under my temporary protection, he has made it especially my duty to serve," was her reply.

In the general ignorance and vice of the population daily pouring into our country from foreign lands, Egeria finds new reason for activity, in the moral and intellectual advancement of all who are brought within her sphere of influence.

Egeria has been accused of being ambitious for her children. "I am ambitious for them," she replies; "ambitious that they should occupy stations that may be as a vantage-ground from which to act for the public good."

Notwithstanding this ambition, she has, to the astonishment of many in her own circle, consented that one of her sons should devote himself to mechanical pursuits. She was at first pitied for this, as a mortification to which she must certainly have been compelled, by her husband's singular notions, to submit.

"You mistake," said Egeria, to one who delicately expressed this pity to her; "my son's choice of a trade had my hearty concurrence. I was prepared for it by the whole bias of his mind from childhood. He will excel in the career he has chosen, I have no doubt; for he has abilities equal to either of his brothers, and he loves the object to which he has devoted them. As a lawyer or physician he would, probably, have but added one to the number of *médiocre* practitioners who lounge through life with no higher aim than their own maintenance."

"But then," it was objected, "he would not have sacrificed his position in society."

Egeria is human, and the sudden flush of indignation must have crimsoned the mother's brow at this; and somewhat of scorn, we doubt not, was in the smile that curled her lip as she replied, "My son can afford to lose the acquaintance of those who cannot appreciate the true nobility and independence of spirit which have made him choose a position offering, as he believes, the highest means of development for his own peculiar powers, and the greatest probability, therefore, of his becoming useful to others."

Our sketches are finished—imperfect sketches we acknowledge them. It would have been a labour of love to have rendered the last complete—to have followed the steps of Egeria—the Christian gentlewoman—through at least one day of her life; to have shown her embellishing her social circle by her graces of manner and charms of conversation, and to have accompanied her from the saloons which she thus adorned, to more humble abodes. In these abodes she was ever a welcome as well as an honoured guest, for she bore thither a respectful consideration for their inmates, which is a rarer and more coveted gift to the poor than any wealth can purchase. Having done this, we would have liked to glance at her in the tranquil evening of a life well spent, and to contrast her then with Flirtilla—old beyond the power of rouge, false teeth, and false hair, to disguise—still running through a round of pleasures that have ceased to charm,—regretting the past, dissatisfied with the present, and dreading the future,—alternately courting and abusing the world, which has grown weary of her.

LYDIA H. SIGOURNEY.

JUSTICE has hardly been done to Mrs. Sigourney as a prose writer. She has been so long, and is so familiarly, quoted as a poet, that the public has in a measure forgotten that her indefatigable pen has sent forth almost a volume of prose yearly for more than a quarter of a century—that her prose works already issued number, in fact, twenty-five volumes, averaging more than two hundred pages each, and some of them having gone through not less than twenty editions. She has indeed produced no one work of a thrilling or startling character, wherewith to electrify the public mind. Her writings have been more like the dew than the lightning. Yet the dew, it is well to remember, is not only one of the most beneficent, but one of the most powerful of nature's agents—far more potential in grand results than its brilliant rival. When account shall be made of the various agencies, moral and intellectual, that have moulded the American mind and heart during the first half of the nineteenth century, few names will be honoured with a larger credit than that of Lydia H. Sigourney.

The maiden name of this most excellent woman was Lydia Howard Huntley. She was born in Norwich, Connecticut, September 1st, 1791, of Ezekiel and Sophia Huntley. Being an only child, she was nurtured with special care and tenderness. But, besides the ordinary parental influences, there was in her early history one circumstance of a peculiar character, which, according to the testimony of those who have known her best, contributed largely and most happily to the moulding of her mind and heart. I refer to the remarkable intimacy that existed between the gifted and brilliant young girl and an aged lady that lived for many years in the same house. Madam Jerusha Lathrop, the lady referred to, was the relict of Dr. Daniel Lathrop, and daughter of Joseph Talcot, one of the Provincial Governors of Connecticut.

Madam Lathrop is reported to have been gifted by nature with strong powers of mind, and a dignity of person and manners that commanded universal respect. Her character had been matured by intercourse with men of powerful intellect, and by participation in great and trying scenes. The parents of Mrs. Sigourney resided under the roof of Madam Lathrop, who had been bereft of her husband and children, and though the households were separate, the latter manifested from the first a tender solicitude for their infant daughter. As the mind of the child began to unfold itself, and to give promise of future richness and depth, the attachment became mutual, and in a few years an enduring confidence, an almost inseparable companionship, was established between the little maiden of six and the venerable woman of eighty.

The following glimpse into the chamber of Madam Lathrop is from one entirely conversant with the subject. For its substantial correctness as to fact, we are permitted to quote the authority of Mrs. Sigourney herself. It is quoted, not only as a beautiful episode in human life, but also as affording a key to some of the most charming peculiarities of Mrs. Sigourney's writings.

"Methinks we stand upon that ancient threshold; we enter those low-browed, but ample rooms; we mark the wood-fire gleaming upon crimson moreen curtains, gilded clock, ebony-framed mirror, and polished wainscot; but what most engages our attention, is the venerable occupant and her youthful companion. There sits the lady in her large arm-chair, and the young friend beside her, with face upturned, and loving eyes fixed on that beaming countenance. We can imagine that we hear, in alternate notes, the quick, gushing voice of childhood, and the tremulous tones of age, as question and reply are freely interchanged. And now we are startled, as the tremulous voice unexpectedly recovers strength and fulness, and breaks forth into some wild or pathetic melody—the ballad or patriotic stanza of former days. The young auditor listens with rapt delight, and now, as the scene changes, with light breath and glowing aspect, she sits attentive to the minute and lively details of some domestic tale of truth, or striking episode of our national history—treasuring up the diamond-dust, to be fused hereafter, by her genius, into pellucid gems. As night closes round, and the light from the two stately candlesticks glimmers through the room, the lady takes the cushioned seat in the corner, and the young inmate spreads out upon the table some well-kept, ancient book, often perused, yet never found wearisome; and beguiles, with incessant reading, all too mature for her years, the long and lonely knitting hours of her aged friend."

This glimpse into the parlour of Madam Lathrop is no fancy sketch. The evening was usually closed by the singing of devotional hymns, and the repetition, from memory, of favourite psalms, or choice specimens of serious verse. The readings were mostly of devotional works. Young's Night Thoughts stood highest upon the list, and had several times been read aloud, from beginning to end, by the young student, at an age in which most children can scarcely read, intelligibly, the simplest verse. Other tomes, and some heavy and sombrous, were also made familiar to her young mind, by repeated perusal; but as the upper shelves of the lady's library contained some volumes of a lighter character, the curiosity of childhood would render it pardonable, if now and then those shelves were furtively explored, or some old play or romance withdrawn, to be read by stealth in the solitary chamber.

The chamber, to the young student, is a sacred precinct. There, not only is the evening problem and the morning recitation faithfully prepared for the school, and the borrowed book pored over in delightful secrecy, with no intrusive eye to note the smiles and tears and unconscious gesticulation, that respond to the moving incidents of the tale—but there, too, in silent and solitary hours, the light-footed muse slips in, and makes her earliest visits, leaving behind those first faintly dotted notes of music, which are for a long time bashfully kept concealed from every eye.

Madam Lathrop watched with entire complacency the dawning genius of her young favourite. The simple, poetic effusion occasionally brought from that solitary chamber and timidly submitted to her inspection, was sure to be received with encouraging praise, and to kindle in the face of her aged friend that glow of approbation which was the highest reward that the imagination of the young aspirant had then conceived.

The death of her venerable benefactress, which took place when she was fourteen years of age, was the first deep sorrow which her young heart had known. It was a disruption of very tender ties—the breaking up of a peculiar intimacy between youth and age, and she could not be easily solaced for the bereavement. Nor has her mind ever lost the influence of this early association. It has kept with her through life, and runs like a fine vein through all her writings. The memory, the image, the teachings of this sainted friend, seem to accompany her like an invisible presence, and wherever the scene may be, she turns aside to commune with her spirit, or to cast a fresh flower upon her grave.

Mrs. Sigourney has been remarkable through life for the steadfastness of her friendships. Besides the venerable companion already commemorated, she became early in life very tenderly attached to one of her own age, whose history has become identified with her own. This was Anna Maria Hyde; a young lady whose sterling worth and fine mental powers were graced and rendered winning by uncommon vivacity and sweetness of disposition, unaffected modesty, and varied acquirements. The friendship of these two young persons for each other was intimate and endearing. They were companions in long rural walks, they sat side by side at their studies, visited at each other's dwellings, read together, wrought the same needle-work pattern, or, with paint and pencil, shaded the same flower. The neighbours regarded them as inseparable; the names of Hyde and

Huntley were wreathed together, and one was seldom mentioned without the other. Youthful friendships are, however, so common, and usually so transient, that this would scarcely demand notice, but for the strength of its foundation. It appeared to be based upon a mutual, strong desire to do good to others; a fixed purpose to employ the talents which God had given them, for the benefit of the world upon which they had entered. In pursuance of this object, they not only addressed themselves to the assiduous cultivation of their mental powers, but they engaged with alacrity in domestic affairs and household duties; and they found time, also, to make garments for the poor, to instruct indigent children, to visit the old and infirm, read with them, and administer to their temporal comfort, and to watch with the sick and dying.

Among the plans for future usefulness which these young friends revolved, none seemed so feasible, or so congenial to their tastes, as that of devoting themselves to the office of instruction. This, therefore, they adopted as their province, their chosen sphere of action, and they resolutely kept this object in view, through the course of their education. The books they read, the studies they pursued, the accomplishments they sought, all had a reference to this main design. After qualifying themselves to teach those English sciences which were considered necessary to the education of young females, together with the elements of the Latin tongue, they went to Hartford and spent the winter of 1810–11 principally in attention to the ornamental branches, which were then in vogue. Returning from thence, they entered at once, at the age of nineteen, upon their grand pursuit. A class of young ladies in their native town gathered joyfully around them, and into this circle they cast not only the affluence of their well stored minds, and the cheering inspiration of youthful zeal, but all the strength of their best and holiest principles. Animated, blooming, happy, linked affectionately arm in arm, they daily came in among their pupils, diffusing love and cheerfulness, as well as knowledge, and commanding the most grateful attention and respect.

The cordial affection between these interesting young teachers was itself a most important lesson to their pupils. One of the privileged few, writing after a lapse of forty years, thus testifies to the lasting impression it produced upon their young hearts. "Pleasant it is to review those dove-like days—to recall the lineaments of that diligent, earnest, mind-expanding group; and to note again the dissimilarity so beautifully harmonious, between those whom we delighted to call our sweet *sister-teachers—the two inseparables, inimitables.* It was a matter of admiration to the pupils, that such oneness of sentiment, opinion, and affection, should co-exist with such a diversity in feature, voice, eyes, expression, manner, and movement, as the two friends exhibited."

After a pleasing association of two years, the young teachers parted, each to pursue the same line of occupation in a different sphere. But another separation, fatal and afflictive, soon took place. The interesting and accomplished Miss Hyde was taken away in the midst of usefulness and promise—mowed down like a rose-tree in bloom, March 26th, 1816, at the age of twenty-four. Of this beloved companion of her youth, Mrs. Sigourney wrote an interesting memoir, soon after her decease; and she again recurs to her with gushing tenderness, in the piece entitled "Home of an early friend," written nearly thirty years after the scene of bereavement. In flowing verse, and prose almost as harmonious as music, she has twined a lasting memorial of the worth of the departed, and of that tender friendship which was a marked incident in her own young life.

Before the death of her friend, she had transferred her residence to Hartford, and again entered, with fresh enthusiasm, upon the task of instruction. In this path she was happy and successful; it was regarded as a privilege to be received into her circle, and many of her pupils became life-long friends, strewing her subsequent pathway with flowers.

In Hartford, she was at once received as a welcome and cherished inmate of the family of Madam Wadsworth, relict of Col. Jeremiah Wadsworth, whose mother was a Talcot, and nearly connected with the revered Madam Lathrop. The mansion-house in which Madam Wadsworth and the aged sisters of her husband dwelt, stood upon the spot now occupied by the Wadsworth Athenæum. It was a spacious structure; unadorned, but deeply interesting in its historic associations. To the young guest it seemed a consecrated roof, whose every room was peopled with images of the past; nor was her ear ever inattentive to those descriptive sketches of the heroic age of our country, with which its venerable inhabitants enlivened the evening hours. The poem, "On the Removal of an Ancient Mansion," is a graphic delineation of the impressions made on her mind by her acquaintance with the threshold and hearth-stone of this fine old house, and her communion with its excellent inmates.

Another member of the same family, Daniel Wadsworth, Esq., had always manifested a lively interest in her mental cultivation. He had known her in childhood, under the roof of Madam Lathrop, and had there seen some of her early effusions, both in prose and verse. At his earnest solicitation, she made a collection of her fugitive pieces, and under his patronage, and with his influence and liberality cast around her as a shield, she first ventured to appear before the public as an author. Mr. Wadsworth's regard for her suffered no diminution till his death, which took place in 1848. Few authors have found a friend so kind and so true. Of her affection for him and his amiable wife, her writings contain many proofs. Her Monody on the death of Mr. Wadsworth has the following noble stanza:—

"Oh, friend! thou didst o'ermaster well
The pride of wealth, and multiply

Good deeds not done for the good word of men,
    But for Heaven's judging ken,
    And clear, omniscient Eye;
And surely where 'the just made perfect' dwell,
    Earth's voice of highest eulogy
Is like the bubble of the far-off sea,—
    A sigh upon the grave
Scarce moving the frail flowers that o'er its surface wave."

We have thus far glanced at the principal scenes and circumstances, which appear to have had an influence in forming the character of Mrs. Sigourney, and preparing her genius for flight. As Miss Huntley, she gave no works to the press except those to which allusion has been made, viz: "Moral Pieces in Prose and Verse," and a memoir of her friend, Miss Hyde. The "Sketch of Connecticut, forty years since," was, however, one of her earliest productions, though not published until 1824. It is honourable to her sensibilities, that so large a portion of these works was prompted by the grateful feelings of the heart. Her later emanations are enriched with deeper trains of thought, and melodies of higher and more varied power, but these are the genuine outpourings of affection—the first fruits of mind, bathed in the dew of life's morning, and laid upon the altar of gratitude.

The marriage of Miss Huntley with Charles Sigourney, Esq., merchant of Hartford, took place at Norwich, June 16th, 1819.

Mrs. Sigourney's domestic life has been varied with frequent excursions and tours, which have rendered her familiar with the scenery and society of most parts of her own country, and in 1840, she went to Europe, and remained there nearly a year, visiting England, Scotland, and France. "Pleasant Memories of Pleasant Lands," published in 1843, and "Scenes in my Native Land," published in 1845, afford sufficient evidence that travelling has had a conspicuous agency in giving richness and variety to her productions.

A personal stranger to Mrs. Sigourney, acquainted only with her varied literary pursuits and numerous writings, might be disposed to think that they occupied her whole time, and that she had accomplished little else in life. Such an assumption would be entirely at variance with the truth. The popular, but now somewhat stale notion, that female writers are, of course, negligent in personal costume, domestic thrift, and all those social offices which are woman's appropriate and beautiful sphere of action, can never prop its baseless and falling fabric with her example. She has sacrificed no womanly or household duty, no office of friendship or benevolence for the society of the muses. That she is able to perform so much in so many varied departments of literature and social obligation, is owing to her diligence. She acquired in early life that lesson—simple, homely, but invaluable—to make the most of passing time. Hours are seeds of gold; she has not sown them on the wind, but planted them in good ground, and the harvest is consequently a hundred fold.

Authentic report informs us that no one better fills the arduous station of a New England housekeeper, in all its various and complicated departments. Nor are the calls of benevolence unheeded. Like that distinguished philanthropist, from whom she derives her intermediate name, she is said to go about doing good. Much of her time is devoted to the practical, silent, unambitious duties of charity. Nor must we omit the crowning praise of all—the report of her humble, unceasing, unpretending, untiring devotion.

We may not conclude this brief review of the life of Mrs. Sigourney, without allusion to a recent afflictive stroke of Providence, which has overshadowed her path with a dark cloud, and almost bowed her spirit to the earth with its weight. She was the mother of two children; the youngest, an only son, had just arrived at the verge of manhood, when he was selected by the Destroying Angel as his own, and veiled from her sight.* A sorrow like this, she had never before known. Such a bereavement cannot take place and not leave desolation behind. Around this early-smitten one, the fond hopes of a mother's heart had clustered; all those hopes are extinguished; innumerable, tender sympathies are cut away; the glowing expectations, nurtured for many years, are destroyed, and the cold urn left in their place. But the Divine Hand knows how to remove branches from the tree without blighting it; and though crushed and wounded, the faith of the Christian sustains the bereaved parent. Her reply to a friend who sympathized in her affliction, will show both the depth of her sorrow, and the source of her consolation—"God's time and will are beautiful, and through bursts of blinding tears I give him thanks."

The amount of Mrs. Sigourney's literary labours may be estimated from the following list of her publications, which is believed to be nearly complete. The works are all prose, and all 12mo., unless otherwise expressly stated: "Moral Pieces in Prose and Verse," 267 pages, 1815; "Biography and Writings of A. M. Hyde," 241 pp., 1816; "Traits of the Aborigines," a poem, 284 pp., 1822; "Sketch of Connecticut, forty years since," 280 pp., 1824; "Poems," 228 pp., 1827; "Biography of Females," 112 pp., small size, 1829; "Biography of Pious Persons," 338 pp., 1832, two editions the first year, now out of print, as are all the preceding volumes; "Evening Readings in History," 128 pp., 1833; "Letters to Young Ladies," 295 pp., 1833, twenty editions; "Memoirs of Phebe Hammond," 30 pp., 1833; "How to be Happy," 126 pp., 1833, two editions the first year, and several in London; "Sketches," 216 pp., 1834; "Poetry for Children," 102 pp., small size, 1834; "Select Poems," 338 pp., 1834, eleven editions; "Tales and Essays for Children," 128 pp., 1834; "Zinzendorff and other Poems," 300 pp., 1834; "History of Marcus Aurelius," 122 pp., 1835; "Olive Buds," 136 pp., 1836;

* Andrew M. Sigourney died in Hartford, June, 1850, aged nineteen years.

"Girls' Reading Book," prose and poetry, 243 pp., 1838, between twenty and thirty editions; "Boys' Reading Book," prose and poetry, 247 pp., 1839, many editions; "Letters to Mothers," 296 pp., 1838, eight editions; "Pocahontas and other Poems," 283 pp., 1841, reprinted in London; "Poems," 255 pp., small size, 1842; "Pleasant Memories of Pleasant Lands," 368 pp., prose and poetry, 1842; "Child's Book," prose and poetry, 150 pp., small size, 1844; "Scenes in my Native Land," prose and poetry, 319 pp., 1844; "Poems for the Sea," 152 pp., 1845; "Voice of Flowers," prose and poetry, 123 pp., small size, 1845, eight editions in five years; "The Lovely Sisters," 100 pp., small size, 1845; "Myrtis and other Etchings," 292 pp., 1846; "Weeping Willow," poetry, 128 pp., small size, 1846, six editions in four years; "Water Drops," prose and poetry, 275 pp., 1847; "Illustrated Poems," 408 pp., 8vo., 1848; "Whisper to a Bride," prose and poetry, 80 pp., small size, 1849; "Letters to my Pupils," 320 pp., 1851; "Olive Leaves," 308 pp., 1851; "Examples of Life and Death," 348 pp., 1851; "The Faded Hope," 264 pp., 1852; "Memoir of Mrs. Harriet Newell Cook," 252 pp., 1852; another about to go to press, &c.

Besides these volumes, forty in number, she has produced several pamphlets, and almost innumerable contributions to current periodical literature. She has moreover maintained a very extensive literary correspondence, amounting in some years to an exchange of sixteen or seventeen hundred letters.

Perhaps no one, who has written so much as Mrs. Sigourney, has written so little to cause self-regret in the review. The secret of this lies in that paramount sense of duty which is the obvious spring of her writings, as of all her conduct. If it has not led her to the highest regions of fancy, it has saved her from all those disgraceful falls that too often mark the track of genius. Along the calm, sequestered vale of duty and usefulness, her writings, like a gentle river fresh from its mountain springs, have gladdened many a quiet home, have stimulated into fertility many a generous heart. Some of her small volumes, like the "Whisper to a Bride," are unpretending in character as they are diminutive in appearance, but they contain a wealth of beauty and goodness that few would believe that have not examined them. Of her larger volumes, none are more widely known than the "Letters to Young Ladies," and "Letters to Mothers." "Letters to my Pupils," just published, will probably be equally popular, as they are equally beautiful. The scraps of autobiography, so gracefully mixed up with her reminiscences of others, will add a special charm to this volume for the thousands who have felt the genial influence of her teachings and writings.

The first of the extracts which follow is from "Myrtis and other Etchings."

THE LOST CHILDREN.

"I ask the moon, so sadly fair,
The night's cold breath through shadows drawn,
'Where are they who were mine? and where?'
A void but answers, 'All are gone.'" Miss H. F. Gould.

There was sickness in the dwelling of the emigrant. Stretched upon his humble bed, he depended on that nursing care which a wife, scarcely less enfeebled than himself, was able to bestow. A child, in its third summer, had been recently laid to its last rest beneath a turf mound under their window. Its image was in the heart of the mother, as she tenderly ministered to her husband.

"Wife, I am afraid I think too much about poor little Thomas. He was so well and rosy when we left our old home, scarcely a year since. Sometimes I feel, if we had but continued there, our darling would not have died."

The tear which had long trembled, and been repressed by the varieties of conjugal solicitude, burst forth at these words. It freely overflowed the brimming eyes, and relieved the suffocating emotions which had striven for the mastery.

"Do not reproach yourself, dear husband. His time had come. He is happier there than here. Let us be thankful for those that are spared."

"It seems to me that the little girls are growing pale. I am afraid you confine them too closely to this narrow house, and to the sight of sickness. The weather is growing settled. You had better send them out to change the air, and run about at their will. Mary, lay the baby on the bed by me, and ask mother to let little sister and you go out for a ramble."

The mother assented, and the children, who were four and six years old, departed, full of delight. A clearing had been made in front of their habitation, and, by ascending a knoll in its vicinity, another dwelling might be seen environed with the dark spruce and hemlock. In the rear of these houses was a wide expanse of ground, interspersed with thickets, rocky acclivities, and patches of forest trees, while far away, one or two lakelets peered up, with their blue eyes deeply fringed. The spirits of the children, as they entered this unenclosed region, were like those of the birds that surrounded them. They playfully pursued each other with merry laughter, and such a joyous sense of liberty, as makes the blood course lightsomely through the veins.

"Little Jane, let us go farther than ever we have before. We will see what lies beyond those high hills, for it is but just past noon, and we can get back long before supper-time."

"Oh! yes, let us follow that bright blue-bird, and see what he is flying after. But don't go in among those briers that tear the clothes so, for mother has no time to mend them."

"Sister, sweet sister, here are some snowdrops in this green hollow, exactly like those in my old, dear garden, so far away. How pure they are, and cool, just like the baby's face, when the wind blows on it! Father and mother will like us to bring them some."

Filling their little aprons with the spoil, and still searching for something new or beautiful, they prolonged their ramble, unconscious of the flight of time, or the extent of space they were traversing. At length, admonished by the chilliness, which often marks the declining hours of the early days of spring, they turned their course homeward. But the returning clue was lost, and they walked rapidly, only to plunge more inextricably in the mazes of the wilderness.

"Sister Mary, are these pretty snow-drops good to eat? I am *so* hungry, and my feet ache, and will not go!"

"Let me lift you over this brook, little Jane; and hold tighter by my hand, and walk as bravely as you can, that we may get home, and help mother set the table."

"We won't go so far next time, will we? What is the reason that I cannot see any better?"

"Is not that the roof of our house, dear Jane, and the thin smoke curling up among the trees? Many times before, have I thought so, and found it only a rock or a mist."

As evening drew its veil, the hapless wanderers, bewildered.

hurried to and fro, calling for their parents, or shouting for help, until their strength was exhausted. Torn by brambles, and their poor feet bleeding from the rocks which strewed their path, they sunk down, moaning bitterly. The fears that overpower the heart of a timid child, who, for the first time finds night approaching, without shelter or protection, wrought on the youngest to insupportable anguish. The elder, filled with the sacred warmth of sisterly affection, after the first paroxysms of grief, seemed to forget herself, and sitting upon the damp ground, and folding the little one in her arms, rocked her with a gentle movement, soothing and hushing her like a nursling.

"Don't cry! oh! don't cry so, dearest; say your prayers, and fear will fly away."

"How can I kneel down here in the dark woods, or say my prayers, when mother is not by to hear me? I think I see a large wolf, with sharp ears, and a mouth wide open, and hear noises as of many fierce lions growling."

"Dear little Jane, do say, 'Our Father, who art in Heaven.' Be a good girl, and, when we have rested here a while, perhaps He may be pleased to send some one to find us, and to fetch us home."

Harrowing was the anxiety in the lowly hut of the emigrant when day drew towards its close, and the children came not. A boy, their whole assistant in the toils of agriculture, at his return from labour, was sent in search of them, but in vain. As evening drew on, the inmates of the neighbouring house, and those of a small hamlet, at considerable distance, were alarmed, and associated in the pursuit. The agony of the invalid parents, through that night, was uncontrollable; starting at every footstep, shaping out of every breeze the accents of the lost ones returning, or their cries of misery. While the morning was yet gray, the father, no longer to be restrained, and armed with supernatural strength, went forth, amid the ravings of his fever, to take part in the pursuit. With fiery cheeks, his throbbing head bound with a handkerchief, he was seen in the most dangerous and inaccessible spots—caverns—ravines—beetling cliffs—leading the way to every point of peril, in the phrensy of grief and disease.

The second night drew on, with one of those sudden storms of sleet and snow, which sometimes chill the hopes of the young spring. Then was a sadder sight—a woman with attenuated form, flying she knew not whither, and continually exclaiming, "My children! my children!" It was fearful to see a creature so deadly pale, with the darkness of midnight about her. She heeded no advice to take care of herself, nor persuasion to return to her home.

"They call me! Let me go! I will lay them in their bed myself. How cold their feet are! What! is Jane singing her nightly hymn without me? No! no! She cries! Some evil serpent has stung her!" and, shrieking wildly, the poor mother disappeared, like a hunted deer, in the depths of the forest.

Oh! might she but have wrapped them in her arms, as they shivered in their dismal recess, under the roots of a tree, uptorn by some wintry tempest! Yet how could she imagine the spot where they lay, or believe that those little wearied limbs had borne them, through bog and bramble, more than six miles from the parental door? In the niche which we have mentioned, a faint moaning sound might till be heard.

"Sister, do not tell me that we shall never see the baby any more. I see it now, and Thomas, too! dear Thomas! Why do they say he died and was buried? He is close by me, just above my head. There are many more babies with him—a host. They glide by me as if they had wings. They look warm and happy. I should be glad to be with them, and join their beautiful plays. But O, how cold I am! Cover me close, Mary. Take my head into your bosom."

"Pray do not go to sleep quite yet, dear Jane. I want to hear your voice, and talk with you. It is so very sad to be waking here alone. If I could but see your face when you are asleep, it would be a comfort. But it is so dark, *so dark!*"

Rousing herself with difficulty, she unties her apron, and spreads it over the head of the child, to protect it from the driving snow; she pillows the cold cheek on her breast, and grasps more firmly the benumbed hand by which she had so faithfully led her, through all their terrible pilgrimage. There they are!—The one moves not. The other keeps vigil, feebly giving utterance, at intervals, to a low suffocating spasm from a throat dried with hunger. Once more she leans upon her elbow, to look on the face of the little one, for whom as a mother she has cared. With love strong as death, she comforts herself that her sister slumbers calmly, because the stroke of the destroyer has silenced her sobbings.

Ah! why come ye not hither, torches that gleam through the wilderness, and men who shout to each other? why come ye not this way? See! they plunge into morasses, they cut their path through tangled thickets, they ford waters, they ascend mountains, they explore forests—but the lost are not found!

The third and fourth nights come and depart. Still the woods are filled with eager searchers. Sympathy has gathered them from remote settlements. Every log-cabin sends forth what it can spare for this work of pity and of sorrow. They cross each other's track. Incessantly they interrogate and reply, but in vain. The lost are not found!

In her mournful dwelling, the mother sat motionless. Her infant was upon her lap. The strong duty to succor its helplessness, grappled with the might of grief, and prevailed. Her eyes were riveted upon its brow. No sound passed her white lips. Pitying women, from distant habitations, gathered around and wept for her. They even essayed some words of consolation. But she answered nothing. She looked not toward them. She had no ear for human voices. In her soul was the perpetual cry of the lost. Nothing overpowered it, but the wail of her living babe. She ministered to its necessities, and that Heaven-inspired impulse saved her. She had no longer any hope for those who had wandered away. Horrid images were in her fancy—the ravening beast—black pits of stagnant water—birds of fierce beak—venomous, coiling snakes. She bowed herself down to them, and travailed as in the birth-hour, fearfully, and in silence. But the hapless babe on her bosom, touched an electric chord, and saved her from despair. Maternal love, with its pillar of cloud and of flame, guided her through the desert, that she perished not.

Sunday came, and the search was unabated. It seemed only

marked by a deeper tinge of melancholy. The most serious felt it fitting to go forth at that sacred season to seek the lost, though not, like their Master, girded with the power to save. Parents remembered that it might have been their own little ones who had thus strayed from the fold, and with their gratitude, took a portion of the mourner's spirit into their hearts. Even the sad hope of gathering the dead for the sepulchre, the sole hope that now sustained their toil, began to fade into doubt. As they climbed over huge trees, which the winds of winter had prostrated, or forced their way among rending brambles, sharp rocks, and close-woven branches, they marvelled how such fragile forms could have endured hardships by which the vigour of manhood was impeded and perplexed.

The echo of a gun rang suddenly through the forest. It was repeated. Hill to hill bore the thrilling message. It was the concerted signal that their anxieties were ended. The hurrying seekers followed its sound. From a commanding cliff, a white flag was seen to float. It was the herald that the lost was found.

There they were—near the base of a wooded hillock, half cradled among the roots of an uptorn chestnut. There they lay, cheek to cheek, hand clasped in hand. The blasts had mingled in one mesh their dishevelled locks, for they had left home with their poor heads uncovered. The youngest had passed away in sleep. There was no contortion on her brow, though her features were sunk and sharpened by famine.

The elder had borne a deeper and longer anguish. Her eyes were open, as though she had watched till death came; watched over that little one, for whom, through those days and nights of terror, she had cared and sorrowed like a mother. Strong and rugged men shed tears when they saw she had wrapped her in her own scanty apron, and striven with her embracing arms to preserve the warmth of vitality, even after the cherished spirit had fled away. The glazed eyeballs were strained, as if, to the last, they had been gazing for her father's roof, or the wreath of smoke that should guide her there.

Sweet sisterly love! so patient in all adversity, so faithful unto the end, found it not a Father's house, where it might enter with

12

the little one, and be sundered no more? Found it not a fold whence no lamb can wander and be lost? a mansion where there is no death, neither sorrow nor crying? Forgot it not all its sufferings for joy at that dear Redeemer's welcome, which, in its cradle, it had been taught to lisp—"Suffer little children to come unto me, and forbid them not, for of such is the kingdom of Heaven."

"I HAVE SEEN AN END OF ALL PERFECTION."

I HAVE seen a man in the glory of his days, and in the pride of his strength. He was built like the strong oak, that strikes its root deep in the earth—like the tall cedar, that lifts its head above the trees of the forest. He feared no danger—he felt no sickness—he wondered why any should groan or sigh at pain. His mind was vigorous like his body; he was perplexed at no intricacy, he was daunted at no obstacle. Into hidden things he searched, and what was crooked he made plain. He went forth boldly upon the face of the mighty deep. He surveyed the nations of the earth. He measured the distances of the stars, and called them by their names. He gloried in the extent of his knowledge, in the vigour of his understanding, and strove to search even into what the Almighty had concealed. And when I looked upon him, I said with the poet, "what a piece of work is man! how noble in reason! how infinite in faculties! in form and moving, how express and admirable! in action how like an angel! in apprehension how like a god!"

I returned—but his look was no more lofty, nor his step proud. His broken frame was like some ruined tower. His hairs were white and scattered, and his eye gazed vacantly upon the passers by. The vigour of his intellect was wasted, and of all that he had gained by study, nothing remained. He feared when there was no danger, and where was no sorrow he wept. His decaying memory had become treacherous. It showed him only broken images of the glory that had departed. His house was to him like a strange land, and his friends were counted as enemies. He thought himself strong and healthful, while his feet tottered on the verge of the grave. He said of his son, "he is my brother;" of his daughter, "I know her not." He even inquired what was his own name. And as I gazed mournfully upon him, one who supported his feeble frame, and ministered to his many wants, said to me, "Let thine heart receive instruction, for thou hast seen an end of all perfection!"

I have seen a beautiful female, treading the first stages of youth, and entering joyfully into the pleasures of life. The glance of her eye was variable and sweet, and on her cheek trembled something like the first blush of the morning. Her lips moved, and there was melody, and when she floated in the dance, her light form, like the aspen, seemed to move with every breeze.

I returned—she was not in the dance. I sought her among her gay companions, but I found her not. Her eye sparkled not there—the music of her voice was silent. She rejoiced on earth no more. I saw a train—sable and slow-paced. Sadly they bore towards an open grave what once was animated and beautiful. As they drew near, they paused, and a voice broke the solemn silence: "Man that is born of a woman, is of few days and full of misery. He cometh up, and is cut down like a flower, he fleeth as it were a shadow, and never continueth in one stay." Then they let down into the deep, dark pit, that maiden whose lips but a few days since were like the half-blown rosebud. I shuddered at the sound of clods falling upon the hollow coffin. Then I heard a voice saying, "Earth to earth, ashes to ashes, dust to dust." They covered her with the damp soil, and the uprooted turf of the valley, and turned again to their own homes. But one mourner lingered to cast himself upon the tomb. And as he wept he said, "There is no beauty, nor grace, nor loveliness, but what vanisheth like the morning dew. I have seen an end of all perfection!"

I saw an infant, with a ruddy brow, and a form like polished ivory. Its motions were graceful, and its merry laughter made other hearts glad. Sometimes it wept,—and again it rejoiced,—when none knew why. But whether its cheek dimpled with smiles, or its blue eyes shone more brilliant through tears, it was beautiful. It was beautiful because it was innocent. And care-worn and sinful men admired, when they beheld it. It was like the first blossom which some cherished plant has put forth, whose cup sparkles with a dew-drop, and whose head reclines upon the parent stem.

Again I looked. It had become a child. The lamp of reason had beamed into its mind. It was simple, and single-hearted, and a follower of the truth. It loved every little bird that sang in the trees, and every fresh blossom. Its heart danced with joy as it looked around on this good and pleasant world. It stood like a lamb before its teachers—it bowed its ear to instruction—it walked in the way of knowledge. It was not proud, nor stubborn, nor envious, and it had never heard of the vices and vanities of the world. And when I looked upon it, I remembered our Saviour's words, "Except ye become as little children, ye cannot enter into the kingdom of Heaven."

I saw a man, whom the world calls honourable. Many waited for his smile. They pointed to the fields that were his, and talked of the silver and gold which he had gathered. They praised the stateliness of his domes, and extolled the honour of his family. But the secret language of his heart was, "By my wisdom have I gotten all this." So he returned no thanks to God, neither did he fear or serve him. As I passed along, I heard the complaints of the labourers, who had reaped his fields—and the cries of the poor, whose covering he had taken away. The sound of feasting and revelry was in his mansion, and the unfed beggar came tottering from his door. But he considered not that the cries of the oppressed were continually entering into the ears of the Most High. And when I knew that this man was the docile child whom I had loved, the beautiful infant on whom I had gazed with delight, I said in my bitterness, "*Now, have I seen an end of all perfection!*" And I laid my mouth in the dust.

SARAH J. HALE.

Mrs. Hale, so widely known by her efforts to promote the intellectual condition of her sex, is a native of Newport, New Hampshire. Her maiden name was Sarah Josepha Buell. Her husband, David Hale, was a lawyer. By his death, she was left the sole protector of five children, the eldest then but seven years old. It was in the hope of gaining for them the means of support and education, that she engaged in authorship as a profession. Her first attempt was a small volume of poems, printed for her benefit by the Freemasons, of which fraternity her husband had been a member. This was followed by "Northwood," a novel in two volumes, published in 1827.

Early in the following year, Mrs. Hale was invited from her native State to Boston, to take charge of the editorial department of "The Ladies' Magazine," the first American periodical devoted exclusively to her sex. She removed to Boston, accordingly, in 1828, and continued to edit the magazine until 1837, when it was united with the "Lady's Book" of Philadelphia. The literary department of the "Lady's Book" was then placed in her charge, and has so remained ever since. She continued, however, for several years to reside in Boston, to superintend the education of her sons, then students at Harvard. In 1841, she removed to Philadelphia, where she still lives.

While living in Boston, Mrs. Hale originated the noble idea of the "Seaman's Aid Society," over which she was called to preside, and of which she continued to be the president until her removal to Philadelphia. This institution, or rather Mrs. Hale as its animating spirit, first suggested the plan of a "Home for Sailors," and showed its practicability by establishing one in Boston, which became completely successful. The many establishments of this kind, now existing in various ports, all took their origin in that of the Boston "Seaman's Aid Society," and in the ideas and reasonings of their first seven annual reports, all of which were from the pen of Mrs. Hale. Nothing that she has ever written, probably, has been more productive of good than this series of annual reports; and though they may be, from their official character, such as to add nothing to her literary laurels, they certainly form an important addition to her general claims to honour as one of the wise and good of the land.

Besides "Northwood," which was republished in London under the title of "A New England Tale," her published works are: "Sketches of American Character;" "Traits of American Life;" "Flora's Interpreter," of which more than forty thousand copies have been sold, besides English reprints; "The Ladies' Wreath," a selection from the female poets of England and America;" "The Good Housekeeper, the way to live well, and to be well while we live," a manual of cookery, of which large and very numerous editions have been printed; "Grosvenor, a Tragedy;" "Alice Ray, a Romance in Rhyme;" "Harry Guy, the Widow's Son, a Romance of the Sea" (the last two written for charitable purposes, and the proceeds given away accordingly); "Three Hours, or the Vigil of Love, and other Poems," in 1848; "A Complete Dictionary of Poetical Quotations," a work of nearly six hundred pages, large octavo, printed in double columns, and containing selections, on subjects alphabetically arranged, from the poets of England and America; "The Judge, a Drama of American Life," published, in numbers, in the Lady's Book, and about to be given to the world in book form. Mrs. Hale has also edited several annuals—"The Opal," "The Crocus," &c., and prepared quite a number of books for the young. A large number of essays, tales, and poems lie scattered among the periodicals of the day, sufficient to fill several volumes. These she proposes to collect and publish, in book form, after concluding her editorial career.

By far the most important and honourable monument of her labour is the volume now passing through the press, entitled "Woman's Record." This is a general biographical dictionary of distinguished women of all nations and ages, filling about nine hundred pages, of the largest octavo size, closely printed in double columns. Mrs. Hale has been engaged for several years upon this undertaking, the labour of which was enough to appal any but a woman of heroic spirit. It needs no prophetic vision to predict that this great work will be an enduring "Record," not only of woman in general, but of the high aims, the indefatigable industry, the varied reading, and just discrimination of its ever to be honoured author.

The first extract from the writings of Mrs. Hale is taken from the work last named, and is in some measure a continuation of the present biographical notice.

FROM "WOMAN'S RECORD."

A FEW words respecting the influences which have, probably, caused me to become the Chronicler of my own sex, may not be considered egotistical. I was mainly educated by my mother, and strictly taught to make the Bible the guide of my life. The books to which I had access were few, very few, in comparison with the number given children now-a-days; but they were such as required to be studied—and I did study them. Next to the Bible and The Pilgrim's Progress, my earliest reading was Milton, Addison, Pope, Johnson, Cowper, Burns, and a portion of Shakspeare. I did not obtain all his works till I was nearly fifteen. The first regular novel I read was "The Mysteries of Udolpho," when I was quite a child. I name it on account of the influence it exercised over my mind. I had remarked that of all the books I saw, few were written by Americans, and none by *women*. Here was a work, the most fascinating I had ever read, always excepting "The Pilgrim's Progress," written by a woman! How happy it made me! The wish to promote the reputation of my own sex, and do something for my own country, were among the earliest mental emotions I can recollect. These feelings have had a salutary influence by directing my thoughts to a definite object; my literary pursuits have had an aim beyond self-seeking of any kind. The mental influence of woman over her own sex, which was so important in my case, has been strongly operative in inclining me to undertake this my latest work, "Woman's Record." I have sought to make it an assistant in home education; hoping the examples shown and characters portrayed, might have an inspiration and a power in advancing the moral progress of society. Yet I cannot close without adverting to the ready and kind aid I have always met with from those men with whom I have been most nearly connected. To my brother* I owe what knowledge I possess of the Latin, of the higher branches of mathematics, and of mental philosophy. He often lamented that I could not, like himself, have the privilege of a

* The late Judge Buell, of Glen's Falls, New York.

college education. To my husband I was yet more deeply indebted. He was a number of years my senior, and far more my superior in learning. We commenced, soon after our marriage, a system of study and reading which we pursued while he lived. The hours allowed were from eight o'clock in the evening till ten; two hours in the twenty-four: how I enjoyed those hours! In all our mental pursuits, it seemed the aim of my husband to enlighten my reason, strengthen my judgment, and give me confidence in my own powers of mind, which he estimated much higher than I. But this approbation which he bestowed on my talents has been of great encouragement to me in attempting the duties that have since become my portion. And if there is any just praise due to the works I have prepared, the sweetest thought is—that *his name* bears the celebrity.

THE MODE.

WHAT a variety of changes there has been in the costumes of men and women since the fig-leaf garments were in vogue! And these millions of changes have, each and all, had their admirers, and every fashion has been, in its day, called *beautiful*. It is evident, therefore, that the reigning fashion, whatever it be, comprehends the essence of the agreeable, and that to continue one particular mode or costume, beautiful for successive ages, it would only be necessary to keep it fashionable. Some nations have taken advantage of this principle in the philosophy of dress, and have, by that means, retained a particular mode for centuries; and there is no doubt the belles of these unfading fashions were, and are, quite as ardently admired, as though they had changed the form of their apparel at every revolution of the moon.

In some important particulars these fixed planets of fashion certainly have the advantage over those who are continually displaying a new phasis. They present fewer data for observation, and consequently, the alterations which time will bring to the fairest person are less perceptible, or, as they always seem the same, less noted. There are few trials more critical to a waning beauty, than the appearing in a new and brilliant fashion. If it becomes her, the whisper instantly runs round the circle, "how young she looks!" —a most invidious way of hinting she is as old as the hills;—if it does not become her, which is usually the case, then you will hear the remark, "what an odious dress!"—meaning, the wearer looks as ugly as the Fates.

The contrast between a new fashion and an old familiar face instantly strikes the beholder, and makes him run over all the changes in appearance he has seen the individual assume; and then, there is danger that the antiquated fashions may be revived—and how provoking it is to be questioned whether one remembers when long waists and hoops, and ruffled-cuffs were worn!—A reference to the parish-register, or the family-record, would not disclose the age more effectually.

Nor are the youthful exempted from their share in the evils of change. It draws the attention of the beholder to the dress, rather than the wearers; and it reminds bachelors, palpably and alarmingly, of the expense of supporting a wife who must thus appear in a new costume every change of the mode.

Now, as it is fashion which makes the pleasing in dress, were one particular form retained ever so long, it would always please, and thus the unnecessary expense of time and money be avoided; and the charges of fickleness and frivolousness entirely repelled. We have facts to support this opinion.

Is not the Spanish costume quite as becoming as our own mode? and that costume has been unchanged, or nearly so, for centuries; while the French and English, from whom we borrow our fashions, (poor souls that we are, to be thus destitute of invention and taste!) have ransacked nature, and exhausted art, for comparisons and terms by which to express the new inventions they have displayed in dress.

We are aware that a certain class of political economists affect to believe that luxury is beneficial to a nation—but it is not so. The same reasoning which would make extravagance in dress commendable, because it employed manufacturers and artists, would also make intemperance a virtue in those who could afford to be drunk, because the preparation of the alcohol employs labourers, and the consumption would encourage trade. All these views of the expediency of tolerating evil are a part of that Machiavellian system of selfishness which has been imposed on the world for wisdom, but which has proved its origin by the corrupting crimes and miseries men have endured in consequence of yielding themselves dupes or slaves of fashion and vice.

We do hope, indeed believe, that a more just appreciation of the true interests and real happiness of mankind will yet prevail. The improvements, now so rapidly progressing, in the intellectual and civil condition of nations must, we think, be followed by a corresponding improvement in the tastes and pursuits of those who are the *élite* of society. Etiquette and the fashions cannot be the engrossing objects of pursuit, if people become reasonable. The excellencies of mind and heart will be of more consequence to a lady than the colour of a riband or the shape of a bonnet. We would not have ladies despise or neglect dress. They should be *always* fit to be seen; personal neatness is indispensable to agreeableness —almost to virtue. A proper portion of time and attention must scrupulously be given to external appearance, but not the whole of our days and energies. Is it worthy of Christians, pretending to revere the precepts of HIM who commanded them not to "take thought what they should put on," to spend their best years in studying the form of their apparel? Trifles should not thus engross us, and they need not, if our citizens would only shake off this tyranny of fashion, imposed by the tailors of Paris and London, and establish a national costume, which would, wherever an American appeared, announce him as a republican, and the countryman of Washington. The men would probably do this, if our ladies would first show that they have sufficient sense and taste to invent and arrange their own costume (without the inspiration of foreign milliners) in accordance with those national principles of comfort, propriety, economy, and becomingness, which are the only true foundation of the elegant in apparel.

It is not necessary to elegance of appearance, nor to the prosperity of trade, that changes in fashion should so frequently occur. Take, for instance, the article of shoes. What good consequence results from a change in the fashion of shoes?

If we have a becoming and convenient mode, why not retain it for centuries, and save all the discussions about square-toed, round or peaked—and all the other *ad infinitum* changes in cut and trimmings? And if the hours thus saved were devoted to reading or exercise, would not the mind and health be more improved than if we were employed in deciding the rival claims of the old and new fashion of shoes to admiration?

Such portions of time may seem very trifling, but the aggregate of wasted hours, drivelled away thus by minutes, makes a large part of the life allotted us.

We by no means advocate an idle and stupid state of society. Excitement is necessary; emulation is necessary; and we must be active if we would be happy. But there are objects more worthy to call forth the energies of rational beings than the tie of a cravat, or the trimming of a bonnet. And when the moral and intellectual beauty of character is more cultivated and displayed, we hope that the "foreign aid of ornament" will be found less necessary; and when all our ladies are possessed of "inward greatness, unaffected wisdom, and sanctity of manners," they will not find a continual flutter of fashion adds anything to the respect and affection their virtues and simple graces will inspire.

EMMA C. WILLARD.

MRS. WILLARD is more known as a woman of action than as an author. She has devoted the greater part of a long and most useful life to the cause of female education, in which her efforts, both as a theorist and a practical teacher, have been crowned with signal success. Her prominence as a writer, however, does not by any means correspond to that assigned to her by common consent as an educator. Still, she has found time in the midst of other duties of a most urgent character, to make several valuable contributions to the cause of letters.

Mrs. Willard is the daughter of the late Samuel Hart, of Berlin, Connecticut, where she was born in February, 1787. Her father was descended on the maternal side, from Thomas Hooker, minister, and on the paternal side, from Stephen Hart, deacon of the original church in Hartford, Connecticut. Minister Hooker and deacon Hart were among that large company of emigrants who came over in 1630, and settled the town of Cambridge, Massachusetts. Five years after its settlement in 1635, a fresh colony swarmed from the parent hive at Cambridge, including the "minister" and the "deacon" just named, and settled the town of Hartford.

The love of teaching appears to have been a ruling passion in Miss Hart's mind, and was developed in her early years. At the age of sixteen she took charge of a district school in her native town. The following year she opened a select school, and in the summer of the next year was placed at the head of the Berlin Academy. During this period, being engaged at home throughout the summer and winter in the capacity of instructress, she managed in the spring and autumn to attend one or other of the two boarding schools at Hartford.

During the spring of 1807, Miss Hart received invitations to take charge of academies in three different states, and accepted that from Westfield, Massachusetts. She remained there but a few weeks, when, upon a second and more pressing invitation, she went to Middlebury, in Vermont. Here she assumed the charge of a female academy, which she retained for two years. The school was liberally patronized, and general satisfaction rewarded the efforts of its preceptress. In 1809, she resigned her academy, and was united in marriage with Dr. John Willard.

In 1814, Mrs. Willard was induced to establish a boarding school at Middlebury, when she formed the determination to effect an important change in female education, by the institution of a class of schools of a higher character than had been established in the country before. She applied herself assiduously to increase her own personal abilities as a teacher, by the diligent study of branches with which she had before been unacquainted. She introduced new studies into her school, and invented new methods of teaching. She also prepared "An Address to the Public," in which she proposed "A Plan for Improving Female Education."

A copy of this plan was sent to Governor De Witt Clinton, who immediately wrote to Mrs. Willard, expressing a most cordial desire that she would remove her institution to the state of New York. He also recommended the subject of her "Plan" in his message to the legislature. The result was the passage of an act to incorporate the proposed institute at Waterford; and another to give to female academies a share of the literary fund; being, it is believed, the first law ever passed by any legislature with the direct object of improving female education.

During the spring of 1819, Mrs. Willard accordingly removed to Waterford, and opened her school. The higher mathematics were introduced, and the course of study was made sufficiently complete to qualify the pupils for any station in life.

In the spring of 1821, difficulties attending the securing of a proper building for the school in Waterford, Mrs. Willard again determined upon a removal. The public-spirited citizens of Troy offered liberal inducements; and in May, 1821, the Troy Female Seminary was opened under flattering auspices; and abundant success crowned her indefatigable exertions. Since that period, the institute has been well known to the public, and the name of Mrs. Willard, for more than a quarter of a century, has been identified with her favourite academy. Dr. Willard died in 1825; Mrs. Willard continued her school till her health was impaired, and in 1830 she visited France. She resided in Paris for several months, and from thence went to England and Scotland, returning in the following year. After her return she published a volume of travels, the avails of which, amounting to twelve hundred dollars, were devoted to the cause of female education in Greece. It may be proper to add, that she gave the avails of one or two other publications to the same object.

In 1838, Mrs. Willard resigned the charge of the Troy Seminary, and returned to Hartford, where she revised her Manual of American History, for the use of schools The merits of this work, of her smaller United

States History, and of her Universal History, have been attested by their very general use in seminaries of education.

Since 1843, she has completed the revision of her historical works, revised her Ancient Geography, and, in compliance with invitations, has written numerous addresses on different occasions, being mostly on educational subjects.

In the winter of 1846, Mrs. Willard prepared for the press a work which has given her more fame abroad, and perhaps at home, than any of her other writings. This work, which was published in the ensuing spring, both in New York and London, developed the result of a study which had intensely occupied her at times for fourteen years. Its title is "A Treatise on the Motive Powers which produce the Circulation of the Blood;" and its object is nothing less than to introduce and to establish the fact, that the principal motive power which produces circulation of the blood is not, as has been heretofore supposed, the heart's action, that being only secondary; but that the principal motive power is respiration, operating by animal heat, and producing an effective force at the lungs. Of this work, the London Critic thus speaks:

"We have here an instance of a woman undertaking to discuss a subject that has perplexed and baffled the ingenuity of the most distinguished anatomists and physiologists who have considered it, from Hervey down to Paxton; and what is more remarkable, so acquitting herself as to show that she apprehended, as well as the best of them, the difficulties which beset the inquiry; perceived as quickly as they did, the errors and incongruities of the theories of previous writers; and lastly, herself propounded an hypothesis to account for the circulation of the blood and the heart's action, eminently entitled to the serious attention and examination of all who take an interest in physiological science."

In addition to the compends of history which she has written, she has invented, for the purpose of teaching and impressing chronology on the mind by the eye, two charts of an entirely original character; one called "The American Chronographic," for American History, and the other for universal history, called the "Temple of Time." In the latter, the course of time from the creation of the world is thrown into perspective, and the parts of this subject wrought into unity, and the more distinguished characters which have appeared in the world are set down, each in his own time. This, in the chart, is better arranged for the memory, than would be that of the place of a city on a map of the world.

In 1849, she published "Last Leaves from American History," containing an interesting account of our Mexican War, and of California.

The poetical compositions of Mrs. Willard are few, and are chiefly comprised in a small volume printed in 1830.

The details in the foregoing sketch are taken chiefly from Mrs. Hale's "Woman's Record."

HOW TO TEACH.

In searching for the fundamental principles of the science of teaching, I find a few axioms as indisputable as the first principles of mathematics. One of these is this:—He is the best teacher who makes the best use of his own time and that of his pupils: for Time is all that is given by God in which to do the work of Improvement.

What is the first rule to guide us in making the best use of Time? It is to seek first and most to improve in the best things. He is not necessarily the best teacher who performs the most labour; makes his pupils work the hardest, and bustle the most. A hundred cents of copper, though they make more clatter and fill more space, have only a tenth of the value of one eagle of gold.

WHAT TO TEACH.

What is the best of all possible things to be taught? Moral Goodness. That respects God and Man: God first, and man second. To infuse into the mind of a child, therefore, love and fear towards God—the perfect in wisdom, justice, goodness, and power—the Creator, Benefactor, and Saviour—the secret Witness and the Judge—this is of all teaching the very best. But it cannot be accomplished merely in set times and by set phrases: it should mingle in all the teacher's desires and actions. The child imbibes it when he sees that the instructor feels and acts on it himself. When the youth is untruthful, when he wounds his companion in body, in mind, in character, or in property, then show him that his offence is against God; that you are God's ministers to enforce his laws, and must do your duty. Be thus mindful in all sincerity; judge correctly, adopt no subterfuge; pretend not to think that he is better than he really is; deal plainly and truly, though lovingly, with him: then his moral approbation will go with you, though it should be against himself, and even if circumstances require you to punish him. The voice of conscience residing in his heart is as the voice of God; and if you invariably interpret that voice with correctness and truth, the child will submit and obey you naturally and affectionately. But if your government is unjust or capricious—if you punish one day what you pass over or approve another, the dissatisfied child will naturally rebel.

Next to moral goodness is Health and Strength, soundness of body and of mind. This, like the former, is not what can be taught at set times and in set phrases; but it must never be lost sight of. It must regulate the measure and the kind of exercise required by the child, both bodily and mental, as well as his diet, air, and accommodations. The regular routine of school duties consists in teaching acts for the practice of future life; or sciences in which the useful or ornamental arts find their first principles; and great skill is required of the teacher in assigning to each pupil an order of studies suitable to his age, and then selecting such books and modes of teaching as shall make a little time go far.

CARE OF HEALTH.

When I am speaking to Young Girls (the Lord bless and keep them), I am in my proper element. Why should it be otherwise? I have had five thousand under my charge, and spent thirty years of my life devoted to their service; and the general reader will excuse me if I add some further advice to them, which the light of this theory will show to be good. If it is so, others may have its benefit as well as they; but it is most natural to me to address myself to them.

Would you, my dear young ladies, do the will of God on earth by being useful to your fellow beings? Take care of health.—Would you enjoy life? Take care of health; for without it existence is, for every purpose of enjoyment, worse than a blank. No matter how much wealth, or how many luxuries you can command, there is no enjoyment without health. To an aching head what is a downy pillow with silken curtains floating above? What is the cushioned landau, and the gardened landscape to her whose disordered lungs can no longer receive the inspirations of an ordinary atmosphere? And what are books, music, and paintings to her whose nervous sufferings give disease to her senses, and agony to her frame?

Would you smooth for your tender parents the pillow of declining life? Take care of health.—And does the "prophetic pencil" sometimes trace the form of one whose name perhaps is now unknown, who shall hereafter devote to you a manly and generous heart, and marriage sanction the bond? Would you be a blessing to such a one? then now take care of your health; or, if you hesitate, let imagination go still further. Fancy yourself feeble, as with untimely age, clad in vestments of sorrow, and leaving a childless home to walk forth with him to the churchyard, there to weep over your buried offspring.

Study, then, to know your frame, that you may, before it is too late, pursue such a course as will secure to you a sound and vigorous constitution.

OF THE FORCE THAT MOVES THE BLOOD.

When circulation is our life, it behoves us to consider well its causes, that we may add reason to instinct in its healthful preservation. That the blood travels through the system by its own volition, none believe; but that it is an inert mass, which will only move as it is moved. What then are the forces which move inert bodies? Are there any which may not be resolved into one of these three:—impulse, gravitation, and heat; of which the latter has the greater range in point of degree, being in the expansion of a fluid from warm to warmer, the most gentle of all imaginable forces, while in other states it is the most powerful of any known to man.

It is, then, to one or more of these forces that we must look for the motive powers which produce the circulation; and the human circulation has peculiar difficulties to encounter. Man does not enjoy his noble erect position without some countervailing disadvantages. The long upright column of his blood, spreading at its base, presents no trifling force to be moved. And this force is to be overcome by means so gentle, that the mind, the dweller in this house of clay, shall not be disturbed by its operations.—Again: the parts of the body are to be used by the mind as instruments, and ten thousand different motions are to be performed at its bidding.—What but Almighty Wisdom could have effected these several objects! And is it not most reasonable to suppose that this wisdom would assign for these purposes, not any one of the forces which move matter, but combine them all?

Gravitation by itself cannot produce a circulation by any machinery. Impulse alone could not carry on a circulation without existing in such an excessive degree that it must disturb the mind and endanger the body. But heat, the antagonist force of gravitation, by the lessening or increasing of the maximum and minimum differences, can operate more or less forcibly as occasion requires, and at the same time so gently and so quietly, that the mind shall take no cognisance of its operation as a moving force. It can be so placed, that by its expansive force it shall lift gravitation when that obstructs the way; and by its transmission, leave to it the course when its presence as a force would become hurtful. Why, then, should we hesitate to conclude that this is the principal force employed, since we know it exists in the human system? And if it is the principal agent which does actually perform this great work, then if the quantity afforded be small, so much the more perfect the machine; for so much the less will it be likely either to endanger the body or disturb the mind, and so much the more praise is due to the Mighty Artificer.

ALMIRA HART LINCOLN PHELPS.

MRS. PHELPS is the daughter of Samuel Hart, already mentioned, and the sister of Mrs. Emma Willard. Like her elder sister, Mrs. Phelps has been engaged most of her life in the business of education, and in the preparation of scientific and educational text books. These, and her miscellaneous writings, entitle her to a place in the present collection.

Mrs. Phelps was born in 1793, at Berlin, Connecticut. She was educated chiefly by her sister, Emma. At the age of eighteen, she spent a year at the Seminary of Miss Hinsdale, at Pittsfield, Massachusetts; and soon after was married to Simeon Lincoln, the editor of the "Connecticut Mirror," Hartford.

Mrs. Lincoln was left a widow at the age of thirty. Being thrown by this event upon her own resources, she commenced preparing herself in the most thorough manner for what was henceforth to be her chosen office, the education of the young. For this purpose she studied the Latin and Greek languages, and the natural sciences, applying herself at the same time to the cultivation of her talents for drawing and painting, and spent seven years in the Troy Seminary, engaged alternately in teaching and study.

In 1831, Mrs. Lincoln was married to the Hon. John Phelps, of Vermont, and the next six years of her life were spent in that State. In 1839, she became Principal of a Female Seminary at Westchester, Pennsylvania. She subsequently removed to Ellicott's Mills, in Maryland, to establish, with the aid of her husband, the Patapsco Female Institute. Mr. Phelps died in 1849.

Mrs. Phelps's first publication was a work known as "Lincoln's Botany." It appeared in 1829, and had a large circulation. The next work, a "Dictionary of Chemistry," though mainly a translation from the French, contained much original matter. After her second marriage, she published "Botany" and "Chemistry" for beginners, and also a course of lectures on education. These lectures were afterwards published as a volume in

Harpers' School Library, under the title of the "Female Student." Some of her other works have been "Natural Philosophy for Schools," "Geology for Beginners," a translation of Madame Necker de Saussure's "Progressive Education," "Caroline Westerly, or the Young Traveller," and "Ida Norman, or Trials and their Uses."

EDUCATION.

The true end of education is to prepare the young for the active duties of life, and to enable them to fill with propriety those stations to which, in the providence of God, they may be called. This includes, also, a preparation for eternity; for we cannot live well without those dispositions of heart which are necessary to fit us for heaven. To discharge aright the duties of life requires not only that the intellect shall be enlightened, but that the heart shall be purified. A mother does not perform her whole duty, even when, in addition to providing for the wants of her children and improving their understanding, she sets before them an example of justice and benevolence, of moderation in her own desires, and a command over her own passions: this may be all that is required of a heathen mother; but the Christian female must go with her little ones to Jesus of Nazareth, to seek his blessing; she must strive to elevate the minds of her offspring by frequent reference to a future state; she must teach them to hold the world and its pursuits in subserviency to more important interests, and to prize above all things that peace which, as the world giveth not, neither can it take away.

ENERGY OF MIND.

Can we find no cause why the children of the rich, setting out in life under the most favourable circumstances, often sink into insignificance, while their more humble competitors, struggling against obstacles, rise higher and higher, till they become elevated in proportion to their former depression? Have we never beheld a plant grow weak and sickly from excess of care, while the mountain pine, neglected and exposed to fierce winds and raging tempests, took strong root and grew into a lofty tree, delighting the eye by its strength and beauty? If we look into our State Legislatures, our National Congress, and the highest executive and judicial offices in the country, we do not find these places chiefly occupied by those who were born to wealth, or early taught the pride of aristocratic distinctions. Most of the distinguished men of our country have made their own fortunes; most of them began life knowing that they could hope for no aid or patronage, but must rely solely upon the energies of their own minds and the blessing of God.

EFFECT OF EXCITEMENTS.

STRONG excitements have an unfavourable effect upon the nerves of young children. We know this to be the case with ourselves, but are apt to forget that things which are common to us may be new and striking to them. My child was, on a certain evening, carried into a large room brilliantly lighted and filled with company. He gazed around with an expression of admiration and delight, not unmixed with perplexity; the latter, however, soon vanished, and he laughed and shouted with great glee; and as he saw that he was observed, exerted himself still farther to be amusing. He was then carried into a room where was music and dancing; this was entirely new, and he was agitated with a variety of emotions; fear, wonder, admiration, and joy seemed to prevail by turns. As the scene became familiar, he again enjoyed it without any mixture of unpleasant feelings.

But the effect of these excitements was apparent when he was taken to his bed-room; his face was flushed, as in a fever, his nervous system disturbed, and his sleep was interrupted by screams.

THE CHILD AND NATURE.

The expression of the emotions of young children, when first viewing the grand scenery of nature, affords a rich treat to the penetrating observer. At eight months old, my child, on being carried to the door during a fall of snow, contemplated the scene with an appearance of deep attention. He had learned enough of the use of his eyes to form some conception of the expanse before him, and to perceive how different it was from the narrow confines of the apartments of the house. The falling snow, with its brilliant whiteness and easy downward motion, was strange and beautiful; and when he felt it lighting upon his face and hands, he held up his open mouth, as if he would test its nature by a third sense.

A few weeks after this he was taken, on a bright winter's day, to ride in a sleigh (this scene was in Vermont). The sleighbells, the horses, the companions of his ride, the trees and shrubs loaded with their brilliant icy gems, the houses, and the people whom we passed, all by turns received his attention. If he could have described what he saw as it appeared to him, and the various emotions caused by these objects, the description would have added a new page in the philosophy of mind. How often are the beauties of nature unheeded by man, who, musing on past ills, brooding over the possible calamities of the future, building castles in the air, or wrapped up in his own self-love and self-importance, forgets to look abroad, or looks with a vacant stare! His outward senses are sealed, while a fermenting process may be going on in the passions within. But if, with a clear conscience, a love of nature, and a quick sense of the beautiful and sublime, we do contemplate the glorious objects so profusely scattered around us by a bountiful Creator, with the interesting changes which are constantly varying the aspect of these objects, still our emotions have become deadened by habit. We do not admire what is familiar to us, and therefore it is that we must be ever ignorant of the true native sympathy between our own hearts and the external world.

LOUISA C. TUTHILL.

AMERICANS have excelled in the preparation of books for the young One of the most successful writers in this line, and a writer of more than ordinary success in other departments of prose composition, is Mrs. Louisa C. Tuthill.

Mrs. Tuthill is descended, on both sides, from the early colonists of New Haven, Connecticut, one of her ancestors, on the father's side, being Theophilus Eaton, the first Governor of the colony. Her maiden name was Louisa Caroline Huggins. She was born, just at the close of the last century, at New Haven, and educated partly at New Haven and partly at Litchfield. The schools for young ladies in both of those towns at that time were celebrated for their excellence, and that in New Haven particularly comprehended a course of study equal in range, with the exception of Greek and the higher Mathematics, to the course pursued at the same time in Yale College. Being the youngest child of a wealthy and retired merchant, she enjoyed to the fullest extent the opportunities of education which these seminaries afforded, as well as that more general, but not less important element of education, the constant intercourse with people of refined taste and cultivated minds.

In 1817, she was married to Cornelius Tuthill, Esq., a lawyer, of Newburgh, New York, who, after his marriage, settled in New Haven. Mr. Tuthill himself, as well as his wife, being of a literary turn, their hospitable mansion became the resort for quite an extensive literary circle, some of whom have since become known to fame. Mr. Tuthill, with two of his friends, the lamented Henry E. Dwight, youngest son of President Dwight of Yale College, and Nathaniel Chauncey, Esq., now of Philadelphia, projected a literary paper, for local distribution, called "The Microscope." It was published at New Haven, and edited by Mr. Tuthill, with the aid of the two friends just named. Through the pages of the Microscope, the poet Percival first became known to the public. Among the contributors were J. C. Brainerd,* Professors Fisher and Fowler, Mrs. Sigourney, and others.

Mrs. Tuthill wrote rhymes from childhood, and as far back as she can remember was devoted to books. One of her amusements during girlhood was to write, stealthily, essays, plays, tales, and verses, all of which, however, with the exception of two or three school compositions, were committed to the flames previous to her marriage. She had imbibed a strong prejudice against literary women, and firmly resolved never to become one. Mr. Tuthill took a different view of the matter, and urged her to a further pursuit of liberal studies and the continued exercise of her pen. At his solicitation, she wrote regularly for the "Microscope" during its continuance, which, however, was only for a couple of years.

Mr. Tuthill died in 1825, at the age of twenty-nine, leaving a widow and four children, one son and three daughters. As a solace under affliction, Mrs. Tuthill employed her pen in contributing frequently to literary periodicals, but always anonymously, and with so little regard to fame of authorship as to keep neither record nor copy of her pieces, though some of them now occasionally float by as waifs on the tide of current literature. Several little books, too, were written by her between 1827 and 1839, for the pleasure of mental occupation, and published anonymously. Some of these still hold their place in Sunday school libraries.

Mrs. Tuthill's name first came before the public in 1839. It was on the title-page of a reading book for young ladies, prepared on a new plan. The plan was to make the selections a series of illustrations of the rules of rhetoric, the examples selected being taken from the best English and American authors. The "Young Ladies' Reader," the title of this collection, has been popular, and has gone through many editions.

The ice being once broken, she began to publish more freely, and during the same year gave to the world the work entitled "The Young Lady's Home." It is an octavo volume of tales and essays, having in view the completion of a young lady's education after her leaving school. It shows at once a fertile imagination and varied reading, sound judgment, and a familiar acquaintance with social life. It has been frequently reprinted.

Her next publication was an admirable series of small volumes for boys and girls, which have been, of all her writings, the most widely and the most favourably known. They are 16mo.'s, of about 150 pages each. "I will be a Gentleman," 1844, twenty-nine editions; "I will be a Lady," 1844, twenty-nine editions; "Onward, right Onward," 1845, fourteen editions; "Boarding School Girl," 1845, eight editions; "Anything for Sport," 1846, eight editions; "A Strike for Freedom, or Law and Order," 1850, three editions in the first year.

In 1852 Mrs. Tuthill commenced a new series, intended for girls and boys in their teens. "Braggadocio," 1852; "Queer Bonnets," 1853;

* See Whittier's Life of J. C. Brainerd.

"Tip Top," 1854; "Beautiful Bertha," 1854. These have passed through several editions, and have been even more popular than the former series.

Had Mrs. Tuthill written nothing but these attractive and useful volumes, she would have entitled herself to an honourable place in any work which professed to treat of the prose literature of the country. They have the graces of style and thought which would commend them to the favourable consideration of the general reader, with superadded charms that make them the delight of children. During the composition of these juvenile works, she continued her occupation of catering for "children of a larger growth," and gave to the world, in 1846, a work of fiction, entitled "My Wife," a tale of fashionable life of the present day, conveying, under the garb of an agreeable story, wholesome counsels for the young of both sexes on the all-engrossing subject of marriage.

A love for the fine arts has been with Mrs. Tuthill one of the ruling passions of her life. At different times, ample means have been within her reach for the cultivation of this class of studies. Partly for her own amusement, and partly for the instruction of her children, she paid special attention to the study of Architecture in its æsthetical character, enjoying, while thus engaged, the free use of the princely library of Ithiel Town, the architect. The result of these studies was the publication, in 1848, of a splendid octavo volume on the "History of Architecture," from which an extract is given. She edited, during the same year, a very elegant octavo annual, "The Mirror of Life," in which several of the contributions were by herself.

"The Nursery Book" appeared in 1849. It is not a collection of nursery rhymes for children, as the title has led many to suppose, but a collection of counsels for young mothers respecting the duties of the nursery. These counsels are conveyed under the fiction of an imaginary correspondence between a young mother, just beginning to dress her first baby, and an experienced aunt. There are few topics in the whole history of the management and the mismanagement of a child, during the first and most important stages of its existence, that are not discussed, with alternate reason and ridicule, in this clever volume.

Mrs. Tuthill is at present engaged upon a series of works, of an unambitious but very useful character, grouped together under the general title of "Success in Life." They are six volumes, 18mo.'s, of about 200 pages each, and each illustrating the method of success in some particular walk in life, by numerous biographical examples. The titles of the several volumes are: "The Merchant," 1849; "The Lawyer," 1850; "The Mechanic," 1850; "The Artist," 1854; "The Farmer," and "The Physician," not yet published.

In 1838, Mrs. Tuthill left her much-loved native city, where until this time she had continually resided, and passed four years in Hartford, Connecticut; from thence she removed to Roxbury near Boston. The health of her family requiring a change of climate, she went, in 1846, to Philadelphia. Since 1848 Mrs. Tuthill has resided at Princeton, New Jersey

DOMESTIC ARCHITECTURE IN THE UNITED STATES.

Domestic architecture in this country must be adapted to the circumstances and condition of the people. As it is an art originating from necessity, the progress of society must change the architecture of every country, from age to age. As wealth and refinement increase, taste and elegance must be consulted, without destroying convenience and appropriateness. We can no more adopt the style of architecture than the dress of a foreign people. We acknowledge the flowing robes of the Persian to be graceful and becoming; they suit the habits and climate of the country. The fur-clad Russian of the north has conformed his dress to his climate, and made it rich and elegant; yet, as he approaches his neighbours of Turkey, his dress becomes somewhat assimilated to theirs. France is said to give the law of fashion in dress to the civilized world; and the absurdities that have resulted from following her dictates, have produced ridiculous anomalies in other countries.

In adopting the domestic architecture of foreign countries, we may be equally ridiculous. England, our fatherland, from some resemblance in habits and institutions, might furnish more suitable models for imitation than any other country; yet they would not be perfectly in accordance with our wants. Our architecture must, therefore, be partly indigenous.

Our associations of convenience, home-comfort, and respectability are connected with a certain style of building, which has been evolved by the wants, manners, and customs of the people. Any great deviations from a style that has been thus fixed, cannot be perfectly agreeable. We must improve upon this style, so that domestic architecture may in time be perfectly American.

Man in his hours of relaxation, when he is engaged in the pursuit of mere pleasure, is less national than he is under the influence of any of the more violent feelings that agitate every-day life.

Hence it is that in our country there is danger that our villas will be anything rather than national. The retired professional man, the wealthy merchant and mechanic, wish to build in the country. Instead of consulting home-comfort and pleasurable association, they select some Italian villa, Elizabethan house, or Swiss cottage, as their model. Ten chances to one the Italian villa, designed for the border of a lake, will be placed near a dusty high-road; the Elizabethan house, instead of being surrounded by venerable trees, will raise its high gables on the top of a bare hill; and the Swiss cottage, instead of hanging upon the mountain-side, will be placed upon a level plain, surrounded with a flower-garden, divided into all manner of fantastic parterres, with box edgings.

Our country, containing as it does, in its wide extent, hills and mountains, sheltered dells and far-spreading valleys, lake-sides and river-sides, affords every possible situation for picturesque villas; and great care should be taken that appropriate sites be chosen for appropriate and comfortable buildings; comfortable, we say, for after the novelty of the exterior has pleased the eye of the owner for a few weeks, if his house wants that half-homely, but wholly indispensable attribute, comfort, he had better leave it to ornament his grounds, like an artificial ruin, and build himself another to live in. Cottages are at present quite "the rage" in many parts of the United States. Some outré enormities are styled Swiss cottages.

The larger and better kind of Swiss cottages are built with roofs projecting from five to seven feet over the sides; these projections are strengthened by strong wooden supports, that the heavy snow which falls upon the roofs need not crush them. Utility and beauty are thus combined; but there is no beauty in such a cottage in a sunny vale, where the snow falls seldom or lightly. On the Green Mountains, or among the White Hills, it might stand as gracefully as it does among its native Alps. Walnut and chestnut trees are always beautiful accompaniments to the Swiss cottage.

The same care should be taken to render the cottage comfortable, as the villa; and in this point, unfortunately, there is often a complete failure. There is no absolute need that this should be the case. A cottage or a farm-house may be picturesque without sacrificing one tittle of its convenience. The great and leading object should be utility, and where that is absolutely sacrificed in architecture, whatever may be substituted in its place, it cannot be considered beautiful.

CAROLINE M. KIRKLAND.

Mrs. Kirkland, formerly Miss Caroline M. Stansbury, was born and bred in the city of New York. After the death of her father, Mr. Samuel Stansbury, the family removed to the western part of the State, where she was married to Mr. William Kirkland, an accomplished scholar, and at one time Professor in Hamilton College. After her marriage she resided several years in Geneva, and in 1835 removed to Michigan; lived two years in Detroit, and six months in the woods—sixty miles west of Detroit. In 1843 she returned to New York, where she has lived ever since, with the exception of a visit abroad in 1849, and another in 1850. Mr. Kirkland died in 1846.

She was first prompted to authorship by the strange things which she saw and heard while living in the backwoods. These things always presented themselves to her under a humorous aspect, and suggested an attempt at description. The descriptions, given at first in private letters to her friends, proved to be so very amusing that she was tempted to enlarge the circle of her readers by publication. "A New Home—Who'll Follow?" appeared in 1839; "Forest Life," in 1842; and "Western Clearings," in 1846. These all appeared under the assumed name of "Mrs. Mary Clavers," and attracted very general attention. For racy wit, keen observation of life and manners, and a certain air of refinement which never forsakes her, even in the roughest scenes, these sketches of western life were entirely without a parallel in American literature. Their success determined in a great measure Mrs. Kirkland's course of life, and she has since become an author by profession.

An "Essay on the Life and Writings of Spenser," prefixed to an edition of the first book of the "Fairy Queen," in 1846, formed her next contribution to the world of letters. The accomplished author appears in this volume quite as shrewd in her observations, and as much at home,

C. M. Kirkland

among the dreamy fantasies of the great idealist, as she had been among the log cabins of the far west.

In July, 1847, the "Union Magazine" was commenced in New York under her auspices as sole editor. After a period of eighteen months, the proprietorship of the Magazine changed hands, its place of publication was transferred to Philadelphia, and its name changed to "*Sartain's* Union Magazine." Under the new arrangement, Mrs. Kirkland remained as associate editor, her duties being limited, however, almost entirely to a monthly contribution. This arrangement continued until July, 1851. Her whole connexion with the Magazine runs through a course of four years, and much of the marked success of that periodical is due to the character of her articles. Having been myself the resident editor of the Magazine during the last two and a half years of that time, and conducted its entire literary correspondence, I suppose I have the means of speaking with some confidence on this point, and I have no hesitation in saying, that of all its brilliant array of contributors, there was not one whose articles gave such entire and uniform satisfaction as those of Mrs. Kirkland. During her first visit to Europe, she wrote incidents and observations of travel, which were published, first in the Magazine, and afterwards in book form, under the title of "Holidays Abroad; or, Europe from the West," in two volumes, 1849. Excepting these, and one or two stories, her contributions have been in the shape of essays, and they form, in my opinion, her strongest claim to distinction as a writer.

THE MYSTERY OF VISITING.

THERE is something wonderfully primitive and simple in the fundamental idea of visiting. You leave your own place and your chosen employments, your slipshod ease and privileged plainness, and sally forth, in special trim, with your mind emptied, as far as possible, of whatever has been engrossing it, to make a descent upon the domicile of another, under the idea that your presence will give him pleasure, and, remotely, yourself. Can anything denote more amiable simplicity? or, according to a certain favourite vocabulary, can anything be more intensely green? What a confession of the need of human sympathy! What *bonhommie* in the conviction that you will be welcome! What reckless self-committal in the whole affair! Let no one say this is not a good-natured world, since it still keeps up a reverence for the fossil remains of what was once the heart of its oyster.

Not to go back to the creation (some proof of self-denial, in these days of research), what occasioned the first visit, probably? Was it the birth of a baby, or a wish to borrow somewhat for the simple householdry, or a cause of complaint about some rural trespass; a desire to share superabundant grapes with a neighbour who abounded more in pomegranates; a twilight fancy for gossip about a stray kid, or a wound from "the blind boy's butt-shaft?" Was the delight of visiting, like the succulence of roast pig, discovered by chance; or was it, like the talk which is its essence, an instinct? This last we particularly doubt, from present manifestations. Instincts do not wear out; they are as fresh as in the days when visiting began—but where is visiting?

A curious semblance of the old rite now serves us, a mere Duessa—a form of snow, impudently pretending to vitality. We are put off with this congelation, a compound of formality, dissimulation, weariness, and vanity, which it is not easy to subject to any test without resolving it at once into its unwholesome elements. Yet why must it be so? Would it require daring equal to that which dashed into the enchanted wood of Ismena, or that which exterminated the Mamelukes, to fall back upon first principles, and let inclination have something to do with offering and returning visits?

A coat of mail is, strangely enough, the first requisite when we have a round of calls to make; not the "silver arms" of fair Clorinda, but the unlovely, oyster-like coat of Pride, the helmet of Indifference, the breastplate of Distrust, the barred visor of Self-Esteem, the shield of "gentle Dulness;" while over all floats the gaudy, tinsel scarf of Fashion. Whatever else be present or lacking, Pride, defensive, if not offensive, must clothe us all over. The eyes must be guarded, lest they mete out too much consideration to those who bear no stamp. The neck must be stiffened, lest it bend beyond the haughty angle of self-reservation in the acknowledgment of civilities. The mouth is bound to keep its portcullis ever ready to fall on a word which implies unaffected pleasure or surprise. Each motion must have its motive; every civility its well-weighed return in prospect. Subjects of conversation must be any but those which naturally present themselves to the mind. If a certain round is not pr*e*scribed, we feel that all beyond it is pr*o*scribed. O, the unutterable weariness of this worse than dumb-show! No wonder we groan in spirit when there are visits to be made!

But some fair, innocent face looks up at us, out of a forest home, perhaps, or in a wide, unneighboured prairie,—and asks what all this means? "Is not a visit always a delightful thing—full of good feeling—the cheerer of solitude—the lightener of labour—the healer of differences—the antidote of life's bitterness?" Ah, primitive child! it is so, indeed, to you. The thought of a visit makes your dear little heart beat. If one is offered, or expected at your father's, with what cheerful readiness do you lend your aid to the preparations! How your winged feet skim along the floor, or surmount the stairs; your brain full of ingenious devices and substitutes, your slender fingers loaded with plates and glasses, and a tidy apron depending from your taper waist! Thoughts of dress give you but little trouble, for your choice is limited to the pink ribbon and the blue one; what the company will wear is of still less moment, so they only come! It would be hard to make you believe that we invite people and then hope they will *not* come! If you omit anybody, it will be the friend who possesses too many acres, or he who has been sent to the legislature from your district, lest dignity should interfere with pleasure; we, on the contrary, think first of the magnates, even though we know that the gloom of their grandeur will overshadow the mirth of everybody else, and prove a wet blanket to the social fire. You will, perhaps, be surprised to learn that we keep a debtor and creditor account of visits, and talk of owing a call, or owing an invitation, as your father does of owing a hundred dollars at the store, for value received. When we have made a visit and are about departing, we invite a return, in the choicest terms of affectionate, or, at least, cordial interest; but if our friend is new enough to take us at our word, and pay the debt too soon, we complain, and say, "Oh dear! there's another call to make!"

A hint has already been dropt as to the grudging spirit of the thing, how we give as little as we can, and get all possible credit for it; and this is the way we do it. Having let the accounts against us become as numerous as is prudent, we draw up a list of our creditors, carefully districted as to residences, so as not to make more cross-journeys than are necessary in going the rounds. Then we array ourselves with all suitable splendour (this is a main point, and we often defer a call upon dear friends for weeks, waiting till the arrivals from Paris shall allow us to endue a new bonnet or mantilla), and, getting into a carriage, card-case in hand, give our list, corrected more anxiously than a price-current, into the keeping of the coachman, with directions to drive as fast as dignity will allow, in order that we may do as much execution as possible with the stone thus carefully smoothed. Arrived at the first house (which is always the one farthest off, for economy of time), we stop—the servant inquires for the lady for whom our civility is intended, while we take out a card and hold it prominent on the carriage door, that not a moment may be lost in case a card is needed. "Not at home?" Ah then, with what pleased alacrity we commit the scrap of pasteboard to John, after having turned down a corner for each lady, if there are several, in this kind and propitious house. But if the answer is "At home," all wears a different aspect. The card slips sadly back again into its silver citadel; we sigh, and say "Oh dear!", if nothing worse—and then, alighting with measured step, enter the drawing-room all smiles, and with polite words ready on our lips. Ten minutes of the weather—the walking—the opera—family illnesses—*on-dits*, and a little spice of scandal, or at least a shrug and a meaning look or two—and the duty is done. We enter the carriage again—urge the coachman to new speed, and go through the same ceremonies, hopes, regrets, and tittle-tattle, till dinner time, and then bless our stars that we have been able to make twenty calls—"so many people were out."

But this is only one side of the question. How is it with us when we receive visits? We enter here upon a deep mystery. Dear simple child of the woods and fields, did you ever hear of *reception*-days? If not, let us enlighten you a little.

The original idea of a reception-day is a charmingly social and friendly one. It is that the many engagements of city life, and the distances which must be traversed in order to visit several friends in one day, make it peculiarly desirable to know when we are sure to find each at home. It may seem strange that this idea should have occurred to people who are confessedly glad of the opportunity to leave a card, because it allows them time to despatch a greater number of visits at one round; but so it is. The very enormity of our practice sometimes leads to spasmodic efforts at reform. Appointing a reception-day is, therefore, or, rather, we should say, *was* intended to make morning-calls something besides a mere form. To say you will always be at home on such a day, is to insure to your friends the pleasure of seeing you; and what a charming conversational circle might thus be gathered, without ceremony or restraint!

No wonder the fashion took at once. But what has fashion made of this plan, so simple, so rational, so in accordance with the best uses of visiting? Something as vapid and senseless as a court drawing-room, or the eternal bowings and compliments of the Chinese! You, artless blossom of the prairies, or belle of some rural city a thousand miles inland, should thank us for putting you on your guard against Utopian constructions of our social canons. When you come to town with your good father, and find that the lady of one of his city correspondents sets apart one morning of every week for the reception of her friends, do not imagine her to be necessarily a "good soul," who hates to disappoint those who call on her, and therefore simply omits going out on that day lest she should miss them. You will find her enshrined in all that is grand and costly; her door guarded by servants, whose formal ushering will kill within you all hope of unaffected and kindly intercourse; her parlours glittering with all she can possibly accumulate that is *recherché* (that is a favourite word of hers), and her own person arrayed with all the solicitude of splendour that morning dress allows, and sometimes something more. She will receive you with practised grace, and beg you to be seated, perhaps seat herself by you and inquire after your health. Then a tall, grave servant will hand you, on a silver salver, a cup of chocolate, or some other permissible refreshment, while your hostess glides over the carpet to show to a new guest or group the identical civilities of which you have just had the benefit. A lady sits at your right hand, as silent as yourself; but you must neither hope for an introduction, nor dare to address her without one, since both these things are forbidden by our code. Another sits at your left, looking wistfully at the fire, or at the stand of greenhouse plants, or, still more likely, at the splendid French clock, but not speaking a word; for she, too, has not the happiness of knowing anybody who chances to sit near her.

Presently she rises; the hostess hastens towards her, presses her hand with great affection, and begs to see her often. She falls into the custody of the footman at the parlour door, is by him committed to his double at the hall door, and then trips lightly down the steps to her carriage, to enact the same farce at the next house where there may be a reception on the same day. You look at the clock, too, rise—are smiled upon, and begged to come again; and, passing through the same tunnel of footmen, reach the door and the street, with time and opportunity to muse on the mystery of visiting.

Now you are not to go away with the idea that those who reduce visiting to this frigid system, are, of necessity, heartless people. That would be very unjust. They are often people of very good hearts indeed; but they have somehow allowed their notions of social intercourse to become sophisticated, so that visiting has ceased with them to be even a symbol of friendly feeling, and they look upon it as merely a mode of exhibiting wealth, style, and desirable acquaintances; an assertion, as it were, of social position. Then they will tell you of the great "waste of time" incurred by the old system of receiving morning calls, and how much better it is to give up one day to it than every day; though, by the way, they never did scruple to be "engaged" or "out" when visits were not desirable. Another thing is—but this, perhaps, they will not tell you,—that the present is an excellent way of refining one's circle; for, as the footman has strict orders not to admit any one, or even receive a card, on other than the regular days, all those who are enough behind the age not to be aware of this, are gradually dropt, their visits passing for nothing, and remaining unreturned. So fades away the momentary dream of sociability with which some simple-hearted people pleased themselves when they heard of reception-days.

But morning calls are not the only form of our social intercourse. We do not forget the claims of "peaceful evening." You have read Cowper, my dear young friend?

> "Now stir the fire, and close the shutters fast,
> Let fall the curtains, wheel the sofa round,
> And while the bubbling and loud hissing urn
> Throws up a steaming column, and the cups
> That cheer, but not inebriate," etc., etc.

And you have been at tea-parties, too, where, besides the excellent tea and coffee and cake and warm biscuits and sliced tongue, there was wealth of good-humoured chat, and, if not wit, plenty of laughter, as the hours wore on towards ten o'clock, when cloaks and hoods were brought, and the gentlemen asked to be allowed to see the ladies home, and, after a brisk walk, everybody was in bed at eleven o'clock, and felt not the worse but the better next morning. Well! we have evening parties, too! A little different, however.

The simple people among whom you have been living really enjoyed these parties. Those who gave them, and those who went to them, had social pleasure as their object. The little bustle, or, perhaps, labour of preparation was just enough to mark the occasion pleasantly. People came together in good humour with themselves and with each other. There may have been some little scandal talked over the tea when it was too strong—but, on the whole, there was a friendly result, and everybody concerned would have felt it a loss to be deprived of such meetings. The very borrowings of certain articles of which no ordinary, moderate household is expected to have enough for extraordinary occasions, promoted good neighbourhood and sociability, and the deficiencies sometimes observable, were in some sense an antidote to pride.

Now all this sounds like a sentimental, Utopian, if not shabby romance to us, so far have we departed from such primitiveness. To begin, we all say we hate parties. When we go to them we groan and declare them stupid, and when we give them we say still worse things. When we are about to give, there is a close calculation either as to the cheapest way, or as to the most *recherché*, without regard to expense. Of course these two views apply to different extent of means, and the former is the more frequent. Where money is no object, the anxiety is to do something that nobody else can do; whether in splendour of decorations or costliness of supper. If Mrs. A. had a thousand dollars' worth of flowers in her rooms, Mrs. B. will strain every nerve to have twice or three times as many, though all the greenhouses within ten miles of the city must be stripped to obtain them. If Mrs. C. bought all the game in market for her supper, Mrs. D.'s anxiety is to send to the prairies for hers,—and so in other matters. Mrs. E. had the *prima donna* to sing at her soirée, and Mrs. F. at once engages the whole opera troupe. This is the principle, and its manifestations are infinite.

But, perhaps, these freaks are characteristic of circles into which wondering eyes like yours are never likely to penetrate. So we will say something of the other classes of party-givers, those who feel themselves under a sort of necessity to invite a great many people for whom they care nothing, merely because these people have before invited them. Obligations of this sort are of so exceedingly complicated a character, that none but a metaphysician could be expected fully to unravel them. The idea of paying one invitation by another is the main one, and whether the invited choose to come or not, is very little to the purpose. The invitation discharges the debt, and places the party-giver in the position of creditor, necessitating, of course, another party, and so on, in endless series.

It is to be observed in passing, that both debtor and creditor in this shifting-scale believe themselves "discharging a duty they owe society." This is another opportunity of getting rid of undesirable acquaintances, since to leave one to whom we "owe" an invitation out of a general party, is equivalent to a final dismissal. This being the case, it is, of course, highly necessary to see that everybody is asked that ought to be asked, and only those omitted whom it is desirable to ignore, and for this purpose, every lady must keep a "visiting list." It is on these occasions that we take care to invite our country friends, especially if we have stayed a few weeks at their houses during the preceding summer.

The next question is as to the entertainment; and this would be a still more anxious affair than it is, if its form and extent were not in good measure prescribed by fashion. There are certainly must-haves, and may-haves, here as elsewhere; but the liberty of choice is not very extensive. If you do not provide the must-haves you are "mean," of course; but it is only by adding the may-haves that you can hope to be elegant. The cost may seem formidable, perhaps; but it has been made matter of accurate computation, that one large party, even though it be a handsome one, costs less in the end than the habit of hospitality for which it is the substitute, so it is not worth while to flinch. We must do our "duty to society," and this is the cheapest way.

Do you ask me if there are among us no old-fashioned people, who continue to invite their friends because they love them and wish to see them, offering only such moderate entertainment as may serve to promote social feeling? Yes, indeed! there are even some who will ask you to dine, for the mere pleasure of your company, and with no intention to astonish you or excite your envy! We boast that it was a lady of our city, who declined giving a large party to "return invitations," saying she did not wish "to exhaust, in the prodigality of a night, the hospitality of a year." Ten such could be found among us, we may hope; leaven enough, perhaps, to work out, in time, a change for the better in our social plan. Conversation is by no means despised, in some circles, even though it turn on subjects of moral or literary interest, and parlour music, which aims at no *eclat*, is to be heard sometimes among people who could afford to hire opera singers.

It must be confessed that the wholesale method of "doing up" our social obligations is a convenient one on some accounts. It prevents jealousy by placing all alike on a footing of perfect indifference. The apportionment of civilities is a very delicate matter. Really, in some cases, it is walking among eggs to invite only a few of your friends at a time. If you choose them as being acquainted with each other, somebody will be offended at being included or excluded. If intellectual sympathy be your touchstone, for every one gratified there will be two miffed, and so on with all other classifications. Attempts have been made to obviate this difficulty. One lady proposed to consider as congenial all those who keep carriages, but the circle proved so very dull, that she was obliged to exert her ingenuity for another common quality by which to arrange her soirées. Another tried the expedient of inviting her fashionable friends at one time, her husband's political friends at another, and the religious friends, whom both were desirous to propitiate, at another; but her task was as perplexing as that of the man who had the fox, the goose, and the bag of oats to ferry over the river in a boat that would hold but one of them at a time. So large parties have it; and in the murky shadow of this simulacrum of sociability we are likely to freeze for some time to come; certainly until all purely mercantile calculation is banished from our civilities.

It is with visiting as with travelling; those who would make the most of either must begin by learning to *renounce*. We cannot do everything; and to enjoy our friends we must curtail our acquaintances. When we would kindle a fire, we do not begin by scattering the coals in every direction; so neither should we attempt to promote social feeling by making formal calls once or twice a year. If we give offence, so be it; it shows that there was nothing to lose. If we find ourselves left out of what is called fashionable society, let us bless our stars, and devote the time thus saved to something that we really like. What a gain there would be if anything drove us to living for ourselves and not for other people; for our friends, rather than for a world, which, after all our sacrifices, cares not a pin about us!

LYDIA M. CHILD.

THE maiden name of this accomplished writer was Lydia Maria Francis. She is a native of Massachusetts, and a sister of the Rev. Conyers Francis, D. D., of Harvard University.

Mrs. Child commenced authorship as early as 1824. Her first production was "Hobomok." It was a novel based upon New England colonial traditions, and was suggested to her mind by an article in the North American Review, in which that class of subjects was urgently recommended as furnishing excellent materials for American works of fiction. Probably, the example of Cooper, who was then in the height of his popularity, and still more, that of Miss Sedgwick, whose "Redwood" was then fresh from the press, had also some influence upon the new author. Her work was well received, and was followed in 1825 by "The Rebels," a tale of the Revolution, very similar in character to the former. Both of these works are now out of print. A new edition of them would be very acceptable.

Her next publication, I believe, was "The Frugal Housewife," containing directions for household economy, and numerous receipts. For this she had some difficulty in finding a publisher, in consequence of the great variety of cookery books already in the market. But it proved a very profitable speculation, more than six thousand copies having been sold in a single year.

Mrs. Child's versatility of talent, and the entire success with which she could pass from the regions of fancy and sentiment to those of fact and duty, still further appeared in her next work, which was on the subject of education. It was addressed to mothers, and was called "The Mother's Book." It contains plain, practical directions for that most important part of education which falls more immediately under the mother's jurisdiction. It has gone through very numerous editions, both in this country and in England, and continues to hold its ground, notwithstanding the number of excellent books that have since appeared on the same subject. It was published in 1831.

The "Girl's Book," in two volumes, followed in 1832, and met with a similar success. Its object was not so much the amusement of children, as their instruction, setting forth the duties of parent and child, but in a manner to attract youthful readers.

She wrote about the same time "Lives of Madame de Staël and Madame Roland," in one volume; "Lives of Lady Russell and Madame Guyon," in one volume; "Biographies of Good Wives," in one volume; and the "History of the Condition of Women in all Ages," in two volumes. All these were prepared for the "Ladies' Family Library," of which she was the editor. They are of the nature of compilations, and therefore do not show much opportunity for the display of originality. But they do show, what is a remarkable trait in all of Mrs. Child's writings, an earnest love of truth. The most original work of the series is the "History of the Condition of Women." They are all very useful and valuable volumes.

In 1833, Mrs. Child published an "Appeal for that Class of Americans called Africans." It is said to be the first work that appeared in this country in favour of immediate emancipation. It made a profound impression at the time.

In the same year, Mrs. Child published "The Coronal." It was a collection of small pieces in prose and verse, most of which had appeared before in periodicals of various kinds.

One of the most finished and original of Mrs. Child's works, though it has not been the most popular, appeared in 1835. It was a romance of Greece in the days of Pericles, entitled "Philothea." Like the "Prophet of Ionia," and some of her other classical tales, the "Philothea" shows a surprising familiarity with the manners, places, and ideas of the ancients. It seems, indeed, more like a translation of a veritable Grecian legend, than an original work of the nineteenth century. While all the externals of scenery, manners, and so forth, are almost faultlessly perfect, perhaps not inferior in this respect to the "Travels of Anacharsis," the story itself has all the freedom of the wildest romance. It is, however, romance of a purely ideal or philosophical cast, such as one would suppose it hardly possible to have come from the same pen that had produced a marketable book on cookery, or that was yet to produce such heart-histories as "The Umbrella Girl," or "The Neighbour-in-law." Indeed, the most remarkable thing in the mental constitution of Mrs. Child, is this harmonious combination of apparently opposite qualities—a rapt and lofty idealism, transcending equally the conventional and the real, united with a plain common sense that can tell in homely phrase the best way to make a soup or lay a cradle—an extremely sensitive organization, that is carried into the third heavens at the sound of Ole Bull's violin, and yet does not shrink from going down Lispenard street to see old Charity Bowery.

Mrs. Child conducted for several years a "Juvenile Miscellany," for which she composed many tales for the amusement and instruction of children. These have since been corrected and re-written, and others added to them, making three small volumes, called "Flowers for Children." One of these volumes is for children from four to six years of age; one, for those from eight to nine; and one, for those from eleven to twelve.

In 1841, Mr. and Mrs. Child went to New York, where they conducted for some time the "Anti-Slavery Standard." Mrs. Child wrote much for this paper, not only upon the topic suggested by the title, but on miscellaneous subjects.

In the same year, 1841, she commenced a series of Letters to the Boston Courier, which contain some of the finest things she has ever written. They were very extensively copied, and were afterwards collected into a volume, under the title of "Letters from New York." This was followed by a second series in 1845.

These Letters are exceedingly various. They contain tales, speculations, descriptions of passing events, biographies, and essays, and bring alternately tears and laughter, according to the varying moods of the writer.

In 1846, she published a volume called "Fact and Fiction," consisting of tales that had previously appeared in the Magazines and Annuals. These are of a miscellaneous character, somewhat like the "Letters," only longer.

OLE BULL.

I HAVE twice heard Ole Bull. I scarcely dare to tell the impression his music made upon me. But casting aside all fear of ridicule for excessive enthusiasm, I will say that it expressed to me more of the infinite, than I ever saw, or heard, or dreamed of, in the realms of Nature, Art, or Imagination.

They tell me his performance is wonderfully skilful; but I have not enough of scientific knowledge to judge of the difficulties he overcomes. I can readily believe of him, what Bettina says of Beethoven, that "his spirit creates the inconceivable, and his fingers perform the impossible." He played on four strings at once, and produced the rich harmony of four instruments. His bow touched the strings as if in sport, and brought forth light leaps of sound, with electric rapidity, yet clear in their distinctness. He made his violin sing with flute-like voice, and accompany itself with a guitar,

9

which came in ever and anon like big drops of musical rain. All this I felt as well as heard, without the slightest knowledge of *quartetto* or *staccato*. How he did it, I know as little as I know how the sun shines, or the spring brings forth its blossoms. I only know that music came from his soul into mine, and carried it upward to worship with the angels.

Oh, the exquisite delicacy of those notes! Now tripping and fairy-like, as the song of Ariel; now soft and low, as the breath of a sleeping babe, yet clear as a fine-toned bell; now high, as a lark soaring upward, till lost among the stars!

Noble families sometimes double their names, to distinguish themselves from collateral branches of inferior rank. I have doubled his, and in memory of the Persian nightingale have named him Ole Bulbul.

Immediately after a deep, impassioned, plaintive melody, an adagio of his own composing, which uttered the soft, low breathing of a mother's prayer, rising to the very agony of supplication, a voice in the crowd called for Yankee Doodle. It shocked me like harlequin tumbling on the altar of a temple. I had no idea that he would comply with what seemed to me the absurd request. But, smiling, he drew the bow across his violin, and our national tune rose on the air, transfigured, in a veil of glorious variations. It was Yankee Doodle in a state of clairvoyance—a wonderful proof of how the most common and trivial may be exalted by the influx of the infinite.

When urged to join the throng who are following this star of the north, I coolly replied, "I never like lions; moreover, I am too ignorant of musical science to appreciate his skill." But when I heard this man, I at once recognised a power that transcends science, and which mere skill may toil after in vain. I had no need of knowledge to feel this subtle influence, any more than I needed to study optics to perceive the beauty of the rainbow. It overcame me like a miracle. I felt that my soul was, for the first time, baptized in music; that my spiritual relations were somehow changed by it, and that I should henceforth be otherwise than I had been. I was so oppressed with "the exceeding weight of glory," that I drew my breath with difficulty. As I came out of the building, the street sounds hurt me with their harshness. The sight of ragged boys and importunate coachmen jarred more than ever on my feelings. I wanted that the angels that had ministered to my spirit should attune theirs also. It seemed to me as if such music should bring all the world into the harmonious beauty of divine order. I passed by my earthly home, and knew it not. My spirit seemed to be floating through infinite space. The next day I felt like a person who had been in a trance, seen heaven opened, and then returned to earth again.

This doubtless appears very excessive in one who has passed the enthusiasm of youth, with a frame too healthy and substantial to be conscious of nerves, and with a mind instinctively opposed to lion-worship. In truth, it seems wonderful to myself; but so it was. Like a romantic girl of sixteen, I would pick up the broken string of his violin, and wear it as a relic, with a half superstitious feeling that some mysterious magic of melody lay hidden therein.

I know not whether others were as powerfully wrought upon as myself; for my whole being passed into my ear, and the faces around me were invisible. But the exceeding stillness showed that the spirits of the multitude bowed down before the magician. While he was playing, the rustling of a leaf might have been heard; and when he closed, the tremendous bursts of applause told how the hearts of thousands leaped up like one.

His personal appearance increases the charm. He looks pure, natural, and vigorous, as I imagine Adam in Paradise. His inspired soul dwells in a strong frame, of admirable proportions, and looks out intensely from his earnest eyes. Whatever may be his theological opinions, the religious *sentiment* must be strong in his nature; for Teutonic reverence, mingled with impassioned aspiration, shines through his honest northern face, and runs through all his music. I speak of him as he appears while he and his violin converse together. When not playing, there is nothing observable in his appearance, except genuine health, the unconscious calmness of strength in repose, and the most unaffected simplicity of dress and manner. But when he takes his violin, and holds it so caressingly to his ear, to catch the faint vibration of its strings, it seems as if "the angels were whispering to him." As his fingers sweep across the strings, the angels pass into his soul, give him their tones, and look out from his eyes, with the wondrous beauty of inspiration. His motions sway to the music, like a tree in the winds; for soul and body accord. In fact, "his soul is but a harp, which an infinite breath modulates; his senses are but strings, which weave the passing air into rhythm and cadence."

If it be true, as has been said, that a person ignorant of the rules of music, who gives himself up to its influence, without knowing whence it comes, or whither it goes, experiences, more than the scientific, the passionate joy of the composer himself, in his moments of inspiration, then was I blest in my ignorance. While I listened, music was to my soul what the atmosphere is to my body; it was the breath of my inward life. I felt, more deeply than ever, that music is the highest symbol of the infinite and holy. I heard it moan plaintively over the discords of society, and the dimmed beauty of humanity. It filled me with inexpressible longing to see man at one with Nature and with God; and it thrilled me with joyful prophecy that the hope would pass into glorious fulfilment.

With renewed force I felt what I have often said, that the secret of creation lay in music. "A *voice* to light gave being." Sound led the stars into their places, and taught chemical affinities to waltz into each other's arms.

> "By one pervading spirit
> Of tones and numbers all things are controlled;
> As sages taught, where faith was found, to merit
> Initiation in that mystery old."

Music is the soprano, the feminine principle, the *heart* of the universe. Because it is the voice of Love,—because it is the highest type, and aggregate expression of passional attraction, therefore it is infinite; therefore it pervades all space, and transcends all being, like a divine influx. What the tone is to the word, what expression is to the form, what affection is to thought, what the heart is to the head, what intuition is to argument, what insight is to policy, what religion is to philosophy, what holiness is to heroism, what moral influence is to power, what woman is to man—is music to the universe. Flexile, graceful, and free, it pervades all things, and is limited by none. It is not poetry, but the *soul* of poetry; it is not mathematics, but it is *in* numbers, like harmonious proportions in cast iron; it is not painting, but it shines *through* colours, and gives them their tone; it is not dancing, but it *makes* all gracefulness of motion; it is not architecture, but the stones take their places in harmony with its voice, and stand in "petrified music." In the words of Bettina—"Every art is the body of music, which is the soul of every art; and so is music, too, the soul of love, which also answers not for its working; for it is the contact of divine with human."

But I must return from this flight among the stars, to Ole Bulbul's violin; and the distance between the two is not so great as it appears.

Some, who never like to admit that the greatest stands before them, say that Paganini played the Carnival of Venice better than his Norwegian rival. I know not. But if ever laughter ran along the chords of a musical instrument with a wilder joy, if ever tones quarrelled with more delightful dissonance, if ever violin frolicked with more capricious grace, than Ole Bulbul's, in that fantastic whirl of melody, I envy the ears that heard it.

THE UMBRELLA GIRL.

In a city, which shall be nameless, there lived, long ago, a young girl, the only daughter of a widow. She came from the country, and was as ignorant of the dangers of a city, as the squirrels of her native fields. She had glossy black hair, gentle, beaming eyes, and "lips like wet coral." Of course, she knew that she was beautiful; for when she was a child, strangers often stopped as she passed, and exclaimed, "How handsome she is!" And as she grew older, the young men gazed on her with admiration. She was poor, and removed to the city to earn her living by covering umbrellas. She was just at that susceptible age, when youth is passing into womanhood; when the soul begins to be pervaded by "that restless principle, which impels poor humans to seek perfection in union."

At the hotel opposite, Lord Henry Stuart, an English nobleman, had at that time taken lodgings. His visit to this country is doubtless well remembered by many, for it made a great sensation at the time. He was a peer of the realm, descended from the royal line, and was, moreover, a strikingly handsome man, of right princely carriage. He was subsequently a member of the British Parliament, and is now dead.

As this distinguished stranger passed to and from his hotel, he encountered the umbrella-girl, and was impressed by her uncommon beauty. He easily traced her to the opposite store, where he soon after went to purchase an umbrella. This was followed up by presents of flowers, chats by the way-side, and invitations to walk or ride; all of which were gratefully accepted by the unsuspecting rustic. He was playing a game for temporary excitement; she, with a head full of romance, and a heart melting under the influence of love, was unconsciously endangering the happiness of her whole life.

Lord Henry invited her to visit the public gardens on the fourth of July. In the simplicity of her heart, she believed all his flattering professions, and considered herself his bride elect; she therefore accepted the invitation with innocent frankness. But she had no dress fit to appear on such a public occasion, with a gentleman of high rank, whom she verily supposed to be her destined husband. While these thoughts revolved in her mind, her eye was unfortunately attracted by a beautiful piece of silk belonging to her employer. Ah, could she not take it without being seen, and pay for it secretly, when she had earned money enough? The temptation conquered her in a moment of weakness. She concealed the silk, and conveyed it to her lodgings. It was the first thing she had ever stolen, and her remorse was painful. She would have carried it back, but she dreaded discovery. She was not sure that her repentance would be met in a spirit of forgiveness.

On the eventful fourth of July she came out in her new dress. Lord Henry complimented her upon her elegant appearance; but she was not happy. On their way to the gardens, he talked to her in a manner which she did not comprehend. Perceiving this, he spoke more explicitly. The guileless young creature stopped, looked in his face with mournful reproach, and burst into tears. The nobleman took her hand kindly, and said, "My dear, are you an innocent girl?" "I am, I am," replied she, with convulsive sobs. "Oh, what have I ever done, or said, that you should ask me that?" Her words stirred the deep fountains of his better nature. "If you are innocent," said he, "God forbid that I should make you otherwise. But you accepted my invitations and presents so readily, that I supposed you understood me." "What *could* I understand," said she, "except that you intended to make me your wife?" Though reared amid the proudest distinctions of rank, he felt no inclination to smile. He blushed and was silent. The heartless conventionalities of life stood rebuked in the presence of affectionate simplicity. He conveyed her to her humble home, and bade her farewell, with a thankful consciousness that he had done no irretrievable injury to her future prospects. The remembrance of her would soon be to him as the recollection of last year's butterflies. With her, the wound was deeper. In her solitary chamber, she wept in bitterness of heart over her ruined air-castles. And that dress, which she had stolen to make an appearance befitting his bride! Oh, what if she should be discovered? And would not the heart of her poor widowed mother break, if she should ever know that her child was a thief? Alas, her wretched forebodings were too true. The silk was traced to her; she was arrested on her way to the store, and dragged to prison. There she refused all nourishment, and wept incessantly.

On the fourth day, the keeper called upon Isaac T. Hopper, and informed him that there was a young girl in prison, who appeared to be utterly friendless, and determined to die by starvation. The kind-hearted Friend immediately went to her assistance. He found her lying on the floor of her cell, with her face buried in her hands, sobbing as if her heart would break. He tried to comfort her, but could obtain no answer.

"Leave us alone," said he to the keeper. "Perhaps she will speak to me, if there is no one to hear." When they were alone together, he put back the hair from her temples, laid his hand kindly on her beautiful head, and said in soothing tones, "My child, consider me as thy father. Tell me all thou hast done. If thou hast taken this silk, let me know all about it. I will do for thee as I would for a daughter; and I doubt not that I can help thee out of this difficulty."

After a long time spent in affectionate entreaty, she leaned her young head on his friendly shoulder, and sobbed out, "Oh, I wish I was dead. What will my poor mother say, when she knows of my disgrace?"

"Perhaps we can manage that she never shall know it," replied he; and alluring her by this hope, he gradually obtained from her the whole story of her acquaintance with the nobleman. He bade her be comforted, and take nourishment; for he would see that the silk was paid for, and the prosecution withdrawn. He went immediately to her employer, and told him the story. "This is her first offence," said he; "the girl is young, and the only child of a poor widow. Give her a chance to retrieve this one false step, and she may be restored to society, a useful and honoured woman. I will see that thou art paid for the silk." The man readily agreed to withdraw the prosecution, and said he would have dealt otherwise by the girl, had he known all the circumstances. "Thou shouldst have inquired into the merits of the case, my friend," replied Isaac. "By this kind of thoughtlessness, many a young creature is driven into the downward path, who might easily have been saved."

The kind-hearted man then went to the hotel and inquired for Henry Stuart. The servant said his lordship had not yet risen. "Tell him my business is of importance," said Friend Hopper. The servant soon returned and conducted him to the chamber. The nobleman appeared surprised that a plain Quaker should thus intrude upon his luxurious privacy; but when he heard his errand, he blushed deeply, and frankly admitted the truth of the girl's statement. His benevolent visiter took the opportunity to "bear a testimony," as the Friends say, against the sin and selfishness of profligacy. He did it in such a kind and fatherly manner, that the young man's heart was touched. He excused himself, by saying that he would not have tampered with the girl, if he had known her to be virtuous. "I have done many wrong things," said he, "but, thank God, no betrayal of confiding innocence rests on my conscience. I have always esteemed it the basest act of which man is capable." The imprisonment of the poor girl, and the forlorn situation in which she had been found, distressed him greatly. And when Isaac represented that the silk had been stolen for *his* sake, that the girl had thereby lost profitable employment, and was obliged to return to her distant home, to avoid the danger of exposure, he took out a fifty dollar note, and offered it to pay her expenses. "Nay," said Isaac, "thou art a very rich man; I see in thy hand a large roll of such notes. She is the daughter of a poor widow, and thou hast been the means of doing her great injury. Give me another."

Lord Henry handed him another fifty dollar note, and smiled as he said, "You understand your business well. But you have acted nobly, and I reverence you for it. If you ever visit England, come to see me. I will give you a cordial welcome, and treat you like a nobleman."

"Farewell, friend," replied Isaac: "Though much to blame in this affair, thou too hast behaved nobly. Mayst thou be blessed in domestic life, and trifle no more with the feelings of poor girls; not even with those whom others have betrayed and deserted."

Luckily, the girl had sufficient presence of mind to assume a false name, when arrested; by which means her true name was kept out of the newspapers. "I did this," said she, "for my poor mother's sake." With the money given by Lord Henry, the silk was paid for, and she was sent home to her mother, well provided with clothing. Her name and place of residence remain to this day a secret in the breast of her benefactor.

Several years after the incidents I have related, a lady called at Friend Hopper's house, and asked to see him. When he entered the room, he found a handsomely dressed young matron with a blooming boy of five or six years old. She rose to meet him and her voice choked, as she said, "Friend Hopper, do you know me?" He replied that he did not. She fixed her tearful eyes earnestly upon him, and said, "You once helped me, when in great distress." But the good missionary of humanity had helped too many in distress, to be able to recollect her without more precise information. With a tremulous voice, she bade her son go into the next room, for a few minutes; then dropping on her knees, she hid her face in his lap, and sobbed out, "I am the girl that stole the silk. Oh, where should I now be, if it had not been for you!"

When her emotion was somewhat calmed, she told him that she had married a highly respectable man, a Senator of his native State. Having a call to visit the city, she had again and again passed Friend Hopper's house, looking wistfully at the windows to catch a sight of him; but when she attempted to enter, her courage failed.

"But I go away to-morrow," said she, "and I could not leave the city, without once more seeing and thanking him who saved me from ruin." She recalled her little boy, and said to him, "Look at that gentleman, and remember him well; for he was the best friend your mother ever had." With an earnest invitation that he would visit her happy home, and a fervent "God bless you," she bade her benefactor farewell.

EMMA C. EMBURY.

Mrs. Embury is a native of New York, and a daughter of an eminent physician of that city, James R. Manley, M. D. She was married on the 10th of May, 1828, to Mr. Daniel Embury of Brooklyn, where she has since resided.

Mrs. Embury has written much, both in prose and verse, and with equal success in both kinds of writing. Her earlier effusions were published under the signature of "Ianthe." A volume of them was collected under the title of "Guido, and other Poems." Her tales, like her poems, have all been published originally in magazines and other periodicals. Were these all collected, they would fill many volumes. The only volumes formed in this way, thus far, have been, "Blind Girl, and other Tales," "Glimpses of Home Life," and "Pictures of Early Life." In 1845 she edited a very elegant gift book, called "Nature's Gems, or American Wild Flowers," with numerous coloured plates, and articles, both in prose and verse, by herself. In 1846, she published another collection of poems, called "Love's Token Flowers." In 1848, "The Waldorf Family" appeared. It is a fairy tale of Brittany, adapted to the meridian of the United States and the present age of the world, being partly a translation and partly original.

If Mrs. Embury never rises so high as some of our female writers sometimes do, no one, on the other hand, who has written so much, approaches her in the ability of writing uniformly well. She seems to have the faculty of never being dull. There is, too, a certain gentle amenity of thought and diction that never forsakes her, taking from the edge of what might otherwise be harsh, and giving a charm to what might be commonplace. If her stories are not deeply tragical or thrilling, they are always beautiful, they always please, they always leave the mind instructed and the heart better.

TWO FACES UNDER ONE HOOD.

"The land hath bubbles as the water hath,
And these are of them."

"Who is she?"

"Ay, that is precisely the question which everybody asks, and nobody can answer."

"She is a splendid-looking creature, be she who she may."

"And her manners are as lovely as her person. Come and dine with me to-morrow; I sit directly opposite her at table, so you can have a fair opportunity of gazing at this new star in our dingy firmament."

"Agreed; I am about changing my lodgings, and if I like the company at your house, I may take a room there.

The speakers were two gay and fashionable men: one a student of law, the other a confidential clerk in a large commercial house. They belonged to that class of youths, so numerous in New York, who, while in reality labouring most industriously for a livelihood, yet take infinite pains to seem idle and useless members of society; fellows who at their outset in life try hard to repress a certain respectability of character, which after a while comes up in spite of them, and makes them very good sort of men in the end. The lady who attracted so much of their attention at that moment, had recently arrived in the city; and, as she wore the weeds of widowhood, her solitary position seemed sufficiently explained. But there was an attractiveness in her appearance and manners which excited a more than usual interest in the stranger's history. She had that peculiar fascination which gentlemen regard as the most exquisite refinement of frank simplicity, but which ladies, better versed in the intricacies of female nature, always recognise as the perfection of art. None but an impulsive, warm-hearted woman, can retain her freshness of feeling and ready responsive sympathy after five-and-twenty; and such a woman never obtains sufficient command over her own sensitiveness to exhibit the perfect adaptability and uniform amiableness of deportment which are characteristics of the skilful fascinator.

Harry Maurice, the young lawyerling, failed not to fulfil his appointment with his friend; and at four o'clock on the following day, he found himself the *vis-à-vis* of the bewitching Mrs. Howard, gazing on her loveliness through the somewhat hazy atmosphere of a steaming dinner-table. If he was struck with her appearance when he saw her only stepping from a carriage, he was now completely bewildered by the whole battery of charms which were directed against him. A well-rounded and graceful figure, whose symmetry was set off by a close-fitting dress of black bombazine; superb arms gleaming through sleeves of the thinnest crape; a neck of dazzling whiteness, only half concealed beneath the folds of a *fichu à la grand'mère;* features not regularly beautiful, somewhat sharp in outline, but full of expression, and enlivened by the brightest of eyes and pearliest of teeth, were the most obvious of her attractions.

The ordinary civilities of the table, proffered with profound respect by Maurice, and accepted with quiet dignity by the lady, opened the way to conversation. Before the dessert came on, the first barriers to acquaintance had been removed, and, somewhat to his own surprise, Harry Maurice found himself perpetrating bad puns and uttering gay *bon-mots* in the full hearing, and evidently to the genuine amusement, of the lovely widow. When dinner was over, the trio found themselves in the midst of an animated discussion respecting the relative capacity for sentiment in men and women. The subject was too interesting to be speedily dropped, and the party adjourned to a convenient corner of the drawing-room. As usual, the peculiar character of the topic upon which they had fallen, led to the unguarded expression of individual opinions, and of course to the development of much *implied* experience. Nothing could have been better calculated to display Mrs. Howard as one of the most sensitive, as well as sensible of her sex. She had evidently been one of the victims to the false notions of society. A premature marriage, an uncongenial partner, and all the thousand-

and-one ills attendant upon baffled sentiment, had probably entered largely into the lady's bygone knowledge of life. Not that she deigned to confide any of her personal experience to her new friends, but they possessed active imaginations, and it was easy to make large inferences from small premises.

Midnight sounded ere the young men remembered that something was due to the ordinary forms of society, and that they had been virtually "talking love," for seven hours, to a perfect stranger. The sudden reaction of feeling, the dread lest they had been exposing their peculiar habits of thought to the eye of ridicule, the frightful suspicion that they must have seemed most particularly "fresh" to the lady, struck both the gentlemen at the same moment. They attempted to apologize, but the womanly tact of Mrs. Howard spared them all the discomfort of such an awkward explanation. She reproached herself so sweetly for having suffered her impulsive nature to beguile her with such unwonted confidence,—she thanked them so gently for their momentary interest in her "melancholy recollections of blighted feelings,"—she so earnestly implored them to forget her indiscreet communings with persons "whose singular congeniality of soul had made her forget that they were strangers," that she succeeded in restoring them to a comfortable sense of their own powers of attraction. Instead of thinking they had acted like men "*afflicted with an extraordinary quantity of youngness,*" they came to the conclusion that Mrs. Howard was one of the most discriminating of her sex; and the tear which swam in her soft eyes as she gave them her hand in parting, added the one irresistible charm to their previous bewilderment.

The acquaintance so auspiciously begun was not allowed to languish. Harry Maurice took lodgings in the same house; and thus, without exposing the fair widow to invidious remark, he was enabled to enjoy her society with less restraint. Unlike most of his sudden fancies, he found his liking for this lady "to grow by what it fed on." She looked so very lovely in her simple white morning dress and pretty French cap, and her manners partook so agreeably of the simplicity and easy negligence of her breakfast attire, that she seemed more charming than ever. Indeed, almost every one in the house took a fancy to her. She won the hearts of the ladies by her unbounded fondness for their children, and her consummate tact in inventing new games for them; while her entire unconsciousness of her own attractions, and apparent indifference to admiration, silenced for a time all incipient jealousy. The gentlemen could not but be pleased with a pretty woman who was so sweet-tempered and so little exacting; while her peculiar talent for putting every one in good humour with themselves,—a talent, which in less skilful hands would have been merely an adroit power of flattery,—sufficiently accounted for her general influence.

There was only one person who seemed proof against Mrs. Howard's spell. This was an old bank clerk, who for forty years had occupied the same post, and stood at the same desk, encountering no other changes than that of a new ledger for an old one, and hating every innovation in morals and manners with an intensity singularly at variance with his usual quietude, or rather stagnation of feeling. For nearly half his life he had occupied the same apartment, and nothing but a fire or an earthquake would have been sufficient to dislodge him. Many of the transient residents in the house knew him only by the *sobriquet* of "the Captain;" and the half-dictatorial, half-whimsical manner in which, with the usual privilege of a humourist, he ordered trifling matters about the house, was probably the origin of the title. When the ladies who presided at the head of the establishment first opened their house for the reception of boarders, he had taken up his quarters there, and they had all grown old together; so it was not to be wondered at if he had somewhat the manner of a master.

The Captain had looked with an evil eye upon Mrs. Howard from the morning after her arrival, when he had detected her French dressing-maid in the act of peeping into his boots, as they stood outside of the chamber-door. This instance of curiosity, which he could only attribute to an unjustifiable anxiety to be acquainted with the *name* of the owner of the said boots, was such a flagrant impropriety, besides being such a gross violation of his privilege of privacy, that he could not forgive it. He made a formal complaint of the matter to Mrs. Howard, and earnestly advised her to dismiss so prying a servant. The lady pleaded her attachment to a faithful attendant, who had left her native France for pure love of her, and besought him to forgive a first and venial error. The Captain had no faith in this being a *first* fault, and as for its veniality, if she had put out an "I," and called it a *venal* affair, it would have better suited his ideas of her. He evidently suspected both the mistress and the maid; and a prejudice in his mind was like a thistle-seed,—it might wing its way on gossamer pinions, but once planted, it was sure to produce its crop of thorns.

In vain the lady attempted to conciliate him; in vain she tried to humour his whims, and pat and fondle his hobbies. He was proof against all her allurements, and whenever by some new or peculiar grace she won unequivocal expressions of admiration from the more susceptible persons around her, a peevish "Fudge!" would resound most emphatically from the Captain's lips.

"Pray, sir, will you be so good as to inform me what you meant by the offensive monosyllable you chose to utter this morning, when I addressed a remark to Mrs. Howard?" said Harry Maurice to him, upon a certain occasion, when the old gentleman had seemed more than usually caustic and observing.

The Captain looked slowly up from his newspaper: "I am old enough, young man, to be allowed to talk to myself, if I please."

"I suppose you meant to imply that I was '*green*,' and stood a fair chance of being '*done brown*,'" said Harry, mischievously, well knowing his horror of all modern slang.

"I am no judge of *colours*," said he, drily, "but I can tell a fool from a knave when I see them contrasted. In old times it was the *woman's* privilege to play the fool, but the order of things is reversed now-a-days." So saying, he drew on his gloves, and walked out with his usual clock-like regularity.

Three months passed away, and Harry Maurice was "full five fathoms deep" in love with the beautiful stranger. Yet he knew no more of her personal history than on the day when they first met, and the old question of "Who is she?" was often in his mind, though the respect growing out of a genuine attachment checked it ere the words rose to his lips. He heard her speak of plantations at the South, and on more than one occasion he had been favoured with a commission to transact banking business for her. He had made several deposits in her name, and had drawn out several small sums for her use. He knew therefore that she had moneys at command, but of her family and connexions he was profoundly ignorant. He was too much in love, however, to hesitate long on this point. Young, ardent, and possessed of that *pseudo*-romance, which, like French gilding, so much resembles the *real* thing that many prefer it, as being cheaper and more durable, he was particularly pleased with the apparent disinterestedness of his affection. Too poor to marry unless he found a bride possessed of fortune, he was now precisely in the situation where alone he could feel himself on the same footing with a wealthy wife. He had an established position in society, his family were among the oldest and most respectable residents of the State, and the offer of his hand under such circumstances to a lone, unfriended stranger, took away all appearance of cupidity from the suitor, while it constituted a claim upon the lady's gratitude as well as affection. With all his assumed self-confidence, Maurice was in reality a very modest fellow, and he had many a secret misgiving as to her opinion of his merits; for he was one of those youths who use puppyism as a cloak for their diffidence. He wanted to assure himself of her preference before committing himself by a declaration, and to do this required a degree of skill in womancraft that far exceeded his powers.

In the mean time the prejudices of the Captain gained greater strength, and although there was no open war between him and the fair widow, there was perpetual skirmishing between them. Indeed it could not well be otherwise, considering the decided contrast between the two parties. The Captain was prejudiced, dogmatic, and full of old-fashioned notions. A steady adherent of ruffled shirts, well-starched collars, and shaven chins, he regarded with contempt the paltry subterfuges of modern fashion. At five-and-twenty he had formed his habits of thinking and acting, and at sixty he was only the same man grown older. A certain indolence of temper prevented him from investigating anything new, and he was therefore content to deny all that did not conform to his early notions. He hated fashionable slang, despised a new-modelled costume, scorned modern morality, and ranked the crime of wearing a moustache and imperial next to the seven deadly sins. His standard of female perfection was a certain "ladye-love" of his youth, who might have served as a second Harriet Byron to some new Sir Charles Grandison. After a courtship of ten years (during which time he never ventured upon a greater familiarity than that of pressing the tips of her fingers to his lips on a New Year's day), the lady died, and the memory of his early attachment, though something like a rose encased in ice, was still the one flower of his life.

Of course, the freedom of modern manners was shocking to him, and in Mrs. Howard he beheld the impersonation of vanity, coquetry, and falsehood. Besides, she interfered with his privileges. She made suggestions about certain arrangements at table; she pointed out improvements in several minor household comforts; she asked for the liver-wing of the chicken, which had heretofore been his peculiar perquisite, as carver; she played the accordeon, and kept an Eolian harp in the window of her room, which unfortunately adjoined his; and, to crown all, she did not hesitate to ask him questions as coolly as if she was totally unconscious of his privileges of privacy. He certainly had a most decided grudge against the lady, and she, though apparently all gentleness and meekness, yet had so adroit a way of saying and doing disagreeable things to the old gentleman, that it was easy to infer a mutual dislike.

The Captain's benevolence had been excited by seeing Harry Maurice on the highroad to being victimized, and he actually took some pains to make the young man see things in their true light.

"Pray, Mr. Maurice, do you spend all your mornings at your office?" said he one day.

"Certainly, sir."

"Then you differ from most young lawyers," was the gruff reply.

"Perhaps I have better reasons than many others for my close application. While completing my studies, I am enabled to earn a moderate salary by writing for Mr. ——, and this is of some consequence to me."

The old man looked inquiringly, and Maurice answered the silent question.

"You know enough of our family, sir, to be aware that my father's income died with him. A few hundred dollars per annum are all that remains for the support of my mother and an invalid sister, who reside in Connecticut. Of course, if I would not encroach upon their small means, I must do something for my own maintenance."

The Captain's look grew pleasanter as he replied, "I do not mean to be guilty of any impertinent intrusion into your affairs, but it seems to me that you share the weakness of your fellows, by thus working like a slave and spending like a prince."

Maurice laughed. "Perhaps my princely expenditures would scarcely bear as close a scrutiny as my slavish toil. I really work, but it often happens that I only *seem* to spend."

"I understand you, but you are worthy of better things; you should have courage to throw off the trammels of fashion, and live economically, like a man of sense, until fortune favours you."

The young man was silent for a moment, then, as if to change the subject, asked, "What was your object in inquiring about my morning walks?"

"I merely wanted to know if you ever met Mrs. Howard in Broadway in the morning."

"Never, sir; but I am so seldom there, that it would be strange if I should encounter an acquaintance among its throngs."

"I am told she goes out every morning at nine o'clock, and does not return until three."

"I suppose she is fond of walking."

"Humph! I rather suspect she has some regular business."

"Quite likely," said Maurice, laughing heartily, "perhaps she is a bank clerk,—occupied from nine to three, you say,—just banking hours."

The Captain looked sternly in the young man's face, then uttering his emphatic "Fudge!" turned upon his heel, and whistling

"A Frog he would a wooing go," sauntered out of the room, thoroughly disgusted with the whole race of modern young men.

The old gentleman's methodical habits of business had won for him the confidence of every one, and as an almost necessary consequence had involved him in the responsibility of several trusteeships. There were sundry old ladies and orphans whose pecuniary affairs he had managed for years with the punctuality of a Dutch clock. Before noon, on the days when their interest moneys were due, he always had the satisfaction of paying them into the hands of the owners. It was only for some such purpose that he ever left his post during business hours; but the claims of the widow and the fatherless came before those of the ledger, and he sometimes stole an hour from his daily duties to attend to these private trusts.

Not long after he had sought to awaken his young friend's suspicions respecting Mrs. Howard, one of these occasions occurred. At midday he found himself seated in a pleasant drawing-room, between an old lady and a young one, both of whom regarded him as the very best of men. He had transacted his business and was about taking leave, when he was detained to partake of a lunch; and, while he was engaged in washing down a biscuit with a glass of octogenarian Madeira, the young lady was called out of the room. She was absent about fifteen minutes, and when she returned, her eyes were full of tears. A pile of gold lay on the table (the Captain would have thought it ungentlemanlike to offer dirty paper to ladies), and taking a five-dollar piece from the heap, she again vanished. This time she did not quite close the door behind her, and it was evident she was conversing with some claimant upon her charity. Her compassionate tones were distinctly heard in the drawing-room, and when she ceased speaking, a remarkably soft, clear, liquid voice responded to her kindness. There was something in these sounds which awakened the liveliest interest in the old gentleman. He started, fidgeted in his chair, and at length, fairly mastered by his curiosity, he stole on tiptoe to the door. He saw only a drooping figure, clad in mourning, and veiled from head to foot, who, repeating her thanks to her young benefactress, gathered up a roll of papers from the hall table, and withdrew before he could obtain a glimpse of her face.

"What impostor have you been feeing now?" he asked, as the young lady entered the room, holding in her hand several cheap French engravings.

"No impostor, my dear sir, but a most interesting woman."

"Oh, I dare say she was very *interesting* and *interested* too, no doubt; but how do you know she was no swindler?"

"Because she shed tears, *real tears.*"

"Humph! I suppose she put her handkerchief to her eyes and snivelled."

"No, indeed, I saw the big drops roll down her cheeks, and I never can doubt such an evidence of genuine sorrow; people can't force tears."

"What story could she tell which was worth five dollars?"

"Her husband, who was an importer of French stationary and engravings, has recently died insolvent, leaving her burdened with the support of two children and an infirm mother. His creditors have seized everything, excepting a few unsaleable prints, by the sale of which she is now endeavouring to maintain herself independently."

"Are the prints worth anything?"

"Not much."

"Then she is living upon charity quite as much as if she begged from door to door; it is only a new method of levying contributions upon people with more money than brains."

"The truth of her statement is easily ascertained. I have promised to visit her, and if I find her what she seems, I shall supply her with employment as a seamstress."

"Will you allow me to accompany you on your visit?"

"Certainly, my dear sir, upon condition that if you find her story true, you will pay the penalty of your mistrust in the shape of a goodly donation."

"Agreed! I'll pay *if* she turns out to be an object of charity. But that voice of hers,—I don't believe there are *two* such voices in this great city."

What notion had now got into the crotchety head of the Captain no one could tell; but he certainly was in wonderful spirits that day at dinner. He was in such good humour that he was even civil to Mrs. Howard, and sent his own bottle of wine to Harry Maurice. He looked a little confounded when Mrs. Howard, taking advantage of his "melting mood," challenged him to a game at backgammon, and it was almost with his old gruffness that he refused her polite invitation. He waited long enough to see her deeply engaged in chess with her young admirer, and then hurried away to fulfil his engagement with the lady who had promised to let him share her errand of mercy.

He was doomed to be disappointed, however. They found the house inhabited by the unfortunate Mrs. Harley; it was a low one-story rear building, in —— Street, the entrance to which was through a covered alley leading from the street. It was a neat, comfortable dwelling, and the butcher's shop in front of it screened it entirely from public view. But the person of whom they were in quest was not at home. Her mother and two rosy children, however, seemed to corroborate her story, and as the woman seemed disposed to be rather communicative, the old gentleman fancied he had now got upon a true trail. But an incautious question from him sealed the woman's lips, and he found himself quite astray again. Finding nothing could be gained, he hurried away, and entering his own door, found Mrs. Howard still deeply engaged in her game of chess, though she did look up with a sweet smile when she saw him.

A few days afterwards his young friend informed him that she had been more successful, having found Mrs. Harley just preparing to go out on her daily round of charity-seeking.

When suspicions are once aroused in the mind of a man like the Captain, it is strange how industriously he puts together the minutest links in the chain of evidence, and how curiously he searches for such links, as if the unmasking of a rogue was really a matter of the highest importance. The Captain began to grow more reserved and incommunicative than ever. He uttered oracular apothegms and dogmatisms until he became positively disagreeable, and at last, as if to show an utter aberration of mind, he determined to obtain leave of absence for a week. It was a most remarkable event in his history, and as such excited much speculation. But the old gentleman's lips were closely buttoned; he quietly packed a valise, and set out upon, what he called, a country excursion.

It was curious to notice how much he was missed in the house. Some missed his kindliness; some his quaint humorousness; some his punctuality, by which they set their watches; and Mrs. Howard seemed actually to feel the want of that sarcastic tone which made the *sauce piquante* of her dainty food. Where he actually went no one knew, but in four days he returned, looking more bilious and acting more crotchety than ever; but with an exhilaration of spirits that showed the marvellous effect of *country* air.

The day after his return, two men, wrapped in cloaks and wearing slouched hats, entered the butcher's shop in —— Street. Giving a nod in passing to the man at the counter, the two proceeded up stairs, and took a seat at one of the back windows. The blinds were carefully drawn down, and they seated themselves as if to note all that passed in the low, one-story building, which opened upon a narrow paved alley directly beneath the window.

"Do you know that we shall have a fearful settlement to make if this turns out to be all humbug?" said the younger man, as they took their station.

"Any satisfaction which you are willing to claim, I am ready to make, in case I am mistaken; but—look there."

As he spoke, a female wearing a large black cloak and thick veil entered the opposite house. Instantly a shout of joy burst from the children, and as the old woman rose to drop the blind at the window, they caught sight of the two merry little ones pulling at the veil and cloak of the mysterious lady.

"Did you see her face?" asked the old man.

"No, it was turned away from the window."

"Then have patience for a while."

Nearly an hour elapsed, and then the door again opened to admit the egress of a person, apparently less of stature than the woman who had so recently entered, more drooping in figure, and clad in rusty and shabby mourning.

"One more kiss, mamma, and don't forget the sugar-plums when you come back," cried one of the children.

The woman stooped to give the required kiss, lifting her veil as she did so, and revealing the whole of her countenance. A groan burst from the lips of one of the watchers, which was answered by a low chuckle from his companion; for both the Captain and Harry Maurice had recognised in the mysterious lady the features of the bewitching Mrs. Howard.

There is little more to tell. The question of "Who is she?" now needed no reply. Mrs. Howard, Mrs. Harley, and some dozen other *aliases*, were the names of an exceedingly genteel adventuress, who is yet vividly remembered by the charitable whom she victimized a few years since. She had resided in several large cities, and was drawing a very handsome income from her ingenuity. Her love of pleasure being as great as her taste for money-making, she devised a plan for living two lives at once, and her extreme mobility of feature, and exquisite adroitness, enabled her to carry out her schemes. How far she would have carried the affair with her young lover it is impossible to say, but the probability is that the "love affair" was only an agreeable episode "*pour passer le tems*," and that whatever might have been the gentleman's intentions, the lady was guiltless of ulterior views.

The Captain managed the affair his own way. He did not wish to injure the credit of the house, which he designed to call his home for the rest of his life, and therefore Mrs. Howard received a quiet intimation to quit, which she obeyed with her usual unruffled sweetness. Harry Maurice paid a visit to his mother and sister in the country, and on his return found it desirable to change his lodgings. The Captain kept the story to himself for several years, but after Maurice was married, and settled in his domestic habitudes, he felt himself privileged to use it as a warning to all gullible young men, against bewitching widows, and mysterious fellow-boarders.

MARY S. B. SHINDLER.

(LATE MRS. MARY S. B. DANA.)

THE Southern muse has had few harps that have awakened a warmer echo than that of Mrs. Mary S. B. Dana, now Mrs. Shindler. Born and nurtured upon Southern soil, her fame has been cherished with peculiar affection in the region of her birth, while her name has been no unfamiliar or unwelcome guest in Northern hearts and homes.

Mrs. Shindler was born in Beaufort, South Carolina, February 15, 1810. Her maiden name was Mary Stanley Bunce Palmer. She was the daughter of the Rev. Benjamin M. Palmer, D. D., who at the time of her birth was pastor of the Independent or Congregational church in Beaufort. In 1814 her parents removed to Charleston, her father having been called to the charge of the Independent church in that city. Her father's congregation consisted principally of planters of the neighbourhood, who spent their summers in the city, and their winters upon their plantations.

In reference to this period of her life, Mrs. Shindler remarks, "I well remember the delight with which we children used to anticipate our spring and Christmas holidays, which we were sure to spend upon some neighbouring plantation, released from all our city trammels, running perfectly wild, as all city children were expected to do, contracting sudden and violent intimacies in all the negro houses about Easter and Christmas times, that we might have a store of eggs for sundry purposes, for which we gave in exchange the most gaudy cotton handkerchiefs that could be bought in Charleston. It was during these delightful rural visits that what little poetry I have in my nature was fostered and developed, and at an early age I became sensible of a something within me which often brought tears into my eyes when I could not, for the life of me, express my feelings. The darkness and loneliness of our vast forests filled me with indescribable emotions, and above all other sounds, the music of the thousand Eolian harps sighing and wailing through a forest of pines, was most affecting to my youthful heart."

Besides the advantage of the best Southern society, she had also the opportunity of most extensive acquaintance with clergymen and others from various Northern States—the hospitality of her parents being unbounded.

She was educated by the Misses Ramsay, the daughters of Dr. David Ramsay, the historian, and grand-daughters, on the maternal side, of Mr. Laurens, who figured so conspicuously in the early history of our Independence. The summer of 1825 her parents spent in Hartford, Conn., and she was placed for six months at the seminary of the Rev. Mr. Emerson, in the neighbouring town of Wethersfield. In 1826 she was placed at a young ladies' seminary in Elizabethtown, New Jersey, with the expectation of remaining eighteen months, in the hope that so long a residence in the North would invigorate her constitution, which was rather delicate; but she pined for her Southern home, and at the expiration of six months was allowed to return to the arms of her parents. She subsequently spent several months at the seminary of the Rev. Claudius Herrick, in New Haven.

On the 19th of June, 1835, she became the wife of Mr. Charles E. Dana, and accompanied him to the city of New York, where they resided for two or three years. During this time she occasionally wrote little pieces of poetry, but did not publish them. Before her marriage, however, she had written considerably for the "Rose-Bud," a juvenile periodical published in Charleston by Mrs. Gilman.

The tone of subdued melancholy that pervades her first publications is explained by the sad story of her afflictions, which can be told in no way so well as in her own simple and affecting language.

"In the fall of the year 1838," says she, in a letter now before me, "accompanied by my parents, we removed to the West. I was then the mother of a beautiful boy, who was born in May, 1837. We spent the winter in Cincinnati, and, as soon as the river rose in the spring, we all went to New Orleans. While in that city, a letter was received from Alabama, acquainting my parents with the fact that my only brother, who was a physician, and was on a tour of inspection for the purpose of finding a pleasant location for the practice of his profession, was in Greene county, sick, and failing rapidly. A favourite sister had died of consumption at my house in New York, just a week after the birth of our little boy, and the news of my brother's illness filled us with the saddest apprehensions. The letter, too, bore rather an old date, having first being mailed to Cincinnati, and forwarded from thence to New Orleans. My afflicted parents immediately hastened to the spot, but they arrived too late even to take a last fond look upon their only son. He had been buried several days when they arrived. Almost heart-broken, yet submissive to the dreadful stroke, they returned to New Orleans, but instead of accompanying us in our western journey, they decided to return to Charleston.

"In a short time we also embarked in a steamer for St. Louis, where we remained for a month or six weeks. We then ascended the Mississippi as far as Bloomington, Iowa; at which place we landed, and we were so much pleased with the appearance of the place, that we decided on spending the summer there. The place had been settled about three years, and contained nearly or quite three hundred inhabitants, and had, so far, proved quite healthy. But the summer of 1839 was a very sickly one. There was a long-continued drought; the Mississippi river was unusually low, and the consequence was the prevalence of congestive fevers in all that region. Indeed, throughout the whole West and South, it was a summer long to be remembered.

"I was the first to take the fever, and had scarcely recovered, when our little Charlie, our only child, became alarmingly ill. The only experienced physician in the village was likewise ill, so that we laboured under a serious disadvantage. After lingering for a fortnight the dear little fellow died. Two days before his death, my husband was taken with the same fever, and also died, after an illness of only four days. Nothing but the consolations of religion could have supported me under this double bereavement. Left entirely alone, thousands of miles away from every relative I had on earth, there was no human arm on which I could lean, and I was to rely on God alone. It was well, perhaps, for me, that I was just so situated. It has taught me a lesson that I have never forgotten, that our heavenly Father will never lay upon us a heavier burthen than he will give us strength to bear. And here I must record my warm and grateful tribute to the genuine kindness and sympathy of Western hearts. If I had been among my own kindred, I could not have received more earnest and affectionate attention.

"As soon as I could settle my affairs, and find suitable protection, I started for my distant home, longing to lay my aching head on the bosom of my own dear mother, and to be encircled in my father's arms.

"I was received in St. Louis with the greatest kindness, and remained there for a week. Placed under the charge of a kind physician, we took a steamer for Cincinnati, but found the river so low, it would be next to impossible to reach there. After sticking fast upon every sand-bar we encountered for a day or two, the captain all the while assuring us that we should soon arrive at Cincinnati, we determined to take advantage of the first boat that passed us, and return to the Mississippi. Nor was it long before we were enabled to put this design into execution.

"In New Orleans the fever was raging to an alarming degree. My kind protector had now reached his home, and could accompany me no further, and I could hear of no one who was going in my direction at that season of the year—the human tide was all setting the other way. At length a friend called to inform me that a schooner was about to sail for Pensacola. Knowing my intense anxiety to reach home, he had called to let me know of the opportunity, thinking that from Pensacola I would be able to reach Charleston without difficulty, though, for his own part, he strongly advised me not to attempt going in the schooner. But I had grown desperate, and caught eagerly at the proposal. Accordingly, that very afternoon, I was conducted to the schooner by my friend, and introduced to the captain, who kindly promised to take good care of me. I must confess my heart almost failed me when, after crossing the deck on the tops of barrels, with which the vessel was loaded, I dived into a cabin, dark, low, and musty, and found that I was the only female on board.

"But the case was a desperate one, and I submitted to necessity, but bade my friend 'farewell' with a heavy heart. We were towed down the canal by horses to the entrance of Lake Ponchartrain, where we were quietly to lie till the next morning. Never shall I forget the sufferings of that dreadful night. The cabin was infested with roaches of an enormous size, and as soon as candles were lighted, they came out of their hiding-places by hundreds and thousands, and literally covered the bed where I was to sleep. Mosquitos also were swarming around; but this was not all. I was taken so ill that it seemed as if I could not live till morning. I shudder even now when I think of it.

"By daylight I called the captain to my side and begged him to get me back to the city. He said there was a schooner which had just come in from the lake, and was going up to the city, and offered to put me aboard of her. I joyfully consented, and he took me in his arms like an infant, carried me on board of the newly-arrived schooner, and seated me in a chair on a pile of wet boards, of which her cargo appeared to consist. After two or three hours of intense suffering, for I was really very sick, I once more reached my friends in New Orleans, who were overjoyed to see me, and who fully determined to prevent me, by force, if necessary, from making any more such travelling experiments. In a few days the steamer between New Orleans and Pascagoula commenced running, and finding company, I at length reached home in safety."

To give herself mental occupation, she now began to indulge in literary pursuits. She had always been very fond of music, and finding very little piano music that was suitable for Sunday playing, she had for several years been in the habit of adapting sacred words to any song which particularly pleased her. To wean her from her sorrows, her parents encouraged her to continue the practice, and this was the origin of the first work she published, "The Southern Harp." At first she had no idea of publishing these little effusions, but having written quite a number of them, she was advised to print a few for the use of herself and friends.

The work, however grew under her hands, till finally, becoming much interested in the design, she decided to publish, not only the words, but the music. She visited New York for this purpose in 1840, and the work appeared early in 1841.

She now used her pen almost incessantly. It is not wonderful that her thoughts ran principally upon the subject of affliction, nor that the scenes through which she had passed during her short sojourn at the West, should have formed the theme of her muse.

In the summer of 1841 she again visited New York for the purpose of publishing a volume of poems. This appeared under the title of "The Parted Family, and other Poems." She undertook, also, at the request of her publishers, to prepare another volume similar in design to the "Southern Harp," to be published under the title of the "Northern Harp." Both of these publications succeeded well. They passed through several large editions, and in a pecuniary way were very profitable, more than twenty-five thousand copies having been sold.

Her next publication was a prose work, entitled "Charles Morton; or, the Young Patriot;" a tale of the American Revolution. This, also, was very successful. It was issued in the early part of the year 1843.

She next published two tales for seamen. The title of the first was "The Young Sailor," and of the other, "Forecastle Tom."

About this time she experienced a change in her religious views, which attracted considerable attention, and led to her next publication. She had been bred a Calvinist, but during the year 1844 she began to entertain doubts about the doctrine of the Trinity, and finally, to the grief of her revered parents, and numerous friends, early in the year 1845, she avowed herself a Unitarian.

The matter having become one of some notoriety, she felt called upon to publish a volume of "Letters to Relatives and Friends," stating the process through which her mind had passed. This, by far the largest of her prose volumes, appeared in Boston, in the fall of 1845, and was republished in London. It went through several editions, and was finally stereotyped.

In 1847 she wrote several "Southern Sketches," the first of which appeared in the "Union Magazine" for October of that year.

At this time another severe affliction befell her. This was the sudden death, within two or three weeks of each other, of both her parents, at Orangeburg, South Carolina.

On the 18th of May, 1848, she became united in marriage to her present husband, the Rev. Robert D. Shindler, a clergyman of the Episcopal Church. Her views on the subject of the Trinity have also experienced a change, or rather have reverted to their original condition, and she is now in communion with the church of her husband.

In April, 1850, Mr. and Mrs. Shindler removed to Upper Marlboro', Maryland, near to his native place, which was Shephardstown, Virginia.

In August, 1851, they removed to Shelbyville, Kentucky, Mr. Shindler having accepted a Professorship in Shelby College.

A DAY IN NEW YORK.

HERE I am in New York—the great, busy, bustling world of New York; and after my year's rustication in a quiet Southern village, you may be sure that my poor little head is almost turned! Even now, while I am writing, there is a diabolical hand-organ, grinding under the window its mechanical music, with a disgusting little monkey—a caricature upon poor humanity—playing its "fantastic tricks before high heaven!" Do not, I entreat you, suppose me in a pet, for after all, I acknowledge that hand-organs, and even monkeys, have their uses, as well as their abuses, and may, by a serious philosophizing mind, be turned to very good account; but, just at this moment, I may perhaps be pardoned for wishing them somewhere else.

Ah! now comes a band of music—*real* music! breathed through various instruments by the breath of human beings, playing in accordance, keeping mutual time, obeying the same harmonious impulses, now delighting the ear and affecting the heart by a soft and plaintive strain, and now stirring the spirit by a burst of martial melody; yes, that *is* music; there is mind, there is soul, there is impulse, there is character in what I now hear, and you must excuse me while I hasten to the open window, and linger there till I catch the faintest echo of the rapidly-retreating harmony. There! It is gone—like so many of life's pleasures—only to linger in the memory. Well! God be praised for *that!*

Day before yesterday I visited Greenwood, your beautiful cemetery. Oh, I wish I could reveal to you all the secret and varied workings of the mind within, as I wandered with a chosen friend—a kindred spirit—through that beautiful and consecrated ground. Thoughts too big for utterance—too spiritual and mysterious to be clothed in words—came crowding thick and fast upon me, till at length I could contain myself no longer, and the tide of softened feeling overflowed its barriers; for tears, not bitter tears, came trickling down each cheek. To add to the solemn interest of the occasion, the bell was tolling for a funeral. It was the funeral of a little Southern boy, who had died while pursuing his studies in one of the city schools. His young school companions, all in uniform, and each with a badge of mourning hanging from the left elbow, marched solemnly and silently to deposit the mortal remains of the youthful stranger in his Northern grave! My busy mind instantly wandered to *his* home and *mine*, in the land of the sunny South! Had he a father? Had he a mother? Had he brothers and sisters who were yet to learn the mournful tidings that the dear little fellow who had left them, recently perhaps, in all the healthful buoyancy of his young existence, had closed his eyes in a land of strangers, and was sleeping his last sleep so far away from his Southern home? Or, was he an orphan, whose young days had been shaded by sorrow? Then, perhaps, he had gone to join the sainted dead! Then, perhaps, he had gone to complete a family in heaven! Glorious, delightful, soothing thought! At any rate, I knew that his young spirit was in the keeping of an infinitely-merciful Father, and there, well cared for, I was content to leave the little Southern boy.

Near the entrance, sat a lady clad in the habiliments of the deepest mourning. She had been, probably, or was going, to the grave of some loved one, "to weep there," as Jesus did! She had been mitigating or increasing the pangs of separation by the views and feelings she had been indulging at that loved one's grave! Perhaps her sorrow was a sanctified sorrow, and she had meekly yielded up the chosen one of her heart, at the summons of her Heavenly Father, resolved to wait patiently for the period of a blissful reunion. If so, she had experienced the truth of the Saviour's words—"*Blessed* are they that mourn, for they shall be comforted!" *But if not*, if, in the insanity of grief, she had been dwelling on the past, disregarding the injunction of the apostle to forget the things which are behind, and press forward to those which are before, how doubly was she to be pitied! Ah, mourning heart! didst thou but know that when we view the matter rightly, the dead are with us, more potently and beneficially than they were in life, thy sorrow would be turned into a pensive joy, creating within thee and around thee precious and purifying influences!

I pass by the splendid monuments which attract the attention of every stranger, to mention one which arrested my footsteps by its exceeding simplicity and beauty. It was a plain white marble shaft, upon which was inscribed one single word, and that was "MARY." I always loved the name, but was never before so struck with its unpretending beauty. It was the name of the virgin-mother of our Lord, it was the name of her whom Jesus loved, and of the erring one whose pardon he pronounced so graciously. And here it was, to designate the resting-place of a youthful wife who had but recently departed to her eternal home. What a world of meaning must that one word convey to the bereaved husband, when, solitary as he must be now, his lonely footsteps seek that sacred spot! Let me tell thee, sorrowing husband, thy Mary is not lost to thee, she has but "gone before;" and if thou hearest and heedest well the voice which issues from that marble tablet, it shall be well with thee! They never can be lost to us, whose memories we love!

Here lie thine ashes, dearest Mary!
While thy spirit shines above;
And this earth so fresh and verdant,
But reminds us of thy love.

Those who knew thy heart, sweet Mary!
Knew how pure its throbbings were;
O'er that heart, which throbs no longer,
Memory sheds her purest tear.

Yes, the tender mourning, Mary!
And the blank felt in thy home,
Live as freshly in our bosoms
As the rose-leaves o'er thy tomb.

Thou wert ever gentle, Mary!
All our comfort and our pride;
Now that thou art gone to heaven,
Oh! to heaven *our* spirits guide!

Be our guardian angel, Mary!
  Be our brilliant polar star!
From earth's storms, and clouds, and darkness,
  Lead us to bright realms afar.

And when from earth's loud turmoil, Mary!
  To this holy spot we turn,
Let the mem'ry of thy meekness
  Teach us, loved one, how to mourn!

I saw, too, the monument which has been recently erected over the grave of Dr. Abeel, the Chinese missionary. I knew and loved him well, and yet my feelings, when I stood beside his grave, had not a tinge of sadness! Indeed, why should they have? He had fought the good fight, he had finished his course, he had kept the faith, and I knew that he was in actual possession of his crown of glory! It was, then, a time and a place for joy and for triumph, and not for mourning and despondency. The Christian hero had gone to his reward, was *that* a cause for sadness?

I have not emptied my heart of half its tide of feeling, but I must forbear; time would fail me, and perhaps your patience also, were I to attempt it. Have you ever noticed, in your Greenwood rambles, a deeply-shaded spot, most appropriately labelled "Twilight Dell?" 'Tis there I would like to lay my weary head, when the toils and cares of life are over! Next to a grave in the far-distant West, where some of my loved ones sleep, or in my own Southern home, where my kindred lie, would I prefer one in the beautifully-shaded Twilight Dell of Greenwood.

CAROLINE LEE HENTZ.

Miss Caroline Lee Whiting (the maiden name of Mrs. Hentz) was born in the romantic village of Lancaster, Massachusetts. She is the daughter of General John Whiting, and the sister of the brave General Whiting, distinguished alike for his literary attainments, and for his services in the army of the United States. She was married in 1825, tc Mr. N. M. Hentz, a French gentleman, of rich and varied talents, who then conducted a seminary of education at Northampton, in conjunction with Mr. Bancroft, the historian. In the early days of their married life, Mr. Hentz was appointed Professor in the College at Chapel Hill, North Carolina. He accepted the honourable post, and remained there several years. Thence they removed to Covington, Kentucky, where she wrote the tragedy of "De Lara, or the Moorish Bride." This play was offered as a competitor for a prize of five hundred dollars, and was successful. It was performed at the Arch Street Theatre, Philadelphia, and I believe elsewhere, with much applause, and for several successive nights. The copyright having reverted to Mrs. Hentz, it was subsequently published in book form.

The family, after living awhile at Covington, removed to Cincinnati, and thence to Florence, Alabama. At this latter place they had for nine years a flourishing Female Academy, which in 1843 they transferred to Tuscaloosa, and again in 1845 to Tuskegee, and once more, in 1848, to Columbus, Georgia, where they now reside. The exhausting labours of their school, much of which fell upon Mrs. Hentz, caused her for several years almost to suspend the exercise of her pen. It is understood that she has recently made arrangements which will give her leisure for the more free exercise of her extraordinary gifts as a writer.

Besides the tragedy already named, Mrs. Hentz has written two others, "Lamorah, or the Western Wilds," published in a Columbus newspaper, and "Constance of Wirtemberg," which has not yet seen the light. She has published many fugitive pieces of poetry, which have been widely copied.

Caroline Lee Hentz

Her prose writings have been chiefly in the form of novelettes for the weekly papers and the monthly magazines. After a wide circulation in this form, they have been generally reprinted as books, and enjoyed the eclat of numerous editions. They are "Aunt Patty's Scrap Bag," 1846; "The Mob Cap," 1848; "Linda, or the Young Pilot of the Belle Creole," 1850; "Rena, or the Snowbird," 1851; "Marcus Warland, or The Long Moss Spring," and "Eoline, or Magnolia Vale," in 1852; "Wild Jack," and "Helen and Arthur, or Miss Thusa's Spinning Wheel," in 1853; and "The Planter's Northern Bride," in 1854. The last work, but recently published, is the longest and most elaborate which has yet issued from her pen, and critics from various parts of the country have united to place it in the first rank of American novels.

Every one practically conversant with the art of composition, knows that those works which, to the uninitiated, seem to have been written *currente calamo*—dashed off at full speed—are ordinarily the fruit of slow and patient labour. Mrs. Hentz appears to be an exception to this rule. The spontaneousness and freedom so apparent in her style are a true exponent of her habit of composition. Her happy facility in this respect reminds us of that most remarkable poetical improvisatrice, Mrs. Osgood. Mrs. Hentz, if we may credit authentic information, writes in the midst of her domestic circle, and subject to constant interruptions, yet with the greatest rapidity, and with a degree of accuracy that seldom requires, as it never receives revision.

One long an inmate of the household, writes to me on this subject as follows: "What has often struck me with wonder in regard to Mrs. Hentz, is the remarkable ease with which she writes. When a leisure moment presents itself, she takes up her pen, as others do their knitting, and it dances swiftly over the paper, as if in vain trying to keep up with the current of her thoughts. 'Aunt Patty's Scrap Bag' was written while I was living in the family, and as at evening I sat at her table, I read it sheet by sheet, ere the ink was dry from her pen, and on every page I saw, in the record of the affectionate family of the Worths, and particularly in the tender relations between Mrs. Worth and her daughters, a faithful transcript of the author's own heart.

"Pardon me if I introduce a few lines which she dashed off hastily for me, while I stood waiting for the coach, the day I left her at Tuskegee. Though simple, they are in many respects a comment upon her heart, and the chief object of her pen. I give them from memory.

"May this ring, when it circles thy finger, remind
Thy heart of the friends thou art leaving behind—
I have breathed on its gold a magical spell—
That, in long after years, of this moment shall tell

"Should snares and temptations around thee entwine,
May the gem on thy finger with warning rays shine—
And whisper of one whose spirit would mourn
If thou from the pathway of virtue shouldst turn.

"Like the eaglet, that fixes its gaze on the sun,
Press upward and on till the bright goal is won—
Let the wings of thy soul never pause in their flight,
Till they bear thee to regions of glory and light."

I am indebted to an accomplished lady of Mobile* for the following additional particulars in relation to Mrs. Hentz.

"Some writer has said, 'Authors should be read—not known.' Mrs. Hentz forms a bright exception to this remark. She is one of those rare magnetic women who attracted my entire admiration at our first interview. The spell she wove around me was like the invisible beauty of music. I yielded willingly and delightfully to its magic influence.

"Never have I met a more fascinating person. Mind is enthroned on her noble brow, and beams in the flashing glances of her radiant eyes She is tall, graceful, and dignified, with that high-bred manner which ever betokens gentle blood.

"She has infinite tact and talent in conversation, and never speaks without awakening interest. As I listened to her eloquent language, I felt she was indeed worthy of the wreath of immortality, which fame has given in other days, and other lands, to a De Genlis, or to a De Sevigné.

"She possesses great enthusiasm of character—the enthusiasm described by Madame De Stael, as '*God within us*,'—the love of the good, the holy, the beautiful. She has neither pretension nor pedantry, and, although admirably accomplished, and a perfect classic and belles lettres scholar, she has all the sweet simplicity of an elegant woman.

"Like the charming Swedish authoress, Fredrika Bremer, her works all tend to elevate the tone of moral feeling. There is a refinement, delicacy, and poetic imagery in all her historiettes, touchingly delightful. A

* Madame Octavia Walton Le Vert. "This accomplished lady has for many years dispensed the refined and elegant hospitalities of Mobile, and is the centre of a circle unsurpassed for its wit, worth, and intelligence. She is the daughter of the no less celebrated Colonel George Walton, formerly Governor of Florida, who now is, we believe, the only surviving son of a signer of the Declaration of Independence.—(Editor of the Spirit of the Times.)

Though Madame Le Vert has not appeared before the world as an authoress, no lady in the Southern States has been more admired for her fascinating powers of conversation, and for those brilliant accomplishments which adorn the social circle. She converses with ease and elegance in several of the modern languages, and excels in all the graces of her sex; foreigners of distinction, who visit Mobile, generally bear letters of introduction to her elegant and hospitable home.

calm and holy religion is mirrored in every page. The sorrow-stricken mourner finds therein the sweet and healing balm of consolation, and the bitter tears cease to flow when she points to that 'better land' where the loved and the lost are waiting for us.

"Many of her works are gay and *spirituel,* full of delicate wit, 'bright as the flight of a shining arrow.' Often have the smiles long exiled from the lips, returned at the bidding of her merry muse. Home, especially, she describes with a truthfulness which is enchanting. She seems to have dipped the pen in her own soul, and written of its emotions. She exalts all that is good, noble, or generous in the human heart, and gives to even the clouds of existence a sunny softness, like the dreamy light of a Claude Lorraine picture." Mrs. Hentz died February 11th, 1856.

AUNT PATTY'S SCRAP BAG.

It was a rainy day, a real, old-fashioned, orthodox rainy day. It rained the first thing in the morning, it rained harder and harder at midday. The afternoon was drawing to a close, and still the rain came down in steady and persevering drops, every drop falling in a decided and obstinate way, as if conscious, though it might be ever so unwelcome, no one had a right to oppose its coming. A rainy day in midsummer is a glorious thing. The grass looks up so green and grateful under the life-giving moisture; the flowers send forth such a delicious aroma; the tall forest-trees bend down their branches so gracefully in salutation to the messengers of heaven. There are beauty, grace, and glory in a midsummer rain, and the spirit of man becomes gay and buoyant under its influence. But a March rain in New England, when the vane of the weather-cock points inveterately to the north-east, when the brightness, and purity, and *positiveness* of winter is gone, and not one promise of spring breaks cheeringly on the eye, is a dismal concern.

Little Estelle stood looking out at the window, with her nose pressed against a pane of glass, wishing it would clear up, it was so pretty to see the sun break out just as he was setting. The prospect abroad was not very inviting. It was a patch of mud and a patch of snow, the dirtiest mixture in nature's olio. A little boy went slumping by, sinking at every step almost to his knees; then a carriage slowly and majestically came plashing along, its wheels buried in mud, the horses labouring and straining, and every now and then shaking the slime indignantly from their fetlocks, and probably thinking none but amphibious animals should be abroad in such weather.

"Oh! it is such an ugly, ugly day!" said Estelle, "I do wish it were over."

"You should not find fault with the weather," replied Emma; "mother says it is wicked, for God sends us what weather seemeth good to him. For my part, I have had a very happy day reading and sewing."

"And I too," said Bessy, "but I begin to be tired now, and I wish I could see some of those beautiful crimson clouds, tinged with gold, that wait upon sunset."

"Bessy has such a romantic mode of expression," cried Edmund, laughing and laying down his book; "I think she will make a poet one of these days. Even now, I see upon her lips 'a prophetess's fire.'"

Bessy's blue eyes peeped at her brother through her golden curls, and something in them seemed to say, "that is not such a ridiculous prophecy as you imagine."

"This is a dreadful day for a traveller," said Mrs. Worth, with a sigh, and the children all thought of their father, exposed to the inclemency of the atmosphere, and they echoed their mother's sigh. They all looked very sad, till the entrance of another member of the family turned their thoughts into a new channel. This was no other than Estelle's kitten, which had been perambulating in the mire and rain, till she looked the most forlorn object in the world. Her sides were hollow and dripping, and her tail clung to her back in a most abject manner. There was a simultaneous exclamation at her dishevelled appearance, but Miss Kitty walked on as demurely as if nothing particular had happened to her, and jumping on her little mistress's shoulder, curled her wet tail round her ears, and began to mew and purr, opening and shutting her green eyes between every purr. Much as Estelle loved her favourite, she was not at all pleased at her present proximity, and called out energetically for deliverance. All laughed long and heartily at the muddy streaks on her white neck, and the muddy tracks on her white apron, and she looked as if she had not made up her mind whether to laugh or cry, when a fresh burst of laughter produced a complete reaction, and a sudden shower of tears fell precipitately on Aunt Patty's lap.

"Take care, Estelle," said Edmund, "Aunt Patty has got on her thunder and lightning calico. She does not like to have it rained on."

Aunt Patty had a favourite frock, the ground-work of which was a deep brown, with zigzag streaks of scarlet darting over it. Estelle called it thunder and lightning, and certainly it was a very appropriate similitude for a child. It always was designated by that name, and Edmund declared, that whenever Aunt Patty wore that dress, it was sure to bring a storm. She was now solicited by many voices to bring out one of her scrap-bags for their amusement. And she, who never wearied of recalling the bright images of her youthful fancy, or the impressions of later years, produced a gigantic satchel, and undrawing the strings, Estelle's little hand was plunged in, and grasping a piece by chance, smiles played like sunbeams on her tears, when she found it was a relic of old Parson Broomfield's banian. It consisted of broad shaded stripes, of an iron-gray colour, a very sober and ministerial-looking calico.

"Ah!" said Aunt Patty—the chords of memory wakened to music at the sight—"I remember the time when I first saw Parson Broomfield wear that banian. I was a little girl then, and my mother used to send me on errands here and there, in a little carriage, made purposely for me on account of my lameness. A boy used to draw me, in the same way that they do infants, and everybody stopped and said something to the poor lame girl. I was going by the parsonage, one warm summer morning, and the parson was sitting reading under a large elm tree, that grew directly in front of his door. He had a bench put all round the trunk, so that weary travellers could stop and rest under its shade. He was a blessed man, Parson Broomfield—of such great piety, that some thought if they could touch the hem of his garment they would have a passport to heaven. I always think of him when I read that beautiful verse in Job: 'The young men saw him and trem bled, the aged arose and stood up.' Well, there he sat, that warm summer morning, in his new striped banian, turned back from his neck, and turned carelessly over one knee, to keep it from sweeping on the grass. He had on black satin lasting pantaloons, and a black velvet waistcoat, that made his shirt collar look as white as snow. He lifted his eyes, when he heard the wheels of my carriage rolling along, and made a sort of motion for me to stop. 'Good morning, little Patty,' said he, 'I hope you are very well this beautiful morning.' We always thought it an honour to get a word from his lips, and I felt as if I could walk without a crutch the whole day. He was very kind to little children, though he looked so grand and holy in the pulpit, you would think he was an angel of light, just come down there from the skies."

"Did he preach in that calico frock?" asked Emma, anxious for the dignity of the ministerial office.

"Oh! no, child—all in solemn black, except his white linen bands. He always looked like a saint on Sunday, walking in the church so slow and stately, yet bowing on the right and left, to the old, white-headed men, that waited for him as for the consolation of Israel. Oh! he was a blessed man, and he is in glory now. Here," added she, taking a piece of spotless linen from a white folded paper, "is a remnant of the good man's shroud. I saw him when he was laid out, with his hands folded on his breast, and his Bible resting above them."

"Don't they have any Bibles in Heaven?" asked little Estelle, shrinking from contact with the funereal sample.

"No, child; they will read there without books, and see without eyes, and know everything without learning. But they put his Bible on his heart, because he loved it so in life, and it seemed to be company for him in the dark coffin and lonely grave."

The children looked serious, and Emma's wistful eyes, lifted towards heaven, seemed to long for that region of glorious intuition, whither the beloved pastor of Aunt Patty's youth was gone. Then the youngest begged her to tell them something more lively, as talking about death, and the coffin, and grave, made them melancholy such a rainy day.

"Here," said Bessy, "is a beautiful pink and white muslin. The figure is a half open rosebud, with a delicate cluster of leaves. Who had a dress like this, Aunt Patty?"

"That was the dress your mother wore the first time she saw your father," answered the chronicler, with a significant smile. Bessy clasped her hands with delight, and they all gathered close, to gaze upon an object associated with such an interesting era.

"Didn't she look sweet?" said Bessy, looking admiringly at her handsome and now blushing mother.

"Yes! her cheeks were the colour of her dress, and that day she had a wreath of roses in her hair; for Emma's father loved flowers, and made her ornament herself with them to please his eye. It was about sunset. It had been very sultry, and the roads were so dusty we could scarcely see after a horse or carriage passed by. Emma was in the front yard watering some plants, when a gentleman on horseback rode slowly along, as if he tried to make as little dust as possible. He rode by the house at first, then turning back, he came right up to the gate, and, lifting up his hat, bowed down to the saddle. He was a tall, dark-complexioned young man, who sat nobly on his horse, just as if he belonged to it. Emma, your mother that is, set down her watering-pot, and made a sort of courtesy, a little frightened at a stranger coming so close to her, before she knew anything about it. 'May I trouble you for a glass of water?' said he, with another bow. 'I have travelled long, and am oppressed with thirst.' Emma courtesied again, and blushed too, I dare say, and away she went for a glass of water, which she brought him with her own hands. Your grandfather had come to the door by this time, and he said he never saw a man so long drinking a glass of water in his life. As I told you before, it had been a terribly sultry day, and there were large thunder pillars leaning down black in the west—a sure sign there was going to be a heavy shower. Your grandfather came out, and being an hospitable man, he asked the stranger to stop and rest till the rain that was coming was over. He didn't wait to be asked twice, but jumped from his horse and walked in, making a bow at the door, and waiting for your mother to walk in first. Well, sure enough, it did rain in a short time, and thunder, and lighten, and blow, as if the house would come down; and the strange gentleman sat down close by Emma, and tried to keep her from being frightened, for she looked as pale as death; and when the lightning flashed bright, she covered up her face with her hands. It kept on thundering and raining till bed-time, when your grandfather offered him a bed, and told him he must stay till morning. Everybody was taken with him, for he talked like a book, and looked as if he knew more than all the books in the world. He told his name, and all about himself—that he was a young lawyer just commencing business in a town near by (the very town we are now living in); that he had been on a journey, and was on his way home, which he had expected to reach that night. He seemed to hate to go away so the next morning, that your grandfather asked him to come and see him again—and he took him at his word, and came back the very next week. This time he didn't hide from anybody what he came for, for he courted your mother in good earnest, and never left her, or gave her any peace, till she had promised to be his wife, which I believe she was very willing to be, from the first night she saw him."

"Nay, Aunt Patty," said Mrs. Worth, "I must correct you in some of your items; your imagination is a little too vivid."

Edmund went behind his mother's chair, and putting his hands playfully over her ears, begged Aunt Patty to go on, and give her imagination full scope.

"And show us the wedding-dress, and tell us all about it," said Bessy. "It is pleasanter to hear of mother's wedding, than Parson Broomfield's funeral."

"But that's the way, darling—a funeral and a wedding, a birth and a death, all mixed up, the world over. We must take things as they come, and be thankful for all. Do you see this white sprigged satin, and this bit of white lace? The wedding-dress was made of the satin, and trimmed round the neck and sleeves with the lace, and the money it cost would have clothed a poor family for a long time. But your grandfather said he had but one daughter, and she should be well fitted out, if it cost him all he had in the world. And, moreover, he had a son-in-law, whom he would not exchange for any other man in the universe. When Emma, your mother that is, was dressed in her bridal finery, with white blossoms in her hair, which hung in ringlets down her rosy cheeks, you might search the country round for a prettier and fairer bride —and your father looked like a prince. Parson Broomfield said they were the handsomest couple he ever married—and, bless his soul, they were the last. He was taken sick a week after the wedding, and never lifted his head afterwards. It is a blessed thing Emma was married when she was, for I wouldn't want to be married by any other minister in the world than Parson Broomfield."

"Where's your husband, Aunt Patty?" said Estelle, suddenly.

Edmund and Bessy laughed outright. Emma only smiled—she feared Aunt Patty's feelings might be wounded.

"I never had any, child," replied she, after taking a large pinch of snuff.

"What's the reason?" persevered Estelle.

"Hush—Estelle," said her mother, "little girls must not ask so many questions."

"I'll tell you the reason," cried Aunt Patty, "for I'm never ashamed to speak the truth. No one ever thought of marrying me, for I was a lame, helpless, and homely girl, without a cent of money to make folks think one pretty, whether I was or not. I never dreamed of having sweethearts, but was thankful for friends, who were willing to bear with my infirmities, and provide for my comfort. I don't care if they do call me an old maid. I'm satisfied with the place Providence has assigned me, knowing it's a thousand times better than I deserve. The tree that stands alone by the wayside offers shelter and shade to the weary traveller. It was not created in vain, though no blossom nor fruit may hang upon its boughs. It gets its portion of the sunshine and dew, and the little birds come and nestle in its branches."

HANNAH ADAMS.

Mrs. Gilman, in her autobiography, page 55 of the present volume, makes a very pleasant allusion to Hannah Adams, the venerated author of the "History of Religions," the pioneer, almost, of American female authorship. The account of her which follows is taken, with very slight verbal alterations, from "Woman's Record," by Mrs. Hale, and may be considered as an additional extract from that valuable work.

"Hannah Adams was born in Medfield, Massachusetts, in 1755. Her father was a respectable farmer in that place, rather better educated than persons of his class usually were at that time; and his daughter, who was a very delicate child, profited by his fondness for books. So great was her love for reading and study, that when very young she had committed to memory nearly all of Milton, Pope, Thomson, Young, and several other poets.

"When she was about seventeen her father failed in business, and Miss Adams was obliged to exert herself for her own maintenance. This she did at first by making lace, a very profitable employment during the revolutionary war, as very little lace was then imported. But after the termination of the conflict she was obliged to resort to some other means of support; and having acquired from the students who had boarded with her father, a competent knowledge of Latin and Greek, she undertook to prepare young men for college; and succeeded so well, that her reputation was spread throughout the State.

"Her first work, entitled "The View of Religions," which she commenced when she was about thirty, is a history of the different sects in religion. It caused her so much hard study and close reflection, that she was attacked before the close of her labours by a severe fit of illness, and threatened with derangement. Her next work was a carefully written "History of New England;" and her third was on "The Evidences of the Christian Religion."

"Though all these works showed great candour and liberality of mind and profound research, and though they were popular, yet they brought her but little besides fame; which, however, had extended to Europe, and she reckoned among her correspondents many of the learned men of all countries. Among these was the celebrated abbé Gregoire, who was then struggling for the emancipation of the Jews in France. He sent Miss Adams several volumes, which she acknowledged were of much use to her in preparing her own work, a "History of the Jews," now considered one of the most valuable of her productions. Still, as far as pecuniary matters went, she was singularly unsuccessful, probably from her want of knowledge of business, and ignorance in worldly matters; and, to relieve her from her embarrassments, three wealthy gentlemen of Boston, with great liberality, settled an annuity upon her, of which she was kept in entire ignorance till the whole affair was completed.

"The latter part of her life passed in Boston, in the midst of a large circle of friends, by whom she was warmly cherished and esteemed for the singular excellence, purity, and simplicity of her character. She died, November 15th, 1832, at the age of seventy-six, and was buried at Mount Auburn; the first one whose body was placed in that cemetery. Through life, the gentleness of her manners and the sweetness of her temper were childlike; she trusted all her cares to the control of her heavenly Father; and she did not trust in vain."

THE GNOSTICS.

THIS denomination sprang up in the first century. Several of the disciples of Simon Magus held the principles of his philosophy, together with the profession of Christianity, and were distinguished by the appellation of Gnostics, from their boasting of being able to restore mankind to the knowledge, γνωσις, of the Supreme Being, which had been lost in the world. This party was not conspicuous for its numbers or reputation before the time of Adrian. It derives its origin from the Oriental philosophy. The doctrine of a soul, distinct from the body, which had pre-existed in an angelic state, and was, for some offence committed in that state, degraded, and confined to the body as a punishment, had been the great doctrine of the eastern sages from time immemorial. Not being able to conceive how evil in so great an extent, could be subservient to good, they supposed that good and evil have different origins. So mixed a system as this is, they therefore thought to be unworthy of infinite wisdom and goodness. They looked upon matter as the source of all evil, and argued in this manner: There are many evils in this world, and men seem impelled by a natural instinct, to the practice of those things which reason condemns; but the eternal Mind, from which all spirits derive their existence, must be inaccessible to all kinds of evil, and also of a most perfect and benevolent nature. Therefore, the origin of those evils, with which the universe abounds, must be sought somewhere else than in the Deity. It cannot reside in him who is all perfection; therefore, it must be without him. Now there is nothing without or beyond the Deity but matter; therefore matter is the centre and source of all evil and of all vice. Having taken for granted these principles, they proceeded further, and affirmed, that matter was eternal, and derived its present form, not from the will of the Supreme God, but from the creating power of some inferior intelligence, to whom the world and its inhabitants owed their existence. As a proof of their assertion, they alleged, that it was incredible the Supreme Deity, perfectly good, and infinitely removed from all evil, should either create, or modify matter, which is essentially malignant and corrupt; or, bestow upon it in any degree, the riches of his wisdom and liberality.

In their system it was generally supposed, that all intelligences had only one source, viz. the divine Mind. And to help out the doctrine concerning the origin of evil, it was imagined, that though the divine Being himself was essentially and perfectly good, those intelligences, or spirits, who were derived from him, and especially those who were derived from them, were capable of depravation. It was further imagined, that the depravation of those inferior intelligent beings from the Supreme, was by a kind of efflux or emanation, a part of the substance being detached from the rest, but capable of being absorbed into it again. To those intelligences derived mediately or immediately from the divine Mind, the author of this system did not scruple to give the name of gods, thinking some of them capable of a power of modifying matter.

The oriental sages expected the arrival of an extraordinary messenger of the Most High upon earth; a messenger invested with a divine authority; endowed with the most eminent sanctity and wisdom; and peculiarly appointed to enlighten with the knowledge of the Supreme Being, the darkened minds of miserable mortals, and to deliver them from the chains of the tyrants and usurpers of this world. When, therefore, some of these philosophers perceived that Christ and his followers wrought miracles of the most amazing kind, and also of the most salutary nature to mankind, they were easily induced to connect their fundamental doctrines with Christianity, by supposing him the great messenger expected from above, to deliver men from the power of the malignant genii, or spirits, to whom, according to their doctrine, the world was subjected, and to free their souls from the dominion of corrupt matter. But though they considered him as the Supreme God, sent from the pleroma, or habitation of the everlasting Father, they deny his divinity, looking upon him as inferior to the Father. They rejected his humanity, upon the supposition that everything concrete and corporeal is in itself essentially and intrinsically evil. Hence the greatest part of the Gnostics denied that Christ was clothed with a real body, or that he suffered really for the sake of mankind, the pains and sorrows which he is said to have endured in the sacred history. They maintained, that he came to mortals with no other view, than to deprive the tyrants of this world of their influence upon virtuous and heaven-born souls, and destroying the empire of these wicked spirits, to teach mankind how they might separate the divine mind from the impure body, and render the former worthy of being united to the Father of spirits.

Their persuasion, that evil resided in matter, rendered them unfavourable to wedlock; and led them to hold the doctrine of the resurrection of the body in great contempt. They considered it as a mere clog to the immortal soul; and supposed, that nothing was meant by it, but either a moral change in the minds of men, which took place before they died; or that it signified the ascent of the soul to its proper abode in the superior regions, when it was disengaged from its earthly encumbrance. The notion, which this denomination entertained, that the malevolent genii presided in nature, and that from them proceed all diseases and calamities, wars, and desolations, induced them to apply themselves to the study of magic, to weaken the powers, or suspend the influences of these malignant agents.

As the Gnostics were philosophic and speculative people, and affected refinement, they did not make much account of public worship, or of positive institutions of any kind. They are said, not to have had any order in their churches.

As many of this denomination thought that Christ had not any real body, and therefore had not any proper flesh and blood, it seems on this account, when they used to celebrate the Eucharist, they did not make any use of wine, which represents the blood of Christ, but of water only.

We have fewer accounts of what they thought or did with respect to baptism, but it seems that some of them at least disused it. And it is said, that some abstained from the Eucharist, and from prayer.

The greatest part of this denomination adopted rules of life, which were full of austerity, recommending a strict and rigorous abstinence, and prescribed the most severe bodily mortifications, from a notion, that they had a happy influence in purifying and enlarging the mind, and in disposing it for the contemplation of celestial things. That some of the Gnostics, in consequence of making no account of the body, might think, that there was neither good nor evil in anything relating to it; and therefore suppose themselves at liberty to indulge in any sensual excesses, is not impossible; though it is more probable, that everything of this nature would be greatly exaggerated by the enemies of this denomination.

ELIZABETH F. ELLET.

Elizabeth Fries Lummis was born at Sodus Point, New York, October, 1818. She was married at an early age to William H. Ellet, M. D., Professor of Chemistry in Columbia College, in the city of New York. Dr. Ellet having accepted, soon after, the appointment of Professor in South Carolina College, Mrs. Ellet resided several years in Columbia. In the beginning of 1849 Dr. and Mrs. Ellet came to reside in New York city.

Her father was Dr. William Nixon Lummis. He was of a highly respectable family, his father and brothers being physicians. He studied medicine in Philadelphia, attending the lectures of Dr. Benjamin Rush, whose friend he was, and whom in person he strongly resembled.

Her mother was Sarah Maxwell, daughter of John Maxwell, and niece of General William Maxwell, who served with distinction until near the close of the Revolutionary war, when he threw up his commission on account of some dissatisfaction.

Mrs. Ellet commenced authorship as early as 1833, since which time she has contributed largely, both in prose and verse, to many of the leading periodicals, besides the publication of several volumes which have met with good success.

A volume of poems appeared in 1835. In 1841 she published "Characters of Schiller," containing an essay on the genius of Schiller, and a critical analysis of his characters. "Joanna of Sicily" soon followed. It was a work partly fictitious, partly historical, intended to exhibit the character and life of the queen whose name it bears. "Rambles about the Country" was a volume intended for children. It describes various scenes in the United States. "Evenings at Woodlawn" is a collection of European legends and traditions, translated and modified to suit American readers. It has had a large sale.

Mrs. Ellet is understood to have written for the North American Review, the American Quarterly, and the Southern Review, but I am unable to designate particularly her articles.

Her largest work is "The Women of the American Revolution," in three volumes. It has gone through seven or eight editions in two years. In this work she has collected, from private sources, with abundant success, all the evidences of special patriotism and nobleness exhibited by her own sex during the period that "tried men's souls." The facts which she has thus rescued from their traditionary state, and placed on permanent record, make a truly valuable addition to our revolutionary story. They are her own noblest and most enduring monument.

Besides these very interesting volumes, Mrs. Ellet has published still another called the "Domestic History of the Revolution," of a character similar to the former in its general tone and point of view, but having a regular and connected narrative, suitable for a text book. Her "Pioneer Women of the West" is a collection of memoirs from original papers and information furnished by the friends of the heroines. Her "Watching Spirits" is an essay on the presence and agency of spirits in the world, as described in the Holy Scriptures.

MARY SLOCUMB.

It was about ten o'clock on a beautiful spring morning, that a splendidly-dressed officer, accompanied by two aids, and followed at a short distance by a guard of some twenty troopers, dashed up to the piazza in front of the ancient-looking mansion. Mrs. Slocumb was sitting there, with her child and a near relative, a young lady, who afterwards became the wife of Major Williams. A few house servants were also on the piazza.

The officer raised his cap, and bowing to his horse's neck, addressed the lady, with the question—

"Have I the pleasure of seeing the mistress of this house and plantation!"

"It belongs to my husband."

"Is he at home?"

"He is not."

"Is he a rebel?"

"No, sir. He is in the army of his country, and fighting against our invaders; therefore not a rebel."

It is not a little singular, that although the people of that day gloried in their rebellion, they always took offence at being called rebels.

"I fear, madam," said the officer, "we differ in opinion. A friend to his country will be the friend of the king, our master."

"Slaves only acknowledge a master in this country," replied the lady.

A deep flush crossed the florid cheeks of Tarleton, for he was the speaker; and turning to one of his aids, he ordered him to pitch the tents and form the encampment in the orchard and field on their right. To the other aid his orders were to detach a quarter guard and station piquets on each road. Then bowing very low, he added: "Madam, the service of his Majesty requires the temporary occupation of your property; and if it would not be too great an inconvenience, I will take up my quarters in your house."

The tone admitted no controversy. Mrs. Slocumb answered: "My family consists of only myself, my sister and child, and a few negroes. We are your prisoners."

While the men were busied, different officers came up at intervals, making their reports and receiving orders. Among others, a tory captain, whom Mrs. Slocumb immediately recognised—for before joining the royal army, he had lived fifteen or twenty miles below—received orders in her hearing to take his troop and scour the country for two or three miles round.

In an hour everything was quiet, and the plantation presented the romantic spectacle of a regular encampment of some ten or eleven hundred of the choicest cavalry of the British monarch.

Mrs. Slocumb now addressed herself to the duty of preparing for her uninvited guests. The dinner set before the king's officers was, in her own words to her friend, "as good a dinner as you have now before you, and of much the same materials." A description of what then constituted a good dinner in that region may not be inappropriate. "The first dish was, of course, the boiled ham, flanked with the plate of greens. Opposite was the turkey, supported by the laughing baked sweet potatoes; a plate of boiled beef, another of sausages, and a third with a pair of baked fowls, formed a line across the centre of the table; half a dozen dishes of different pickles, stewed fruit, and other condiments, filled up the interstices of the board." The dessert, too, was abundant and various. Such a dinner, it may well be supposed, met the particular approbation of the royal officers, especially as the fashion of that day introduced stimulating drinks to the table, and the peach brandy, prepared under Lieutenant Slocumb's own supervision, was of the most excellent sort. It received the unqualified praïse of the party; and its merits were freely discussed. A Scotch officer, praising it by the name of whiskey, protested that he had never drunk as good out of Scotland. An officer speaking with a slight brogue, insisted it was not whiskey, and that no Scotch drink ever equalled it. "To my mind," said he, "it tastes as yonder orchard smells."

"Allow me, madam," said Colonel Tarleton, "to inquire where the spirits we are drinking is procured."

"From the orchard where your tents stand," answered Mrs. Slocumb.

"Colonel," said the Irish captain, "when we conquer this country, is it not to be divided out among us?"

"The officers of this army," replied the colonel, "will undoubtedly receive large possessions of the conquered American provinces."

Mrs. Slocumb here interposed. "Allow me to observe and prophesy," said she, "the only land in these United States which will ever remain in possession of a British officer, will measure but six feet by two."

"Excuse me, madam," remarked Tarleton. "For your sake I regret to say—this beautiful plantation will be the ducal seat of some of us."

"Don't trouble yourself about me," retorted the spirited lady. "My husband is not a man who would allow a duke, or even a king, to have a quiet seat upon his ground."

At this point the conversation was interrupted by rapid volleys of fire-arms, appearing to proceed from the wood a short distance to the eastward. One of the aids pronounced it some straggling scout, running from the picket-guard; but the experience of Colonel Tarleton could not be easily deceived.

"There are rifles and muskets," said he, "as well as pistols; and too many to pass unnoticed. Order boots and saddles, and you, captain, take your troop in the direction of the firing."

The officer rushed out to execute his orders, while the colonel walked into the piazza, whither he was immediately followed by the anxious ladies. Mrs. Slocumb's agitation and alarm may be imagined; for she guessed but too well the cause of the interruption. On the first arrival of the officers she had been importuned, even with harsh threats—not, however, by Tarleton—to tell where her husband, when absent on duty, was likely to be found; but after her repeated and peremptory refusals, had escaped further molestation on the subject. She feared now that he had returned unexpectedly, and might fall into the enemy's hands before he was aware of their presence.

Her sole hope was in a precaution she had adopted soon after the coming of her unwelcome guests. Having heard Tarleton give the order to the tory captain as before mentioned, to patrol the country, she immediately sent for an old negro, and gave him directions to take a bag of corn to the mill, about four miles distant, on the road she knew her husband must travel if he returned that day. "Big George" was instructed to warn his master of the danger of approaching his home. With the indolence and curiosity natural to his race, however, the old fellow remained loitering about the premises, and was at this time lurking under the hedge-row, admiring the red coats, dashing plumes, and shining helmets of the British troopers.

The colonel and the ladies continued on the look-out from the piazza. "May I be allowed, madam," at length said Tarleton, "without offence, to inquire if any part of Washington's army is in this neighbourhood?"

"I presume it is known to you," replied Mrs. Slocumb, "that the Marquis and Greene are in this State. And you would not of course," she added, after a slight pause, "be surprised at a call from Lee, or your old friend Colonel Washington, who, although a perfect gentleman, it is said shook your hand (pointing to the scar left by Washington's sabre) very rudely, when you last met."

This spirited answer inspired Tarleton with apprehensions that the skirmish in the woods was only the prelude to a concerted attack on his camp. His only reply was a loud order to form the troops on the right; and springing on his charger, he dashed down the avenue a few hundred feet, to a breach in the hedge-row, leaped the fence, and in a moment was at the head of his regiment, which was already in line.

Meanwhile, Lieutenant Slocumb, with John Howell, a private in his band, Henry Williams, and the brother of Mrs. Slocumb, Charles Hooks, a boy of about thirteen years of age, was leading a hot pursuit of the tory captain who had been sent to reconnoitre the country, and some of his routed troop. These were first discerned in the open grounds east and north-east of the plantation, closely pursued by a body of American mounted militia; while a running fight was kept up with different weapons, in which four or five broadswords gleamed conspicuous. The foremost of the pursuing party appeared too busy with the tories to see anything else; and they entered the avenue at the same moment with the party pursued. With what horror and consternation did Mrs. Slocumb recognise her husband, her brother, and two of her neighbours, in chase of the tory captain and four of his band, already half-way down the avenue, and unconscious that they were rushing into the enemy's midst!

About the middle of the avenue one of the tories fell; and the course of the brave and imprudent young officers was suddenly arrested by "Big George," who sprang directly in front of their horses, crying, "Hold on, massa! de debbil here! Look yon!"* A glance to the left showed the young men their danger: they were within pistol shot of a thousand men drawn up in order of battle. Wheeling their horses, they discovered a troop already leaping the fence into the avenue in their rear. Quick as thought they again wheeled their horses, and dashed down the avenue directly towards the house, where stood the quarter-guard to receive them. On reaching the garden fence—a rude structure formed of a kind of lath, and called a wattled fence—they leaped that and the next, amid a shower of balls from the guard, cleared

* Yon, for yonder.

the canal at one tremendous leap, and scouring across the open field to the north-west, were in the shelter of the wood before their pursuers could clear the fences of the enclosure. The whole ground of this adventure may be seen as the traveller passes over the Wilmington railroad, a mile and a half south of Dudley depôt.

A platoon had commenced the pursuit; but the trumpets sounded the recall before the flying Americans had crossed the canal. The presence of mind and lofty language of the heroic wife, had convinced the British colonel that the daring men who so fearlessly dashed into his camp were supported by a formidable force at hand. Had the truth been known, and the fugitives pursued, nothing could have prevented the destruction not only of the four who fled, but of the rest of the company on the east side of the plantation.

Tarleton had ridden back to the front of the house, where he remained eagerly looking after the fugitives till they disappeared in the wood. He called for the tory captain, who presently came forward, questioned him about the attack in the woods, asked the names of the American officers, and dismissed him to have his wounds dressed, and see after his men. The last part of the order was needless; for nearly one-half of his troop had fallen. The ground is known to this day as the Dead Men's Field.

Another anecdote, communicated by the same friend of Mrs. Slocumb, is strikingly illustrative of her resolution and strength of will. The occurrence took place at a time when the whole country was roused by the march of the British and loyalists from the Cape Fear country, to join the royal standard at Wilmington. The veteran Donald McDonald issued his proclamation at Cross Creek, in February, 1776, and having assembled his Highlanders, marched across rivers and through forests, in haste to join Governor Martin and Sir Henry Clinton, who were already at Cape Fear. But while he had eluded the pursuit of Moore, the patriots of Newbern and Wilmington Districts were not idle. It was a time of noble enterprise, and gloriously did leaders and people come forward to meet the emergency. The gallant Richard Caswell called his neighbours hastily together; and they came at his call as readily as the clans of the Scotch mountains mustered at the signal of the burning cross. The whole country rose in mass; scarce a man able to walk was left in the Neuse region. The united regiments of Colonels Lillington and Caswell encountered McDonald at Moore's Creek;* where, on the twenty-seventh, was fought one of the bloodiest battles of the Revolution. Colonel Slocumb's recollections of this bravely-contested field were too vivid to be dimmed by the lapse of years. He was accustomed to dwell but lightly on the gallant part borne by himself in that memorable action; but he gave abundant praise to his associates; and well did they deserve the tribute. "And," he would say—"*my wife was there!*" She was indeed; but the story is best told in her own words:

"The men all left on Sunday morning. More than eighty went from this house with my husband; I looked at them well, and I could see that every man had mischief in him. I know a coward as soon as I set my eyes upon him. The tories more than once tried to frighten me, but they always showed coward at the bare insinuation that our troops were about.

"Well, they got off in high spirits; every man stepping high and light. And I slept soundly and quietly that night, and worked hard all the next day; but I kept thinking where they had got to —how far; where and how many of the regulars and tories they would meet; and I could not keep myself from the study. I went to bed at the usual time, but still continued to study. As I lay—whether waking or sleeping I know not—I had a dream; yet it was not all a dream. (She used the words, unconsciously, of the poet who was not then in being.) I saw distinctly a body wrapped in my husband's guard-cloak—bloody—dead; and others dead and wounded on the ground about him. I saw them plainly and distinctly. I uttered a cry, and sprang to my feet on the floor; and so strong was the impression on my mind, that I rushed in the direction the vision appeared, and came up against the side of the house. The fire in the room gave little light, and I gazed in every direction to catch another glimpse of the scene. I raised the light;

* Moore's Creek, running from north to south, empties into the South River, about twenty miles above Wilmington.

everything was still and quiet. My child was sleeping, but my woman was awakened by my crying out or jumping on the floor. If ever I felt fear it was at that moment. Seated on the bed, I reflected a few moments—and said aloud: 'I must go to him.' I told the woman I could not sleep, and would ride down the road. She appeared in great alarm; but I merely told her to lock the door after me, and look after the child. I went to the stable, saddled my mare—as fleet and easy a nag as ever travelled; and in one minute we were tearing down the road at full speed. The cool night seemed after a mile or two's gallop to bring reflection with it; and I asked myself where I was going, and for what purpose. Again and again I was tempted to turn back; but I was soon ten miles from home, and my mind became stronger every mile I rode. I should find my husband dead or dying—was as firmly my presentiment and conviction as any fact of my life. When day broke, I was some thirty miles from home. I knew the general route our little army expected to take, and had followed them without hesitation. About sunrise I came upon a group of women and children, standing and sitting by the roadside, each one of them showing the same anxiety of mind I felt. Stopping a few minutes, I inquired if the battle had been fought. They knew nothing, but were assembled on the road to catch intelligence. They thought Caswell had taken the right of the Wilmington road, and gone towards the north-west (Cape Fear). Again was I skimming over the ground through a country thinly settled, and very poor and swampy; but neither my own spirits nor my beautiful nag's failed in the least. We followed the well-marked trail of the troops.

"The sun must have been well up, say eight or nine o'clock, when I heard a sound like thunder, which I knew must be cannon. It was the first time I ever heard a cannon. I stopped still; when presently the cannon thundered again. The battle was then fighting. What a fool! my husband could not be dead last night, and the battle only fighting now! Still, as I am so near, I will go on and see how they come out. So away we went again, faster than ever; and I soon found by the noise of guns that I was near the fight. Again I stopped. I could hear muskets, I could hear rifles, and I could hear shouting. I spoke to my mare and dashed on in the direction of the firing and the shouts, now louder than ever. The blind path I had been following brought me into the Wilmington road leading to Moore's Creek Bridge, a few hundred yards below the bridge. A few yards from the road, under a cluster of trees were lying perhaps twenty men. They were the wounded. I knew the spot; the very trees; and the position of the men I knew as if I had seen it a thousand times. I had seen it all night! I saw all at once; but in an instant my whole soul was centred in one spot; for there, wrapped in his bloody guard-cloak, was my husband's body! How I passed the few yards from my saddle to the place I never knew. I remember uncovering his head and seeing a face clothed with gore from a dreadful wound across the temple. I put my hand on the bloody face; 'twas warm; and an *unknown voice* begged for water. A small camp-kettle was lying near, and a stream of water was close by. I brought it; poured some in his mouth; washed his face; and behold—it was Frank Cogdell. He soon revived and could speak. I was washing the wound in his head. Said he, 'It is not that; it is that hole in my leg that is killing me.' A puddle of blood was standing on the ground about his feet. I took his knife, cut away his trousers and stocking, and found the blood came from a shot-hole through and through the fleshy part of his leg. I looked about and could see nothing that looked as if it would do for dressing wounds but some heart-leaves. I gathered a handful and bound them tight to the holes; and the bleeding stopped. I then went to the others; and —Doctor! I dressed the wounds of many a brave fellow who did good fighting long after that day! I had not inquired for my husband; but while I was busy Caswell came up. He appeared very much surprised to see me; and was with his hat in hand about to pay some compliment: but I interrupted him by asking—'Where is my husband?'

"'Where he ought to be, madam; in pursuit of the enemy. But pray,' said he, 'how came you here?"

"'Oh, I thought,' replied I, 'you would need nurses as well as soldiers. See! I have already dressed many of these good fellows;

and here is one'—going to Frank and lifting him up with my arm under his head so that he could drink some more water—'would have died before any of you men could have helped him.'

"'I believe you,' said Frank. Just then I looked up, and my husband, as bloody as a butcher, and as muddy as a ditcher,* stood before me.

"'Why, Mary!' he exclaimed, 'What are you doing there? Hugging Frank Cogdell, the greatest reprobate in the army?'

"'I don't care,' I cried. 'Frank is a brave fellow, a good soldier, and a true friend to Congress.'

"'True, true! every word of it!' said Caswell. 'You are right, madam!' with the lowest possible bow.

"I would not tell my husband what brought me there. I was so happy; and so were all! It was a glorious victory; I came just at the height of the enjoyment. I knew my husband was surprised, but I could see he was not displeased with me. It was night again before our excitement had at all subsided. Many prisoners were brought in, and among them some very obnoxious; but the worst of the tories were not taken prisoners. They were, for the most part, left in the woods and swamps wherever they were overtaken. I begged for some of the poor prisoners, and Caswell readily told me none should be hurt but such as had been guilty of murder and house-burning. In the middle of the night I again mounted my mare and started for home. Caswell and my husband wanted me to stay till next morning and they would send a party with me; but no! I wanted to see my child, and I told them they could send no party who could keep up with me. What a happy ride I had back! and with what joy did I embrace my child as he ran to meet me!"

What fiction could be stranger than such truth! And would not a plain unvarnished narrative of the sayings and doings of the actors in Revolutionary times, unknown by name, save in the neighbourhood where they lived, and now almost forgotten even by their descendants, surpass in thrilling interest any romance ever written!

* It was his company that forded the creek, and penetrating the swamp, made the furious charge on the British left and rear, which decided the fate of the day.

In these days of railroads and steam, it can scarcely be credited that a woman actually rode alone, in the night, through a wild unsettled country, a distance—going and returning—of a hundred and twenty-five miles; and that in less than forty hours, and without any interval of rest! Yet even this fair equestrian, whose feats would astonish the modern world, admitted that one of her acquaintances was a better horsewoman than herself. This was Miss Esther Wake, the beautiful sister-in-law of Governor Tryon, after whom Wake County was named. She is said to have ridden eighty miles—the distance between Raleigh and the Governor's head-quarters in the neighbourhood of Colonel Slocumb's residence—to pay a visit; returning the next day. What would these women have said to the delicacy of modern refinement, fatigued with a modern drive in a close carriage, and looking out on woods and fields from the windows!

E. OAKES SMITH.

About twelve miles from the city of Portland, in Maine, a pretty cottage just on the edge of a thick wood is pointed out by the neighbours with a feeling of pride, as the birth-place of Mrs. E. Oakes Smith. Her maiden name was Elizabeth Oakes Prince. One of the earliest of the settlers of Maine was an ancestor of hers by the name of Prince, and there is a tract of land in Maine, called "Prince's Point," where her ancestors settled in 1630, having gone there from Massachusetts. Her grandfather died in the year 1849, at the age of ninety-seven. He is described as having been a tall, handsome, patriarchal man, in appearance. Her mother, too, is described as an imperious, intellectual woman, with strong characteristics, and exceedingly beautiful. Her name was Blanchard, and she is of Huguenot descent. On the father's side Mrs. Smith is of a puritan family.

She gave early indications of genius. The only circumstance of her childhood, however, that seems particularly noticeable, is her habit while a mere girl, of dramatizing little extempore plays, when as yet she had never seen or heard of such a thing, and in a family where Shakspeare was regarded as an abomination, and his readers as——no better than they should be!

She was married at the early age of sixteen to Mr. Seba Smith, so widely known as the original "Jack Downing." Mr. Smith at the time of his marriage was the editor of the leading political journal of Maine. They are at present living in New York.

Mrs. Smith's poems have never been fully collected. One small volume has been published, and has run through seven or eight editions. "The Sinless Child" has been greatly admired, as also have been her "Sonnets," and many other small occasional pieces. Her largest work in verse is a tragedy, called "The Roman Tribute," which was acted in New York, but I believe has never been printed. Another play, "Jacob Leisler, or Old New York," has been well received by the critics, having been acted several times with entire success.

As a prose writer, Mrs. Smith has been for several years a frequent contributor to the leading Magazines. Her contributions of this sort, chiefly stories and sketches, would make several volumes. Her magazine stories are chiefly of a legendary character, and many of them are connected with the history of her native State. She purposes collecting and publishing them under the title of "Legends of Maine."

Her largest story, "The Lost Angel," was published in a volume in 1848. She has chosen for the scene of this story the romantic valley of the Ramapo, in the State of New York, and dated it about two centu ries back. It is, however, purely an imaginative, not an historical work There may be facts embodied in the narrative, of which types are to be found in the early history of the Dutch colony, as there may be descriptions of scenery corresponding to what actually exists in the Ramapo valley. But the ideas which form the staple of the book, and which give it all its significance, are no more American, than the ideas of the "Midsummer Night's Dream" are English. The work, in other words, is purely of an imaginative character. It is founded on those dark mysterious legends—half Christian, half pagan—which prevailed in central Germany during the middle ages. Out of these wild myths, Mrs. Smith has produced a fiction, somewhat over-bold in speculation, occasionally careless in execution, but full of significance, brilliant—almost dazzling—in some of its conceptions, and everywhere teeming with grace and beauty.

"Woman and her Needs" discusses the vexed question of woman's rights, and is a text book with those of the progressive party. "Hints on Dress and Beauty" has been received with much favour. The same may be remarked of "Shadow Land," in which the author gives her views of the spiritual element of our nature. "Bertha and Lily," 1854, likewise developes the author's views on the great moral and social questions of the age. It is represented by that accomplished critic, Mr. Ripley, as being far beyond any of Mrs. Smith's previous writings. "Riches without Wings," "Western Captive," "Moss Cup," and "Dandelion," are the titles of some of her smaller volumes.

THE MYSTERY OF THE MOUNTAIN.

While Hugo saw these things where he stood high up in the mountain, his eyes followed the sparks from the furnace, and he began to wonder that he should hear the sound of the flame at such a distance. Then he bethought himself and looked around, for, what he had supposed the sound from the heat of the forge, proceeded from something close to his feet, at which he marvelled, seeing nothing. It was a short tinkling sound as if many metallic substances rang against one another, and crystals clicked their angles fretfully, yet all making most clear and beautiful melody. Observing more closely, Hugo beheld a toad squatted close to his ear upon a shelf of the rock, whose eyes were brighter than sapphires, and every spot upon his mottled sides had become a gem while he sang:—

In the cavern we lie hidden,
  Gem, and crystal, diamond stone,
Buried are we, and forbidden
  To lay bare our glittering throne.
Mystic numbers, sacred symbols,
  Break the spell that now enthralls us.
Hark the tabor and the timbrels;
  Up, my braves, the music calls us.

Instantly the toad began to move itself up and down, thrusting out its short loose legs in the strangest fashion, and with great apparent glee. Its head moved from side to side, keeping time to the music, and its eyes grew every moment more brilliant. While Hugo looked on laughing, and he laughed in the loudest manner, for he was a bluff hearty man, he began to move to and fro, and wag his head with the toad. Then he saw that another had joined them in the shape of a serpent, whereat he drew back in terror; but the snake came on, erecting his head and glowing in his burnished folds, till he came opposite to the man Hugo, when he began to move from side to side, and Hugo did the same, with wonderful ease and pleasure; the dance growing more and more rapid, and the snake, no more a snake, but a column of rubies and diamonds and all precious stones, changing and flashing and tinkling their sharp points, and rolling and writhing in the ecstasy of light; just as a skilful youth tosses many marbles into the air, catching them before they fall to the ground, and they ring sharply as they click one against another.

There was a slight crash, and Hugo saw as it were into the bowels of the mountain. He stooped himself and peered down, wondering from whence came so great a light. Then he saw that the earth opened, revealing a great funnel, the sides of which consisted of projections or little shelves upon which rested swarthy creatures, whose eyes were gems, and lighted the cavern. As Hugo looked, they each turned themselves heavily and rolled their eyes upon him; and as they did so, each lifted a filmy paw, and showed a jewel which he held beneath, so bright as to dazzle the eyes and cast a flash like that of the firefly when he lifteth his wings. Hugo felt his heart burning with desire; he longed to reach out his hand and seize the wealth held under those black claws; but he was at a loss which to take, for every moment one more gorgeous than the last met his eyes.

Still peering downward, he beheld upon the floor of the cavern a huge brown creature studded with crimson, which clung to the ground as the haliotis clings to the rock; but seeing the eager desire of Hugo, he lifted himself and showed what he held concealed; and the man saw *a burning triangle, with a word written in fire*, and he knew that that was the word, which spoken gives dominion over the whole earth.

Hugo roused himself with a great shout, trying to pronounce the word; three times did he shout, and three times did the word escape him; as when a person would sneeze and the power is lost just in the act, so was it with him, and he was filled with a great rage. When he would have tried again, he felt a finger soft and cool laid in the shape of a cross upon his lips, whereat the oaths which were gathering there fell backward, and he saw the fair stately form of his wife looking tenderly upon him, but she did not speak. When Hugo would have spread forth his arms to her, he met only the night air; the pale stars were shining reproachfully upon him, and the summer air lifted his locks from his bare head. He saw the toad plump itself into a hole, and the tail of the serpent twirl spirally as he slunk away among the rocks. Hugo thought of his wife, and for awhile the vision of the mountain lost its power, for his true human heart yearned with an exceeding love, which made all things else poor and unworthy.

Next day Hugo placed his daughter upon a white palfrey, while he mounted a heavy black charger, and they went forth together, following the river as it wound itself out of the glen into the open plain. Mary forgot her grief, and carolled like a bird, hoping to make her father smile. She darted ahead at full speed, and then returned showering roses in her path, and bound the head of her father's horse with a gay chaplet. Hugo smiled at the fooleries of the girl, for he bethought himself of her mother, and restrained his moodiness.

When they came out where the country spread itself into a broad meadow, with the river rolling onward and the silent forest, and the high mountains lay against the sky, the girl drew with feelings of awe to the side of her father, and rode on in silence. Ever and anon the clear sound of a bugle swelled out, and then died away in the distance—while the baying of hounds told of courtly sport. Mary looked on every side, but neither dwelling nor human being was to be seen, but jangling the bells of her harness she caught the spirit of life which the bugle implied, and rode gayly onward.

Reaching a lovely glade where the birches trembled lightly over a stream, Hugo dismounted, and they sat down upon the bank. The girl feared to disturb the silence of her father, so she nestled to his side and pulled the violets for lack of something to do. At length he said:

"Mary, what is the word which the spirit keeps up in the mountain? I have tried to speak it, and am not able."

"It is an ill word, dear father, that removes the soul from God."

"Nevertheless, speak it," said Hugo.

"I dare not speak a word, that will mix my nature with earth-spirits, dear father."

"Thou art but a cowardly girl," cried Hugo; "did I not see wealth such as the greatest monarch might envy, and did I not see thrones and power within my grasp, save that this palsied tongue could not seize the word?"

While her father spoke in this wise, Mary grew pale, and knelt with her hands folded in silence. At length she spoke:

"It is a fearful word, dear father, which causes the crystal gates of Paradise to glide upon their hinges and shut the utterer out for ever."

Hugo ground his teeth firmly, and said in a voice terrible, it was so firm and loud—

"Speak, child—I would know it."

Then Mary prayed, saying, "Oh, my God! let the knowledge fade out from my soul, that I may never be guilty of this great sin."

"Speak," said her father, turning pale with a great rage.

The clear face of the child was turned to that of the dark man, and a fair smile was on her lips as she answered,

"God has heard my prayer, dear father—I know it not."

"Thou liest," answered the fierce man, and he struck the child with his heavy palm.

Mary threw her arms around the neck of her father, pale and trembling, whereat a sudden pang of remorse filled him with shame and grief; but when he saw how still she lay in his arms, he grew fearful, and raised her up and looked into her face. She lay without breath or motion, and although he sprinkled water in her face from the brook, and called her passionately back to life, she did not lift up the fringes of her lids.

THE ANGEL AND THE MAIDEN.

After this scene upon the mountain, the stranger no longer wore that appearance of extreme sadness, which before had created a painful interest in his behalf: he no longer seemed weighed by those deep and mysterious thoughts, that shadow forth the unseen world, and leave us without the sympathy which alone makes this life cheerful; now a fair serenity diffused itself in his mien, and his face wore a placid and benign candour most lovely to behold There was a joyful upwardness in his look, and a genial outwardness in his eyes, as if they rested lovingly upon God's creatures, and no longer were content with selfish introversion.

Mary saw the change in the youth with untold delight, she walked by his side and listened to his voice, gathering a higher aspiration from her noble companionship. Light as a fawn, she sported beside the clear brook, and the melody of her song waked the echoes of the glen to sweeter harmonies.

Mary and the youth were wandering beyond the valley where the river opened into the plain, talking as they were wont; they had gone onward, beguiled by their sweet discourse, and did not perceive how the great red sun burnished the hills with golden powder, for the dense trees were about them, and only his sharp light flecked the leaves and glanced upon the boles of the trees, now glinting the shoulders of the red-bird, and now flashing the green mail of the lizard, or turning the wings of the dragon-fly to rainbows—anon the coquettish squirrel caught the beam in his full soft eye, and the timid hare showed the tracery of blood in his pink ears as he darted across their path; the mosses were like velvet beneath, and the frail wild flowers, vestal worshippers, meek beautifiers of the wilderness, lifted themselves in their solitude, content only with the blessing of the good Father.

Mary drew to the side of the youth, and laid her hand in his, but he gently removed his own and placed it upon the jewelled hilt of his sword. Mary's cheek turned to crimson; she faltered, and, stung with pride, the tears gushed to her eyes. At this moment, they heard a low growl above their heads, and splinters of bark were scattered at their feet; looking up, they perceived a panther just in the act to spring, with his terrible eyes fixed upon the victims below. Instantly the sword of the young man sprang from its sheath, and the ferocious beast alighted, in his deadly leap, upon its point.

When Mary recovered from the swoon into which she had fallen, she found the youth standing over the prostrate animal whose blood was dripping from his sword and garments, and she shrieked with terror, supposing that he must have been wounded. With kindly and respectful courtesy, he lifted her from the ground, and seating himself by her side, implored her to be tranquil.

"I must leave thee, Mary; for I feel assured that my pilgrimage is near its close."

Mary could only weep.

"There is much that I would tell thee, Mary; but I know not whether thou art able to bear it," the youth at length said.

"Shall we meet again?" faltered the child in a low voice. His face contracted with a sharp pang, and he murmured, "Oh, my God! deliver thou me."

"Mary, I am in deadly peril; I beseech thee question me not," he replied.

Mary looked into his eyes, so full of their clear unearthly light; so full of all that makes a human heart a well-spring of ineffable blessedness, and overcome with the flood of girlish sympathy, she cast her arms about his neck, and murmured, "Do not leave me."

Poor child! the youth arose sternly from the ground, and placing one foot upon the shoulder of the beast he had just slain, turned his back to the girl, who shrank to the earth, and buried her face in the masses of curls that clustered about her neck. At length, the sobs of the child touched even his stern heart, and he turned himself around: but oh! the grief and agony on his face had done in minutes the work of years—he who a moment before had been fair and smooth as the boy of eighteen summers, was now rigid, stern, and marked by those outlines of thought, which come only when the soul has wrestled with some mighty grief, even like unto that of the Patriarch of old, when he wrestled all night with the Angel of God.

"Mary," he said, sinking on his knees beside the girl, "I must tell thee all, and then if thou dost weep, and lament, the judgment of the Eternal will be completed in me."

Mary lifted her head—"Thou wilt go—shall we not meet again?"

The youth groaned heavily.

Mary's pure nature taught her that she was giving pain, and casting her selfishness aside, she said:

"Wilt thou pardon my folly? forget me, unless thou canst also forget this unmaidenly scene."

The youth buried his face in his hands, and through the fingers

Mary saw the tears trickle, but the nature of them was soothing and holy.

"I shall never forget thee, Mary; wherever in the mysteries of God I may be transferred, the holiness of thy affection will cause this cheerless earth, in which and for which I have suffered so much, to be none other than the Paradise of God;" and stooping downward he touched the tears, which had fallen upon the earth, and they became a chaplet of lilies with which he bound the head of Mary.

"Dost thou remember the gems I once gave thee, Mary? Then I had power over only the element of fire, which burns and consumes, or hardens to the rock, but now the water and the life are mine—behold these lilies—wear them—for thou art worthy."

He turned his steps as if to depart.

"Shall we meet again?" implored the child.

The youth lifted his head sorrowfully. "Shall we meet again?" he repeated; "for thy sake, for mine, I have questioned too. The knowledge of the future was once mine, but I resigned it as thou didst thy dangerous knowledge, and now the eternal world is hidden from me; I tread the valley of darkness more dismayed, than even a human soul; now—now, O that I could see! What is faith to the once prescient Archangel?" and he cast himself to the earth, overcome with his terrible thoughts.

"Shall we not meet again? Oh! in the long eternal years shall I not yearn for the look, the tone, for which even now I peril my redemption? What is that terrible future? How shall the soul exist floating onward for ever and for ever, with a universe of suns receding from its path, if it bear not with it the known and the loved? How will it shiver and shrink from the gray twilight of the eternal, unless folded in the wings of a love which, though born of earth, leads onward to God? Mary, Mary"—his voice ceased, and he fell prostrate to the earth.

LOUISA S. M'CORD.

MRS. M'CORD was born in Charleston, South Carolina, Dec. 3, 1810 She is the daughter of Langdon Cheves, Esq., so well known in our public and political history. She was educated in Philadelphia, at the celebrated school of Mr. Charles Picot, during her father's residence in that city; resided a short time in Lancaster, Pennsylvania; and in 1828, returned to the South, where in May, 1840, she was married to D. J. M'Cord, Esq., of Columbia, South Carolina; a gentleman of considerable local distinction—an admirable lawyer, an able public speaker, a good writer—the editor of the Statutes at large of South Carolina, and a frequent contributor to the Southern Quarterly Review. Like his accomplished wife, he delights in political economy, and is one of the best writers of the country, on the Free Trade side of the question. She is living at present at a plantation about thirty miles below Columbia, the site well known in revolutionary history as Fort Motte, distinguished by the patriotic sacrifice of her dwelling by the famous lady of that name, who handed to Marion the bow and arrows with which the blazing torches were conveyed to the shingles, and the British driven from the fastness. Mrs. M'Cord is herself a woman capable of this very sort of heroism, noble of person, warm, impulsive of spirit, and with a lofty and generous nature.

Mrs. M'Cord has not collected her writings, which are comparatively numerous, and which usually take the shapes of reviews and essays. The writings by which she is chiefly known are of a sort to show that the advantages of birth and education so liberally granted her, have not been without fruit. She is one of the few women who have undertaken to write on the difficult subject of political economy. Her contributions on this subject to the Southern Quarterly Review are characterized by masculine vigour and an enlarged acquaintance with the subject. Among them may be named particularly "Justice and Fraternity," July, 1849; "The Right to Labour," Oct., 1849; "Diversity of Races, its Bearing upon Negro Slavery," April, 1851. She has published also a small volume, called "Sophisms of Political Economy," translated from the French of Frederick Bastiat.

Mrs. M'Cord is also favourably known as a poet. A volume of her poetry, entitled "My Dreams," appeared in 1848; and in 1851, she published "Caius Gracchus, a Tragedy," by far the most elaborate and important of her writings. Her miscellaneous poems are mostly of a didactic character, and therefore do not justly illustrate the higher properties of her mind, which is marked by the energies of an eager, sanguine temperament. This characteristic is more fully developed in her tragedy, where her poetical genius appears to more advantage.

THE RIGHT TO LABOUR.

We are not ultra-reformists;—far from it;—and yet we are of those who see, in the present condition of the world, the waking up of a new era. We are of those who believe in,—if not the perfectibility of man,—at least his great, lasting, and boundless improvement. Thought is roused, mind is awakened, which never again can sleep. Vainly are we told that preceding ages have shown equal civilization and similar improvement. Vainly is our attention directed to the great Nineveh, to Egypt, to Greece, and to Rome. These certainly do show—these have shown—progression and retrogression, rise and fall, as the great pulse of humanity has throbbed in its breathing of ages; but never has the world-soul been roused, as now, by the expansion of thought, circulating to distant points of our globe, whose very existence was not dreamed of by the wise of ancient days. Never has the great heart of civilization cast, as now, by its every pulsation, its life-blood to the farthest extremes of a universe, rousing itself from unconscious infancy to the full action of a reasoning being. Great as were the efforts of the ancients—great as were the results of those efforts—they were confined to little corners of a world, which now basks under the full radiance of extended and extending light. And yet, even of these efforts, nothing has been lost. The soul of their civilization, as each sank in its ruins, was breathed into the survivor, until at last, in the great crash of Roman power, the shattered remnants of its pride and its knowledge, scattering through Europe, laid the basis of modern civilization.

Yet not for this, alas! are we now exempt from the wildest

follies, the grossest vices. France, in her present struggles, shows a mingling chaos of all that is best and wisest, of all that is maddest and worst. Among the most rampant of her run-mad fancies is this wild dream of "fraternity" and socialism, with their Icarias and Utopian worlds. Would that these were confined to France alone! Unfortunately, we see their extravagant madness striding the Atlantic and stamping its too plainly marked foot-tracks on our own shores. That terrible fallacy compacted in the words, "The right to labour," is rapidly working its mischief. "The right of man to labour, and of land whereon to labour,"—what is it, as our communists interpret it, but the right to rob? They would not labour for nothing, nor yet for such compensation as the true value of their labour, given where it is wanted and paid for as it is needed, will produce. They have the right to labour, be it for good or for ill. They have the right to be paid for that labour, let the capital they force into their use be theirs or another's. You do not want my work,—it matters not,—"I have a right to work, and you, having capital, must pay me for such work, be it to your detriment or your benefit. I have the right to labour!"

Within this specious formula—"the right to labour"—lie concentrated the greater number of those terrible fallacies which now threaten to overrun and devastate civilized society. The hydra of communism holds struggling in its deadly folds the Hercules of truth. That the latter conquers, who can doubt? Man's nature, his soul, and instinct, alike lead him to the light. The world is progressive. The past shows, the present hopes for, and the future promises this; but fearful are the doubts, the despondencies, and the agonies, through which society must pass to attain its highest tone! Around each great truth is gathered a crowd of errors—deceitful reflections of its beauty—giving to the mischievous a pretext for ill, and often, with *ignis fatuus* light, misleading even the true-hearted and the good.

There are crises in the world's course, when, rousing from temporary lethargy, reason seems more than usually wide awake to the influence of truth and light. But, in this very waking, is she also more subject to the misleading influence of error. The craving heart—the longing, seeking, hungering for truth—is roused; and, in its eager search, how often, alas! is the will-o'-the-wisp mistaken for the star-beam! Through one of these crises are we now struggling. The world is in labour of a great truth, but its sick fancy is cheated with the bewildering dazzle of its own delirious dreams.

One of society's closest guards—a kind of shepherd's dog, as it were, of the flock—stands political economy. Watching, barking, wrangling at every intruder, suspicious of outward show, nor satisfied with skin-deep inspection, it examines, before admitting all pretenders as true prophets, and strips many a wolf of his sheep's clothing. The evil-inclined, thus, naturally, hoot and revile it. The ignorant mistrust it. What do we, its advocates, ask in its defence? Simply nothing, but that the world should learn to know it. We wish no law for its imposition—no tax for its protection. Let truth be but heard: there is in the heart of man an instinct to know and to seize it. Error is simply negative; like shadow, it is only want of light. Heaven's sunbeam on the material world—reason's effulgence on the thinking soul—alone suffice to work God's purposes. Man, his humble instrument, cannot make the light; he can but strive to remove the obstacles which intercept its abundant flow.

We ask, then, only to be heard. Let the world know us. Let the people know us. Let political economy be the science of the crowd. It is neither incomprehensible nor abstruse. It requires but that each individual man should think,—think—not imagine, not dream, not utopianize—but think, study, and understand for himself. Where the masses are ignorant, what more natural than that they stumble into wrong? Mind must act; and more and more, as the world advances, does it call for the right of exerting and developing its power. In earlier ages, learning, information, thought, being limited to the few, the masses took the word from these high-priests of reason, whose veiled holy of holies was sacred from the intrusion of the crowd. But, now, the veil is rent asunder. Not you, nor we, nor he—nor any chosen one—nor ten, nor twenty—but man,—now claims the right to think for himself. He claims it; he will have it; he ought to have it. Let but those who are ahead in the race of knowledge give to those who need; guide those who stumble in the dark; and each, thus putting in his mite of well-doing in the cause, ward off, as much as possible, the calamities which necessarily hover round the great and progressive change through which the world is passing. Great changes are oftenest wrought out only through great convulsions. It is a man's work, and man's heart is in it, when the humblest individual, with shoulder to the wheel, stands boldly and honestly forth, to raise his hand in warding off the avalanche of evil.

France, which now stands before the world, in the agonies of her struggles—great alike in truth and in error—France has experimented, and written for us, in her sufferings, a mighty lesson. May we but read and learn it! Revelling in the madness of newly-gained freedom, her people not knowing the use of what they had seized, for them it became the synonyme of license. Rushing from extreme to extreme, they forgot that liberty was but enfranchisement; and, with "democracy" for their watchword, exercised a despotism much more fearful than that of the single tyrant, because its power, like its name, was "*legion.*"

And what is the result? Credit dead; industry paralyzed; commerce annihilated; her starving people now sinking despondent under their difficulties—now driven to the madness of revolt, against they know not whom—asking, they know not what. France, terrified at her own acts, calls out for succour, and on every side resound the answers of her best and wisest citizens: "Step back from your errors; give truth its way"—"*laissez passer*"—"*laissez faire.*"

Amidst the throng of confused theories, each of which burns into the very vitals of the suffering State, its brand of crime and folly,

"While lean-looked prophets whisper fearful change,"

political economy alone, with its great and simple truths, seems to hold forth some hope of a real regeneration. It alone enjoins upon its disciples to follow, step by step—to sift to the bottom its theories and their remotest effects—before launching the world upon untried experiments. It alone gropes patiently its way, grappling with doubts and difficulties, making sure and clear its footing, before calling upon society to follow. Its opponents—socialists of every grade—leaping blindfold to their conclusions, and taking impulse for inspiration, recklessly drag on their devotees from one wild dream to another, until

> "Contention, like a horse,
> Full of high feeding, madly doth break loose,
> And bears down all before him."

They do not mean the evil which they do. Very possibly, their hearts are of the purest—but their ideas, unfortunately, not of the clearest. Without examining into the practicability of their own schemes, they give way to a misty vision of goodness—a kind of foggy virtue—which, often but the rush-light of their own unregulated fancy—too indolent or too cowardly to probe to its source, and follow to its end—they imagine an inward light, a transmitted beam of heaven, and so dream on!

ANN S. STEPHENS.

Mrs. Stephens, according to a writer in Graham's Magazine,* was born about the year 1810, in an interior village of the State of Connecticut. She was married at an early age, and soon after removed with her husband to Portland, Maine. Subsequently, they changed their residence to New York, where they have lived ever since.

Mrs. Stephens's literary career commenced in Portland. Among the first of her friends there, was John Neal, who early appreciated her genius. She projected, and for some time published, the "Portland Magazine," to which she gave considerable celebrity, chiefly through her own contributions. On removing to New York, she engaged in writing for a more extensive circle of readers, and her fame rapidly widened. An event occurred soon after which gave to her name a special eclat. This was the winning of a prize of four hundred dollars, for the story of "Mary Derwent." Whatever she has written since that time has been in great demand among periodical publishers. Her tales, sketches, and poems, published in this way, would fill several volumes. Unfortunately, they have never been collected into any more enduring form than that in which they originally appeared.

Mrs. Stephens has a remarkable talent for description, seizing always the strongest points in a picture and bringing them out into bold relief. In the conception and delineation of character, too, she is clear and comprehensive, yet working out her views more by descriptive than dramatic effect, telling how her characters act, rather than setting them into action. In regard to plot, her stories are simple, and rather bare of incident, as if aiming to hurry forward the reader by a strong, torrent-like impulse, rather than to entangle him in a curious and complicated maze. She has shown great versatility, apparently vibrating at will between a vein of the richest humour, as in the story of the "Patch-Work Quilt," and that deep and startling tragedy on which she more commonly relies.

"Fashion and Famine," the largest of Mrs. Stephens's stories, being a full sized novel, has made its appearance just as the revised edition of this work is going to the press, July, 1854. The story is understood to be one

* Charles J. Peterson.

Ann S Stephens

of the present time, bringing into strong contrast the varied scenes of splendour and of squalor, of riotous wealth and of starving poverty, that mark the state of society in our large cities. It is a fruitful theme, and one well suited to Mrs. Stephen's genius.

THE QUILTING PARTY.

A THREE-SEATED sleigh, gorgeous with yellow paint and gilding, drawn by two horses and a leader, stopped with a dash by the door-yard gate. A troop of girls, cloaked and hooded to the chin, were disengaging themselves from the buffalo-robes and leaping cheerily out on either side, while the driver stood in front, bending backward in a vigorous effort to hold in his horses, which every instant gave a leap and a pull upon the lines, which set the bells a-ringing and the girls a-laughing with a burst of music that went through the old house like a flash of sunshine. The sleigh dashed up the lane in quest of a new load, while the cargo it had just left were busy as so many humming-birds in Julia's dressing-room. Cloaks were heaped in a pile on the bed, hoods were flung off, and half a dozen bright, smiling faces were peeping at themselves in the glass. Never was an old-fashioned mirror so beset. Flaxen and jetty ringlets, braids of chestnut, brown and ashy gold flashed on its surface—white muslins, rose-coloured crapes, and silks of cerulean blue floated before it like a troop of sunset clouds—eyes glanced in and out like stars reflected in a fountain, and soft, red lips trembled over its surface like rosebuds flung upon the same bright waters.

Again the sleigh dashed up to the gate, and off once more. Then we all gathered to the out room, sat demurely down by the quilt, and began to work in earnest. Such frolic and fun and girlish wit —such peals of silvery laughter as rang through that old house were enough to make the worm-eaten rafters sound again—such a snipping of thread and breaking of needles—such demand for cotton and such graceful rolling of spools across the "rising sun"* could only be witnessed in a New England quilting frolic. The fire snapped and blazed with a sort of revel cheerfulness; it danced up and down over the old mirror that hung in a tarnished frame oppo-

* The name of the pattern which they were quilting.

site, and every time the pretty girl nearest the hearth-rug lifted the huge tailor's shears, appropriated to her use, the flame flashed up and played over them till they seemed crusted with jewels. One young lady, with a very sweet voice, sung "I'd be a Butterfly," with tumultuous applause. Miss Narissa exercised her sharp voice in "I won't be a Nun," and two young ladies, who had no places at the quilt, read conversation cards by the fire.

Toward night-fall, Miss Elizabeth, who had hovered about the quilt at intervals all the afternoon, appeared from the middle room and whispered mysteriously to Narissa, who got up and went out. After a few minutes the amiable sisters returned, and with smiling hospitality announced that tea was ready.

The door was flung wide open, and a long table, covered to the carpet with birds-eye diaper, stood triumphantly in view. We moved toward the door, our garments mingling together, and some with linked arms, laughing as they went.

Miss Elizabeth stood at the head of the table, supported by a huge Britannia teapot and conical-shaped sugar-bowl, which had officiated at her grandmother's wedding supper. She waved her hand with a grace peculiarly her own, and we glided to our chairs, spread out our pocket-handkerchiefs, and waited patiently while Miss Elizabeth held the Britannia teapot in a state of suspension and asked each one separately, in the same sweet tone, if she took sugar and cream. Then there was a travelling of small-sized China cups down the table. As each cup reached its destination, the recipient bathed her spoon in the warm contents, timidly moistened her lips, and waited till her neighbour was served. Then two plates of warm biscuit started an opposition route on each side the board, followed by a train of golden butter, dried beef and sago cheese.

About this time Miss Narissa began to make a commotion among a pile of little glass plates that formed her division of command. Four square dishes of currant jelly, quince preserves, and clarified peaches, were speedily yielding up their contents. The little plates flashed to and fro, up and down, then became stationary, each one gleaming up from the snow-white cloth like a fragment of ice whereon a handful of half-formed rubies had been flung. There was a hush in the conversation, the tinkling of tea-spoons, with here and there a deep breath as some rosy lip was bathed in the luscious jellies. After a time the China cups began to circulate around the tea-tray again, conical-shaped loaf cakes became locomotive, from which each guest extracted a triangular slice with becoming gravity. Then followed in quick succession a plate heaped up with tiny heart-shaped cakes, snow-white with frosting and warmly spiced with carraway seed, dark-coloured ginger-nuts and a stack of jumbles, twisted romantically into true lover's knots and dusted with sugar.

Last of all came the crowning glory of a country tea-table. A plate was placed at the elbow of each lady, where fragments of pie, wedge-shaped and nicely fitted together, formed a beautiful and tempting Mosaic. The ruby tart, golden pumpkin, and yet more delicate custard, mottled over with nutmeg, seemed blended and melting together beneath the tall lights, by this time placed at each end of the table. We had all eaten enough, and it seemed a shame to break the artistical effect of these pie plates. But there sat Miss Elizabeth by one huge candlestick entreating us to make ourselves at home, and there sat Miss Narissa behind the other, protesting that she should feel quite distressed if we left the table without tasting everything upon it. Even while the silver tea-spoons were again in full operation, she regretted in the most pathetic manner the languor of our appetites, persisted that there was nothing before us fit to eat, and when we arose from the table, she continued to expostulate, solemnly affirming that we had not made half a meal, and bemoaned her fate in not being able to supply us with something better, all the way back to the quilting-room.

Lights were sparkling, like stars, around the "rising sun," but we plied our needles unsteadily and with fluttering hands. One after another of our number dropped off and stole up to the dressing-chamber, while the huge mirror in its tarnished frame seemed laughing in the firelight, and enjoying the frolic mightily as one smiling face after another peeped in, just long enough to leave a picture and away again.

The evening closed in starlight, clear and frosty. Sleigh-bells were heard at a distance, and the illuminated snow which lay beneath the windows was peopled with shadows moving over it, as one group after another passed out, anxious to obtain a view up the lane.

A knock at the nearest front door put us to flight. Three young gentlemen entered and found us sitting primly around the quilt, each with a thimble on and earnestly at work, like so many birds in a cherry-tree. Again the knocker resounded through the house, as if the lion's head that formed it were set to howling by the huge mass of iron belabouring it so unmercifully. Another relay of guests, heralded in by a gush of frosty wind from the entry, was productive of some remarkably long stitches and rather eccentric patterns on the "rising sun," which, probably, may be pointed out as defects upon its disc to this day. Our fingers became more hopelessly tremulous, for some of the gentlemen bent over us as we worked, and a group gathered before the fire, shutting out the blaze from the huge mirror, which seemed gloomy and discontented at the loss of its old playmate, though a manly form slyly arranging its collar and a masculine hand thrust furtively through a mass of glossy hair did, now and then, glance over its darkened surface.

The lion's head at the door continued its growls, sleigh-bells jingled in the lane, smiles, and light and half-whispered compliments circulated within doors. Every heart was brim full of pleasurable excitement, and but one thing was requisite to the general happiness—the appearance of Old Ben, dear old black Ben, the village fiddler. Again the lion-knocker gave a single growl, a dying hoarse complaint, as if it were verging from the lion rampant to the lion couchant. All our guests were assembled except the doctor; it must be he or Cousin Rufus, with Old Ben. A half score of sparkling eyes grew brighter. There was a heavy stamping of feet in the entry, which could have arisen from no single person. The door opened, and Cousin Rufus appeared, and beyond him, still in the dusk, stood the fiddler, with a huge bag of green baize in his hand, which rose up and down as the old negro deliberately stamped the snow, first from one heavy boot, then from the other, and, regardless of our eager glances, turned away into the supper-room, where a warm mug of gingered cider waited his acceptance.

What a time the fiddler took in drinking his cider! We could fancy him tasting the warm drink, shaking it about in the mug, after every deep draught, and marking its gradual diminution, by the grains of ginger clinging to the inside, with philosophical calmness—all the time chuckling, the old rogue, over the crowd of impatient young creatures waiting his pleasure in the next room.

At length, Cousin Rufus flung open the door leading to the long kitchen, arms were presented, white hands trembling with impatience eagerly clasped over them, and away we went, one and all, so restless for the dance that two-thirds of us took a marching step on the instant.

The old kitchen looked glorious by candlelight. Everywhere the wreathing evergreens flung a chain of tremulous and delicate shadows on the wall. A huge fire roared and flashed in the chimney, till some of the hemlock boughs on either side grew crisp and began to shower their leaves into the flames, which crackled the more loudly as they received them, and darting up sent a stream of light glowing through the upper branches and wove a perfect net-work of shadows on the ceiling overhead. The birds gleamed out beautifully from the deep green, the tall candles glowed in their leafy chandeliers till the smooth laurel leaves and ground pine took more than their natural lustre from the warm light, and the whole room was filled with a rich fruity smell left by the dried apples and frost grapes just removed from the walls.

Old Ben was mounted in his chair, a huge seat which we had tangled over with evergreens. He cast his eye down the columns of dancers with calm self-complacency, took out his fiddle, folded up the green baize satchel, and began snapping the strings with his thumb with a sort of sly smile on his sharp features which, with broken music sent from his old violin, was really too much for patient endurance.

Miss Narissa Daniels led off with the first stamp of old Ben's foot, and Elizabeth stood pensively by, evidently reluctant to engage herself before the doctor's arrival; Julia had Cousin Rufus for a partner, and I, poor wretch, stood up half pouting with Ebenezer Smith, who distorted his already crooked countenance, with a desperate effort to look interesting, and broke into a disjointed double shuffle every other moment.

The night went on merrily. It seemed as if the warm gingered cider had released the stiffened fingers of our fiddler, for the old-fashioned tunes rung out from his instrument loud and clear, till every nook in the farm-house resounded with them. There was dancing in that long kitchen, let me assure you, reader, hearty, gleeful dancing, where hearts kept time cheerily to the music, and eyes kindled up with a healthier fire than wine can give.

I have been in many a proud assembly since that day, where the great and the beautiful have met to admire and be admired, where lovely women glided gracefully to and fro in the quadrille with so little animation that the flowers in their hands scarcely trembled to the languid motion. But we had another kind of amusement at Julia Daniels's quilting frolic, and to say truth a better kind—the grace of warm, unstudied, innocent enjoyment, spiced perhaps with a little rustic affectation and coquetry.

EMMA D. E. N. SOUTHWORTH.

By ancestry Mrs. Southworth is both French and English, being descended through her father from Charles, le Comte Nevitte, and through ner mother from Sir Thomas Grenfeldt, a knight of the days of James I. When the American Revolution broke out, her forefathers were among the first to fly to arms, and the names of Covington, Wailes, and Nevitt are not unhonoured in the Revolutionary annals of Maryland and Virginia.

She was the eldest daughter of Captain Charles L. Nevitt, of Alexandria, Virginia, and of his second wife, Susannah George Wailes, of St. Mary's county, Maryland. Her father was an importing merchant of Alexandria. During the naval difficulties with France, his ships and cargoes were seized by the French, and consequently his affairs thrown into inextricable embarrassment. During the last war with Great Britain he served at the head of a company of volunteers, and received a wound in the chest, of which he never fully recovered. About the year 1816, Captain Nevitt married his second wife, then a girl of fifteen years of age, who was the only child of a widowed mother, and who could not well be separated from her. They therefore removed together to Washington city, having leased conjointly the commodious house on New Jersey Avenue, formerly occupied as a residence by General Washington.

"Here," says Mrs. Southworth, "I was born, on the 26th of December, 1818, in the very chamber once tenanted by General Washington. I was a child of sorrow from the very first year of my life. Thin and dark, I had no beauty except a pair of large, wild eyes—but even this was destined to be tarnished. At twelve months old I was attacked with an inflammation of the eyes, that ended in total, though happily temporary, blindness; thus my first view of life was through a dim, mysterious 'cathedral light,' in which every object in the world looked larger, vaguer, and more distant and imposing than it really was. Among the friends around me, the imposing form and benignant face of my dear grandmother made the deepest impression. At three years of age my sight began to clear. About this time my only *own* sister was born. She was a very beautiful child, with fair and rounded form, rosy complexion, soft blue eyes, and golden hair, that in after years became of a bright chestnut. She was of a lively, social, loving nature, and, as she grew, won all the hearts around her—parents, cousins, nurses, servants, and all who had been wearied to death with two years' attendance on such a wierd little elf as myself—yes—and *who made me feel it too.*

"I was wildly, passionately attached to my father—and even his partiality—it was the natural and general partiality—in favour of my younger sister, his 'dove-eyed darling,' as he called her, did not affect my love for him. But he was very often from home for months at a time, and all my life then was divided into two periods,—when he was home, and when he was gone; and every event dated from one of two epochs—joyfully, 'since father came home'—sadly, 'since father went away.' But at last my father, who had never recovered from the effects of his wound, got a cold which fell upon his lungs. His health declined rapidly. And my joys and sorrows now took these forms—'Father is able to walk about;' 'Father is sick in bed.'

"My father was a Roman Catholic, my mother an Episcopalian. This accounts for what occurred about this time. One day my sister and myself were dressed and taken into our father's room. We found all the family assembled, with several neighbours around our father's bed. The priest was there in his sacred vestments. He had come to administer the last consolations of the Church to our father, and was now about to christen my sister and myself by his dying bed. After these rites of baptism were over, we were taken from the room, but not before our father had laid his dying hands upon our heads and blessed us. I do not know how long it was after this, or where we were standing, when some one—I know not who—came and said, 'Emma, your father is dead.' I remember I felt as if I had received a sudden stunning blow upon the brow. I reeled back from the blow an instant, unable to meet it, and then—with an impulse to fly, to escape from the calamity—turned and fled—fled with my utmost speed, until, at some distance from home, I fell upon my face exhausted, insensible. That is all I remember except the dark pageantry of the funeral that seemed to me like a hideous dream. I was then about four years old, my sister one year old. For months and even years after, I ruminated on life, death, heaven, and hell, with a painful intensity of thought, impossible to describe.

"After my father's death, my grandmother and mother were in very straitened circumstances, and found it extremely difficult to keep up the style of living to which they had been accustomed. My grandmother had some property that brought her in a moderate income; they had besides the house leased, and, for that day, very sumptuously furnished. My grandmother yielded to the advice of her friends, and received a few very select boarders. But she was a lady of the lofty old school, and never could learn to present a bill; so the end of it was, she gave it up in a year.

"At the age of six, I was a little, thin, dark, wild-eyed elf, shy, awkward and unattractive, and in consequence was very much—*let alone.* I spent much time in solitude, reverie, or mischief—took to attics, cellars, and cock-lofts, consorting with cats and pigeons—or with the old negroes in the kitchen, listening with open ears and mind to ghost stories, old legends, and tales of the times when 'Ole mist'ess was rich and saw lots of grand company'—very happy when I could get my little sister to share my queer pleasures; but 'Lotty' was a parlour favourite, and was better pleased with the happy faces of our young country cousins, some of whom were always with us on long visits. The brightest lights of those days were the frequent visits we would make down into St. Mary's county, sometimes sailing down the majestic Potomac as far as St. Clement's Isle and Bay, where we generally landed, and sometimes going in the old family carriage through the grand old forest between the District of Columbia and the shores of the Chesapeake. We often received visits also from our country kinsfolks—visits of months' and even of years' duration.

"At this time of my life, rejoicing in the light and liberty and gladness of nature, I should have been very happy also in the love of my friends and relations, if they had permitted it, but—no matter! Year after year, from my eighth to my sixteenth year, I grew more lonely, retired more into myself, until, notwithstanding a strong, ardent, demonstrative temperament, I became cold, reserved, and abstracted, even to absence of mind—even to apparent insensibility.

* * * * * * *

"Let me pass over in silence the stormy and disastrous days of my wretched girlhood and womanhood—days that stamped upon my brow of youth the furrows of fifty years—let me come at once to the time when I found myself broken in spirit, health, and purse—a widow in fate but not in fact—with my babes looking up to me for a support I could not give them. It was in these darkest days of my *woman's* life, that my *author's* life commenced. I wrote and published 'Retribution,' my first novel, under the following circumstances.

"In January, 1849, I had been appointed teacher of the Fourth District Primary School. The school was kept in the two largest rooms in my house—those upon the ground floor. I had eighty pupils. A few months previous to this I had written a few short tales and sketches for the National Era. It was while I was organizing my new school that Dr. Bailey applied to me for *another* story. I promised one that should go through two papers. I called up several subjects of a profoundly moral and philosophical nature upon which the very trials and sufferings of my own life had led me to reflect, and from among them selected that of *moral retri-*

bution, as I understood it. I designed to illustrate the idea by a short tale. I commenced, and, somehow or other, my head and heart were teeming with thought and emotion, and the idea that had at first but glimmered faintly upon my perceptions, blazed into a perfect glory of light—but which I fear I have not been able to transmit to others with the brightness with which it shone upon myself—no, it was dimmed by the dullness of the medium. My story grew into a volume. Every week I would supply a portion to the paper, until weeks grew into months, and months into quarters, before it was finished.

"The circumstances under which this, my first novel, was written, and the success that afterwards attended its publication, is a remarkable instance of 'sowing in tears and reaping in joy;' for, in addition to that bitterest sorrow with which I may not make you acquainted—that great life-sorrow—I had many minor troubles. My small salary was inadequate to our comfortable support. My school numbered eighty pupils, boys and girls, and I had the whole charge of them myself. Added to this, my little boy fell dangerously ill and was confined to his bed in perfect helplessness until June. He would suffer no one to move him but myself—in fact no one else *could* do so without putting him in pain. Thus my time was passed between my housekeeping, my school-keeping, my child's sick-bed, and my literary labours. The time devoted to writing was the hours that should have been given to sleep or to fresh air. It was too much for me. It was too much for any human being. My health broke down. I was attacked with frequent hemorrhage of the lungs. Still I persevered. I did my best by my house, my school, my sick child, and my publisher. Yet neither child, nor school, nor publisher received justice. The child suffered and complained—the patrons of the school grew dissatisfied, annoying and sometimes insulting me—and as for the publisher, he would reject whole pages of that manuscript which was written amid grief, and pain, and toil that he knew nothing of (pages, by the way, that were restored in the republication).

"This was indeed the very *melee* of the 'Battle of Life.' I was forced to keep up struggling when I only wished for death and for rest.

"But look you how it terminated. That night of storm and darkness came to an end, and morning broke on me at last—a bright glad morning, pioneering a new and happy day of life. First of all, it was in this very tempest of trouble that my 'life-sorrow' was, as it were, carried away—or *I* was carried away from brooding over it. Next, my child, contrary to my own opinion and the doctor's, got well. Then my book, written in so much pain, published besides in a newspaper, and, withal, being the *first* work of an obscure and penniless author, was, contrary to all probabilities, accepted by the first publishing house in America, was published and (subsequently) noticed with high favour even by the cautious English reviews. Friends crowded around me—offers for contributions poured in upon me. And I, who six months before had been poor, ill, forsaken, slandered, *killed* by sorrow, privation, toil, and friendliness, found myself born as it were into a new life; found independence, sympathy, friendship, and honour, and an occupation in which I could delight. All this came very suddenly, as after a terrible storm, a sun burst."

Mrs. Southworth's novels have been extremely popular, and they have been poured forth from her teeming brain with a rapidity perfectly amazing. "Retribution" appeared in book form in 1849, "The Deserted Wife" in 1850, "Shannondale" and "The Mother-in-Law" in 1851, "Children of the Isle" and "The Foster Sisters" in 1852, "The Curse of Clifton," "Old Neighbourhoods and New Settlements," and "Mark Sutherland," in 1853, "The Lost Heiress" and "Hickory Hall," now in press, 1854—eleven large works of fiction in less than five years! Nearly all her novels have gone through numerous and large American editions, and at least four of them have been reproduced in England.

The following estimate of Mrs. Southworth's writings is taken from "Woman's Record," by Mrs. Hale, written after the appearance of the first four of the works quoted above.

"Mrs. Southworth is yet young, both as a woman and an author; but she is a writer of great promise, and we have reason to expect that the future productions of her pen will surpass those works with which she has already favoured the reading community—works showing great powers of the imagination, and strength and depth of feeling, it is true, but also written in a wild and extravagant manner, and occasionally with a freedom of expression that almost borders on impiety. This we are constrained to say, though we feel assured that no one would shrink more reluctantly than the young writer herself from coolly and calmly approaching, with too familiar a hand, the persons and places held sacred by all the Christian world. She seems carried, by a fervid imagination, in an enthusiasm for depicting character as it is actually found (in which she excels) beyond the limits prescribed by correct taste or good judgment. In other respects her novels are deeply interesting. They show, in every page, the hand of a writer of unusual genius and ability. In descriptions of southern life, and of negro character and mode of expression, she is unequalled. She writes evidently from a full heart and an overflowing brain, aud sends her works forth to the criticisms of an unimpassioned public without the advantage which they would receive from a revision, and careful pruning at some moment when calmer reflection was in the ascendancy."

THE NEGLECTED CHILDREN IN THE ATTIC.

HAGAR was driven in from her rambles by the arising of a furious storm. She betook herself to the garret, her place of refuge in times of trouble. Poor little Rose, repulsed by the gloom and ill-temper of "uncle," had already hidden herself there; and the children sat before the fireless hearth—the desolate children in the desolate scene. It was a large, low, square room, with two deep dormer windows facing the east, and looking far out upon the bay—with a dark cuddie under the eaves of the western wall—with a rude fireplace on the south, and opposite on the north, the door leading from the room into the narrow passage and down the stairs. The walls were very dark, and the plastering broken here and there. Between the two dormer windows, and close to the floor, was a large crevice in the wall, through which you might look into the long dark space between the wall and the edge of the roof, a space corresponding to the cuddie on the opposite side. Strange sounds were sometimes heard in this place, and through the crevice. Hagar, that child of shadows, would look with mysterious awe—for with its boundaries lost in obscurity, to her it seemed a dark profound sinking through the house down to the centre of the earth, while her imagination loved to people it with ghosts, gnomes, and all the subterranean demons she had read of in her favourite book, the Arabian Nights. "Listen! listen to the spirits," she would sometimes whisper in wantonness to her little cousin.

"I hear nothing but the rats in the cuddie," would the matter of fact Rose reply. The floor of the attic was bare, the planks rude and rough, and worn apart in some places, leaving dark apertures, down which Hagar would look as into an interminable abyss, the haunt of her favourite gnomes. There was no furniture in this room except an old trunk without a top, that sometimes served Rosalie for a baby-house, and sometimes reversed, for a seat. Upon this trunk the children were now seated. The storm still raged around the old house-top—the shingles were reft off, whirled aloft, and sent clattering, like hail-stones, to the ground; the wind howled and shrieked about the walls, and the old windows and rafters writhed and groaned in the blast, like the wail of lost souls, and the laugh of exultant fiends. The rain was dashed in floods against the crazy windows, and the children sprinkled through their crevices. The water began to stream from the leakages in the ceiling, and to collect in puddles in the corners of the room. These puddles enlarging and approaching each other, threatened to overflow the floor. The children drew their trunk upon the fireless hearth. Rose's little chubby arms and legs were red with cold.

"Oh! how the wind's a-blowing. I am almost frozen," wept Rose. And they were. "Let's go into the parlour," suggested Rose.

Hagar looked at her with astonishment, that she should propose to "beard the lion" in his present mood.

"Yes, into the parlour," persisted the child. "I'll bet you anything that uncle will let us stay in the parlour this evening, and warm ourselves at the fire; it is so very cold you know."

"Well! it is *my* house, anyhow, and so, for your sake, Rose, we *will* go down."

And hand in hand the shivering children left the attic, passed down four flights of back stairs, and went to the parlour door, and Rosalie peeped timidly in. It was the same old parlour, papered with the Christian martyrs, that I have before described; and there sat the tall thin figure of Mr. Withers, dark, solemn, and lowering; and opposite sat Sophie, with her soft brown eyes bent over her knitting. And, oh! sight of luxury to the half-frozen child,—there was a glorious, glowing hickory fire, crackling, blazing, and roaring in the chimney. The children opened the door and passed in, carefully closing it after them; they approached the fire, Hagar with an air of defiance, Rose with a look of deprecation. Sophie looked at the children with remorseful tenderness, and made room for them, unluckily, between herself and Withers, thereby attracting his attention. He turned, and knitting his brows until they met across his nose, and fixing his eyes sternly on the children, he asked, in a rough tone—

"What are you doing here?"

"Warming ourselves!" exclaimed Hagar, raising her eyes, flashing, to his face.

He frowned darkly on her, and half started from his seat, while Rose cowered at her side, and Sophie grew pale.

"Be off with yourselves," he said, in a stern undertone.

Hagar planted her feet firmly on the ground, while Rosalia slunk away. Sophie arose, and saying, in a low tone, "Take Rose to the kitchen fire, dear Hagar," prepared to follow them.

"Come back, Sophie!" exclaimed Withers, in an excited tone. And she sat down with a patient, despairing look, merely motioning to Hagar, by an imploring gesture, to leave the room.

"Well! let's go into the kitchen and warm ourselves at Aunt Cumbo's fire," suggested the ever hopeful Rosalia.

They left the parlour by a back door that led through a sort of closet into the kitchen. The storm was still raging, but a good fire was burning on the kitchen hearth, and the tea-kettle was singing over the blaze, and old Cumbo was standing at a table kneading dough.

"Are you going to have biscuits for supper, Aunt Cumbo?" asked Rosalia, in a coaxing tone, as she approached the table.

"Now, what you comin' out here botherin' arter me for, when I am gettin' supper—go 'long in de house wid you."

The old woman happened to be in a bad humour.

"But, Aunt Cumbo, we are cold—we want to warm ourselves," coaxed Rose. "Mayn't we warm ourselves by your fire?"

"No, no, no! kitchen ain't no place for white children, no how you can fix it, so go 'long in wid you." And the rough old woman came bustling up to the fireplace, drove the little girls away, and began to set her spider and spider lid to heat.

"No; this *is* no place for us," said Hagar, who disdained a controversy with a menial; and the children left the passage.

Rosalia's teeth were chattering, and she felt as though the cold had reached her heart.

"I wish that we were both dead, Hagar," said she, in a whimpering tone.

"I don't," said Hagar, looking half in pity, half in scorn, at the wailing child. "Nor must you. You must live. You are to marry the President of the United States, you know."

"Oh, yes!" exclaimed the vain child, suddenly brightening up, "so I am! Cumbo, when she ain't cross, says I'm pretty enough to marry him or his betters! And then, Hagar! oh, Hagar! then I am going to have a good fire all the time, in every room in the house; and I will wear *whole* shoes and stockings *every* day, and *always* have biscuits for supper. And—never mind, Hagar, you shall live with me, too; and when I think of that, oh, Hagar! When I think of that, I have such a—such a—what do you call it, that keeps people up, and keeps 'em alive?"

"Hope."

"Yes! 'never give up.' You know Gusty Wilde says 'never give up,' and I am agoing to 'never give up.' I am going down into the cellar, now, to pick up chips. Tarquins has been down there sawing wood, and I know there must be chips there; and we can pick up enough to make us a fire, and we can make a nice fire and tell stories."

And with the elasticity of childhood she led the way down to the cellar. It was a large, dark, musty old place, with an area partitioned off, in which milk, butter, fresh meat, &c., were kept in summer; in winter it was usually two feet deep in water; now, however, it was nearly dry. It was originally intended for a kitchen, and was built in the old-fashioned English style, with a large grate in the fireplace, with ovens each side, having heavy iron doors. These deep ovens, the bounds of which were out of sight in the darkness, seemed to Hagar like the entrances to subterranean caverns, the abode of ghosts. To Rose they were merely brick closets, that smelt very musty and unpleasant. The brick pavement of the cellar was decayed away, and green with mould. It was, however, a favourite resort with the children, for there they were free from persecution. They entered, and Rosalia began to fill her apron with chips, when Hagar spied an old worn-out flag basket, and drew it towards them. They both went to work, and soon filled the little basket, and Rosalia, taking it up in her chubby arms, began to toil up stairs with it. Hagar would have taken it from her —but "No, Hagar," said she, "I am afraid to go into the kitchen again. I'll carry this, and *you* go and steal a coal of fire, and bring the broom, so that we can sweep up the slop."

Hagar went into the kitchen, which she found vacant. Cumbo had gone to the spring. Taking a coal of fire in the tongs, and seizing the broom, she fled up stairs into the attic, where little Rose was already busied in clearing the damp rubbish from the fireplace. She received the coal from Hagar, and, kneeling down, placed it on the hearth, collected around it the smallest chips, and blew it. A little blaze soon flickered on the hearth. She continued to add more chips as the weak flame would bear it. In the meantime Hagar had swept up the room. The storm had subsided. The little fire was burning cheeringly. The children drew the old trunk before it and sat down, their arms round each other's waist; their little toes stretched out to the fire; their countenances wearing that satisfied consciousness of having toiled for and won the comforts they were enjoying. And after all, it was but a little fire in a dreary old attic. They were not permitted to enjoy this long. Steps were heard approaching their retreat. The door opened, and Tar, or as he called himself, Tarquinius Superbus—the coloured boy of all work—entered. Rose ran to her basket of chips, and placed herself before it.

"What you-dem do wid dat broom you stole from de kitchen, you little t'ieves, you? Nex' time you gim me trouble for come up here arter you dem's nonsense, I tell Mrs. Widders, an' ef dat don't do I tell *Mr.* Widders—*you* see!"

With that he espied the broom, and in going around to take it, his eyes fell upon the little fire, and the small basket of chips.

Poor Rose looked guilty and dismayed, but held desperately on to her property. Hagar watched him with a steady eye.

"My good gracious 'live—did any *soul* ever see de like? What *will* Mr. Widders say? A-wastin' all de wood! Here's chips enough to kindle all de fires in de mornin'."

And with a perspective glance at his morning's work, when the basket of chips would be very convenient, the rude boy stooped down to take possession of the prize. Rosalia held tight her treasure. He jerked it from her, and in doing so, tore her little tender arms with the rough flags of the old basket. Having lost his temper in the struggle, the boy then went to the chimney, and taking the tongs scattered the blazing chips, and raking the damp rubbish from the corners, extinguished the fire. Then with his prize he marched out of the room. Rose was sobbing and wiping the blood from her wounded arm. Hagar was still and silent, but the fire was kindling in her dark eyes; her gipsy blood was rising; at last she started after him, overtook him half way down the stairs, and seized the basket; he pulled it from her hold and fled, she pursuing him into the kitchen. To end the matter, he went up to the chimney, turned up the basket, and shook down the chips into the fire. Her gipsy blood was up! She ran to him as he was stooping over his work of wanton cruelty, and giving him a sudden push, sent him into the fire. The basket was crushed under his hands, and saved them from being badly burnt. He struggled, recovered himself, and arose. Just at this moment Cumbo re-entered the kitchen, and Rosalia, who had followed her cousin, came in.

"What's de matter now?" inquired the old woman.

Hagar was too proud and Rosalia too frightened to speak.

Tar gave an exaggerated account of the whole affair, as he brushed the smut and ashes from his sleeves. He dwelt particularly on the *waste* with which "de childer had burned up all de light wood for kindlin'."

Cumbo turned up the whites of her eyes in horror at the depredation.

"It was only a few little chips that we picked up, and they were damp; and see how he scratched my arms!" said Rosalia, holding them up to view.

Cumbo having sent in supper, felt herself in a better humour; and thought herself prepared to render judgment with marvellous impartiality and wisdom, which, seating herself, and resting her hands on her knees, she did to the following effect:

"Tarquinus Perbus, you go right in house an' wait on table. Massa Widders, he callin' for you. An' Rose, you putty little angel, you come here an' sit on old mammy's lap, and toast your poor little footy toes before dis nice fire; mammy's got a warm biscuit for you in her bosom, too. An' Hagar, you ugly, bad ting, go 'long right trait out dis here kitchen wid yourself. You're so bad I can't a-bear you—but ugly people always *is* bad."

Now, if she had said bad people always are ugly, she might have come nearer the truth, or at least taught a better lesson.

"I did not make myself, God made me," said Hagar.

"He didn't! He never made anything half so ugly and bad! De debil made you. *He* made my beautiful, lovely, good, little Rose. Some ob dese days she shall be de Presiden's wife, and *you*—you shall be her waitin' maid, 'cause nobody's ever gwine to marry *you*—you're too ugly and hateful. Go 'long trait out dis here kitchen now, I don't want nuffin 'tall to do wid you."

Hagar left the kitchen, casting back a look of inquiry at Rosalia; but the little girl was petted, coaxed, flattered, and tempted by the warm fire, and the prospect of the nice biscuit, and preferred to keep her seat.

Hagar took her lonely way up the four flights of stairs that led to the attic. Arrived there she sat down moodily upon the trunk, resting her elbows upon her knees, and holding her thin face between the palms of her hands; her black elf-locks were hanging wildly about her shoulders, and her eyes were wide open and fixed upon the floor in a stare. She was bitterly reflecting that with a really kind-hearted aunt she was suffering all the evils of orphanage, abused by menials, pinched with hunger, and half frozen with cold. She was wondering, too, how it was that the good God had made her so ugly that she could not be loved, and therefore could not be good. Poor child, she never dreamed of general admiration, she only wished to be loved; and she had no one to tell her that the beauty which wins permanent affection is the beauty of goodness; that goodness will soften the hardest, and intellect light up the dullest features; that though physical beauty may excite passion, and intellect attract admiration, only goodness can win everlasting love.

When I recollect the strong and decided bias given in childhood to my own character by people and circumstances over which I had no sort of control, and against whose evil influence I could make no sort of resistance; when I suffer by the effect of impressions received in infancy, which neither time, reason, nor religion have been able to efface—which only sorrow could impair by bruising the tablet; knowing as I know the tender impressibility of infancy, feeling as I feel the indelibility of such impressions, I tremble for the unseen influences that may surround my own young children—ay, even for the chance word dropped by stranger lips, and heard by infant ears; for that word may be a fruitful seed that shall spring up into a healthful vine, or a upas tree, twenty years after it is sown. Infancy is a fair page upon which you may write—goodness, happiness, heaven, or—sin, misery, hell. And the words once written, no chemical art can erase them. The substance of the paper itself must be rubbed through by the file of suffering before the writing can be effaced. Infancy is the soft metal in the moulder's hands; he may shape it in the image of a fiend, or the form of an angel—and when finished, the statue hardens into rock, which nothing but the hammer of God's providence can break; nothing but the fire of God's providence can melt for remoulding.

THERESE LOUISE ALBERTINE ROBINSON.

(TALVJ.)

MRS. ROBINSON, the wife of the accomplished Orientalist, and herself a very accomplished philologist and scholar, is a German by birth. But so much of the outgrowth of her mind has been American in its origin, that it seems but meet to give her a place in the present work.

The maiden name of Mrs. Robinson was Therese Louise Albertine von Jacob. The initials of her name, with a slight change in the arrangement of the letters, form the word Talvj, which has hitherto been her chief *nom de plume*. She is the daughter of the distinguished Professor von Jacob, of Halle. She was born at that place, on the 26th of January, 1797. Her father became a Professor in a Russian University, first at Charkow, in 1806, afterwards at St. Petersburg, in 1811. It was during her ten years' residence at these two places, that she acquired her profound knowledge of the Slavic languages and literatures. On the return of her father to Halle, in 1816, she acquired a knowledge of the Latin. In 1822, she translated into German two of Scott's novels, "Old Mortality" and "Black Dwarf." In 1825, she published several original tales, under the title of "Psyche." Her next publication was "Popular Songs of the Servians," in two volumes, in 1826. They consisted of translations from the Servian, a language to which her attention had been accidentally turned, and which she mastered for the purpose of exploring its hidden treasures.

She was married to Professor Robinson in 1828. On coming to her home in the New World, her philological zeal followed her, and led her to undertake researches into the aboriginal languages of this continent, and to translate into German the work of Mr. Pickering on the "Indian Tongues of North America." This translation was published in 1834, at Leipsic. She published about the same time an historical view of the Slavic languages. This appeared first in 1834, in the form of contributions to the

"Biblical Repository." It was afterwards revised and enlarged, and published as a separate volume in 1850, under the following title, "Historical View of the Languages and Literatures of the Slavic Nations, with a Sketch of their Popular Poetry."

With the exception of a few articles in the Reviews and Periodicals, the "Historical View" is Mrs. Robinson's only original English work. Her novels, "Heloise, or the Unrevealed Secret," "Life's Discipline," and "The Exiles," though composed in this country, were all written in German, and translated into English by her daughter, who has the advantage of *two native languages*. In works of the imagination, where so much depends upon idiomatic expressions and the niceties of diction, Mrs. Robinson has not felt willing to trust herself to write in what is to her after all a foreign tongue. But in works partaking more of a scientific character, the case seemed to her different, and she has honoured the country of her adoption by making its language the vehicle of the profound and original work that has just been named.

During a temporary visit to Germany, in 1837, Mrs. Robinson prepared and published an "Historical Characterization of the Popular Songs of the Germanic Nations, with a Review of the Songs of the Extra-European Races;" also a work on "The Falseness of the Songs of Ossian."

Among the results of her American studies, may be mentioned a "History of John Smith," published in Germany in 1845, and "The Colonization of New England," likewise published in Germany, in 1847. These are both works of great research. They were prepared with a view to make her countrymen better acquainted with the ante-revolutionary history of this country.

As a German writer, Talvi had the good fortune to be introduced to the public by Goethe, whose friendship she enjoyed, and who remarked of her, that "she had the heart of a woman, but the brain of a man."

SLAVIC SUPERSTITIONS.

The strong and deeply-rooted superstitions of the Slavic nations are partly manifest in their songs and tales; these are full of foreboding dreams, and good or bad omens; witchcraft of various kinds is practised; and a certain oriental fatalism seems to direct will and destiny. The connexion with the other world appears nevertheless much looser than is the case with the Teutonic nations. There is no trace of spirits in Russian ballads; although spectres appear occasionally in Russian nursery tales. In Servian, Bohemian, and

Slovakian songs, it occurs frequently that the voices of the dead sound from their graves; and thus a kind of soothing intercourse is kept up between the living and the departed. The superstition of a certain species of blood-sucking spectres, known to the novel-reading world under the name of *vampyres*, a superstition retained chiefly in Dalmatia, belongs also here. In modern Greek, such a spectre is called *Brukolacas*, in Servian *Wukodlak*. We do not however recollect the appearance of a vampyre, in any genuine production of modern Greek or Servian poetry. It seems as if the sound sense of the common people had taught them that this superstition is too shocking, too disgusting, to be admitted into poetry; while the oversated palates of the fashionable reading world crave the strongest and most stimulating food, and can only be satisfied by the most powerful excitement.

In the whole series of Slavic ballads and songs, which lie before our eyes, we meet with only one instance of the return of a deceased person to this world in the like gloomy and mysterious way in which the Christian nations of the North and West are wont to represent such an event. This is in the beautiful Servian tale, "Jelitza and her Brothers." As it is too long to be inserted here entire, we must be satisfied with a sketch of it. Jelitza, the beloved sister of nine brothers, is married to a Ban on the other side of the sea. She departs reluctantly, and is consoled only by the promise of her brothers to visit her frequently. But "the plague of the Lord" destroys them all; and Jelitza, unvisited and apparently neglected by her brothers, pines away and sighs so bitterly from morning to evening, that the Lord in heaven takes pity on her. He summons two of his angels before him;

"Hasten down to earth, ye my two angels,
To the white grave where Jovan lies buried,
The lad Jovan, Jelitza's youngest brother;
Into him, my angels, breathe your spirit,
Make for him a horse of his white grave-stone,
Knead a loaf from the black mould beneath him,
And the presents cut out from his grave-shroud;
Thus equip him for his promised visit."

The angels do as they are bidden. Jelitza receives her brother with delight, and asks of him a thousand questions, to which he gives evasive answers. After three days are past, he must away; but she insists on accompanying him home. Nothing can deter her. When they come to the churchyard, the lad Jován's home, he leaves her under a pretext and goes back into his grave. She waits long, and at last follows him. When she sees the nine fresh graves, a painful presentiment seizes her. She hurries to the house of her mother. When she knocks at the door, the aged mother, half distracted, thinks it is "the plague of the Lord," which, after having carried off her nine sons, comes for her. The mother and daughter die in each other's arms.

This simple and affecting tale affords, then, the only instance in Slavic popular poetry, of a regular apparition; but even here that apparition has, as our readers have seen, a character very different from that of a Scotch or German ghost. The same ballad exists also in modern Greek; although in a shape perhaps not equal in power and beauty to the Servian.

But the very circumstance that its subject is so isolated among the Slavic nations, who are so ready to seize other poetical ideas and to mould them in various ways, leads us to believe that the Servian poet must have heard somehow or other the Greek ballad, or a similar one; and that the subject of the Servian ballad, although this is familiar to all classes, was originally a stranger in Servia. Nowhere indeed, in the whole range of Slavic popular poetry, do we meet with that mysterious gloom, with those enigmatical contradictions, which are peculiar to the world of spirits of the Teutonic North; and which we think find their best explanation in the antithesis between the principles of Christianity, and the ruins of paganism on which it was built.

It is true, that, wherever Christianity has been carried, similar contradictions must necessarily have taken place; but the mind of the Slavic nations, so far as it is manifest in their poetry, seems never to have been perplexed by these contradictions. History shows that the Slavic nations, with the exception of those tribes who were excited to headstrong opposition by the cruelty and imprudence of their German converters, received Christianity with childlike submission; in most cases principally because their superiors adopted it. Vladimir the Great, to whom the Gospel and the Koran were offered at the same time, was long undecided which to choose; and was at last induced to embrace the former, because "his Russians could not live without the pleasure of drinking." The wooden idols, it is true, were solemnly destroyed; but numerous fragments of their altars were suffered to remain undisturbed at the foot of the cross; and the passion-flower grew up in the midst of the wild broom, the branches of which, tied together, the Tshuvash considers, even at the present day, as his tutelary spirit or Erich. No struggle seems ever to have taken place to reconcile these contradictory elements; while the more philosophical spirit of the Teutonic nations, and their genius for meditation and reflection, could not be so easily satisfied. The character of the Teutonic world of spirits is the reflex of this struggle. The foggy veil which covers their forms, the mysterious riddles in which their existence is wrapped, the anxious pensiveness which forms a part of their character, all are the results of these fruitless and mostly unconscious endeavours to amalgamate opposing elements. We cannot approach the region of their mysterious existence without an awful shuddering; while the few fairies which Slavic poetry and superstition present us, strike us by the distinctness and freshness of their forms, and give us the unmingled impression either of the ludicrous or of the wild and fantastic.

FRANCES S. OSGOOD.

THE maiden name of Mrs. Osgood was Frances Sargent Locke. She was a native of Boston, and born (we believe) about the year 1813. Her early life was passed chiefly in the village of Hingham. She gave very early indications of poetical talent. Her abilities in this respect were first recognised by Mrs. Lydia M. Child, who was then editing a Juvenile Miscellany. Miss Locke became a regular contributor to this work, and subsequently to other works, under the name of "Florence." She was married in 1834 to Mr. Osgood, the painter, and accompanied him soon after to London. They remained in the great metropolis for four years, Mr. Osgood acquiring an enviable reputation as an artist, and Mrs. Osgood as a writer. After their return to the United States, they resided chiefly in New York. although Mr. Osgood has been occasionally absent on professional tours to different parts of the country. In 1841, Mrs. Osgood edited an Annual, "The Flowers of Poetry, and the Poetry of Flowers," and in 1847, "The Floral Offering." She published a collection of her poems in 1846, and in 1850 a complete collection of her poetical works in one large octavo volume. This work, which was issued in sumptuous style, contains all of her poems, up to that date, which she thought worthy of preservation. She, however, after that time produced some few other poems, which will probably take their place in future editions of her works.

Her prose contributions to the Magazines were numerous, and would make, if collected, one or two volumes. Though prose in name, they are all essentially poetical, far more so than much that goes under the name of poetry. Her whole life, indeed, as it has been well remarked, was a continual poem. "Not to write poetry—not to think it—act it—dream it—and *be* it, was entirely out of her power."

Mrs. Osgood died, greatly lamented, in May 1850.

THE MAGIC LUTE.

My beauty! sing to me and make me glad!
Thy sweet words drop upon the ear as soft
As rose-leaves on a well.—Festus.

On a low stool at the feet of the Count de Courcy sat his bride, the youthful Lady Loyaline. One delicate, dimpled hand hovered over the strings of her lute, like a snowy bird, about to take wing with a burst of melody. The other she was playfully trying to release from the clasp of his. At last, she desisted from the attempt, and said, as she gazed up into his proud "unfathomable eyes"—

"Dear De Courcy! how shall I thank you for this beautiful gift? How shall I prove to you my love, my gratitude, for all your generous devotion to my wishes?"

Loyaline was startled by the sudden light that dawned in those deep eyes; but it passed away and left them calmer, and prouder than before, and there was a touch of sadness in the tone of his reply—

"Sing to me, sweet, and thank me so!"

Loyaline sighed as she tuned the lute. It was ever thus when she alluded to her love. His face would lighten like a tempest-cloud, and then grow dark and still again, as if the fire of hope and joy were suddenly kindled in his soul to be as suddenly extinguished. What could it mean? Did he doubt her affection? A tear fell upon the lute, and she said, "I will sing

THE LADY'S LAY."

The deepest wrong that thou couldst do,
Is thus to doubt my love for thee,
For questioning that thou question'st too
My truth, my pride, my purity.

'Twere worse than falsehood thus to meet
Thy least caress, thy lightest smile,

Nor feel my heart exulting beat
  With sweet, impassioned joy the while.

The deepest wrong that thou couldst do,
  Is thus to doubt my faith professed;
How should I, love, be less than true,
  When *thou* art noblest, bravest, best?

The tones of the Lady Loyaline's voice were sweet and clear, yet so low, so daintily delicate, that the heart caught them rather than the ear. De Courcy felt his soul soften beneath those pleading accents, and his eyes, as he gazed upon her, were filled with unutterable love and sorrow.

How beautiful she was! With that faint colour, like the first blush of dawn, upon her cheek—with those soft, black, glossy braids, and those deep blue eyes, so luminous with soul! Again the lady touched her lute—

For thee I braid and bind my hair
  With fragrant flowers, for only thee;
Thy sweet approval, all my care,
  Thy love—the world to me!

For thee I fold my fairest gown,
  With simple grace, for thee, for thee!
No other eyes in all the town
  Shall look with love on me.

For thee my lightsome lute I tune,
  For thee—it else were mute—for thee!
The blossom to the bee in June
  Is less than thou to me.

De Courcy, by nature proud, passionate, reserved, and exacting, had wooed and won, with some difficulty, the young and timid girl, whose tenderness for her noble lover was blent with a shrinking awe, that all his devotion could not for awhile overcome.

At the time my story commences, he was making preparations to join the Crusaders. He was to set out in a few days, and, brave and chivalric as he was, there were both fear and grief in his heart, when he thought of leaving his beautiful bride for years, perhaps for ever. Perfectly convinced of her guileless purity of purpose, thought and deed, he yet had, as he thought, reason to suppose that her heart was, perhaps unconsciously to herself, estranged from him, or rather that it never had been his. He remembered, with a thrill of passionate grief and indignation, her bashful reluctance to meet his gaze—her timid shrinking from his touch—and thus her very purity and modesty, the soul of true affection, were distorted by his jealous imagination into indifference for himself and fondness for another. Only two days before, upon suddenly entering her chamber, he had surprised her in tears, with a page's cap in her hand, and on hearing his step, she had started up blushing and embarrassed, and hidden it beneath her mantle, which lay upon the couch. Poor De Courcy! This was indeed astounding; but while he had perfect faith in her honour, he was too proud to let her see his suspicions. That cap! that crimson cap! It was not the last time he was destined to behold it!

The hour of parting came, and De Courcy shuddered as he saw a smile—certainly an exulting smile—lighten through the tears in the dark eyes of his bride, as she bade him for the last time "farewell."

A twelvemonth afterward, he was languishing in the dungeons of the East—a chained and hopeless captive.

"Ah! fleeter far than fleetest storm or steed,
Or the death they bear,
The heart, which tender thought clothes, like a dove,
With the wings of care!"

The Sultan was weary; weary of his flowers and his fountains—of his dreams and his dancing-girls—of his harem and himself. The banquet lay untouched before him. The rich chibouque was cast aside. The cooling sherbet shone in vain.

The Almas tripped, with tinkling feet,
Unmarked their motions light and fleet!

His slaves trembled at his presence; for a dark cloud hung lowering on the brows of the great Lord of the East, and they knew from experience, that there were both thunder and lightning to come ere it dispersed.

But a sound of distant plaintive melody was heard. A sweet voice sighing to a lute. The Sultan listened. "Bring hither the minstrel," he said in a subdued tone; and a lovely, fair-haired boy, in a page's dress of pale-green silk, was led blushing into the presence.

"Sing to me, child," said the Lord of the East. And the youth touched his lute, with grace and wondrous skill, and sang, in accents soft as the ripple of a rill,

THE VIOLET'S LOVE.

Shall I tell what the violet said to the star,
While she gazed through her tears on his beauty, afar?
She sang, but her singing was only a sigh,
And nobody heard it, but Heaven, Love, and I,
A sigh, full of fragrance and beauty, it stole
Through the stillness up, up, to the star's beaming soul.

She sang—"Thou art glowing with glory and might,
And I'm but a flower, frail, lowly, and light.
I ask not thy pity, I seek not thy smile;
I ask but to worship thy beauty awhile;
To sigh to thee, sing to thee, bloom for thine eye,
And when thou art weary, to bless thee and die!"

Shall I tell what the star to the violet said,
While ashamed, 'neath his love-look, she hung her young head?
He sang—but his singing was only a ray,
And none but the flower and I heard the dear lay.
How it thrilled, as it fell, in its melody clear,
Through the little heart, heaving with rapture and fear!

Ah no! love! I dare not! too tender, too pure,
For me to betray, were the words he said to her;
But as she lay listening that low lullaby,
A smile lit the tear in the timid flower's eye;
And when death had stolen her beauty and bloom,
The ray came again to play over her tomb.

Long ere the lay had ceased, the cloud in the Sultan's eye had dissolved itself in tears. Never had music so moved his soul.

"The lute was enchanted! The youth was a Peri, who had lost his way! Surely it must be so!"

"But sing me now a bolder strain!" And the beautiful child flung back his golden curls—and swept the strings more proudly than before, and his voice took a clarion-tone, and his dark, steel-blue eyes flashed with heroic fire as he sang

THE CRIMSON PLUME.

Oh! know ye the knight of the red waving plume?
Lo! his lightning smile gleams through the battle's wild gloom,
Like a flash through the tempest; oh! fly from that smile!
'Tis the wild-fire of fury—it glows to beguile!
And his sword-wave is death, and his war-cry is doom!
Oh! brave not the knight of the dark crimson plume!

His armour is black, as the blackest midnight;
His steed like the ocean-foam, spotlessly white;
His crest—a crouched tiger, who dreams of fierce joy—
Its motto—"Beware! for I wake—to destroy!"
And his sword-wave is death, and his war-cry is doom!
Oh! brave not the knight of the dark crimson plume!

"By Allah! thou hast magic in thy voice! One more! and ask what thou wilt. Were it my signet-ring, 'tis granted!"

Tears of rapture sprung to the eyes of the minstrel-boy, as the Sultan spoke, and his young cheek flushed like a morning cloud. Bending over his lute to hide his emotion, he warbled once again—

THE BROKEN HEART'S APPEAL.

Give me back my childhood's truth!
Give me back my guileless youth!
Pleasure, Glory, Fortune, Fame,
These I will not stoop to claim!
Take them! All of Beauty's power,
All the triumph of this hour
Is not worth one blush you stole—
Give me back my bloom of soul!

Take the cup and take the gem!
What have I to do with them?
Loose the garland from my hair!
Thou shouldst wind the night-shade there

Thou who wreath'st, with flattering art,
Poison-flowers to bind my heart!
Give me back the rose you stole!
Give me back my bloom of soul?

"Name thy wish, fair child. But tell me first what good genius has charmed thy lute for thee, that thus it sways the soul?"

"A child-angel, with large melancholy eyes and wings of lambent fire—we Franks have named him Love. He led me here and breathed upon my lute."

"And where is he now?"

"I have hidden him in my heart," said the boy, blushing as he replied.

"And what is the boon thou wouldst ask?"

The youthful stranger bent his knee, and said in faltering tones —"Thou hast a captive Christian knight; let him go free, and Love shall bless thy throne!"

"He is thine—thou shalt thyself release him. Here, take my signet with thee."

And the fair boy glided like an angel of light through the guards at the dungeon-door. Bolts and bars fell before him—for he bore the talisman of Power—and he stood in his beauty and grace at the captive's couch, and bade him rise and go forth, for he was free.

De Courcy, half-awake, gazed wistfully on the benign eyes that bent over him. He had just been dreaming of his guardian angel; and when he saw the beauteous stranger boy—with his locks of light—his heavenly smile—his pale, sweet face—he had no doubt that this was the celestial visitant of his dreams, and, following with love and reverence his spirit-guide, he scarcely wondered at his sudden disappearance when they reached the court.

"Pure as Aurora when she leaves her couch,
Her cool, soft couch in Heaven, and, blushing, shakes
The balmy dew-drops from her locks of light."

Safely the knight arrived at his castle-gate, and as he alighted from his steed, a lovely woman sprang through the gloomy archway, and lay in tears upon his breast.

"My wife! my sweet, true wife! Is it indeed thou! Thy cheek is paler than its wont. Hast mourned for *me*, my love?" And the knight put back the long black locks and gazed upon that sad, sweet face. Oh! the delicious joy of that dear meeting! Was it too dear, too bright to last?

At a banquet, given in honour of De Courcy's return, some of the guests, flushed with wine, rashly let fall in his hearing an insinuation which awoke all his former doubts, and, upon inquiry, he found to his horror that during his absence the Lady Loyaline had left her home for months, and none knew whither or why she went, but all could guess, they hinted.

De Courcy sprang up, with his hand on the heft of his sword, and rushed toward the chamber of his wife. She met him in the anteroom, and listened calmly and patiently as he gave vent to all his jealous wrath, and bade her prepare to die. Her only reply was—"Let me go to my chamber; I would say one prayer; then do with me as you will."

"Begone!"

The chamber door closed on the graceful form and sweeping robes of the Lady de Courcy. But in a few moments it opened again, and forth came, with meekly folded arms, a stripling in a page's dress and *crimson cap!*—the bold, bright boy with whom he had parted at his dungeon-gate! "Here! in her very chamber!" The knight sprang forward to cleave the daring intruder to the earth. But the stranger flung to the ground the cap and the golden locks, and De Courcy fell at the feet, not of a minstrel-boy, but of his own true-hearted wife, and begged her forgiveness, and blessed her for her heroic and beautiful devotion.

ELIZABETH C. KINNEY.

Mrs. Kinney is a native of New York, and the daughter of Mr. David L. Dodge, a wealthy and retired merchant of that city. She was married in 1840 to Mr. William B. Kinney, so well known as the editor of the Newark Daily Advertiser, and as the leading political writer in the State of New Jersey.

To Mrs. Kinney, the language of song seems to have been one of the instincts of her nature, and, if she did not actually "lisp in numbers," her poetical temperament was very early manifest, and has always been very strong. Her poems, which have been profusely scattered through the pages of the Knickerbocker, Graham, and Sartain, have, unfortunately, never been collected into any more enduring shape. She commenced publishing under the name of "Stedman," dating from "Cedar Brook," the country residence of her father, near Newark, New Jersey.

With the exception of "Aunt Rachel," published in Sartain's Magazine; "The Parsonage Gathering," "My Aunt Polly," and "Mrs. Tiptop," in Graham, and some few other tales and sketches, her prose writings have appeared in the Newark Daily, the literary department of which has been for several years committed to her hands. The critiques and essays of various kinds that have graced these columns are among the best things that Mrs. Kinney has written.

Mrs. Kinney, in 1850, went to Italy, her husband having received from the United States Government the appointment to the Sardinian mission. Her talents and her literary reputation have secured for her a very flattering reception among the savants and the court circle to which she has been accredited. Their residence is at Turin.

OLD MAIDS.

We might say "maiden ladies!"—but wish to redeem two plain monosyllables from a certain undefinable stigma that they have borne too long. *Old* implies years, and *years* imply wisdom; why should we despise the one and not the other? Why, unless it be that the word old, when coupled with maid, is held up as a bugbear to frighten girls into hasty and injudicious marriages; or is perverted into another term for a shrivelled, vinegar-faced spinster, in whose nature the milk of human kindness has been soured by disappointment, and turns to acid every sweet that it comes in contact with. Words being but signs of ideas, if such is the apparition conjured to the mind of any by the phrase old maid, we cannot wonder that it seems formidably odious. To us, very different associations are connected with it: the stigmatized name seems almost sacred, conveying to the mind, as it does, the image of a pure, patient, doing, and enduring spirit, well nigh divested of the selfishness that, innate, controls the infant, the child, the belle, and even the wife and mother—that ideal of perfected woman!—in short, the embodiment of *disinterestedness.*

And who that will take off the glasses of prejudice, look around, and call up recollections of domestic life either at home, or in other homes, can fail to discover some female form and face—possibly attenuated and wrinkled by time and care—moving about the house from morning till night, ever bent on some errand of good to its inmates: now nursing the sick; now contriving some delicacy for the table, or to gratify the juvenile appetite; now bravely leading on to the fight a soap and water regiment, at that semi-annual internal revolution called house-cleaning, herself in the thickest of the fray; now arranging wardrobes for the Spring and Autumn comfort of all the household—save *herself;* now remaining through the heat and noxious atmosphere of a summer in the city, to keep the house in safety, while its proprietor, children, and even servants are enjoying cool sea-breezes, drinking at fountains of health, or roving in the free air of the country; now out watching the moon, with weary but sleepless eyes, the uninvited, awaiting the return of invited guests from some party or masquerade; in brief, spending and being spent in the service of perhaps a sister, a cousin, or a niece, whose return for untiring, disinterested affection, is the selfish love that considers its recipient invaluable, not as a gentle, unpretending associate, but as a reliable convenience!

But let us look at the causes, as well as effects, of single life in women. If the histories of all old maids were written, what disclosures of female heroism would be made! In how many cases could celibacy be traced, not to want of personal or mental attractions; nor of admiration or love; but to that heroic nature which, though capable of the deepest and most enduring passion, has the fortitude to live alone, rather than be *bound*, not *united*, to an uncongenial being. And if "He that ruleth his spirit be greater than he that taketh a city," surely she that ruleth her heart is greater than she that taketh a name for the sake of a name; or to avoid one stigmatized indiscriminately.

Love is the instinct of the female heart: almost every woman who has lived to see thirty years, has felt the outgoings of affection's well-spring; but hers is not often the power of choosing, though it is of refusing. Who may tell the inward conflicts, the unuttered agonies, the protracted soul-sickness of conquered passion? But when a true woman once triumphs over an inexpedient or unreciprocated attachment, she triumphs over *self*, and becomes, that noblest of feminine spirits, the disinterested friend of mankind! Be sure that the scandal-monger, the tart-mouthed old maid, is one whose inner heart has never felt the wound that opens a passage for human sympathies to flow out; but is smarting under superficial mortifications, that, like poison introduced only skin-deep, fester and irritate continually. Rare are such cases, and yet few as they are, they infect the general mind, so that old maid, thus considered, is a noun of multitude, including all who choose or are destined to live single lives. And how many unhappy marriages are the con sequence of this opprobrium!

Even the single-hearted piety of unmarried females is derided.

Who has not heard such ribaldry as this, "O, she's getting *religion* now that she can't get a *husband?*" But it is the inspired Apostle who says, "The unmarried woman careth for the things of the Lord, that she may be holy both in body and in spirit." Thus do we see oftenest in the single woman that perfect love to God, which manifests itself in love to all his creatures.

For our part, we venerate the very name of Old Maid—its heroism, its benevolence, its piety! Ye, who are blessed with an Aunt Fanny, an Aunt Polly, or an Aunt Betsy—names too venerable to be spelled with the modern *ie*, which in your own, perchance, is substituted for the old-fashioned *y*—do ye ever think that, though unwedded, she has a heart alive with all human sympathies? Ah, you cannot but feel this in her countless ministrations for your comfort. But do you ever realize that she feels, not loved for *herself* in return, but for her *deeds*, and weeps silently under the consciousness that when her lonely, loving life ceases on earth, not she, but her offices of kindness will be missed and mourned for?

Such are some of the obscurer subjects of the vulgar prejudice against "Old Maids;" and if these noiseless, yet immortalized individuals, "whose names are written in the Book of Life," are such invaluable members of the household and of society; what shall we say of Hannah More, of Joanna Baillie, of Maria Edgeworth, of Jane Taylor, of our own Miss Dix, and of a host of others, whose names are written in the universal heart; some of whom "do rest from their labours," and all of whose works shall live after them? For ever honoured, and through these renowned, be the sisterhood of Old Maids.

THE SONNET.

THERE are people who seem to think that an intellectual taste for certain kinds of poetry, or an ear for Italian music are to be *acquired;* like a physical relish for olives, tomatoes, or macaroni! That even cultivated minds cannot appreciate some styles of poetic composition, so as to feel the sentiment conveyed in them, till familiarized to the form of conveyance: and that no ear—however delicately attuned by the great Master—can naturally enjoy the soul of melody that gushes from the throats of Italia's songsters, because Art commingles the melting strains into harmonious passages, giving unity to multiplicity of sound; as it weaves into musical feet the inborn idea—the breathing thought of poesy. We should like to have all who *say* they can enjoy natural, but not artistic music, visit an aviary in the season of song; when some fifty vocal throats—pitched on as many keys—are striving to drown one another's tones: we never hear such a *discord* "of sweet sounds" from Nature's undrilled troupe, without thinking, if it were possible for Art to harmonize the warblers' voices together, what a tide of affluent melody would overpower the senses! And would it be less *Nature's* music than before?

The truth is, that such as hear only artificial tones from Italy's *born*-songsters—made artists by study and practice—have not the ear for natural melody that they boast of; but one in sympathy with discordant sounds. So he that cannot recognise at once the native soul of poetry, in whatever form presented, has imagined himself an admirer of poetry, when only in love with certain forms of expression and musical cadences, while insensible to the spirit and power of the poetic thought they embody; and he is so constituted in mind as never to acquire any true appreciation of at least one form of the beautiful. We noticed recently in a periodical paper a Sonnet introduced by the following paragraph:

"We have an utter, relentless, unmitigated dislike, aversion, horror, for those fourteen-lined effusions, called Sonnets. They remind us of a child struggling to walk in swaddling clothes. They are puny ideas on stilts. They have a central thought, which, like the centre of gravity, is never seen. The poor thing flounders about like a man running tied up in a sack. It is a puzzle for children of a larger growth. Like a glass thread, one wonders how it is spun, or how the apple got into the dumplings!"

Nor is the above the expression of an uncommon sentiment regarding Sonnets. Now, no lover of the Sonnet will affirm that even its beautiful form of composition, ever so artistically wrought out of rich material, can affect the human mind, unless the vital spark animates the whole, any more than other forms of art through which no spiritual meaning is conveyed. But he, who in a *true* Sonnet can see nothing but the imaginary laborious process of its execution, would probably stand before a Grecian temple calculating the labour and manner of its construction; while the lover of Art, blind to its processes, in silent awe worshipped the grandeur of its complete manifestation.

A Sonnet, in the highest sense, naturally obeys the law of art, which is to conceal its processes. And where, in the Sonnets of Petrarch, of Milton, of Shakspeare, of Coleridge, or of Wordsworth, can any "anointed eye" see the least shadow of constraint, or trace of effort? So unconstrainedly do the poetic language and imagery arrange their metrical feet in the beautiful order of the Sonnet,—while the one luminous idea, like electricity, runs through the whole,—that the mind which can perceive, sees only the radiant thought, yet feels that a harmonious chain is its conductor.

Nor is the Sonnet such an effort to the poet, as the machine poetaster or mechanical reader may suppose. All will allow that love utters itself through the most natural forms of expression. Petrach's love for Laura gave birth to the Sonnet: it was not the invention of mechanical genius; but a living creation, that owes its being to the strong emotions of hopeless passion. And, if, when reproduced in its original likeness, its beauty and vital power are unfelt, depend upon it, the fault is not in the Sonnet.

Born in Italy—and how can anything lack music or warmth that originated under those glowing skies?—and introduced into England by Lord Surrey, the Sonnet has for centuries been the medium of conveying and receiving the richest gems of poetic thought and fancy. In our opinion, Wordsworth's Sonnets, save one or two Odes, are worth all his other poems; and he has said,

"Scorn not the Sonnet; Critic, you have frowned,
Mindless of its just honours; with this key
Shakspeare unlocked his heart; the melody
Of this small lute gave ease to Petrarch's wound;

A thousand times this pipe did Tasso sound;
  Camoens soothed with it an exile's grief;
  The Sonnet glittered a gay myrtle leaf
Amid the cypress with which Dante crowned
  His visionary brow: a glow-worm lamp,
It cheered mild Spenser, called from Fairy-land
  To struggle through dark ways; and, when a damp
Fell round the path of Milton, in his hand
  The thing became a trumpet, whence he blew
  Soul-animating strains—alas, too few!"

But the Sonnet is not confined to the Old World:—certain also of our own poets have with this magic "key" unlocked the heart; with this "glow-worm lamp," shed light into the enshrouded mind; with this "pipe," awakened tones musical as the shepherd god sent through Arcadian vales; with this "myrtle leaf," made green again the cypress-crowned brow; with this "trumpet," sounded the victory of the spirit over human passions and earth-born hopes.

"And what shall we say more? Time would fail us to tell of" all that the Sonnet has effected—of all who have made it the mighty instrument for the soul's unwritten music.

HARRIET FARLEY.

SOON after the commencement of the present century, a young minister, named Stephen Farley, was settled in the beautiful town of Claremont, New Hampshire, his native State; and, as the rich soil on the banks of the Connecticut was full of good things for the present, and good promise for the future; as the lively falls of Sugar river could be induced to turn their active energies to the accumulation of comforts and wealth; the new preacher was easily persuaded to bring a young bride to alleviate his cares and heighten his joys. She was born in Massachusetts, the child of a father who had derived so rich an inheritance that, in her early childhood, it might not have been supposed the daughter would ever be called upon to eke out a frugally genteel subsistence by school teaching. Such, however, was her employment in Maine, where she went to reside with her mother, after the sudden death of her father. That mother was of the celebrated "Moody" family, so well known once throughout New England, and not yet extinct, being still, whether on the high seas, or near the forests of their native State, or in the metropolis of that section of the country, or at the capital of the Union, or away in the new cities of the far West—being everywhere distinguished for cultivation, urbanity, hospitality, family pride, patriotism, and all those qualities which distinguish the gentry of the "old school."

"Father Moody," so often quoted in the provincial history of New England, was the ancestor of this family. "Handkerchief Moody," his son, the hero of Hawthorne's story of "The Minister's Veil," is embalmed in many memories for his piety and affliction. He committed an accidental murder, and ever after covered his face from his fellow men. "Master Moody," the celebrated preceptor of "Dummer Academy," wished that his niece had been a man, that he might have given her a collegiate education. She was remarkable not only for intellectual qualities, but for the graceful dignity becoming to any woman.

After her husband's death, she went with her children to the old town of York, in the District of Maine, and thither the young New Hampshire minister repaired to find, in her daughter, his future helpmeet. She was a beautiful and very animated woman, with fine taste, much wit, and unusual conversational powers. Among her rejected admirers were those who have since become Judges, and otherwise "potent, grave, and reverend seigniors." The calm, studious, sober minister, was her choice; and, in an humble country cottage, she reared her little brood of children.

But afflictions came. Ill health and mental disquiet, the conflict of a speculative mind with venerated creeds and cherished belief, impaired the energies of the father. And then the dark cloud, that had cast its gloom over Handkerchief Moody's life, and settled in blackness over the close of her father's, cast its fearful shadow upon the mother's mind; and, through her, a sombre shade upon her family. Some years after, the mental sun broke through this cloud, and shone for a long time within the homestead; then again came the sad eclipse which, in this world, may never pass away. During the interval of brightness, came the tenth, and last, of the household band, more than half of whom have been taken away.

Harriet Farley was the sixth of these children. She was born amidst the beautiful scenery of the Connecticut valley, but educated, principally, in the quiet town of Atkinson, New Hampshire, where her father was both pastor of the parish and preceptor of the academy.

Prior to her fifteenth year, her advantages were good for obtaining an English and classical education. But she often expresses her regret that these advantages were not duly appreciated; that she was deprived in a great measure of a mother's influence, and gave to light literature and social enjoyment too much of the golden hours that should have been devoted to more solid intellectual acquisitions.

At the age of fifteen the truth came home to the poor minister's daughter, that upon herself she must henceforth depend for her subsistence. School teaching, sewing, straw plaiting, and shoe binding, were successively tried, but none suited; and so she went to the factory. Here she perseveringly laboured for several years, returning home when the sick or dying required her presence, and once leaving the mills for several months to attend school.

In 1840 the "Improvement Circle" was established, to which she became a constant contributor. Soon after, the establishment of the "Lowell Offering" disseminated the knowledge of these mill-girls' efforts throughout our own and other countries. Though the work first attracted attention as a mere literary novelty, it was not destitute of intrinsic merit; and the writers were stimulated by praise and patronage. Miss Farley was invited to edit the third volume, a task which she combined with mill-labour. With editorial labours she combined the care of the "Home Department," in publishing the fourth, fifth, and sixth volumes.

The seventh volume she edited and published alone, charging herself with all the duties of editor, publisher, and agent. The book-keeping, mailing, canvassing, and all else, devolved on her. Since that time she has employed an assistant, to mail the numbers, keep office, and accounts, and do the stitching and folding.

She has contributed but little to other publications. Her literary claims and history are pretty much confined to that of the "Offering." This work has gained kind notices, in Great Britain, Germany, and France, from eminent literati. Compilations from it have been published in England and Scotland, and there have been some translations in foreign tongues.

The first article, written expressly for publication, was "Abby's Year in Lowell," a story which was reprinted in Edinburgh, by the Messrs. Chambers, in their series of cheap publications for the million. It is, perhaps, as good a specimen of her style as can be given.

ABBY'S YEAR IN LOWELL.

"Mr. Atkins, I say! Husband, why can't you speak? Do you hear what Abby says?"

"Anything worth hearing?" was the responsive question of Mr. Atkins; and he laid down the New Hampshire Patriot, and peered over his spectacles with a look which seemed to say, that an event so uncommon deserved particular attention.

"Why, she says that she means to go to Lowell, and work in the factory."

"Well, wife, let her go;" and Mr. Atkins took up the Patriot again.

"But I do not see how I can spare her; the spring cleaning is not done, nor the soap made, nor the boys' summer clothes; and you say that you intend to board your own 'men-folks,' and keep two more cows than you did last year; and Charley can scarcely go alone. I do not see how I can get along without her."

"But you say she does not assist you any about the house."

"Well, husband, she *might*."

"Yes, she might do a great many things which she does not think of doing; and as I do not see that she means to be useful here, we will let her go to the factory."

"Father! are you in earnest? May I go to Lowell?" said Abby; and she raised her bright black eyes to her father's with a look of exquisite delight.

"Yes, Abby, if you will promise me one thing; and that is, that you will stay a whole year without visiting us, excepting in case of sickness, and that you will stay but one year."

"I will promise anything, father, if you will only let me go; for I thought you would say that I had better stay at home and pick rocks, and weed the garden, and drop corn, and rake hay; and I do not want to do such work any longer. May I go with the Slater girls next Tuesday, for that is the day they have set for their return?"

"Yes, Abby, if you will remember that you are to stay a year, and only one year."

Abby retired to rest that night with a heart fluttering with pleasure; for ever since the visit of the Slater girls with new silk dresses, and Navarino bonnets trimmed with flowers, and lace veils, and gauze handkerchiefs, her head had been filled with visions of fine clothes; and she thought if she could only go where she could dress like them, she should be completely happy. She was naturally very fond of dress, and often, while a little girl, had she sat on the grass bank by the roadside watching the stage which went daily by her father's retired dwelling; and when she saw the gay ribbons and smart shawls, which passed like a bright phantom before her wondering eyes, she had thought that, when older, she too would have such things; and she looked forward to womanhood as to a state in which the chief pleasure must consist in wearing fine clothes.

But as years passed over her, she became aware that this was a source from which she could never derive any enjoyment whilst she remained at home; for her father was neither able nor willing to gratify her in this respect, and she had begun to fear that she must always wear the same brown cambric bonnet, and that the same calico gown would always be her "go-to-meeting dress." And now what a bright picture had been formed by her ardent and uncultivated imagination! Yes, she would go to Lowell, and earn all that she possibly could, and spend those earnings in beautiful attire; she would have silk dresses—one of grass green, and another of cherry red, and another upon the colour of which she would decide when she purchased it; and she would have a new Navarino bonnet, far more beautiful than Judith Slater's; and when at last she fell asleep, it was to dream of satin and lace, and her glowing fancy revelled all night in a vast and beautiful collection of milliners' finery.

But very different were the dreams of Abby's mother; and when she awoke the next morning, her first words to her husband were, "Mr. Atkins, were you serious last night when you told Abby that she might go to Lowell? I thought at first that you were vexed because I interrupted you, and said it to stop the conversation."

"Yes, wife, I was serious, and you did not interrupt me, for I had been listening to all that you and Abby were saying. She is a wild, thoughtless girl, and I hardly know what it is best to do with her; but perhaps it will be as well to try an experiment, and let her think and act a little while for herself. I expect that she will spend all her earnings in fine clothes; but after she has done so, she may see the folly of it; at all events, she will be rather more likely to understand the value of money when she has been obliged to work for it. After she has had her own way for one year, she may possibly be willing to return home and become a little more steady, and be willing to devote her active energies (for she is a very capable girl) to household duties, for hitherto her services have been principally out of doors, where she is now too old to work. I am also willing that she should see a little of the world, and what is going on in it; and I hope that, if she receives no benefit, she will at least return to us uninjured."

"Oh, husband, I have many fears for her," was the reply of Mrs. Atkins, "she is so very giddy and thoughtless; and the Slater girls are as hairbrained as herself, and will lead her on in all sorts of folly. I wish you would tell her that she must stay at home."

"I have made a promise," said Mr. Atkins, "and I will keep it; and Abby, I trust, will keep hers."

Abby flew round in high spirits to make the necessary preparations for her departure, and her mother assisted her with a heavy heart.

The evening before she left home, her father called her to him, and fixing upon her a calm, earnest, and almost mournful look, he said, "Abby, do you ever think?" Abby was subdued and almost awed by her father's look and manner. There was something unusual in it—something in his expression which was unexpected in him, but which reminded her of her teacher's look at the Sabbath school, when he was endeavouring to impress upon her mind some serious truth.

"Yes, father," she at length replied, "I have thought a great deal lately about going to Lowell."

"But I do not believe, my child, that you have had one serious reflection upon the subject, and I fear that I have done wrong in consenting to let you go from home. If I were too poor to maintain you here, and had no employment about which you could make yourself useful, I should feel no self-reproach, and would let you go, trusting that all might yet be well; but now I have done what I may at some future time severely repent of; and, Abby, if you do not wish to make me wretched, you will return to us a better, milder, and more thoughtful girl."

That night Abby reflected more seriously than she had ever done in her life before. Her father's words, rendered more impressive by the look and tone with which they were delivered, had sunk into her heart as words of his had never done before. She had been surprised at his ready acquiescence in her wishes, but it had now a new meaning. She felt that she was about to be abandoned to herself, because her parents despaired of being able to do anything for her; they thought her too wild, reckless, and untameable to be softened by aught but the stern lessons of experience. I will surprise them, said she to herself; I will show them that I have some reflection; and after I come home, my father shall never ask me if I *think*. Yes, I know what their fears are, and I will let them see that I can take care of myself, and as good care as they have ever taken of me. I know that I have not done as well as I might have done; but I will begin *now*, and when I return, they shall see that I am a better, milder, and more thoughtful girl. And the money which I intended to spend in fine dress shall be put into the bank; I will save it all, and my father shall see that I can earn money, and take care of it too. Oh how different I will be from what they think I am; and how very glad it will make my father and mother to see that I am not so very bad after all!

New feelings and new ideas had begotten new resolutions, and Abby's dreams that night were of smiles from her mother, and words from her father, such as she had never received nor deserved.

When she bade them farewell the next morning, she said nothing of the change which had taken place in her views and feelings, for she felt a slight degree of self-distrust in her own firmness of purpose.

Abby's self-distrust was commendable and auspicious; but she had a very prominent development in that part of the head where phrenologists locate the organ of firmness; and when she had once determined upon a thing, she usually went through with it. She had now resolved to pursue a course entirely different from that which was expected of her, and as different from the one she had first marked out for herself. This was more difficult, on account of her strong propensity for dress, a love of which was freely gratified by her companions. But when Judith Slater pressed her to purchase this beautiful piece of silk, or that splendid piece of muslin, her constant reply was, "No, I have determined not to buy any such things, and I will keep my resolution."

Before she came to Lowell, she wondered, in her simplicity, how people could live where there were so many stores, and not spend all their money; and it now required all her firmness to resist being overcome by the tempting display of beauties which met her eyes whenever she promenaded the illuminated streets. It was hard to walk by the milliners' shops with an unwavering step; and when she came to the confectionaries, she could not help stopping. But she did not yield to the temptation; she did not spend her money in them. When she saw fine strawberries, she said to herself, "I can gather them in our own pasture next year;" when she looked upon the nice peaches, cherries, and plums, which stood in tempting array behind their crystal barriers, she said again, "I will do without them *this* summer;" and when apples, pears, and nuts, were offered to her for sale, she thought that she would eat none of them till she went home. But she felt that the only safe place for her earnings was the savings' bank, and there they were regularly deposited, that it might be out of her power to indulge in momentary whims. She gratified no feeling but a newly-awakened desire for mental improvement, and spent her leisure hours in reading useful books.

Abby's year was one of perpetual self-contest and self-denial; but it was by no means one of unmitigated misery. The ruling desire of years was not to be conquered by the resolution of a moment; but when the contest was over, there was for her the triumph of victory. If the battle was sometimes desperate, there was so much more merit in being conqueror. One Sabbath was spent in tears, because Judith Slater did not wish her to attend their meeting with such a dowdy bonnet; and another fellow-boarder thought her gown must have been made in "the year one." The colour mounted to her cheeks, and the lightning flashed from her eyes, when asked if she had "*just come down;*" and she felt as though she should be glad to be away from them all, when she heard their sly innuendoes about "bush-whackers." Still she remained unshaken. It is but for a year, said she to herself, and the time and money that my father thought I should spend in folly shall be devoted to a better purpose.

At the close of a pleasant April day, Mr. Atkins sat at his kitchen fireside, with Charley upon his knee. "Wife," said he to Mrs. Atkins, who was busily preparing the evening meal, "is it not a year since Abby left home?"

"Why, husband, let me think: I always clean up the house thoroughly just before fast-day, and I had not done it when Abby went away. I remember speaking to her about it, and telling her that it was wrong to leave me at such a busy time; and she said, 'Mother, I will be at home to do it all next year.' Yes, it is a year, and I should not be surprised if she should come this week."

"Perhaps she will not come at all," said Mr. Atkins, with a gloomy look; "she has written us but few letters, and they have been very short and unsatisfactory. I suppose she has sense enough to know that no news is better than bad news; and having nothing pleasant to tell about herself, she thinks she will tell us nothing at all. But if I ever get her home again, I will keep her here. I assure you her first year in Lowell shall also be her last."

"Husband, I told you my fears, and if you had set up your authority, Abby would have been obliged to stay at home; but perhaps she is doing pretty well. You know she is not accustomed to writing, and that may account for the few and short letters we have received; but they have all, even the shortest, contained the assurance that she would be at home at the close of the year."

"Pa, the stage has stopped here," said little Charley, and he bounded from his father's knee. The next moment the room rang with the shout of "Abby has come! Abby has come!"

In a few moments more she was in the midst of the joyful throng. Her father pressed her hand in silence, and tears gushed from her mother's eyes. Her brothers and sisters were clamorous with delight, all but little Charley, to whom Abby was a stranger, and who repelled with terror all her overtures for a better acquaintance. Her parents gazed upon her with speechless pleasure, for they felt that a change for the better had taken place in their once wayward girl. Yes, there she stood before them, a little taller and a little thinner, and, when the flush of emotion had faded away, perhaps a little paler; but the eyes were bright in their joyous radiance, and the smile of health and innocence was playing around the rosy lips. She carefully laid aside her new straw-bonnet, with its plain trimming of light-blue ribbon, and her dark merino dress showed to the best advantage her neat symmetrical form. There was more delicacy of personal appeärance than when she left them, and also more softness of manner; for constant collision with so many young females had worn off the little asperities which had marked her conduct while at home.

"Well, Abby, how many silk gowns have you got?" said her father, as she opened a large new trunk.

"Not *one*, father," said she, and she fixed her dark eyes upon him with an expression which told all. "But here are some little books for the children, and a new calico dress for mother; and here is a nice black silk handkerchief for you to wear around your neck on Sundays. Accept it, dear father, it is your daughter's first gift."

"You had better have bought me a pair of spectacles, for I am sure I cannot see anything." There were tears in the rough farmer's eyes, but he tried to laugh and joke, that they might not be perceived. "But what did you do with all your money?"

"I thought I had better leave it there," said Abby, and she placed her bank-book in her father's hand. Mr. Atkins looked a moment, and the forceḋ smile faded away. The surprise had been too great, and tears fell thick and fast from the father's eyes.

"It is but a little," said Abby.

"But it was all you could save," replied her father, "and I am proud of you, Abby; yes, proud that I am the father of such a girl. It is not this paltry sum which pleases me so much, but the prudence, self-command, and real affection for us which you have displayed. But was it not sometimes hard to resist temptation?"

"Yes, father, *you* can never know how hard; but it was the thought of *this* night which sustained me through it all. I knew how you would smile, and what my mother would say and feel; and though there have been moments, yes, hours, that have seen me wretched enough, yet this one evening will repay for all. There is but one thing now to mar my happiness, and that is the thought that this little fellow has quite forgotten me," and she drew Charley to her side. But the new picture-book had already effected wonders, and in a few moments he was in her lap, with his arms around her neck, and his mother could not persuade him to retire that night until he had given "Sister Abby" a hundred kisses.

"Father," said Abby, as she arose to retire when the tall clock struck eleven, "may I not some time go back to Lowell? I should like to add a little to the sum in the bank, and I should be glad of *one* silk gown."

"Yes, Abby, you may do anything you wish. I shall never again be afraid to let you spend a year in Lowell. You have shown yourself to be possessed of a virtue, without which no one can expect to gain either respect or confidence—SELF-DENIAL."

MARY H. EASTMAN.

MARY HENDERSON, now Mrs. Mary H. Eastman, was born in Warrenton, Fauquier county, Virginia. Her father is Dr. Thomas Henderson, of the U. S. Army; her mother is a daughter of the well known naval commander, Commodore Truxtun. Her parents left Warrenton while she was still young, and removed to the city of Washington, where she lived till the time of her marriage, which took place at West Point, in 1835. Her husband, Captain S. Eastman, of the U. S. Army, is a graduate of the West Point Academy. Since his graduation, which was in 1829, he has spent most of his time in frontier stations, chiefly at Fort Snelling, where he was for a period of nine years. Mrs. Eastman was with him the greater part of this time. While there she had more favourable opportunities, probably, for studying the Indian character and customs than were ever possessed by any lady before. Having enjoyed while young the advantages of an excellent education, and possessing intellectual gifts of a high order, as well as much natural shrewdness of observation, she employed herself in gathering up curious Indian lore, which, since her return to the abodes of civilization, she has communicated to the public in several very interesting publications. The first of these was published in 1849, and entitled "Dahcotah, or Legends of the Sioux." The second series of papers was published in 1851, of the same character as "Dahcotah." These all consist of stories, sketches, poems, &c., relating to the Sioux and Chippeway Indians, whom she saw at and near Fort Snelling. A third work, called the "Aboriginal Portfolio," in quarto, appeared in 1853; and still a fourth, of the same general character, but relating chiefly to the Indian tribes of Pueblos in New Mexico, is now in press (1854).

Of all the portraitures of Indian life and character that have been given to the public, none, probably, have come more nearly to the truth than those by Mrs. Eastman. Her books are among the very best contributions to our native literature that have lately appeared. Her descriptions are happily free from the prevailing bombast and extravagance. She has the faculty—rare among her sex—of saying much in little space, and of saying that much with commendable precision. She conceives strongly what she means to say, and says it directly and in good English.

Besides her Indian books, Mrs. Eastman made, in 1852, a successful hit in another walk of literature. When "Uncle Tom's Cabin" was at the height of its popularity, she published a reply, under the title of "Aunt Phillis's Cabin," a novel in form, but abounding in sharp retort and hard argument. Eighteen thousand copies of this work were sold in a few weeks.

SHAH-CO-PEE.

No one who has lived at Fort Snelling can ever forget Shah-co-pee, for at what house has he not called to shake hands and smoke, to say that he is a great chief, and that he is hungry and must eat before he starts for home? If the hint is not immediately acted upon, he adds that the sun is dying fast, and it is time for him to set out.

Shah-co-pee is not so tall or fine looking as Bad Hail, nor has he the fine Roman features of Old Man in the Cloud. His face is decidedly ugly; but there is an expression of intelligence about his quick black eye and fine forehead, that makes him friends, notwithstanding his many troublesome qualities.

When he speaks he uses a great deal of gesture, suiting the action to the word. His hands, which are small and well formed, are black with dirt; he does not descend to the duties of the toilet.

He is the orator of the Dahcotahs. No matter how trifling the occasion, he talks well; and assumes an air of importance that would become him if he were discoursing on matters of life and death.

Some years ago, our government wished the Chippeways and Dahcotahs to conclude a treaty of peace among themselves. Frequently have these two bands made peace, but rarely kept it any length of time. On this occasion many promises were made on both sides; promises which would be broken by some inconsiderate young warrior before long, and then retaliation must follow.

Shah-co-pee has great influence among the Dahcotahs, and he was to come to Fort Snelling to be present at the council of peace. Early in the morning he and about twenty warriors left their village on the banks of the St. Peter's, for the Fort.

When they were very near, so that their actions could be distinguished, they assembled in their canoes, drawing them close together, that they might hear the speech which their chief was about to make to them.

They raised the stars and stripes, and their own flag, which is a staff adorned with feathers from the war eagle; and the noon-day sun gave brilliancy to their gay dresses, and the feathers and ornaments that they wore.

Shah-co-pee stood straight and firm in his canoe—and not the less proudly that the walls of the Fort towered above him.

"My boys," he said (for thus he always addressed his men) "the Dahcotahs are all braves; never has a coward been known among the People of the Spirit Lakes. Let the women and children fear their enemies, but we will face our foes, and always conquer.

"We are going to talk with the white men; our great Father wishes us to be at peace with our enemies. We have long enough shed the blood of the Chippeways; we have danced round their scalps, and our children have kicked their heads about in the dust. What more do we want? When we are in council, listen to the words of the Interpreter as he tells us what our great Father says, and I will answer him for you; and when we have eaten, and smoked the pipe of peace, we will return to our village."

The chief took his seat with all the importance of a public benefactor. He intended to have all the talking to himself, to arrange matters according to his own ideas; but he did it with the utmost condescension, and his warriors were satisfied.

Besides being an orator, Shah-co-pee is a beggar, and one of a high order too, for he will neither take offence nor refusal. Tell him one day that you will not give him pork and flour, and on the next he returns, nothing daunted, shaking hands, and asking for pork and flour. He always gains his point, for you are obliged to give in order to get rid of him. He will take up his quarters at the Interpreter's, and come down upon you every day for a week just at meal time—and as he is always blessed with a ferocious appetite, it is much better to capitulate, come to terms by giving him what he wants, and let him go. And after he has once started, ten to one if he does not come back to say he wants to shoot and bring you some ducks; you must give him powder and shot to enable him to do so. That will probably be the last of it.

It was a beautiful morning in June when we left Fort Snelling to go on a pleasure party up the St. Peter's, in a steamboat, the first that had ever ascended that river. There were many drawbacks in the commencement, as there always are on such occasions. The morning was rather cool, thought some, and as they hesitated about going, of course their toilets were delayed till the last moment. And when all were fairly in the boat, wood was yet to be found. Then something was the matter with one of the wheels—and the mothers were almost sorry they had consented to come; while the children, frantic with joy, were in danger of being drowned every moment, by the energetic movements they made near the sides of the boat, by way of indicating their satisfaction at the state of things.

In the cabin, extensive preparations were making in case the excursion brought on a good appetite. Everybody contributed loaf upon loaf of bread and cake; pies, coffee, and sugar; cold meats of every description; with milk and cream in bottles. Now and then, one of these was broken or upset, by way of adding to the confusion, which was already intolerable.

Champagne and old Cogniac were brought by the young gentlemen, only for fear the ladies should be sea-sick; or, perhaps, in case the gentlemen should think it positively necessary to drink the ladies' health.

When we thought all was ready, there was still another delay.

Shah-co-pee and two of his warriors were seen coming down the hill, the chief making an animated appeal to some one on board the boat; and as he reached the shore he gave us to understand that his business was concluded, and that he would like to go with us. But it was very evident that he considered his company a favour.

The bright sun brought warmth, and we sat on the upper deck admiring the beautiful shores of the St. Peter's. Not a creature was to be seen for some distance on the banks, and the birds as they flew over our heads seemed to be the fit and only inhabitants of such a region.

When tired of admiring the scenery, there was enough to employ us. The table was to be set for dinner; the children had already found out which basket contained the cake, and they were casting admiring looks towards it.

When we were all assembled to partake of some refreshments, it was delightful to find that there were not enough chairs for half the party. We borrowed each others' knives and forks, too, and etiquette, that petty tyrant of society, retired from the scene.

Shah-co-pee found his way to the cabin, where he manifested strong symptoms of shaking hands over again; in order to keep him quiet, we gave him plenty to eat. How he seemed to enjoy a piece of cake that had accidentally dropped into the oyster-soup! and with equal gravity would he eat apple-pie and ham together. And then his cry of "wakun"* when the cork flew from the champagne bottle across the table!

How happily the day passed—how few such days occur in the longest life!

As Shah-co-pee's village appeared in sight, the chief addressed Colonel D———, who was at that time in command of Fort Snelling, asking him why we had come on such an excursion.

"To escort you home," was the ready reply; "you are a great chief, and worthy of being honoured, and we have chosen this as the best way of showing our respect and admiration of you."

The Dahcotah chief believed all; he never for a moment

* Mysterious.

thought there was anything like jesting on the subject of his own high merits; his face beamed with delight on receiving such a compliment.

The men and women of the village crowded on the shore as the boat landed, as well they might, for a steamboat was a new sight to them.

The chief sprang from the boat, and swelling with pride and self-admiration he took the most conspicuous station on a rock near the shore, among his people, and made them a speech.

We could but admire his native eloquence. Here, with all that is wild in nature surrounding him, did the untaught orator address his people. His lips gave rapid utterance to thoughts which did honour to his feelings, when we consider who and what he was.

He told them that the white people were their friends; that they wished them to give up murder and intemperance, and to live quietly and happily. They taught them to plant corn, and they were anxious to instruct their children. "When we are suffering," said he, "during the cold weather, from sickness or want of food, they give us medicine and bread."

And finally he told them of the honour that had been paid him. "I went, as you know, to talk with the big Captain of the Fort, and he, knowing the bravery of the Dahcotahs, and that I was a great chief, has brought me home, as you see. Never has a Dahcotah warrior been thus honoured!"

Never, indeed! But we took care not to undeceive him. It was a harmless error, and as no efforts on our part could have diminished his self-importance, we listened with apparent, indeed with real admiration of his eloquent speech. The women brought ducks on board, and in exchange we gave them bread; and it was evening as we watched the last teepee of Shah-co-pee's village fade away in the distance.

Shah-co-pee has looked rather grave lately. There is trouble in the wigwam.

The old chief is the husband of three wives, and they and their children are always fighting. The first wife is old as the hills, wrinkled and haggard; the chief cares no more for her than he does for the stick of wood she is chopping. She quarrels with everybody but him, and this prevents her from being quite forgotten.

The day of the second wife is past too, it is of no use for her to plait her hair and put on her ornaments; for the old chief's heart is wrapped up in his third wife.

The girl did not love him, how could she? and he did not succeed in talking her into the match; but he induced the parents to sell her to him, and the young wife went weeping to the teepee of the chief.

Hers was a sad fate. She hated her husband as much as he loved her. No presents could reconcile her to her situation. The two forsaken wives never ceased annoying her, and their children assisted them. The young wife had not the courage to resent their ill treatment, for the loss of her lover had broken her heart. But that lover did not seem to be in such despair as she was—he did not quit the village, or drown himself, or commit any act of desperation. He lounged and smoked as much as ever. On one occasion, when Shah-co-pee was absent from the village, the lovers met.

They had to look well around them, for the two old wives were always on the lookout for something to tell of the young one; but there was no one near. The wind whistled keenly round the bend of the river as the Dahcotah told the weeping girl to listen to him.

When had she refused? How had she longed to hear the sound of his voice when wearied to death with the long boastings of the old chief!

But how did her heart beat when Red Stone told her that he loved her still—that he had only been waiting an opportunity to induce her to leave her old husband, and go with him far away!

She hesitated a little, but not long; and when Shah-co-pee returned to his teepee his young wife was gone—no one had seen her depart—no one knew where to seek for her. When the old man heard that Red Stone was gone too, his rage knew no bounds.

He beat his two wives almost to death, and would have given his handsomest pipe-stem to have seen the faithless one again.

His passion did not last long; it would have killed him if it had. His wives moaned all through the night, bruised and bleeding, for the fault of their rival; while the chief had recourse to the pipe, the never-failing refuge of the Dahcotah.

"I thought," said the chief, "that some calamity was going to happen to me" (for, being more composed, he began to talk to the other Indians who sat with him in his teepee, somewhat after the manner and in the spirit of Job's friends). "I saw Unk-a-tahe, the great fish of the water, and it showed its horns; and we know that that is always a sign of trouble."

"Ho!" replied an old medicine man, "I remember when Unk-a-tahe got in under the falls" (of St. Anthony) "and broke up the ice. The large pieces of ice went swiftly down, and the water forced its way until it was frightful to see it. The trees near the shore were thrown down, and the small islands were left bare. Near Fort Snelling there was a house where a white man and his wife lived. The woman heard the noise, and, waking her husband, ran out; but as he did not follow her quick enough, the house was soon afloat and he was drowned."

There was an Indian camp near this house, for the body of Wenona, the sick girl who was carried over the Falls, was found here. It was placed on a scaffold on the shore, near where the Indians found her, and Checkered Cloud moved her teepee, to be near her daughter. Several other Dahcotah families were also near her.

But what was their fright when they heard the ice breaking, and the waters roaring as they carried everything before them? The father of Wenona clung to his daughter's scaffold, and no entreaties of his wife or others could induce him to leave.

"Unk-a-tahe has done this," cried the old man, "and I care not. He carried my sick daughter under the waters, and he may bury me there too." And while the others fled from the power of Unk-a-tahe, the father and mother clung to the scaffold of their daughter.

They were saved, and they lived by the body of Wenona until they buried her. The power of Unk-a-tahe is great!" So spoke the medicine-man, and Shah-co-pee almost forgot his loss in the fear and admiration of this monster of the deep, this terror of the Dahcotahs.

He will do well to forget the young wife altogether; for she is far away, making mocassins for the man she loves. She rejoices at her escape from the old man, and his two wives; while he is always making speeches to his men, commencing by saying he is a great chief, and ending with the assertion that Red Stone should have respected his old age, and not have stolen from him the only wife he loved.

Shah-co-pee came, a few days ago, with twenty other warriors, some of them chiefs, on a visit to the commanding officer of Fort Snelling.

The Dahcotahs had heard that the Winnebagoes were about to e removed, and that they were to pass through their hunting-grounds on their way to their future homes. They did not approve of this arrangement. Last summer the Dahcotahs took some scalps of the Winnebagoes, and it was decided at Washington that the Dahcotahs should pay four thousand dollars of their annuities as an atonement for the act. This caused much suffering among the Dahcotahs; fever was making great havoc among them, and to deprive them of their flour and other articles of food was only enfeebling their constitutions, and rendering them an easy prey for disease. The Dahcotahs thought this very hard at the time; they have not forgotten the circumstance, and they think that they ought to be consulted before their lands are made a thoroughfare by their enemies.

They accordingly assembled, and, accompanied by the Indian agent and the interpreter, came to Fort Snelling to make their complaint. When they were all seated (all on the floor but one, who looked most uncomfortable, mounted on a high chair), the agent introduced the subject, and it was discussed for a while; the

Dahcotahs paying the most profound attention, although they could not understand a word of what was passing; and when there was a few moments' silence, the chiefs rose each in his turn to protest against the Winnebagoes passing through their country. They all spoke sensibly and well; and when one finished, the others all intimated their approval by crying "Ho!" as a kind of chorus. After a while Shah-co-pee rose; his manner said "I am Sir Oracle." He shook hands with the commanding officer, with the agent and interpreter, and then with some strangers who were visiting the fort.

His attitude was perfectly erect as he addressed the officer.

"We are the children of our great Father, the President of the United States; look upon us, for we are your children too. You are placed here to see that the Dahcotahs are protected, that their rights are not infringed upon."

While the Indians cried "Ho! ho!" with great emphasis, Shah-co-pee shook hands all round again, and then resumed his place and speech.

"Once this country all belonged to the Dahcotahs. Where had the white man a place to call his own on our prairies? He could not even pass through our country without our permission!

"Our great Father has signified to us that he wants our lands. We have sold some of them to him, and we are content to do so, but he has promised to protect us, to be a friend to us, to take care of us as a father does of his children.

"When the white man wishes to visit us, we open the door of our country to him; we treat him with hospitality. He looks at our rocks, our river, our trees, and we do not disturb him. The Dahcotah and the white man are friends.

"But the Winnebagoes are not our friends, we suffered for them not long ago; our children wanted food; our wives were sick; they could not plant corn or gather the Indian potato. Many of our nation died; their bodies are now resting on their scaffolds. The night birds clap their wings as the winds howl over them!

"And we are told that our great Father will let the Winnebagoes make a path through our hunting-grounds: they will subsist upon our game; every bird or animal they kill will be a loss to us.

"The Dahcotah's lands are not free to others. If our great Father wishes to make any use of our lands, he should pay us. We object to the Winnebagoes passing through our country; but if it is too late to prevent this, then we demand a thousand dollars for every village they shall pass."

"Ho!" cried the Indians again; and Shah-co-pee, after shaking hands once more, took his seat.

I doubt if you will ever get the thousand dollars a village, Shah-co-pee; but I like the spirit that induces you to demand it. May you live long to make speeches and beg bread—the unrivalled orator and most notorious beggar of the Dahcotahs!

S. MARGARET FULLER,

(MARCHIONESS OF OSSOLI.)

SARAH MARGARET FULLER was born at Cambridge, Massachusetts, May 23, 1810. She was the daughter of the Hon. Timothy Fuller, a lawyer of Boston, but nearly all his life a resident of Cambridge, and a Representative of the Middlesex District in Congress from 1817 to 1825. Mr. Fuller, upon his retirement from Congress, purchased a farm at some distance from Boston, and abandoned law for agriculture, soon after which he died. His widow and six children still survive.

Margaret was the first-born, and from a very early age evinced the possession of remarkable intellectual powers. Her father regarded her with a proud admiration, and was from childhood her chief instructor, guide, companion, and friend. At eight years of age he was accustomed to require of her the composition of a number of Latin verses per day, while her studies in philosophy, history, general science, and current literature were in after years extensive and profound. After her father's death, she applied herself to teaching as a vocation, first in Boston, then in Providence, and afterwards in Boston again, where her "Conversations" were for several seasons attended by classes of women, some of them married, and including many from the best families of that city.

In the autumn of 1844, she accepted an invitation to take part in the conduct of "The Tribune," with especial reference to the department of Reviews and Criticisms on current Literature and Art, a position which she filled with eminent ability for nearly two years. Her reviews of Longfellow's Poems, Wesley's Memoirs, Poe's Poems, Bailey's "Festus," Douglas's Life, &c., may be mentioned with special emphasis. She had previously found "fit audience, though few," for a series of remarkable papers on "The Great Musicians," "Lord Herbert of Cherbury," "Woman," &c., in "The Dial," of which she was at first co-editor

Margaret Fuller.

with Ralph Waldo Emerson, but which was afterwards edited by him only, though she continued a contributor to its pages. In 1843, she accompanied some friends on a tour by Niagara, Detroit, and Mackinac to Chicago, and across the Prairies of Illinois, and her resulting volume, entitled "Summer on the Lakes," is considered one of the best works in its department ever issued from the American press. Her "Woman in the Nineteenth Century"—an extension of her essay in "The Dial"—was published early in 1845, and a moderate edition sold. The next year a selection from her "Papers on Literature and Art" was issued by Wiley & Putnam, in two fair volumes of their "Library of American Books." These "Papers" embody some of her best contributions to "The Dial," "The Tribune," and perhaps one or two which had not appeared in either.

In the summer of 1845, Miss Fuller accompanied the family of a devoted friend to Europe, visiting England, Scotland, France, and passing through Italy to Rome, where they spent the ensuing winter. She accompanied her friends next spring to the north of Italy, and there stopped, spending most of the summer at Florence, and returning at the approach of winter to Rome, where she was soon after married to Giovanni, Marquis d'Ossoli, who had made her acquaintance during her first winter in the Eternal City. They afterwards resided in the Roman States until the summer of 1850, after the surrender of Rome to the French army of assassins of liberty, when they deemed it expedient to migrate to Florence, both having taken an active part in the Republican movement. Thence in June they departed and set sail at Leghorn for New York, in the Philadelphia brig Elizabeth, which was doomed to encounter a succession of disasters. They had not been many days at sea when the captain was prostrated by a disease which ultimately exhibited itself as confluent small-pox of the most malignant type, and terminated his life soon after they touched at Gibraltar, after a sickness of intense agony and loathsome horror. The vessel was detained some days in quarantine by reason of this affliction, but finally set sail again just in season to bring her on our coast on the fearful night between the 18th and 19th of July, 1850, when darkness, rain, and a terrific gale from the south-west conspired to hurl her into the very jaws of destruction. She struck during the night, and before the next evening was a mass of drifting sticks and planks, while her passengers and part of her crew were buried in the boiling surges.

Among those drowned in this fearful wreck were the Marquis and Marchioness d'Ossoli, and their only child.

Miss Fuller was more remarkable for strength and vigour of thought, and a certain absolute and almost scornful independence, than for the graces of style and diction. She had the reputation of being "the best talker since Madame de Staël," and by those who knew her most intimately her conversational powers were considered more brilliant even than her talents as a writer. She was, without doubt, in both respects, one of the most remarkable women of the present century. Her friends, R. W. Emerson and W. H. Channing, published in 1851 an interesting Memoir of her life and writings, in two volumes.

A SHORT ESSAY ON CRITICS.

An essay on Criticism were a serious matter; for, though this age be emphatically critical, the writer would still find it necessary to investigate the laws of criticism as a science, to settle its conditions as an art. Essays, entitled critical, are epistles addressed to the public, through which the mind of the recluse relieves itself of its impressions. Of these the only law is, "Speak the best word that is in thee." Or they are regular articles got up to order by the literary hack writer, for the literary mart, and the only law is to make them plausible. There is not yet deliberate recognition of a standard of criticism, though we hope the always strengthening league of the republic of letters must ere long settle laws on which its Amphictyonic council may act. Meanwhile let us not venture to write on criticism, but, by classifying the critics, imply our hopes and thereby our thoughts.

First, there are the subjective class (to make use of a convenient term, introduced by our German benefactors). These are persons to whom writing is no sacred, no reverend employment. They are not driven to consider, not forced upon investigation by the fact, that they are deliberately giving their thoughts an independent existence, and that it may live to others when dead to them. They know no agonies of conscientious research, no timidities of self-respect. They see no ideal beyond the present hour, which makes its mood an uncertain tenure. How things affect them now they know; let the future, let the whole take care of itself. They state their impressions as they rise, of other men's spoken, written, or acted thoughts. They never dream of going out of themselves to seek the motive, to trace the law of another nature. They never dream that there are statures which cannot be measured from their point of view. They love, they like, or they hate; the book is detestable, immoral, absurd, or admirable, noble, of a most approved scope;—these statements they make with authority, as those who bear the evangel of pure taste and accurate judgment, and need be tried before no human synod. To them it seems that their present position commands the universe.

Thus the essays on the works of others, which are called criticisms, are often, in fact, mere records of impressions. To judge of their value you must know where the man was brought up, under what influences,—his nation, his church, his family even. He himself has never attempted to estimate the value of these circumstances, and find a law or raise a standard above all circumstances, permanent against all influence. He is content to be the creature of his place, and to represent it by his spoken and written word. He takes the same ground with a savage, who does not hesitate to say of the product of a civilization on which he could not stand, "It is bad," or "It is good."

The value of such comments is merely reflex. They characterize the critic. They give an idea of certain influences on a certain act of men in a certain time or place. Their absolute, essential value is nothing. The long review, the eloquent article by the man of the nineteenth century, are of no value by themselves considered, but only as samples of their kind. The writers were content to tell what they felt, to praise or to denounce without needing to convince us or themselves. They sought not the divine truths of philosophy, and she proffers them not if unsought.

Then there are the apprehensive. These can go out of themselves and enter fully into a foreign existence. They breathe its life; they live in its law; they tell what it meant, and why it so expressed its meaning. They reproduce the work of which they speak, and make it better known to us in so far as two statements are better than one. There are beautiful specimens in this kind. They are pleasing to us as bearing witness of the genial sympathies of nature. They have the ready grace of love with somewhat of the dignity of disinterested friendship. They sometimes give more pleasure than the original production of which they treat, as melodies will sometimes ring sweetlier in the echo. Besides there is a peculiar pleasure in a true response; it is the assurance of equipoise in the universe. These, if not true critics, come nearer the standard than the subjective class, and the value of their work is ideal as well as historical.

Then there are the comprehensive, who must also be apprehensive. They enter into the nature of another being, and judge his work by its own law. But having done so, having ascertained his design and the degree of his success in fulfilling it, thus measuring his judgment, his energy, and skill, they do also know how to put that aim in its place, and how to estimate its relations. And this the critic can only do who perceives the analogies of the universe, and how they are regulated by an absolute, invariable principle. He can see how far that work expresses this principle, as well as how far it is excellent in its details. Sustained by a principle, such as can be girt within no rule, no formula, he can walk around the work, he can stand above it, he can uplift it, and try its weight. Finally, he is worthy to judge it.

Critics are poets cut down, says some one by way of jeer; but, in truth, they are men with the poetical temperament to apprehend, with the philosophical tendency to investigate. The maker is divine; the critic sees this divine, but brings it down to humanity by the analytic process. The critic is the historian who records the order of creation. In vain for the maker, who knows without learning it, but not in vain for the mind of his race.

The critic is beneath the maker, but is his needed friend. What tongue could speak but to an intelligent ear, and every noble work demands its critic. The richer the work, the more severe should be its critic; the larger its scope, the more comprehensive must be his power of scrutiny. The critic is not a base caviller, but the younger brother of genius. Next to invention is the power of interpreting invention; next to beauty the power of appreciating beauty.

And of making others appreciate it; for the universe is a scale of infinite gradation, and below the very highest, every step is explanation down to the lowest. Religion, in the two modulations of poetry and music, descends through an infinity of waves to the lowest abysses of human nature. Nature is the literature and art of the divine mind; human literature and art the criticism on that; and they, too, find their criticism within their own sphere.

The critic, then, should be not merely a poet, not merely a philosopher, not merely an observer, but tempered of all three. If he criticise the poem, he must want nothing of what constitutes the poet, except the power of creating forms and speaking in music. He must have as good an eye and as fine a sense; but if he had as fine an organ for expression also, he would make the poem instead of judging it. He must be inspired by the philosopher's spirit of inquiry and need of generalization, but he must not be constrained by the hard cemented masonry of method to which philosophers are prone. And he must have the organic acuteness of the observer, with a love of ideal perfection, which forbids him to be content with mere beauty of details in the work or the comment upon the work.

There are persons who maintain, that there is no legitimate criticism, except the reproductive; that we have only to say what the work is or is to us, never what it is not. But the moment we look for a principle, we feel the need of a criterion, of a standard; and then we say what the work is *not*, as well as what it *is*; and this is as healthy though not as grateful and gracious an operation of the mind as the other. We do not seek to degrade but to classify an object, by stating what it is not. We detach the part from the whole, lest it stand between us and the whole. When we have ascertained in what degree it manifests the whole, we may safely restore it to its place, and love or admire it there ever after.

The use of criticism, in periodical writing, is to sift, not to stamp a work. Yet should they not be "sieves and drainers for the use of luxurious readers," but for the use of earnest inquirers, giving voice and being to their objections, as well as stimulus to their sympathies. But the critic must not be an infallible adviser to his reader. He must not tell him what books are not worth reading, or what must be thought of them when read, but what he read in them. Woe to that coterie where some critic sits despotic, entrenched behind the infallible "We." Woe to that oracle who has infused such soft sleepiness, such a gentle dulness into his atmosphere, that when he opes his lips no dog will bark. It is this attempt at dictatorship in the reviewers, and the indolent acquiescence of their readers, that has brought them into disrepute. With such fairness did they make out their statements, with such dignity did they utter their verdicts, that the poor reader grew all too submissive. He learned his lesson with such docility, that the greater part of what will be said at any public or private meeting can be foretold by any one who has read the leading periodical works for twenty years back. Scholars sneer at and would fain dispense with them altogether; and the public, grown lazy and helpless by this constant use of props and stays, can now scarce brace itself even to get through a magazine article, but reads in the daily paper laid beside the breakfast-plate a short notice of the last number of the long-established and popular review, and thereupon passes its judgment and is content.

Then the partisan spirit of many of these journals has made it unsafe to rely upon them as guide-books and expurgatory indexes. They could not be content merely to stimulate and suggest thought, they have at last become powerless to supersede it.

From these causes and causes like these, the journals have lost much of their influence. There is a languid feeling about them, an inclination to suspect the justice of their verdicts, the value of their criticisms. But their golden age cannot be quite past. They afford too convenient a vehicle for the transmission of knowledge; they are too natural a feature of our time to have done all their work yet. Surely they may be redeemed from their abuses, they may be turned to their true uses. But how?

It were easy to say what they should *not* do. They should not have an object to carry or a cause to advocate, which obliges them either to reject all writings which wear the distinctive traits of individual life, or to file away what does not suit them, till the essay, made true to their design, is made false to the mind of the writer. An external consistency is thus produced, at the expense of all salient thought, all genuine emotion of life, in short, and all living influence. Their purpose may be of value, but by such means was no valuable purpose ever furthered long. There are those, who have with the best intention pursued this system of trimming and adaptation, and thought it well and best to

"Deceive their country for their country's good."

But their country cannot long be so governed. It misses the pure, the full tone of truth; it perceives that the voice is modulated to coax, to persuade, and it turns from the judicious man of the world, calculating the effect to be produced by each of his smooth sentences, to some earnest voice which is uttering thoughts, crude, rash, ill-arranged it may be, but true to one human breast, and uttered in full faith, that the God of Truth will guide them aright.

And here, it seems to me, has been the greatest mistake in the conduct of these journals. A smooth monotony has been attained, an uniformity of tone, so that from the title of a journal you can infer the tenor of all its chapters. But nature is ever various, ever new, and so should be her daughters, art and literature. We do not want merely a polite response to what we thought before, but by the freshness of thought in other minds to have new thought awakened in our own. We do not want stores of information only, but to be roused to digest these into knowledge. Able and experienced men write for us, and we would know what they think, as they think it not for us but for themselves. We would live with them, rather than be taught by them how to live; we would catch the contagion of their mental activity, rather than have them direct us how to regulate our own. In books, in reviews, in the senate, in the pulpit, we wish to meet thinking men, not schoolmasters or pleaders. We wish that they should do full justice to their own view, but also that they should be frank with us, and, if now our superiors, treat us as if we might some time rise to be their equals. It is this true manliness, this firmness in his own position, and this power of appreciating the position of others, that alone can make the critic our companion and friend. We would converse with him, secure that he will tell us all his thought, and speak as man to man. But if he adapts his work to us, if he stifles what is distinctively his, if he shows himself either arrogant or mean, or, above all, if he wants faith in the healthy action of free thought, and the safety of pure motive, we will not talk with him, for we cannot confide in him. We will go to the critic who trusts Genius and trusts us, who knows that all good writing must be spontaneous, and who will write out the bill of fare for the public as he read it for himself,---

> "Forgetting vulgar rules, with spirit free
> To judge each author by his own intent,
> Nor think one standard for all minds is meant."

Such an one will not disturb us with personalities, with sectarian prejudices, or an undue vehemence in favour of petty plans or temporary objects. Neither will he disgust us by smooth obsequious flatteries, and an inexpressive, lifeless gentleness. He will be free and make free from the mechanical and distorting influences we hear complained of on every side. He will teach us to love wisely what we before loved well, for he knows the difference between censoriousness and discernment, infatuation and reverence; and while delighting in the genial melodies of Pan, can perceive, should Apollo bring his lyre into audience, that there may be strains more divine than those of his native groves.

CATHERINE E. BEECHER.

MISS BEECHER's literary history is remarkable, and illustrates one of her own favourite maxims in regard to education. Until the age of twenty, her reading, so far as left to her own choice, was confined to works of imagination and humour, she had written nothing but letters and poetry, had a decided aversion to the practical duties of domestic life, was so disinclined to metaphysical inquiries, though living in a family where such inquiries formed the staple of daily conversation, as never to have given the subject any connected attention, and withal was so averse to mathematical studies as not even to have learned the multiplication table, or to have mastered the simplest arithmetical process. Yet this woman has become distinguished as a writer on some of the most abstruse questions of mental and moral science, has prepared one of the clearest manuals extant for teaching the rationale of arithmetic, has written most acceptably on domestic economy, and she is most favourably known, throughout the length and breadth of the land, by the sober and practical character of her views as an educator and a philanthropist.

Miss Beecher is the daughter of the eminent theologian, the Rev. Lyman Beecher, D. D. She was born at East Hampton, Long Island, Sept. 6, 1800. In 1810, the family removed to Litchfield, Connecticut, where Catherine was placed at Miss Pierce's school for young ladies, then the most celebrated in the country.

About the age of twenty, according to Mrs. Hale, "an event occurred that ended for ever all Miss Beecher's youthful dreams of poetry and romance, and changed the whole course of thought and feeling as regarded her destiny in life. But the Providence that withdrew her heart from the world of woman's hopes, has proved a great blessing to her sex and her country."

In consequence of the event thus delicately alluded to, Miss Beecher directed her whole energies to the subject of education. She founded, in

1823, the Hartford Female Seminary, which received pupils from every State in the Union, numbering at one time as high an attendance as one hundred and sixty.

In 1832, she accompanied her father to Cincinnati, and established there, in 1833, the Western Female Institute. Her more recent efforts towards organizing a general plan for popular education, though highly important in themselves and honourable to her, do not lie strictly within the scope of the present article.

Miss Beecher's first published work was entitled "Suggestions on Education," a small volume of eighty-four pages, which appeared in 1829. The next was the "Arithmetic" already referred to, which appeared in 1830. It was designed to make teachers more thorough in explaining the rationale of arithmetical processes, and was quoted with high commendation by Prof. Olmstead of Yale College. Her next work was printed in 1831, but has never been published. It was an octavo of 452 pages, on the "Elements of Mental and Moral Philosophy, as founded on Reason, Experience, and the Bible." The extract which is given is from this work. It was printed privately for the use of her own pupils, the author always intending to rewrite and publish it as the chief literary labour of her life. "Letters on Difficulties in Religion," 351 pp., appeared in 1836. It was occasioned by the author's meeting in her travels with many sceptical persons of high character, with whom she had carried on earnest discussions, both oral and written. "The Moral Instructor," 194 pp., appeared in 1838. It was designed as a text-book to teach a complete system of Christian morals to young children. She next published a small volume on the slavery question, discussing the duty of American women in reference to this subject. "Domestic Economy for Young Ladies," which appeared soon after, has had the largest circulation of all of Miss Beecher's works, and the author boasts, that, notwithstanding her early distaste for the subject, there is not a household or culinary process described in her book with which she is not practically familiar. A memoir of her brother, the Rev. George Beecher, 345 pp., appeared in 1844. "Truth Stranger than Fiction," 294 pp., 1850, was intended to redress an individual wrong, exposing the conduct of a young clergyman who had been guilty of a virtual breach of promise of marriage. Miss Beecher's last work, "The True Remedy for the Wrongs of Woman," 263 pp., 1851, contains a history of her views and efforts in regard to female education.

HABIT.

HABIT is a facility in performing physical or mental operations, gained by the repetition of such acts. As examples of this facility gained in *physical* operations, may be mentioned the power of walking, which is acquired only by a multitude of experiments; the power of speech, which is a slow process of repeated experiments at imitation; and the power of writing, gained in the same way. Success in every pursuit of life is attained by oft-repeated attempts, which finally induce a habit. As examples of the formation of *intellectual* habits, may be mentioned the facility which is gained in acquiring knowledge, by means of repeated efforts, and the accuracy and speed with which the process of reasoning is performed after long practice in this art. As examples of the formation of *moral* habits, may be mentioned those which are formed by the exercise of self-government, of justice, veracity, obedience, and industry. After the long practice of these virtues they become such fixed habits, that it is much more easy and natural to practise them than it was before such habits were formed. On the contrary, the indulgence of indolence, pride, envy, selfishness, and deceit, forms habits of mind which are equally manifest and powerful.

The happiness of man, in the present state of existence, depends not solely upon the circumstances in which he is placed, nor upon the capacities with which he is endowed, but almost entirely upon the *formation of his habits.* A man might have the organ of sight bestowed, and be surrounded with all the beauties of nature, and yet if he did not form the *habit* of judging of the form, distance, and size of bodies, all pleasure and all use from this sense would be destroyed. The world and all its beauties would be a mere confused mass of colours. If the habits of walking, and of speech, were not acquired, the faculties, and the circumstances for employing them, would not furnish the enjoyment they were made to secure. It is the formation of intellectual habits by mental discipline and study, also, which opens the vast resources for intellectual enjoyment that otherwise would be for ever closed, and it is by practising obedience to parents that moral habits of subordination are formed, which are indispensable to our happiness as citizens, and as subjects of the Divine government. There is no enjoyment which can be pointed out, that is not, to a greater or less extent, dependent upon the formation of habits, and upon this, all *increase* of happiness is equally dependent.

The formation of the habits depends upon the leading desire or governing purpose, because, whatever the mind desires the most, it will *act* the most to secure, and thus by repeated acts will form its habits. The character of every individual depends upon the mode of seeking happiness selected by the will. Thus, the ambitious man has selected the attainment of power and admiration as his leading purpose, and whatever modes of enjoyment interfere with this are sacrificed. The man of pleasure seeks his happiness from the various gratifications of sense, and sacrifices other modes of enjoyment that interfere with this. The man devoted to intellectual pursuits, and seeking reputation and influence through this medium, sacrifices other modes of enjoyment to secure this gratification. The man who has devoted his affections and the service of his life to God and the good of his fellow-men, sacrifices all other enjoyments to secure that which results from the fulfilment of such obligations. Thus, a person is denominated an ambitious man, a man of pleasure, a man of literary ambition, or a man of piety, according to the governing purpose or leading desire of the mind. There are some minds, however, which seem destitute of any leading purpose or characteristic; who seem to be creatures of circumstance, and merely seek enjoyment from any object that happens to offer, without any definite purpose of life.

There is one fact in regard to the choice of the leading object of desire, or the governing purpose of life, that is very peculiar. Certain modes of enjoyment, in consequence of repetition, increase the desire, but lessen the *capacity* of happiness from this source; while, at other sources of enjoyment, gratification increases the *desire*, and at the same time increases the *capacity* for enjoyment.

The pleasure of sensitive enjoyments is of the first kind. It will be found as a matter of universal experience, that where this has been chosen as the main purpose of life, though the desire for such enjoyments is continually increased, yet owing to the physical effects of excessive indulgence the capacity for emotions of enjoyment is decreased. Thus the man who so degrades his nature as to make the pleasures of eating and drinking the great pursuit of life, while his desires never abate, finds his zest for such enjoyments continually decreasing;—finds a perpetual need for new devices to stimulate appetite and awaken the dormant capacities for enjoyment. The pleasures of sense always pall from repetition, grow "stale, flat, and unprofitable," though the deluded being who has slavishly yielded to such appetites, feels himself bound by chains of habit which, even when enjoyment ceases, seldom are broken.

The pleasures derived from the exercise of power, when the attainment of this gratification becomes the master passion, are also of this description. We find our fellow-creatures toiling and striving for the attainment of this good; the statesman, the politician, the conqueror, are all seeking for this, and desire never abates while anything of the kind remains to be attained. We do not find that enjoyment increases in proportion as power is attained. On the contrary, it seems to cloy in possession. Alexander, the conqueror of the world, when he had gained *all* for which he had sought, wept that objects of desire were extinct, and that possession could not satisfy. Intemperate gratification of this desire always lessens the capacity of enjoyment.

But there are other sources of happiness, which while sought, the desire ever continues, and possession only increases the capacity for more enjoyment. Of this class is the susceptibility of happiness from *giving and receiving affection.* Here, the more is given and received, the more is the power of giving and receiving increased, and the more is the susceptibility of gratification refined and strengthened. We find that this principle outlives the decay of every other, and even the decays of nature itself. When tottering age on the borders of the grave is just ready to resign its wasted tenement, often from its dissolving ashes the never-dying spark of affection has burst forth with new and undiminished lustre. This is that immortal fountain of happiness always increased by imparting, never surcharged by receiving.

Another principle which is never weakened by exercise, is the power of enjoyment from being the *cause of happiness to others*, and to this may be added, as partially involved in it, the happiness which results from *conscious rectitude*. Never was an instance known of regret for the pursuit of rectitude, or for devotion to the happiness of others. On the contrary, the more these holy and delightful principles are in exercise, the more the desires are increased, and the more are the susceptibilities for enjoyment enlarged. While the votaries of pleasure are wearing down with the exhaustion of abused nature, and the votaries of ambition are sighing over its thorny wreath, the benevolent spirit is exulting in the success of its accomplished plans of good, and reaching forth to still purer and more accomplished bliss.

The pleasures which result from *sympathy*, depend almost entirely on the circumstances in which a person is placed, and on the mode of happiness he has chosen to secure. If he is surrounded by those he is aiding to comfort and bless, their happiness is his, in a measure peculiarly delightful. If he is the cause of sorrow, suffering, and crime, his power of sympathy is only a cause of suffering. A benevolent mind, even while surrounded by sorrow and suffering, while agitated with sympathizing grief, is solaced and cheered with the assurance that this painful sympathy is a source of comfort and relief to the wounded spirit that for ever seeks this balm.

The pleasures which result from *activity* of body and mind, depend very much upon the object of pursuit which occupies the mind. If the objects pursued are found to be unsatisfactory, and ever mingled with sorrow and disappointment, the pleasures of activity are very much decreased. If, on the contrary, activity is ever found to insure success in attaining good to ourselves and others, enjoyment from this source is increased.

It thus appears that there are *two* sources of happiness, which, if made the chief objects of life, always increase desire, while they *lessen the capacity* for enjoyment. There are *three* sources of happiness which always increase the desire, and also *increase the capacity* for enjoyment, so long as they are sought, while there are *two* sources of happiness which depend entirely upon the nature of that species of enjoyment from which the mind chooses to derive its chief happiness.

But there is another fact in regard to habit, which has an immense bearing on the well-being of our race. When a habit of seeking happiness in some one particular mode is once formed, the change of this habit becomes difficult just in proportion to the degree of repetition which has been practised. After a habit is once formed, it is no longer an easy matter to choose between that mode of securing happiness pursued, and another, which the mind may be led to regard as much superior. Thus, after a habit has been formed of gratifying the appetite, a man may feel that instead of increasing his happiness, it is continually diminishing it, and that, by sacrificing it, he may secure much greater enjoyment from another source; yet the force of habit is such, that decisions of the will seem perpetually to yield to its power. Thus also if a man has found his chief enjoyment in that admiration and applause of men so ardently desired, even after it has ceased to charm, and seems like emptiness and vanity, still when nobler objects of pursuit and happiness are offered, the chains of habit bind him to his wonted path, and though he looks and longs for the one that his conscience and his intellect assure him is brightest and best, the conflict with bad habits often ends in fatal defeat and ruin. It is true that every habit can be corrected and changed, but nothing requires greater firmness of purpose and energy of will. For it is not *one* resolution of mind that can conquer habit, it must be a constant series of long-continued efforts.

From this it appears that all the happiness of life is dependent on the early formation of right habits; and the revelations of another world give fearful evidence that the happiness of an eternal existence is resting on the same foundation.

The influence of habit in reference to *emotions* is very peculiar, and deserves special attention, as having a direct influence upon character and happiness. All pleasurable emotions of mind, being grateful, are indulged and cherished, and are not weakened by repetition unless they become excessive. If the pleasures of sense are indulged beyond a certain extent, the bodily system is exhausted, and satiety is the consequence. If the love of power and admiration is indulged and becomes the leading purpose of life, they are found to be cloying. But within certain limits all pleasurable emotions do not seem to lessen in power by repetition.

But, in regard to painful emotions, the reverse is true. The mind instinctively resists or flies from them, so that after a frequent repetition of the same cause, a habit of resisting such emotions is formed, until the susceptibility appears almost entirely destroyed. The mind seems to be able to turn its attention from painful emotions, or in some way to suppress them, after continued repetition. Thus, a person often exposed to danger ceases to be troubled by emotions of fear, because he forms a habit of suppressing them. A person frequently in scenes of distress and suffering learns to suppress the emotions of sympathy and pity. The surgeon is an example of the last case, where, by repeated operations, he has learned to suppress emotions until they seldom recur. A person inured to guilt gradually deadens the pangs of remorse, until, as the Scripture expresses it, the conscience becomes "seared as with an hot iron." Thus also with the emotion of shame. After a person has been repeatedly exposed to contempt, and feels that he is universally despised, he grows hardened and callous to any such emotions.

The mode by which the mind succeeds in forming such a habit, seems to be by that implanted principle which makes ideas that are most in consonance with the leading desire of the mind become vivid and distinct, while those which are less interesting fade away. Now, no person desires to witness pain except from the hope of alleviating it, unless it be that from anger the mind is sometimes gratified with the infliction of suffering. But in ordinary cases the sight of suffering is avoided except where relief can be administered. In such cases, the desire of admistering relief is the one which is the leading desire, so that the mind is turned off from the view of the suffering to dwell on conceptions of modes of relief; and thus the surgeon and physician gradually form such habits that the sight of pain and suffering lead the mind to conception of modes of relief, whereas a mind not thus interested dwells on the more painful ideas. The mind also can form a habit of inattention to our own bodily sufferings by becoming interested in other things, and thus painful sensations go unnoticed. Some persons will go for years with a chronic headache, and yet appear to enjoy nearly as much as those who never suffer from such a cause. Thus those also who violate conscience seem to relieve themselves from suffering by forming a habit of dwelling on other themes, and of turning the mind entirely from those obligations, which, when contemplated, would upbraid and pain them. Thus, too, the sense of shame is lost. A habit is formed of leading the mind from whatever pains it, to dwell on more pleasurable contemplations.

The habits of life are all formed either from the desire to secure happiness or to avoid pain, and the *fear of suffering* is found to be a much more powerful principle than the *desire of happiness.* The soul flies from pain with all its energies, even when it will be inert at the sight of promised joy. As an illustration of this, let a person be fully convinced that the gift of two new senses would confer as great an additional amount of enjoyment as is now secured by the eye and ear, and the promise of this future good would not stimulate with half the energy that would be caused by the threat of instant and entire blindness and deafness.

If, then, the mind is stimulated to form good habits and to avoid the formation of evil ones most powerfully by the activity of *painful* emotions, if they are called into exercise, and their legitimate object is not effected in producing such good habits or in removing bad ones, by the very constitution of mind they must continually decrease in vividness, and so the hope of good to one who thus resists them must continually diminish. If a man is placed in circumstances of danger, and fear leads to the formation of habits of caution and carefulness, the object of exciting this emotion is accomplished, and the diminution of the emotion is attended with no evil. But if fear is continually excited and no such habits are formed, then the susceptibility is lessened, while the good to be secured by it is lost. Thus also with emotions of sympathy. If we witness pain and suffering, and it leads to the formation of habits of active devotion to the good of those who suffer, the diminution of the suceptibility is a blessing and no evil. But if we simply indulge emotion, and do not form the habits they were intended to secure, the power of sympathy is weakened, and the benefit to be secured by it is lost. Thus again with shame. If this painful emotion does not lead us to form habits of honour and rectitude, it is continually weakened by repetition, and the object for which it was bestowed is not secured. And thus also with remorse. If this emotion is awakened without leading to the formation of habits of benevolence and virtue, it constantly decays in power, and the good it would have secured is for ever lost.

It does not appear, however, that the power of emotion in the soul, is thus *destroyed*. Nothing is done but to form habits of inattention to painful emotions, by allowing the mind to be engrossed in other and more pleasurable subjects. This appears from the fact that the most hardened culprits, when brought to the hour of death, where all plans of future good cease to charm the mental eye, are often overwhelmed with the most vivid emotions of sorrow, shame, remorse, and fear. And often in the course of life there are seasons when the soul returns from its pursuit of deluding visions, to commune with itself in its own secret chambers. At such seasons, shame, remorse, and fear, take up their abode in their long-banished dwelling, and ply their scorpion whips, till they are obeyed, and the course of honour and virtue is resumed; or till the distracted spirit again flies abroad for comfort and relief.

This peculiarity of our mental character leads to the most anxious and painful reflections. Does every act of indolence, selfishness, pride, envy, and revenge, lead to the formation of one of these powerful fetters, these habits of crime so easily formed and so difficult to break? Does the resistance of the admonitions of fear, shame, and conscience, tend to form another terrible habit which removes the most powerful restraints of guilt? Is every act of meekness, self-denial, justice, magnanimity, and obedience necessary, not only to immediate rectitude and peace, but necessary as a golden link in the bright chain of some habit indispensable to our happiness? Is the soul so constituted that its susceptibilities can never be destroyed? Is there an hour coming when all the illusions of life will cease, and the soul must return to commune with itself, and understand and feel all its iron chains of guilt and miserable captivity? What terrific anticipations for a mind estranged from the only foundation of safety and of hope, the favour and guidance of Him who formed the undying spirit, and who offers, when sought, to guide it aright; but who, when forsaken, can never afford His almighty aid!

HARRIET BEECHER STOWE.

Harriet Elizabeth Beecher is the daughter of Rev. Lyman Beecher D. D., and seems to have inherited much of the splendid talents of her father. She was born at Litchfield, Connecticut, June 15, 1812. She went to Cincinnati with her father's family in the autumn of 1832. In the winter of 1836 she was married to Professor Calvin E. Stowe, of the Theological Seminary of that place. In 1850 Professor Stowe accepted a professorship in Bowdoin College, Brunswick, Maine, where the family resided for one or two years, when he was transferred to a chair in the Theological Seminary, at Andover, Massachusetts.

Mrs. Stowe's writings are found principally in the various literary and religious periodicals of the country, and in a volume of tales, called "The Mayflower," published in 1843. She has not written so much as some of our female authors, but what she has written has left a profound impression. She is remarkable for the qualities of force and clearness. Few readers can resist the current of her argument, and none can mistake her meaning. She possesses also a great fund of wit, and a delicate play of fancy not inferior to our most imaginative writers.

The foregoing paragraphs were published in 1851, the year before the appearance of Mrs. Stowe's great work. In revising our article for the present edition (1854), we have concluded to let the verdict stand unaltered, merely adding, in the briefest possible manner, such remarks as subsequent events seem to call for.

"Uncle Tom's Cabin" was published in March, 1852. Its success was unprecedented in the annals of literature. In less than nine months, the sale had exceeded a million of copies; the author and her publishers had made fortunes out of it; more than thirty rival editions of it had been published in London alone, besides numerous other editions in different parts of Scotland and Ireland; it was translated into every living language that possessed a popular literature; and Harriet Beecher Stowe, before comparatively unknown even in her own country, became as familiar a name in every part of the civilized world, as Homer or Shakespeare.

It is absurd to attribute such extraordinary success to the abolition character of the book. This feature of the work has probably repelled quite as many readers as it has attracted. The anti-slavery sentiment, obtruded by the author in her own person, is the greatest blemish of the book as a work of art. It is an undoubted proof of the extraordinary skill of the author in other respects, that she has been able so completely to fascinate millions of readers, to whom her anti-slavery opinions have been utterly offensive. The whole secret of the matter simply is, Mrs. Stowe is a woman of genius, and her book is one of consummate skill. No living writer equals her in abilities as a mere story-teller, seizing the reader's attention, as she does, on the very first page, and holding it captive, without any let-up to the very last. Her delineations of character are perfectly life-like. Even those personages that are introduced incidentally in a single scene, stand out clear and distinct upon the canvass, like the charcoal sketches in the contours of a great master. Of her dramatic power—generally considered the highest walk of genius—it is superfluous to speak, when hundreds of theatres have been kept thronged for months in succession, by the exhibition of her story even in the crude form given to it by some bungling playwright. Her mastery of pathos is apparently unbounded. The springs of emotion are touched at will; the heart throbs, the eyes swim, without a moment's notice, and without any apparent effort or preparation on the part of the writer.

Blackwood, in an article of more than thirty pages, devoted to the examination of the literary merits of "Uncle Tom's Cabin," viewing it solely as a work of art, and apart entirely from the social and political questions which it suggests, thus sums up its opinion of the author.

"Mrs. Stowe is unquestionably a woman of GENIUS; and that is a word which we always use charily: regarding genius as a thing *per se*—different from talent, in its highest development, altogether, and in kind. Quickness, shrewdness, energy, intensity, may, and frequently do accompany, but do not constitute genius. Its divine spark is the direct and special gift of God: we cannot completely analyze it, though we may detect its presence, and the nature of many of its attributes, by its action; and the skill of high criticism is requisite, in order to distinguish between the feats of genius and the operation of talent. Now, we imagine that no person of genius can read *Uncle Tom's Cabin*, and not feel in glowing contact with genius—generally gentle and tender, but capable of rising, with its theme, into very high regions of dramatic power. This Mrs. Stowe has done several times in the work before us—exhibiting a passion, an intensity, a subtle delicacy of perception, a melting tenderness, which are as far out of the reach of mere talent, however well trained and experienced, as the prismatic colours are out of the reach of the born blind.

But the genius of Mrs. Stowe is of that kind which instinctively addresses itself to the affections; and though most at home with the gentler, it can be yet fearlessly familiar with the fiercest passions which can agitate and rend the human breast. With the one she can exhibit an exquisite tenderness and sympathy; watching the other, however, with stern but calm scrutiny, and delineating both with a truth and simplicity, in the one case touching, in the other really *terrible*."

In 1853, "Uncle Tom" being then in the very acme of his renown, the author visited England, and several countries of Europe. The enthusiasm of her reception abroad is still too fresh upon the minds of all to need repetition. In the British Isles, particularly, it was a regular ovation. Since her return, she has prepared and published a book of travels, called "Sunny Memories of Foreign Lands," now just from the press. It is in two volumes, 12mo., and is having a rapid sale. These volumes are very unequal in style and execution. Parts of them are devoted to the exposition of the various religious and philanthropic institutions of Great Britain. These are of course plain and practial, as they should be. But in those parts, as in the visits to Melrose Abbey, to Abbotsford, to Stratford-upon-Avon, to Warwick Castle, and to various other places and persons of historical renown, the imaginative temperament of the author has had free play, and she has written in a manner not surpassed by anything in "Uncle Tom." One would have supposed it impossible to write with such freeness on such hackneyed topics. The incidental remarks, interspersed here and there in the midst of her narrative, contain some of the finest specimens of aesthetic criticism to be found anywhere. What she says, for instance of Shakspeare, and of Gothic architecture, as exhibited in the various cathedrals which she visited, is in the very highest style of criticism. These criticisms, oftentimes profound as they are brilliant, seem to gush forth in the simplest and most natural manner, as if from an overflowing fountain, giving an indescribable charm to the parts of her book in which they occur.

THE TEA ROSE.

THERE it stood, in its little green vase, on a light ebony stand, in the window of the drawing-room. The rich satin curtains, with their costly fringes, swept down on either side of it, and around it glittered every rare and fanciful trifle which wealth can offer to luxury, and yet that simple rose was the fairest of them all. So pure it looked, its white leaves just touched with that delicious creamy tint peculiar to its kind: its cup so full, so perfect; its head bending as if it were sinking and melting away in its own richness—oh! when did ever man make anything to equal the living, perfect flower!

But the sunlight that streamed through the window revealed something fairer than the rose. Reclined on an ottoman, in a deep recess, and intently engaged with a book, rested what seemed the counterpart of that so lovely flower. That cheek so pale, that fair forehead so spiritual, that countenance so full of high thought, those long, downcast lashes, and the expression of the beautiful mouth, sorrowful, yet subdued and sweet—it seemed like the picture of a dream.

"Florence! Florence!" echoed a merry and musical voice, in a sweet, impatient tone. Turn your head, reader, and you will see a light and sparkling maiden, the very model of some little wilful elf, born of mischief and motion, with a dancing eye, a foot that scarcely seems to touch the carpet, and a smile so multiplied by dimples that it seems like a thousand smiles at once. "Come, Florence, I say," said the little sprite, "put down that wise, good, and excellent volume, and descend from your cloud, and talk with a poor little mortal."

The fair apparition, thus adjured, obeyed; and, looking up, revealed just such eyes as you expected to see beneath such lids—eyes deep, pathetic, and rich as a strain of sad music.

"I say, cousin," said the "light ladye," "I have been thinking what you are to do with your pet rose when you go to New York, as, to our consternation, you are determined to do; you know it would be a sad pity to leave it with such a scatterbrain as I am. I do love flowers, that is a fact; that is, I like a regular bouquet, cut off and tied up, to carry to a party; but as to all this tending and fussing, which is needful to keep them growing, I have no gifts in that line."

"Make yourself easy as to that, Kate," said Florence, with a smile; "I have no intention of calling upon your talents; I have an asylum in view for my favourite."

"Oh, then you know just what I was going to say. Mrs. Marshall, I presume, has been speaking to you; she was here yesterday, and I was quite pathetic upon the subject, telling her the loss your favourite would sustain, and so forth; and she said how delighted she would be to have it in her green-house, it is in such a fine state now, so full of buds. I told her I knew you would like to give it to her, you are so fond of Mrs. Marshall, you know."

"Now, Kate, I am sorry, but I have otherwise engaged it."

"Who can it be to? you have so few intimates here."

"Oh, it is only one of my odd fancies."

"But do tell me, Florence."

"Well, cousin, you know the pale little girl to whom we give sewing."

"What! little Mary Stephens? How absurd! Florence, this is just another of your motherly, old-maidish ways—dressing dolls for poor children, making bonnets and knitting socks for all the dirty little babies in the region round about. I do believe you have made more calls in those two vile, ill-smelling alleys back of our house, than ever you have in Chestnut street, though you know everybody is half dying to see you; and now, to crown all, you must give this choice little bijou to a sempstress-girl, when one of your most intimate friends, in your own class, would value it so highly. What in the world can people in their circumstances want with flowers?"

"Just the same as I do," replied Florence, calmly. "Have you not noticed that the little girl never comes here without looking wistfully at the opening buds? And, don't you remember, the other morning she asked me so prettily if I would let her mother come and see it, she was so fond of flowers?"

"But, Florence, only think of this rare flower standing on a table with ham, eggs, cheese, and flour, and stifled in that close little room where Mrs. Stephens and her daughter manage to wash, iron, cook, and nobody knows what besides."

"Well, Kate, and if I were obliged to live in one coarse room, and wash, and iron, and cook, as you say—if I had to spend every moment of my time in toil, with no prospect from my window but a brick wall and dirty lane, such a flower as this would be untold enjoyment to me."

"Pshaw! Florence—all sentiment: poor people have no time to be sentimental. Besides, I don't believe it will grow with them; it is a greenhouse flower, and used to delicate living."

"Oh, as to that, a flower never inquires whether its owner is rich or poor; and Mrs. Stephens, whatever else she has not, has sunshine of as good quality as this that streams through our window. The beautiful things that God makes are his gift to all alike. You will see that my fair rose will be as well and cheerful in Mrs. Stephens's room as in ours."

"Well, after all, how odd! When one gives to poor people, one wants to give them something *useful*—a bushel of potatoes, a ham, and such things."

"Why, certainly, potatoes and ham must be supplied; but, having ministered to the first and most craving wants, why not add any other little pleasures or gratifications we may have it in our power to bestow? I know there are many of the poor who have fine feeling and a keen sense of the beautiful, which rusts out and dies because they are too hard pressed to procure it any gratification. Poor Mrs. Stephens, for example: I know she would enjoy birds, and flowers, and music, as much as I do. I have seen her eye light up as she looked on these things in our drawing-room, and yet not one beautiful thing can she command. From necessity, her room, her clothing, all she has, must be coarse and plain. You should have seen the almost rapture she and Mary felt when I offered them my rose."

"Dear me! all this may be true, but I never thought of it before. I never thought that these hard-working people had any ideas of *taste!*"

"Then why do you see the geranium or rose so carefully nursed in the old cracked teapot in the poorest room, or the morning-glory planted in a box and twined about the window. Do not these show that the human heart yearns for the beautiful in all ranks of life? You remember, Kate, how our washerwoman sat up a whole night, after a hard day's work, to make her first baby a pretty dress to be baptized in."

"Yes, and I remember how I laughed at you for making such a tasteful little cap for it."

"Well, Katy, I think the look of perfect delight with which the poor mother regarded her baby in its new dress and cap, was something quite worth creating; I do believe she could not have felt more grateful if I had sent her a barrel of flour."

"Well, I never thought before of giving anything to the poor but what they really needed, and I have always been willing to do that when I could without going far out of my way."

"Well, cousin, if our heavenly Father gave to us after this mode, we should have only coarse, shapeless piles of provisions lying about the world, instead of all this beautiful variety of trees, and fruits, and flowers."

"Well, well, cousin, I suppose you are right—but have mercy on my poor head; it is too small to hold so many new ideas all at once—so go on your own way." And the little lady began practising a waltzing step before the glass with great satisfaction.

It was a very small room, lighted by only one window. There was no carpet on the floor; there was a clean, but coarsely-covered bed in one corner; a cupboard, with a few dishes and plates, in the other; a chest of drawers; and before the window stood a small cherry stand, quite new, and, indeed, it was the only article in the room that seemed so.

A pale, sickly-looking woman of about forty was leaning back in her rocking-chair, her eyes closed and her lips compressed as if in pain. She rocked backward and forward a few minutes, pressed her hand hard upon her eyes, and then languidly resumed her fine stitching, on which she had been busy since morning. The door opened, and a slender little girl of about twelve years of age entered, her large blue eyes dilated and radiant with delight as she bore in the vase with the rose-tree in it.

"Oh! see, mother, see! Here is one in full bloom, and two more half out, and ever so many more pretty buds peeping out of the green leaves."

The poor woman's face brightened as she looked, first on the rose and then on her sickly child, on whose face she had not seen so bright a colour for months.

"God bless her!" she exclaimed, unconsciously.

"Miss Florence—yes, I knew you would feel so, mother. Does it not make your head feel better to see such a beautiful flower? Now you will not look so longingly at the flowers in the market, for we have a rose that is handsomer than any of them. Why, it seems to me it is worth as much to us as our whole little garden used to be. Only see how many buds there are! Just count them, and only smell the flower! Now where shall we set it up?" And Mary skipped about, placing her flower first in one position and then in another, and walking off to see the effect, till her mother gently reminded her that the rose-tree could not preserve its beauty without sunlight.

"Oh yes, truly," said Mary; "well, then, it must stand here on our new stand. How glad I am that we have such a handsome new stand for it; it will look so much better." And Mrs. Stephens laid down her work, and folded a piece of newspaper, on which the treasure was duly deposited.

"There," said Mary, watching the arrangement eagerly, "that will do—no, for it does not show both the opening buds; a little farther around—a little more; there, that is right;" and then Mary walked around to view the rose in various positions, after which she urged her mother to go with her to the outside, and see how it looked there. "How kind it was in Miss Florence to think of giving this to us!" said Mary; "though she had done so much for us, and given us so many things, yet this seems the best of all, because it seems as if she thought of us, and knew just how we felt; and so few do that, you know, mother."

What a bright afternoon that little gift made in that little room! How much faster Mary's fingers flew the livelong day as she sat sewing by her mother; and Mrs. Stephens, in the happiness of her child, almost forgot that she had a headache, and thought, as she sipped her evening cup of tea, that she felt stronger than she had done for some time.

That rose! its sweet influence died not with the first day. Through all the long cold winter, the watching, tending, cherishing of that flower awakened a thousand pleasant trains of thought, that beguiled the sameness and weariness of their life. Every day the fair, growing thing put forth some fresh beauty—a leaf, a bud, a new shoot, and constantly awakened fresh enjoyment in its possessors. As it stood in the window, the passer-by would sometimes stop and gaze, attracted by its beauty, and then proud and happy was Mary; nor did even the serious and careworn widow notice with indifference this tribute to the beauty of their favourite.

But little did Florence think, when she bestowed the gift, that there twined about it an invisible thread that reached far and brightly into the web of her destiny.

One cold afternoon in early spring, a tall and graceful gentleman called at the lowly room to pay for the making of some linen by the inmates. He was a stranger and wayfarer, recommended through the charity of some of Mrs. Stephens's patrons. As he turned to go, his eye rested admiringly on the rose-tree, and he stopped to gaze at it.

"How beautiful!" said he.

"Yes," said little Mary, "and it was given to us by a lady as sweet and beautiful as that is."

"Ah!" said the stranger, turning upon her a pair of bright dark eyes, pleased and rather struck by the communication; "and how came she to give it to you, my little girl?"

"Oh, because we are poor, and mother is sick, and we never can have anything pretty. We used to have a garden once, and we loved flowers so much, and Miss Florence found it out, and so she gave us this."

"Florence!" echoed the stranger.

"Yes—Miss Florence l'Estrange—a beautiful lady. They say

she was from foreign parts; but she speaks English just like other ladies, only sweeter."

"Is she here now? Is she in this city?" said the gentleman, eagerly.

"No; she left some months ago," said the widow, noticing the shade of disappointment on his face; "but," said she, "you can find out all about her at her aunt's, Mrs. Carlysle's, No. 10 —— street."

A short time after, Florence received a letter in a handwriting that made her tremble. During the many early years of her life spent in France, she had well learned to know that writing—had loved as a woman like her loves only once; but there had been obstacles of parents and friends, long separation, long suspense, till, after anxious years, she had believed the ocean had closed over that hand and heart; and it was this that had touched with such pensive sorrow the lines in her lovely face.

But this letter told that he was living,—that he had traced her, even as a hidden streamlet may be traced, by the freshness, the verdure of heart, which her deeds of kindness had left wherever she had passed.

Thus much said, my readers need no help in finishing the story for themselves.

SARA H. BROWNE.

SARA HALL BROWNE, the subject of this sketch, was born in Sunderland, Massachusetts, during one of those calamitous periods which not unfrequently interrupt the prosperity of families, where the husband and father is engaged in the mercantile profession. A series of misfortunes and losses had reduced her parents, at the time of her birth, to circumstances of difficulty and embarrassment, which ultimately led to the abandonment of trade for the safer and surer pursuit of agriculture. With this design they removed to Hyde Hillside, a pleasant maternal estate in the retired town of Templeton, Massachusetts, which has ever since been the family residence.

A very quiet place is the Hillside; beautiful and picturesque in its environments. Sequestered like a nest among the hills, it is a sweet, wild, rural abode, every way fitted to be a child's paradise, and the nursery and school of that species of genius which feasts on natural beauty and unfolds most successfully in solitude.

Hyde Hillside is, some might affirm, a very lonely abode, on the southern slope of a rocky hill, yet surrounded by scenery of remarkable beauty. On the east, the descent is quite abrupt for a few hundred yards to a beautiful expanse of water, partly lying in the shadow of dark pine woods, and again spread out in the sunshine, sparkling like a lake of molten diamonds. Another hill rises from this watery interval, with a smooth and gradual ascent, for a mile or two, on the summit of which stands the pleasant village of Templeton, in full view, with its trees, its church spires, and its white dwellings.

Mount Monadnock rises, hoary and cloud-capped, to the north, while on the south and west the prospect is bounded by hill and woodland.

The venerable ancestral mansion is a large commodious dwelling, which has offered the hospitalities of nearly a century to friend and stranger.

In this rural retreat was passed Miss Browne's childhood; here was she instructed by an excellent mother in all those domestic virtues which are appropriate to the female character, in all stations and circumstances; here were laid the foundations of every valuable attainment which after years may have more fully developed; here dawned those aspirations, which, kindled by the fire of inborn genius, quickened and expanded by judicious parental encouragement, have borne her ever onward in a career certainly not after the ordinary level of common workday life, and which promises to give her a still widening sphere of influence and usefulness.

By the aid of advanced preparation in the home school-room, and the practice of rigorous economy—for her pecuniary resources were by no means abundant—Miss Browne was able to complete an extensive course of study, in one of our best female seminaries, in 1841. For a short time subsequently she engaged in teaching, but a severe and protracted bronchial affection ultimately prohibited effort in that department of congenial labour.

In 1846 occurred her first great sorrow, in the death of a father whose moral and intellectual worth and experience were always a safe anchorage for the doubts and difficulties of children who ever had occasion to rise up and call him blessed, alike for the prudent and judicious policy exercised in their mental training and direction, as for those lessons of piety and benevolence which he was faithful to instil and to exemplify.

Within the last few years Miss Browne has devoted herself mainly to the literary profession, both as a means of giving scope to her inclinations and tastes, and of gaining an independent livelihood. Having encountered trials and overcome difficulties which would have daunted a less courageous heart, she seems particularly prepared to contend in that race in which mind measures with mind, and ultimately to put on the laurels which belong to the victor.

Though yet at the very commencement of her literary career, Miss Browne has won very unequivocal favour both as a vigorous painter of illustrative fiction and a teacher of religious truth.

Her prose is characterized by a very marked originality, force, and point. The moral she invariably inculcates is always apparent in its meaning and strong in its application. The characters she delineates are clearly individualized, and usually contrasted finely with one another, while a tendency to, and keen relish of, the humorous is distinctly perceptible. She unfolds truthfully and happily the workings of the purest and tenderest human sensibilities, yet her style never verges towards sentimentalism, and the entire survey of her published writings would not furnish a single sickly feature, or a single example which would lay her open to the charge of moral cowardice. Light and shadow, joy and sorrow, tears and laughter, tragedy and comedy, follow in the wake of her versatile pen.

As a religious writer, no one can mistake the earnest loving warmth of the Christian heart. Baptized into the spirit of that piety she commends to others, especially to the young, her success in this department of letters has been truly encouraging. Her "Book for the Eldest Daughter," has had and will continue to have a wide circulation; and she has received from time to time most grateful assurances of its popularity and usefulness. It is indeed a felicitous compound of physical, intellectual, moral, and religious instruction, given in a clear, affectionate, attractive style, which falls on the young ear and heart like those sweet "mother tones" which irresistibly constrain to the path of virtue and holiness.

As a poetess, Miss Browne is not remarkably prolific; she writes deliberately and cautiously, rather than abundantly. She is a poetic sculptor rather than painter—patient to chisel into perfect harmony and proportion, the outline and lineaments of every image whose glowing ideal adorns the inner chambers of her imagination.

A list of Miss Browne's publications is given in the subjoined note.

For Sartain's Union Magazine, Miss Browne has furnished various articles of prose and poety, viz.: In 1849, a "Salutation to Fredrika Bremer;" "Waters of Marah," (poem); in 1850, "The Goblet of Revenge," (poem); "Song of the Winter Serenaders," (poem); "Death Bed of Schiller;" in 1851, "The Token of Hope," (poem); "Sing to me," (poem). For the Dollar Newspaper, Philadelphia—1847, a prose tale, "Reforming a Husband;" in 1848, "Fretting for a Secret;" "Prescribed by a Physician;" in 1849, "Maying in December;" in 1850, "The Iron Grays." For the Boston Rambler and National Library, Boston—1847, "Capt. Gage's Cousins;" "The First Falsehood;" "The Pauper Bride;" in 1848, "Things Old," Nos. I. II. III; in 1849, "Mary Stuart's last Pageant," (poem); "The Two Homes;" "The Snow Buried," (poem). For the American Cabinet and Atheneum—1848, "One Among a Thousand;" "John Quincy Adams," (poem); in 1849, "Mendelssohn's last Composition," (poem); "The First Crime," (poem); in 1850, "Mode and Tense." For the Lady's Book several poems: 1845, "Last of the Asmonians," (poem); in 1843, "The Unknown Flower," (poem); in 1847, "Madame Roland," (poem); "The Wife's Dowry," (poem); in 1845, "The Costliest Gift," (poem). Besides a great many other fugitive articles of both prose and poetry for various magazines, papers, and annuals. In 1847, her first volume was published, entitled "My Early Friends;" 1849, "Book for the Eldest Daughter," a work of between two and three hundred pages; 1850, "Recollections of my Sabbath School Teachers," besides others now in press, and a volume of poems in course of preparation.

A SALUTATION TO FREDRIKA BREMER.

When America bids you welcome, sweet Lady of the Norseland, it is not as a stranger. With the lineaments of your countenance, to be sure, she cannot assert familiarity, but then how small a portion of one's individuality is the face! Useful indeed it is to its possessor, and pleasant to look upon as the medium of noble, or gentle, or playful emotions; but ah! how much may be learned of a human being with no knowledge of the physical outline! The soul can speak with a voice so clear and far-resounding that "nations, and tongues, and people," catch the strain and echo it from heart to heart till the speaker is lost in what she has spoken! Thus is it, Lady of the Norseland, between you and America, when she takes you by the hand to greet your first footstep on the soil.

The great, the rich, the titled sometimes come from the Fatherland to view our cities, our forests, our lakes, our foaming cataracts, our lofty mountains, our interminable caverns. The splendour of their retinue and appointments dazzles the eye as they dash from object to object. They stare at this, wonder at that, dance a few measures at somebody's fancy ball, dine with a bevy of our millionaires, shake hands with their wives and daughters, and are off in the next steamer to write a book of travels! And it is well thought of, this book of travels; for it reminds the American reader of what he had otherwise speedily forgotten, viz., that the author has actually been and gone! Few heard of him before he came—few saw him—few cared to recollect him when he had taken leave, and, save a smile or two awakened by the book of travels, he is altogether as though he were not. Such travellers must ever be strangers—when they come, and while they tarry, and when they depart. No bosom swells joyfully at the mention of their names, if indeed they are mentioned out of the small circle which has been in personal contact. They have done nothing, said nothing, attempted nothing which deserves daguerreotyping in a nation's memory, how lofty soever their station, how noble their descent; and they must be content with the tribute of forgetfulness!

But when Fredrika Bremer declares her resolution to cross the world of waves which roll between us and the Norseland, and the papers, circulating in the huts and hamlets all over our broad land, echo that intention, an emotion of a different kind is stirred, and thousands of glad young voices from the cabin as well as from the villa, exclaim, "Welcome to her!" There is no need to explain who she is, or whence she comes—there is not a hamlet in all the land where the question could not be intelligently answered, accompanied with a hearty "God bless her!"

What has made the difference between them? between these scores of gay, and proud, and rich, and great, who move among us like meteors from time to time, and this one woman, whose soft and steady starlight has reached us long before the path of her orbit had brought her hitherward, to shine brighter and brighter unto the perfect day?

He has made it, Lady of the Norseland, who anointed you high priestess of the affections in their truest and purest exercise! He, who inspired your pen to consecrate and sanctify the Home! He, who constrained you to pour out from its full fountain such rills and rivers of Love and Concord, of Peace and Hope, and every element of the better life!

Then come among us, and be sure of a benediction. Come to our cots as well as to our palaces—to our wild woods as well as to our gardens—to our hearts as well as to our hearths, and you shall find that we too have our "Homes," our "Brothers and Sisters," our "Neighbours," our Lares and Penates, with their shrines and vestals, our loves and lovers, our jealousies and fears, as well as all gentler and lovelier emotions. Come and see.

From the class which the writer of these lines would represent, a welcome especially sincere and warm will everywhere await you. Homes like hers you have entered again and again with a soft and soothing tread—communicating a peace and joy, a contentedness with life and labour and care—a knowledge that others have borne our burdens of grief and disappointment, have wept our tears and endured our agonies, have cherished our hopes and aimed at our mark; impressing too a conviction that others will yet find strength and courage, faith and fruition, from balmy words welling up from a loving heart, and dropping like diamonds from sweet sympathizing lips! Lone dwellers with nature are we—afar from tower and town, from noise and bustle and business; with forest and lake, hill and village for our wild landscape, with needle and books, music and flowers for society, through the long winter without a "Midnight Sun." Lights that have burned around the hearthstone have been here and there put out. A silvery head has lately gone from its "old arm-chair" to heaven. Alas! alas! in what Home will you not find one ever vacant chair? Hedvig too has gone, to make a heaven in a newly consecrated household; and sometimes we, the small remnant, repine for a little while, but anon, we are cheered, for we look joyfully onward and aloft, awaiting a sure reunion day; and sweet words, which your dear pen has traced, teach us lessons of Life, of inner, deeper, spiritual Life, whose peace and repose, like a broad still river, sweeps along until it is lost in the ocean depths of Eternity and God!

Yes, you have made blessed such homes as ours. Come to them, and make them lighter and lovelier, by starting an echo of your own human voice, and a reflection of your own human smile, and we will love you better—and for ever!

MARIA J. B. BROWNE.

MARIA JANE BANCROFT BROWNE is a native of the beautiful town of Northampton, Mass. In her early childhood, however, her parents removed from that place to the retired inland town of Templeton, Mass., which has since been her home.

Miss Browne's parents belonged to that judicious class, who, while their pecuniary means were restricted, considered the acquisition of a liberal education by their children of vastly more value than the inheritance of that wealth which so proverbially spreads its pinions and flies away, or, what is worse, enchains the energies to frivolity and indolence. To facilitate so desirable an object, these excellent parents did what they could. They had already transmitted to their daughters their own characteristics of energy, resolution, and perseverance, and having removed obstacles out of the way, they left those qualities, under the sunshine of encouraging words and smiles, to their own irrepressible expansiveness and eventual success. Thrown thus mainly on their own resources, Miss Browne and her two elder sisters succeeded in completing an extensive course of study, and were graduated with distinction at the Mount Holyoke Seminary in 1841. Since that time Miss Browne has devoted herself principally to the instruction and training of young ladies in the various departments of moral, intellectual, and physical culture; a profession for which, by the structure of her own mind, and the nature of her acquirements, she is very happily adapted.

Her tastes, however,—the bent of those tastes having unfolded itself in very early life,—incline her to the pursuit of letters. Endowed with a vigorous and varied imagination, gifted with clear, quick, and discriminating perceptions, which penetrate beneath the surface of things for principles and conclusions; with eye, and ear, and heart, alive to all that is lovely and truthful in nature, art, and the peculiar province of intellect—possessing a wide humanity which earnestly labours for, and expects moral renovation to follow the wheels of progress; possessing also the courage and the skill to hold the mirror before the face of folly, and to paint the silly lineaments of its deformity; we scarcely need wonder at the tendency of her mind to this species of labour, in a "field which is the world."

Miss Browne's literary career is however, comparatively, but just begun. The efforts of her pen have been very favourably received by the public, and these tones of kindness and welcome from the popular voice, encourage the hope that hers has not been an adventurous launch amidst the shoals and breakers of authorship.

Miss Browne's style of writing contains many popular elements as well as intrinsic beauties. In portraying the incidents of actual life, in depicting scenes of familiar occurrence in the family or the neighbourhood, she has few equals, and no superiors. That sterling common sense which strips off the mask of frivolity and conventionalism, which falls with withering and mortifying weight upon false pretensions, which holds up to derision and contempt those hollow and heartless principles and practices, which obtain in so-called "fashionable" society, lends a peculiar charm of satisfaction to the perusal of her tales. Of these qualities her "Town and Country," "Marrying for the Parish," and "Looking up in the World," furnish eminent examples. No one can rise from the perusal of these excellent life-pictures, having fairly imbibed their spirit and meaning, without a thrill of gratification at the well-ordered finale, and its admirable point and truthfulness.

She is playful, pathetic, serious, earnest, full of life and intensity, never prosaic, never tedious, never common-place, deeply imbued with the religious, largely read in that school of sensibility which enables her to sympathize with all forms of human sorrow and suffering; her writings, consequently, find their way directly to the heart and bosom of the reader. In argument, she is clear, persuasive, and convincing; in satire, keen, and cutting, and a remarkable coherency and unity runs through the whole, so as to make it a difficult thing to isolate a passage in any given article, on which something antecedent or subsequent does not materially depend; every passage is linked with its neighbour so necessarily and appropriately, that an extractor finds his task a perplexing one. Harmony and felicity of diction is another invariable attribute of Miss Browne's style of composition. Her command of language is so affluent, that it sometimes insensibly leads her into a redundancy of epithet tending toward the superlative; but the finished elegance of her periods compensates amply for this defect, which time and experience will eradicate.

In Miss Browne's religious writings appears an element of depth and fervour which has made them decided favourites with the serious and devout. Her little volumes for the young are replete with pathos, tenderness, and truthfulness, conveying lessons of piety and virtue in a manner peculiarly calculated to impress the heart and conscience. In all there is something so obviously instructive, so high-toned a morality, so transparent a purity, so heartfelt a Christianity, which never once condescends to utter a low thought, an equivocal idea, or an objectionable word, that they are eminently proper to place in the hands of children and youth by the most careful parent, which is, perhaps, the truest compliment which can be paid to a popular writer.

Miss Browne has furnished for Sartain's Union Magazine, to which she is an engaged contributor, the following articles: April, 1849—"Marrying for the Parish;" October and November, 1849—"The Ace of Hearts," Parts I. and II.; November, 1850—"Looking Up in the World;" July, 1851—"The Rabbit on the Wall." For Graham's Magazine, Philadelphia: February, 1849—"Lessons in German;" September, 1849—"Jessie Lincoln, or The City Visiters." For the Dollar Magazine, New York: November, 1849—"Going into Winter Quarters;" February, 1850—"Condescending to Marry." For the Ladies' Magazine, Boston: November, 1846—"Precept and Example;" February, March, and April, 1847—"Choosing how to Die," Parts I., II., III., IV.; October, 1847—"Not Wealth, but Worth;" November, 1847—"The Disappointed Husband;" March, April, May, June, 1848—"Self-Conquest;" February, 1849—"En Dishabille, a Story for Young Wives." For the Dollar Newspaper, Philadelphia: July, 1848—"Town and Country;" August, 1849—"Reversed Decision;" November, 1849—"Thanksgiving Carols;" February, 1850—"The One-Horned Dilemma." For the New York Organ: March, 1850—"The Misadventure;" July, 1850—"The Bachelor's Criticisms;" July, 1851—"The Promise and the Pledge."

Several other fugitive sketches have appeared, from Miss Browne's pen, through various channels: "The Fatal Jest," "The Bride of the Buccaneer," "Elizabeth Falconer," "Love and Policy," &c. The religious press has also brought out a variety of articles from the same source, and three small volumes for the young: 1848—"Margaret McDonald, or The True Sister;" 1849—"Story of a Western Sabbath School;" 1850—"Laura Huntley;" 1850—"The Youth's Sketch Book" (of which Miss Browne and her sisters are joint authoresses). The "Snow Flake," an annual for 1851, has also an article entitled "The Contrast," of 18 pages.

LOOKING UP IN THE WORLD.

Something must be done to escape from the inevitable disgrace and odium of labouring at such a disgraceful and odious business as shoemaking. James Skates should not be a shoemaker any longer, nor Katy a shoemaker's wife! "O yes, to be sure, something must be done," said Cousin Sophronia, "it was a shame they were not getting above their neighbours, and looking up in the world, when Katy had natural abilities to make so much of an appearance, and cut such a dash in the city. Mr. Skates must be persuaded; and she guessed between them, they could manage it, as he was not the readiest with arguments or decision, in matters where the odds of logic were so decidedly on the other side. Yes, Skates must be brushed up, and persuaded to go to the city with his family, board them at a hotel or boarding-house, and then engage himself in some employment which would furnish spending money—money was to be made so easy in the city. And then it would be so much more *respectable* than to burrow in the country, where one never was heard of, and *shoemake* for a living! She herself would introduce them into the 'first society,' and bestow favours of that important kind upon them in such profusion, a lifetime would not be long enough to cancel the debt of gratitude they would owe her!"

Katy and Sophronia "cut and dried" the whole affair, while Sophronia sat in the rocking-chair with her mits on, and fanned herself; and Katy ran about as if she had been put upon an extra pair of springs in every limb, to wait upon her. When it was all ready and propped up on all sides with invincible arguments, Mr. Skates was cautiously and warily "towed in," to become the lion in the scheme; while Sophronia and her cousin worked vigorously at the long arm, till all obstacles were finally thrust out of the way. Indeed, such had been the silent effect of Sophronia's "continual dropping" about gentility and respectability, even upon a mind so slowly perceptive, and so absolutely common-place as Mr. Skates's, that the difficulty of gaining him over to their side, was far less formidable than the ambitious cousins had anticipated. To the unconcealed surprise and consternation of all his neighbours and friends, and in the very face of remonstrance, and forebodings of ruin, Mr. Skates did let his house and shop, and consent to emigrate upon uncertainties, to the great city—the great city, which stood out in alto relievo before the vision of his wife, like the veritable Paradise. To his praise, however, be it spoken, it was not without many inward misgivings, and hours of almost tearful reluctance, that he started upon such a wildgoose chase; and if his wife, who was the polestar of his being, though now dangerously out of her true position, had not been on the wing, fluttering up almost out of his sight in the track of her foolish ambition, the peaceful scenes that had always encircled him, and bounded his desires, and the almost irresistible attractions of his pleasant labour, would have won him back from his illusion, and left him a quiet, useful, and valuable citizen.

These arrangements were very suddenly got up, and of course must be executed while at a fever heat, or they would be likely to fail, as Mr. Skates, though his neighbours had never called him "shifty-minded" before, might possibly sicken of the prospective change, and overturn the whole just on the very eve of accomplishment. When Katy was so near the enchanted circle, it would be death to be obliged to withdraw. Sophronia considerately protracted her stay a week longer than she had at first meditated, to mind the children, and do some "light chores," to facilitate the preparations which Mr. and Mrs. Skates were so busy and so animated in making. And when the "things" were nearly all removed from their places, and packed away into the chambers, and all the rooms began to look stripped and melancholy, and there began to be gloomy and ill-omened echoes shooting through the unfurnished apartments—echoes that would croak of desolation, and would sometimes strike like a knell on James's simple heart in spite of himself—in spite of the bustling and gleefulness of his triumphant little wife—in spite of the glare of Cousin Sophronia's fancy paintings, which she took care to hold up before him to the very last moment of her tarrying,—when matters were in such a train, and she had given the unsophisticated aspirants all necessary directions,—quite a catalogue, by the way,—Cousin Sophronia took her departure, and in a few days Mr. and Mrs. Skates were ready to follow.

Mrs. Skates was happy as a queen when they were all seated in the cars going to the city—the city at last!—and when the coach drew up before the splendid entrance of a great castle-like hotel, and the servants came out and overwhelmed them with attentions and services, and conducted them in as if they were indeed the Hon. Captain Somebody and lady, she was quite bewildered with excitement and triumph. "Let my neighbours sneer now if they will," thought Katy, as she tossed her vain little head, and sat down with a mixture of confusion, diffidence, and complacency, in the long, brilliantly illuminated, and magnificent drawing-room. Oh, such a gorgeous carpet, her feet fairly sunk in its plushy softness, as if she had been treading on a bed of fresh moss! Such luxurious furniture!—such dazzling lamps and mirrors! While her bewildered vision was struggling to take in all this grandeur at one grasp, another sense carried in a throb of bitter mortification to her heart.

"Name, sir?" said a servant to her husband, who was standing still with mouth and eyes wide open, looking about him in amazement, trying to collect himself, and to decide whether he was in the body or out of the body, so like an unreal panorama seemed all that was around him to his simplicity. "Name, sir?" politely repeated the servant, his face looking the personation of a subdued chuckle.

"Oh, Squire James and Miss Skates!" replied Mr. Skates very audibly; and then, on second thought, as if something of the most absolute importance had been forgotten, he added, "and the children, too,—put them in."

The servant retreated instantly, and saved himself a hemorrhage, perhaps, by indulging his overcharged mirthfulness, and recorded on the book of arrivals for the morning paper, "—— James, Esq., and Miss Skates."

Now Mr. Skates had been instructed—specifically instructed—to say, when his name was called for at the hotel, "James Skates, Esq., lady and children," but his mind and memory were topsy-turvy with this dashing so suddenly into gentility, and no wonder he could not concentrate his ideas to a proper focus. Mrs. Skates felt badly about it, for she feared the whole city would be misled when they came to read it, and she thought best to have the mistake corrected; but she would consult Cousin Sophronia. By the time she had an opportunity to consult her oracle, however, the unfortunate edition of the paper had gone by, and everybody in the world but themselves had forgotten the announcement, if, indeed, they ever noticed it.

It was already evening when Mr. and Mrs. Skates arrived; Katy was very much excited, and cruelly exhausted—her cheeks burned like a fever, and her arms trembled with fatigue, as she tossed the baby hither and thither to quiet him, and alternately soothed and scolded poor little terrified James. Mr. Skates indicated, as soon as he could collect his recreant faculties, that they would like to engage board "for a spell, and see if they liked;" and the landlord, whose keen eye was so familiarly educated to the mensuration of pretensions, and who could detect at a glance the spurious from the genuine coin, after some demurring and some adroitly directed regrets that his house was so crowded he should not be able to accommodate the gentleman for a few days as well as he could desire, to all of which Mr. Skates obligingly replied "it was just as wal," he ordered a servant to conduct Mr. and Mrs. Skates to No. 150!

Oh what a journey it was, superadded to the day's weariness, to reach No. 150, and through what a labyrinth of endless halls, walled up on both sides by rows of green window-blind-looking doors! and up, up, up what flights and flights of stairs, and round what numbers of corners! Katy felt as if she should drop down, and Mr. Skates, whose good temper outlasted everything, jocosely remarked to his baggage-laden conductor, "Wal, sir, if it's much further, we'll stop in somewhere and rest. I hope when you get us up here you'll be sure to come and show us the way out again!"

Poor Katy was sick enough by the time she reached her room; and as she entered it, her thoughts would revert to her own bedchamber at the cottage home—vastly larger than this little hot "six by eight" enclosure—so pleasantly and commodiously furnished, and commanding a view of such a green and flowing landscape from its windows; here she could see from the one window, she knew not what it was, some great dark object, which gradually developed into the brick wall of a neighbouring building, and that bounded the prospect. But she was too ill to care much that night,—her head ached violently, and spun round with dizziness, and all she could do was just to go to bed, sweltering and fainting, and leave the charge of unrobing and quieting the children to her husband. Mr. Skates thought the undertaking too hopeless to get down stairs and up again alone, so he went without his supper, and bathed Katy's burning forehead, and whistled and hummed the old home lullabys to the children, till all were uneasily slumbering, and then, as the noise in the streets died away, all but the occasional rattle of a vehicle on the pavement, or the echoing tramp of a solitary foot-fall breaking in on the midnight hush of the city, and the lamps one by one flickered and expired, Mr. Skates too, his mind in a whirl, and his purposes and expectations all misty and intangible, composed himself into a restless and half-watchful repose. Even that was broken ever and anon, by a sudden scream from one or both of the children, whose sleep itself was fritted away by the stifling heat of the small, close room, and the excitement and fatigue their own little frames were suffering.

But they all rose quite as vigorous as could reasonably be anticipated, and novelty supplied abundantly the stimulus that otherwise would have been lacking. Mrs. Skates was somewhat faint, and felt some disagreeable visitings of nausea now and then, but she managed with her husband's good offices, in matters pertaining to the toilet, to get herself and the children all ready in full dress for breakfast, some minutes before it was announced. When the terrific notes of the gong—it had a giant voice—were heard pealing and groaning and moaning and growling and howling through the long empty halls, affrighting the very echoes, such a chorus of unaffected terror as issued from the throats of the two young Skateses was appalling! Mr. and Mrs. Skates, too, were startled and alarmed, and thought at first that all the wild beasts in the world were in desperate battle just outside of their own door, and the children shrieked as if every sense were but an inlet to the most excruciating torture. In vain did papa and mamma hush and hug and soothe and threaten after the cause of the alarm was ascertained; every measure weighed light as a feather in the balance with the fright and horror they experienced at the sudden acquaintanceship of this unearthly noise. The poor children refused to be comforted till it was too late for the regular breakfast, so Mr. Skates, lady and children, breakfasted alone.

Cousin Sophronia was good enough to come quite early, and

spend all the morning with Mrs. Skates, congratulating her on having emerged from a living burial in the country, welcoming her to the unutterable delights of a city life, and giving her lessons in gentility, while Mr. Skates went out into the street to look up some kind of "genteel business;" for he was made distinctly to understand, that none other would answer his purpose, though his simple ideas were at the lowest possible ends concerning the boundary lines between a genteel and an ungenteel occupation. But Sophronia assured him that such as he was in pursuit of was "plenty as quails," and he supposed it must be of course, if he had only been sufficiently acquainted in the city to know where to look for it. Everywhere he inquired he was informed by the industrious and laborious business men, that "they did not keep the article," and he came to his hotel from his unsuccessful tour quite discouraged and disheartened. But he was soon called to forget his ill success in obtaining employment, by the necessity of preparation for dinner. Cousin Sophronia had apprised Mrs. Skates that "folks did not dress much for breakfast, but dinner at hotels and fashionable bordin' houses" was a great affair, and conducted with a marvellous display of state and ceremony—that they must be dressed in their very best and gayest clothes, and be on the alert to "see just how other folks did," or coming from the country so fresh, they would be liable to some gross violations of dinner-table etiquette, and the "folks would think so strange of it."

Katy felt less apprehension for her own ability to manage than she did for her husband and children. Mr. Skates was mortally awkward, there was no disputing, and the children would be most likely to do as children always will—behave worst when they are put upon their *best* behaviour—cry when it is indispensable they should be quiet,—seize upon things they should let alone, and sometimes, by the simplest prattle, uncover family secrets it takes the practised ingenuity of parents to conceal—the plain-spoken little wretches!

Mr. Skates was sent to the barber to get himself shaved after the most approved fashion, and then he was trimmed out in his new suit of blue broadcloth, with his fancy silk vest and his new blue and white plaid neckerchief, and his white linen handkerchief shaken out of its neat folds, and stuffed with fashionable carelessness into his coat pocket, by Sophronia's own competent hands. Indeed, he looked very much dressed up, and you would hardly have suspected his occupation but for the peculiar stoop in the shoulders craftsmen of his calling are apt to acquire, and for certain dark-coloured and very incorrigible labour-lines and calluses on his hands, which perseveringly resisted all the influence of soap and sand which could be brought to bear upon them. Honourable labour-lines and calluses they were, too; he was in no danger of losing the good opinion and respect of any whose respect and good opinion were worth preserving, for these; he might be, for suffering himself to be persuaded to blush for them, to be coaxed, and not very reluctantly, into his present apish and incongruous transition!

Katy Skates robed herself in her new changeable silk, flounced and rosetted in the skirt, and decorated about the low neck and short sleeves in the very latest style. Her hair shone and waved and curled deliciously, her eyes sparkled, and her cheeks glowed like roses; and if she had been going to figure at a magnificent entertainment on some great and special occasion, by invitation from an affluent host, she would have looked not only suitably but beautifully habited; for Mrs. Skates was really handsomer in person than many renowned beauties who make considerable sensation in the world. Moreover, to set off her charms still more effectually, Cousin Sophronia—obliging soul!—had been so good as to loan Mrs. Skates a very gay bracelet and brooch, with great glaring, hot-looking purple stones in them, and a chain from which dangled a gold pencil. And when these were all fixed on in their places, and Katy looked in the mirror to see herself, she was sensible of a glow of real admiration, and her little vain heart swelled with pride and satisfaction. I am sorry her pride and satisfaction had no nobler groundwork to base themselves upon!

Mr. Skates, I need not say, admired her too, and could hardly forbear kissing her, as if he were a lover, or she a bride.

The horrible notes of the gong were at length heard grumbling along through the halls. This time the children only turned pale, and clung closer to their parents, with their eyes stretched open, staring wonderingly. Mr. Skates carried the baby, and Mrs. Skates led James and hung on her husband's arm, till, with a crowd that kept swelling all the way from "No. 150" down, they found themselves floating into the spacious dining-hall of the hotel; and somehow, they hardly realized how, they were seated at the table. Everything was new and strange. Mr. Skates innocently stared at the services and ceremonies he could not understand, and Mrs. Skates increased and made manifest her confusion, by trying to appear at ease, and accustomed to it all. The "great towel" laid by his plate Mr. Skates had no use for, with a good white handkerchief in his pocket, so he "doubled it up," and put it behind him, to keep it out of little James's hands.

That hopeful young "scion" opened the table scene by being vastly troublesome. He refused to be seated on his father's knee, and clamoured bravely for his "high chair." Mr. Skates's arguments for some time were of no avail, but at length he succeeded in persuading his small but resolute antagonist that "they did not have high chairs here in the city," and he must either be good, or be sent to No. 150 to stay alone. James surrendered; but as soon as he was fairly settled in his place, and had looked a long inquisitive stare into the faces of the company on the opposite side of the table, he seized a silver fork that lay by his father's plate, and began raking it over his cheeks and his protruded tongue.

"What's this, pa? what's this thing?" he inquired, holding it still more fast, while his father attempted to take it out of his determined grasp.

"You mustn't meddle with it—let it alone, James. It looks some like a spoon!" replied Mr. Skates, forcing it away from the little hand, and laying it down on the cloth. But James, with the children's universal license to misbehave on the most important occasions, instantly took it up again, and began ringing the elegant champagne glass which a servant that moment presented to a gentleman who sat next.

"We han't got no such 'poons to home, have we, pa?" interrogated the youngster.

"Ah, James!" interrupted Mrs. Skates, who had had more than she could do thus far to keep her borrowed finery out of the hands and mouth of the astonished baby, "Ah, James; what did I tell you?"

"You said you should trounce me if I wasn't still," confessed the child, rapping his head with the fork, and making it do the service of a comb in frizzling up his nicely-smoothed hair. But the memory of the threat silenced him for a few minutes, while a fiery-red blush of three-fold mortification, suffused the before glowing cheeks of his exasperated mamma—mortification that her son had exposed his ignorance of the purposes for which silver forks are used—that he should disclose so publicly, and without remorse, the unfortunate and disgraceful fact that he was a stranger to such luxuries at home, and lastly, that he should be so explicit in his delineation of her peculiar mode of family discipline!

But Mrs. Skates's cheeks tingled worse and worse, and her forehead burned hotter and hotter, when she heard her unsophisticated spouse remark to a waiter who handed him a well-filled plate,

"Thank'ee, thank'ee, sir, but you've loaded 'most too heavy of that; I can't eat all this and taste of all them other sorts, too. I see you've got lots back there yet!" Mrs. Skates set her satin slipper hard down on Mr. Skates's boot, under the table, telegraphing that he was guilty of something, he hardly knew what; but it made him silent, and left her to blush and flutter at the impertinent smile she saw running from lip to lip on the other side of the table, —a cruel but very common way of exposing the real vulgarity and grossness of mind which would pass itself for high breeding, and a contempt for what, by a kind of false comparison, appears unrefined or uncultivated in the manners of others.

Little James by this time had recovered from the shock he had experienced from the recollection of what was in store for him, if he "wasn't still," and he found his curiosity was by no means satisfied concerning the new things that were about him. He proceeded with his investigation by seizing a "bill of fare," which the nearest neighbour had just laid down.

"What's this, pa?" he inquired, bringing the smooth, clean paper into contact with his greasy mouth. It was a fixed habit of Master James's this, of introducing everything to the acquaintanceship of his facial orifice, whether said orifice was in receiving order or not.

"I do' know, child; let it alone, and hand it right straight back to the gentleman—it's his'n," replied Mr. Skates, getting not a little impatient at his son's inquisitiveness.

"But what is it, pa?" persisted James, pouting and scowling that the dawning of his curiosity should be so cruelly repressed.

"I do' know, I tell you; it looks like a little newspaper about vittles. Now hold your tongue!" retorted Mr. Skates, as he took the soiled paper out of James's hand, and administered a box on his ear sufficiently expressive to set him snivelling.

This scene of course added to the amusement of the gay young people across the table. They discoursed very audibly about "Jonathans," and "bumpkins," and "country animals," and one young woman, more bold and vulgar-souled and ill-bred than her companions, though her face was royally beautiful, and her voice as soft and sweet as the song of a siren, and her diction, even in rude sarcasm, as polished and musical as the diction of an orator, called quite aloud, "Waiter, do give me that little newspaper about vittles!" Her party joined in the joke with boisterous merriment, and poor Katy, instead of feeling honest contempt, rejoiced that her baby screamed just then, for even an uncomfortable and annoying circumstance relieved the bitter confusion of a consciousness that she and her well-meaning husband were the unfortunate objects of such unprincipled ridicule.

"That's what we call a bill of fare, mum, not a newspaper," replied the waiter, obsequiously, placing the paper in her fair hand.

"Oh, I understand, sir!" retorted the disconcerted beauty, a flush of indignation mounting to her very temples, that a servant should dare to presume her ignorant; "your explanation is unnecessary, quite;" but before she could deliver the rebuke she meditated, the offending waiter was out of hearing on the other side of the hall.

Mrs. Skates now began to hope that her sufferings for this once were at an end, but scarcely was the baby quieted, when James caught hold of the chain that depended from his mother's neck, and inquired with the most provoking innocence, "Whose is this, ma? 'Taint yours, is it? Cousin 'Phrony lent it to you; didn't she, ma?"

"Sh-h-h, James!" fretted Mrs. Skates. I think at that moment she would have enjoyed the "trouncing business" right heartily! It was too vexatious that he should expose what one felt the keenest anxiety to conceal—the fact that she was really glittering in "borrowed plumage!"

"Shall you whip me, ma?" pursued the little wretch, taking alarm from his mother's severe expression, and cowering down in the chair behind his father, where he had been standing; while that uncomfortable and embarrassed worthy was trying to clear his plate of its contents, and at the same time working industriously to keep the perspiration from streaming in rivulets over his face. James managed to entertain himself in his new situation with his own perpetual chatter, and with scratching the chair with his fork, till the meal was finished. Oh, how glad were Mr. and Mrs. Skates when that event happened! Poor Katy felt that her little No. 150 would be an asylum, indeed, she was so thoroughly disconcerted; and Mr. Skates felt that he should never desire to dine again as long as he lived! Visions of his own quiet and social table at the forsaken home danced through his mind with a kind of tantalizing mockery; and then the precious absence of *ceremony* there! Sick, indeed, he was of so much ceremony, that "he didn't know nothing what they meant by!" He would have relished Katy's very poorest "washing-day hash," done up in "pot-skimmings," a thousand times better than those elaborately served viands, and their multitude of French gastronomic accompaniments, and "feel so all shook-up in his mind," as he declared he had done at this first city dinner.

ELIZABETH BOGART.

MISS BOGART has written only a few tales in prose, but they have all been of sterling excellence.

Her first tale, "The Effect of a Single Folly," obtained a prize in the "Memorial," an Annual published in Boston, 1828. It was her first attempt at story writing, and was completed and sent secretly, without being submitted to any of her friends for correction or improvement. In the course of a few months afterward, she received a copy of the book from the publishers, and found, to her surprise, that she had been successful in obtaining one of the two prizes offered. From that circumstance, she was induced to write occasional tales for her own amusement, and convey them through the medium of different periodicals to the public. In 1830 she obtained a second prize for a tale entitled "The Forged Note;" in 1844 another, for a domestic story, entitled "Arlington House;" and in 1849 the fourth, for "The Heiress, or Romance of Life."*

She has written much more poetry than prose. The history of her mind in this respect is sketched with much beauty and simplicity in the following extract from a letter in reply to one making inquiries on this point. "My rhyming propensity," says she, "commenced, I believe, with my earliest powers of thought, as I remember nothing previous to my first attempts at scribbling verses; but those youthful productions were invariably destroyed from a feeling of diffidence, and an utter impossibility of satisfying myself. My ideas of excellence in metrical composition, so

* The titles of her other stories are as follows: "The Secrets of the Heart," 1828; "The Cloaked Gentleman," 1829; "Decourcy," 1829; "The Family of Meredith," 1830; "Traditions of the Visions of Armies in the Heavens," 1844; "The Bachelor's Wedding," 1846; "Gertrude Wurtemburg," 1848; "Love and Politics," 1849; "Rose Winters," 1849; "The Widow's Daughter," 1851; "The Auction, or the Wedding Coat," and "Ada Danforth, or the Will," not yet published.

far exceeded my own efforts, that I was frequently tempted to give up the Muse in despair, and probably I would have done so, had not the poetic passion been too strongly implanted in my nature. The indulgence of this love for embodying my thoughts and feelings in verse, was the happiness of my life. It was often cherished in the place of friends or lovers. It was my resource in solitude, my consolation in trials, my reward for disappointments, my relief in weariness, my recreation in idleness, and my delight in every change of residence, by which new scenes and scenery have been presented to my view."

Miss Bogart was born in the city of New York, which was also the birth-place of her father and his ancestors for several generations back. They are descended on the paternal side from the Huguenots who fled to Holland after the revocation of the edict of Nantz, and emigrated from Holland to America.

Her father was the Rev. David Schuyler Bogart, a graduate of Columbia College, and a minister of the gospel. In his profession, he was highly respected and esteemed, and exceedingly beloved by the people of his charge. Soon after entering on his profession he accepted a call to a Presbyterian church at Southampton, an isolated town, on the eastern part of Long Island, where he resided for fifteen years. There, in the village school-house, Miss Bogart received all her education, excepting what was given her by her father, whose instructions were continued even to the close of his life. From Southampton they removed, in 1813, to Hempstead Harbour, a wild and lovely spot, some eighty miles further west, and on the north side of the island.

"The scenery of the two places," says Miss Bogart, in the letter already quoted, "presented a perfect contrast. The country at Southampton was entirely level, and the town situated immediately on the Atlantic, within sight of its foaming surf, and sound of its ceaseless roar—while Hempstead Harbour was located at the head of a beautiful bay running in from the Long Island Sound, and surrounded with high hills, covered with forest trees and evergreens. It was truly a place to charm the eye, and enrich the imagination; and thus it was, that while my first love was for the grand and magnificent ocean, my *second* was for the more fascinating and picturesque beauty of nature's scenery; amid which the early romance of my disposition was nurtured into an enduring character. The name of the little village of Hempstead Harbour has since been changed to that of Roslyn, but it seems to me an unmeaning appellation, and no improvement; although it will doubtless receive an *eclat* from the fact of our poet Bryant having fixed his residence there.

"It was from my home in that place, in 1825, that I sent forth my first poem, simply headed 'Stanzas,' on a venture to the press. It was published in the 'Long Island Star,' under the signature of 'Adelaide,' and made the subject of a complimentary poetical address in the same paper. I soon afterward commenced writing for 'The New York Mirror,' which was at that time in its most flourishing state, under the able management of its proprietor, George P. Morris. My signature was then changed to that of 'Estelle,' a *nom de plume,* which I have ever since retained; and which, before my real name was known, procured me a poetical correspondent in the 'Mirror,' the history of which is quite a little romance. The correspondence was carried on at intervals, for nearly four years; the writer being all the while utterly unknown to me, excepting inasmuch as his poems declared him to be a gentleman of taste, talent, and education. He had mistaken me for another person, and notwithstanding my repeated denials of the identity, he persisted in addressing me as *the* 'Estelle' of his love, whose name I had unwittingly stolen. My curiosity became at length considerably excited, but he maintained his incognito; and it was not until several years after he had ceased writing, that I accidentally learned his name, and that by means of *his* initials, and the signature of 'Estelle' to the pieces passing between us in the 'Mirror,' he had recovered his *true ladye love,* and married her."

Miss Bogart was particularly fond of these little literary mysteries. They amused and interested her, and gave her both subject and occupation. In the country she had always leisure, as well as love for the Muses. "Without this love," says she, "my life would have been divested of half its pleasures; and without the leisure to indulge it, I think I should have felt as if time, however otherwise employed, were only wasted." Her fugitive poems have now accumulated to a number sufficient to fill a large volume, although they have never been collected and prepared for publication in that form.

In 1826 her father removed, with his family, into the city of New York, where he continued to reside during the remainder of his life. Miss Bogart lives there still.

The first of the extracts which follow, is from "The Forged Note." It is a description of Arthur Mowbray, the hero of the "tale," given from the impression which the author, while a child, had received from seeing him. He had been a country boy, born and educated in humble life, and the history of his school days is first told.

ARTHUR MOWBRAY.

It was years after that period, that Arthur Mowbray came to my father's house, a travelled and polished gentleman. The rusticity of country manners was entirely obliterated. Not a word or action betrayed his early habits, and those who knew him not would never have suspected his humble parentage. The grace and ease of his behaviour made an impression on my childish fancy; and though then incapable of judging of character or talent, I listened to his fluent and fascinating conversation with wonder and delight. He was indeed a young man of most astonishing powers. His Proteus mind assumed a thousand different shapes, from its inexhaustible store of knowledge, observation, and uncommon originality. The current of his ideas never ceased to flow for an instant; and what was more remarkable, they passed over nothing in their course without adding a new touch of brilliancy, beauty, or vigour. No subject escaped his attention, nor was beyond his mastery. His giant intellect grasped the whole range of literature and science, and held them as nothing in its strength: and while others were seeking with weary labour their hidden treasures, he drew forth the pearls from their unfathomed depths, and cast them around him with an unsparing hand. His face and figure were eminently handsome; but the expression of his eyes I have never forgotten. It was wily, dark, and unstable. His sudden glance was like the lightning flash, which carries with it an involuntary thrill of fear. It told that the *heart* was not right. The seeds of vice had fallen promiscuously on its prolific soil, and choked, in their wild luxuriance, the early growth of virtue. * * * * *

[This character is justified by his after-course in life. He is convicted of forgery, and sentenced to the State Prison, from which "durance vile" he is released after three years, by a pardon from the Governor.] It was a bright and beautiful morning, when the bars were removed, and the bolts withdrawn from his prison doors; and he came forth from the gloomy and frowning edifice, a solitary being in the midst of a gay and populous city. The clear heavens, and the bright earth, and the varied objects which met his eager gaze, yielded him no thought of pleasure;

"For bitter shame had spoiled the sweet world's taste."

He knew that he could have no communion with those whom he had once known: and as he wandered on among the multitude of busy and happy faces, he experienced a feeling of hatred to mankind, mingled with a sense of desolation more withering to his heart than even the dreary and hopeless solitude of his prison cell. In the bitterness of his soul he cursed himself and his destiny. True, he was again free to walk the earth, and look upon his fellow-men; but Cain-like, he was cast out as a fugitive and vagabond from among them. The mark of disgrace was set upon him. The stain of guilt and ignominy could never more be wiped from his name; and he saw himself cut off from that part of society which nature and education had fitted him to enjoy. His former visions of greatness could return to him no more; and with the terrible consciousness of his irretrievable fall, his heart became hardened, and his conscience callous to the stings of reproach.

[He was subsequently convicted of a similar crime in another State, and fated to die at last in a prison. A fragment of his history is given, as having been written by himself in his cell, in which he says,] "I know no dates for time. The days, and weeks, and months, are all alike to me. There is but one thought in my bosom continually, from the rising to the setting of the sun; and it gnaws with ceaseless and corroding power on my heart. The tormenting thought that I am always in one place—that I cannot move beyond a certain limit, and that here I must remain until death closes my disgraceful career. My glass is nearly run, and I rejoice at it; although I ought now to have been in the very prime of manhood: but my constitution has given way to the midnight revel, and the unnatural excitement of the gaming table. The inebriating bottle has mingled its deadly poison in my blood; gray hairs have scattered an untimely frost upon my head; and the life of man already appears to me like a little speck in the ocean of eternity. *Eternity!* No—there is no eternity! I believe it not! I am a renegade from the faith of my fathers! I have laughed at all religion, and derided the idle terrors of a *hell*, as the mere bugbear of canting hypocrites. Why, then, did I speak of *eternity?* We die, are laid in the grave, and are as if we had never been. . . . . . Even now, my brain is on fire. Reason totters. Philosophy trembles—and I sink—am lost." * * *

RECOLLECTIONS OF CHILDHOOD.

THERE are, perhaps, no scenes which make so strong an impression on the mind, as those with which our early recollections are associated. Other things may pass from the memory, and be lost amid the vicissitudes of the world; but these will still recur at intervals, as some wandering thought or truant feeling comes home to the heart. In such moments, I have frequently felt a strong and irrepressible desire to revisit the scenes of my childhood; and it was with mingled emotions of pleasure and impatience that I at length prepared for the journey. Every spot was familiar to my imagination, and I even fancied on the way, that I could already hear the voices of welcome, and that I possessed the sight of Lynceus to look through the distant space. It was at the close of a summer afternoon that we arrived at the place of our destination. The sun was setting in full splendour over the same local scenes which were engraven on the first page of my memory, and the changing hues of the clouds reminded me of those hours when I delighted to watch them till their gorgeous colours were lost in darkness. The moon looked down with bright, unaltered face, on the same green fields and clear waters, and the stars peeped out from their hidden worlds, as if to return my gaze of recognition. There was a kind of imaginary happiness connected with real objects in my mind, as I walked through the quiet town. The little school-house where I was first taught the pleasant use of my pen, and the perplexing mysteries of figures, brought back many reminiscences both ludicrous and interesting. The idea of the ingenious and burlesque punishments, invented by our benevolent and good-natured teacher, for his mischievous, unruly boys, occasioned an involuntary burst of laughter, and the images of "Lew," "Tom," and "Bob," with their inked hands and shamed faces, seemed instantly to rise before me, but it was only for a moment. The question, Where is now our indulgent and beloved preceptor? darted across my mind, and I felt a pang of self-reproach, as I turned my eyes to the grave-yard, and remembered that he "rested from his labours," in the silent tomb.

JANE ELIZABETH LARCOMBE.

Miss Larcombe has, within the last few years, won an honourable place among the magazinists of the country. Her tales are sprightly and piquant, and show a degree of originality and a fertility of invention, which augur well for her future and more elaborate efforts. Her stories thus far have appeared in Neal's Gazette, Godey, Peterson, Sartain, as well as in the Annuals, and all under the assumed name of "Kate Campbell." She is at present engaged as a regular contributor to some of the religious periodicals of the church to which she belongs—the Baptist.

Miss Larcombe was born January 13, 1829, at Colebrook, Connecticut. The family removed in 1831, to Danbury, Connecticut; in 1834, to Saugerties, New York; and in 1835, to Philadelphia, where they still reside. She is descended, on the mother's side, of a Scottish family, staunch covenanters. Her father, who is a clergyman, and who, the greater part of his life, has been chaplain to the Eastern Penitentiary of Pennsylvania, is of French descent, from the Waldenses of Piedmont. The family left France at the revocation of the Edict of Nantes, and settled in Bristol, England, and thence emigrated to Hartford, Connecticut.

On the 4th of November, 1851, Miss Larcombe was married to the Rev. Heman Lincoln, of the Baptist church.

THOUGHTS BY THE WAYSIDE.

A summer twilight! who enjoys it? or rather, who can resist the magnetism which draws one to the open window, beneath which the leaves of the trees tremble in the quiet air, while the Heaven above lies so hushed and smiling, with a calmness as though it had been shedding tears, and, worn and exhausted, could do nought but smile languidly on the broad, sinful earth?

Yet we can remember, when a little child, thinking the twilight hour the gloomiest of the twenty-four—a dark spirit commanding us to give up work or play, and loiter restlessly around the house, till the first welcome glimmer of a light released us from its dismal thraldom. It seemed to us the most particularly unpleasant arrangement of nature to be conceived, and often and often did we wonder ourself stupid, trying to solve the phenomenon.

It was equally puzzling to see with what a spirit of enjoyment the "old folks" settled themselves comfortably in their easy chairs, and with eyes fixed on the fading heavens, seemed soaring away from earthly cares and joys. Instinctively we felt that mirth and mischief must be postponed to a more convenient season.

When we grew older, wise enough to *contrive*, we got along much better; the gathering gloom of evening was the signal for a general muster; out we flew from the quiet parlour to the dim hall and passages, where, with stifled shouts and shrieks of mysterious merriment, we indulged in all the excitement of a game at hide and seek, or, when tired out, gathered in a compact knot at the foot of the stairs, and with elbows on our knees, heads supported by our hands, and eyes widely dilated, listened to the delicious horrors of some marvellous tale of ghost or ogre. Such stories! no one else ever dreamed of such delights! Such giants as we had! such fairies! such a quantity of winding-sheets as our favourite narrator provided for us!—our brother, with his wide, smiling mouth, and glistening teeth! We can see him now, his rosy face ever in a perpetual grin, even while skilfully depicting scenes which made "each individual hair to stand on end" among his entranced audience! Our brother!—"gone, but not lost."

Sometimes, too, of a winter's evening, we found our way into the warm, bright, cozy kitchen, bringing our noise and mirth with us, which was speedily quelled, however, through the influence of the presiding spirit of the place—a tidy, thrifty servant girl, who loved us all dearly—troublesome as we were—and who, despite her unattractive appearance, stole a place for herself in our kind memories. She was an Irish girl, with features strongly marked with small-pox, and a most disastrous hump between her shoulders; short in person, somewhat short in speech, but withal, the kindest heart that ever beat! Dearly did she love to gather the unruly crowd of boys and girls around her glowing, social fire, and hush them to a grave-like stillness with the wild legends of her native isle.

Ah, well! those days have passed and gone now, for ever. We can only sit quietly by the open window and think of the "now, and what has been," and remember with a blending of the mirthful and sorrowful—a kind of *comic* sadness—how we grew out of those pleasant ways; how our first influx of sentimentalism crept in about the time we put up our "elf-locks wildly floating," and imbibed a strong disgust for long-sleeved checked aprons; how we took to reading newspaper poetry, descriptive of the "shining stars" and "silver moon," and naturally enough, went from that to looking in the gray heavens for them; how we laid aside the favourite book, smoothed down the folds of our dress, and seated ourself methodically at the window, *vis-à-vis* to our mother, and gazed perseveringly at the steadfast skies, persuading ourself that we were immeasurably happy, while all the time, had we listened to the heart's truth, tears would have been dropping for the good old times—the "joyous days of yore"—with the romp in the hall, the blazing kitchen fire, the hump-backed servant girl, and the merry playmates, now slumbering beneath the sod.

So, after all, it took Time, patient teacher, to instil a full appreciation of the delights of twilight. Time brought the thousand things which make at once the charm and the sadness of that mystic hour;—the fleeting, intangible Past, the ideal hues which form a fairy halo round the most common-place occurrences; the real Present, contrasting vividly with the buried life; the last friends beyond the skies to draw our thoughts thither, and more than all, the feeling that we have tasted through experience somewhat of existence, and have earned a right to moralize upon its fleeting pleasures.

EMILY C. JUDSON,

(FANNY FORRESTER.)

EMILY C. CHUBBUCK was born in the pleasant town of Morrisville, in the central part of New York. This is the "Alderbrook" so familiar to her readers. Here she made a profession of religion, and connected herself with the Baptist church.

From Morrisville she went to Utica, to engage in teaching. While living at Utica, she made her first essays at authorship. These consisted of some small volumes of a religious character published by the Baptist Publication Society, and poetical contributions to the Knickerbocker. None of these, however, attracted any special attention. The first production of her pen that is at all noticeable was a light article which she wrote, without any very definite design, under the assumed name of "Fanny Forrester," to the "New Mirror," while on a visit to the city of New York. This was in June, 1844. The editor had the sagacity, in this, as in several other instances, to perceive at once the evidences of genius that appeared in this playful bagatelle, and by a warm and judicious commendation, led the author to a continued, and, in the end, most successful, exploration of the vein thus accidentally brought to light. A series of essays, sketches, and poems followed, of a very brilliant character, which in 1846 were collected and published in two volumes under the title of "Alderbrook."

In the beginning of 1846, the venerable missionary Judson returned to America, to visit the churches. On coming to Philadelphia, he was directed to Miss Chubbuck as a suitable person to prepare a memoir of his lately deceased wife, the second Mrs. Judson. Miss Chubbuck, then resident in Philadelphia, cheerfully undertook the grateful task. Being thus thrown much together, a mutual affection sprung up between them, and the favoured child of literature joyfully laid aside the laurels then fresh upon her brow, to go, as the wife of Dr. Judson, on a self-denying mission to the Burmans They were married, at Hamilton, New York, June 2, 1846, and soon after sailed for Burmah. The "Memoir" was published in 1848. Dr. Judson died at Maulmain, in Burmah, in 1850. Soon after the death of her husband, Mrs. Judson returned to the United States. Her health soon began to decline, and on the first of June, 1854, after a lingering illness, she died at the residence of her brother, at Hamilton, Madison county, New York.

LUCY DUTTON.

It was an October morning, warm and sunny, but with even its sunshine subdued into a mournful softness, and its gorgeous drapery chastened by a touch of the dreamy atmosphere into a sympathy with sorrow. And there was a sorrowing one who needed sympathy on that still, holy morning—the sympathy of the great Heart which beats in Nature's bosom—for she could hope no other. Poor Lucy Dutton!

There was a funeral that morning—a stranger would have judged by the gathering that the great man of the village was dead, and all that crowd had come out to do his ashes honour—but it was not so. Yet the little, old-fashioned church was filled to overflowing. Some there were that turned their eyes devoutly to the holy man that occupied the sacred desk, receiving from his lips the words of life; some looked upon the little coffin that stood, covered with its black pall, upon a table directly below him, and perhaps thought of their own mortality, or that of their bright little ones; while many, very many, gazed with cold curiosity at the solitary mourner occupying the front pew. This was a young creature, in the very spring-time of life,—a frail, erring being, whose only hope was in Him who said, "Neither do I condemn thee—go, and sin no more." There was a weight of shame upon her head, and woe upon her heart, that together made the bereaved young mother cower almost to the earth before the prying eyes that came to look upon her in her distressing humiliation. Oh! it was a pitiful sight! that crushed, helpless creature's agony.

But the year before, and this same lone mourner was considered a sweet, beautiful child, whom everybody was bound to protect and love; because, but that she was the pet lamb of a doting old wo man, she was without friend and protector. Lucy Dutton was the last blossom on a tree which had boasted many fair ones. When the grave opened to one after another of that doomed family, till none but this bright, beautiful bud was left, she became the all in all, and with the doting affection of age was she cherished. When poverty came to Granny Dutton's threshold, she drew her one priceless jewel to her heart, and laughed at poverty. When sorrows of every kind compassed her about, and the sun went down in her heaven of hope, another rose in a holier heaven of love; and Lucy Dutton was this fountain of love-born light. The old lady and her pretty darling occupied a small, neat cottage, at the foot of the hill, with a garden attached to it, in which the child flitted all day long, like a glad spirit among the flowers. And, next to her child-idol, the simple-hearted old lady loved those flowers, with a love which pure natures ever bear to the beautiful. It was by these, and the fruit produced by the little garden, that the twain lived. Many a fine carriage drew up before the door of the humble cottage, and bright ladies and dashing gentlemen sauntered beneath the shade, while the rosy fingers of Lucy adjusted bouquets for them, her bright lips wreathed with smiles, and her sunny eye turning to her grandmother at the placing of every stem, as though for approbation of her taste. Not a child in all the neighbourhood was so happy as Lucy. Not a child in all the neighbourhood was so beautiful, so gentle, and so good. And nobody ever thought of her as anything but a child. Though she grew to the height of her tallest geranium, and her form assumed womanly proportions, nobody, not even the rustic beaux around her, thought of her as anything but a child. Lucy was so artless, and loved her dear old grandmother so truly, that the two were somehow connected in people's minds, and it seemed as impossible that the girl should grow older, as that the old lady should grow younger.

Lucy was just booked for fifteen, with the seal of innocence upon her heart, and a rose-leaf on her cheek, when "the Herman property," a fine summer residence that had been for years unoccupied, was purchased by a widow lady from the metropolis. She came to Alderbrook early in the spring, accompanied by her only son, to visit her new possessions, and finding the spot exceedingly pleasant, she determined to remain there. And so Lucy met the young metropolitan; and Lucy was beautiful and trusting, and thoughtless; and he was gay, selfish, and profligate. Needs the story to be told?

When the Howards went away, Lucy awoke from her dream. She looked about her, and upon herself, with the veil taken from her eyes; and then she turned from all she had ever loved; for, in the breaking up of those dreams, was broken poor Lucy's heart.

Nay, censor, Lucy was a child—consider how very young, how very untaught—oh! her innocence was no match for the sophistry of a gay city youth! And young Howard stole her unthinking heart the first day he looked in to purchase a bouquet. Poor, poor Lucy!

Before the autumn leaves fell, Granny Dutton's bright pet knelt in her little chamber, and upon her mother's grave, and down by the river-side, where she had last met Justin Howard, and prayed for death. Sweet, joyous Lucy Dutton, asking to lay her bright head in the grave! Spring came, and shame was stamped upon the cottage at the foot of the hill. Lucy bowed her head upon her bosom, and refused to look upon anything but her baby; and the old lady shrunk, like a shrivelled leaf, before this last and greatest of her troubles. The neighbourhood had its usual gossip. There were taunts, and sneers, and coarse jests, and remarks severely true; but only a little, a very little, pity. Lucy bore all this well, for she knew that it was deserved; but she had worse than this to bear. Every day she knelt by the bed of the one being who had doted upon her from infancy, and begged her blessing, but in vain.

"Oh! that I had laid you in the coffin, with your dead mother, when all around me said that the breath had passed from you!" was the unvarying reply; "then my gray hairs might have gone down to the grave without dishonour from the child that I took from the gate of death, and bore for years upon my bosom. Would you had died, Lucy!"

And Lucy would turn away her head, and, in the bitterness of her heart, echo, "Ay! would that I had died!" Then she would take her baby in her arms, and, while the scalding tears bathed its unconscious face, pray God to forgive the wicked wish, and preserve her life for the sake of this sinless heir to shame. And sometimes Lucy would smile—not that calm, holy smile which usually lingers about an infant's cradle, but a faint, sicklied play of the love-light within, as though the mother's fond heart were ashamed of its own throbbings. But, before the autumn passed, Lucy Dutton was fearfully stricken. Death came! She laid her last comfort from her bosom into the coffin, and they were now bearing it to the grave,—she, the only mourner. It mattered but little that the grandmother's forgiveness and blessing came now; Lucy scarce knew the difference between these words and those last spoken; and most earnestly did she answer, "Would, would that I had died!" Poor, poor, Lucy!

She sat all through the sermon, and the singing, and the prayer, with her head bowed upon the side of the pew; and when at last they bore the coffin to the door, and the congregation began to move forward, she did not raise it until the kind clergyman came and led her out to take a last look at her dead boy. Then she laid her thin, pale face against his within the coffin, and sobbed aloud. And now some began to pity the stricken girl, and whisper to their neighbours that she was more sinned against than sinning. Still none came forward to whisper the little word which might have brought healing, but the holy man whose duty it was. He took her almost forcibly from the infant clay, and strove to calm her, while careless eyes came to look upon that dearer to her than her own heart's blood. Finally, curiosity was satisfied; they closed the coffin, screwed down the lid, spread the black cloth over it, and the procession began to form. Minister Green left the side of the mourner, and took his station in advance, accompanied by some half dozen others; then four men followed, bearing the light coffin in their hands, and all eyes were turned upon the mourner. She did not move.

"Pass on, madam," said Squire Field, who always acted the part of marshal on such occasions; and, though little given to the weakness of feeling, he now softened his voice as much as it would bear softening. "This way—right behind the—the—pass on!"

Lucy hesitated a moment, and many a generous one longed to step forward and give her an arm; but selfish prudence forbade. One bright girl, who had been Lucy's playmate from the cradle, but had not seen her face for many months, drew impulsively towards her; but she met a reproving eye from the crowd, and only whispering, "I *do* pity you, Lucy!" she shrunk back, and sobbed almost as loud as her erring friend. Lucy started at the words, and, gazing wildly round her, tottered on after the coffin.

Loud, and slow, and fearfully solemn, stroke after stroke, the old church-bell doled forth its tale; and slowly and solemnly the crowd moved on with a measured tread, though there was many a careless eye and many a smiling lip, turning to other eyes and other lips, with something like a jest between them. On moved the crowd after the mourner; while she, with irregular, laboured step, her arms crossed on her bosom, and her head bent to the same resting-place, just kept pace with the body of her dead boy. Winding through the opened gate into the church-yard, they went trailing slowly through the long, dead grass, while some of the children crept slily from the procession, to pick up the tufts of scarlet and yellow leaves, which made this place of graves strangely gay; and several young people wandered off, arm in arm, pausing as they went, to read the rude inscriptions lettered on the stones.

On went the procession, away to the farthermost corner, where slept the stranger and the vagabond. Here a little grave had been dug, and the coffin was now set down beside it, while the long procession circled slowly round. Several went up and looked into the dark, damp cradle of the dead child; one observed to his neighbour that it was very shallow; and another said that Tom Jones always slighted his work when there was nobody to see to it; anyhow, it was not much matter, the child would stay buried; and another let drop a jest, a hard, but not very witty one, though it was followed by a smothered laugh. All this passed quietly; nothing was spoken above a low murmur; but Lucy heard it all;

and, as she heard and remembered, what a repulsive thing seemed to her the human heart! Poor Lucy Dutton!

Minister Green stood at the head of the grave and said a prayer, while Lucy leaned against a sickly-looking tree, alone, and pressed her cold hands against her temples, and wondered if she should ever pray again—if God would hear her if she should. Then they laid the little coffin upon ropes, and gently lowered it. The grave was too short, or the men were careless, for there was a harsh grating against the hard earth, which made Lucy start and extend her arms; but she instantly recollected herself, and, clasping her hands tightly over her mouth, lest her agony should make itself heard, she tried to stand calmly. Then a handful of straw was thrown upon the coffin, and immediately a shovelful of earth followed. Oh! that first sinking of the cold clod upon the bosom we have loved! What a fearful, shivering sensation, does it send to the heart and along the veins! And then the benumbing faintness which follows, as though our own breath were struggling up through that damp covering of earth! Lucy gasped and staggered, and then she twined her arm about the body of the little tree, and laid her cheek against its rough bark, and strove hard to keep herself from falling.

Some thought the men were very long in filling up the grave, but Lucy thought nothing about it. She did not, after that first shovelful, hear the earth as it fell; and when, after all was done and the sods of withered grass had been laid on, Minister Green came to tell her, she did not hear his voice. When she did, she pushed back the hair from her hollowed temples, looked vacantly into his face, and shook her head. Others came up to her—a good-natured man who had been kind to her grandmother; then the deacon's wife, followed by two or three other women; but Lucy only smiled and shook her head. Glances full of troubled mystery passed from one to another; there was an alarmed look on many faces, which those more distant seemed to comprehend; and still others came to speak to Lucy. It was useless—she could find no meaning in their words—the star of intellect had gone out—the temple was darkened. Poor, poor Lucy Dutton!

They bore her home—for she was passive and helpless—home to the sick old grandmother, who laid her withered hand on those bright locks, and kissed the cold cheek, and took her to her bosom, as though she had been an infant. And Lucy smiled, and talked of playing by the brook, and chasing the runaway bees, and of toys for her baby-house, and wondered why they were all weeping, particularly dear grandmamma, who ought to be so happy. But this lasted only a few days, and then another grave was made, and yet another, in the poor's corner; and the grandmother and her shattered idol slept together. The grave is a blessed couch and pillow to the wretched. Rest thee there, poor Lucy!

MY FIRST GRIEF.

I LAUGHED and crowed above this water, when I was a baby, and, therefore, I love it. I played beside it, when the days were years of summer-time, and the summers were young eternities of brightness, and, therefore, I love it. It was the scene of my first grief, too. Shall I tell you? There is not much to tell, but I have a notion that there are people above us, up in the air, and behind the clouds, that consider little girls' doings about as important as those of men and women. The birds and the angels are great levellers.

It was a dry season; the brook was low, and a gay trout in a coat of golden brown, dotted over with crimson, and a silver pinafore, lay, weather-bound, on the half-dry stones, all heated and panting, with about a tea-spoonful of lukewarm water, turning lazily from its head, and creeping down its back at too slow a pace to afford the sufferer hope of emancipation. My sympathies—little girls, you must know, are made up of love and sympathy, and such like follies, which afterwards contract into—*n'importe!* I was saying, my sympathies were aroused; and, quite forgetting that water would take the gloss from my new red morocco shoes, I picked my way along, and laying hold of my fine gentleman in limbo, succeeded in burying him, wet face and all, in the folds of my white apron! But *such* an uneasy prisoner! More than one frightened toss did he get into the grass, and then I had an infinite deal of trouble to secure him again. His gratitude was very like that of humans', when you do them unasked service.

When I had reached a cool, shaded, deep spot, far adown, where the spotted alders lean, like so many self-enamoured narcissuses, over the ripple-faced mirror, I dropped my apron, and let go my prize. Ah! he was grateful *then!* He must have been! How he dived, and sprang to the surface, and spread out his little wings of dark-ribbed gossamer, and frisked about, keeping all the time a cool, thin sheet of silver between his back and the sun-sick air! I loved that pretty fish, for I had been kind to it; and I thought it would love me, too, and stay there, and be a play-fellow for me; so I went every day and watched for it, and watched until my little eyes ached; but I never saw it again. That was my first grief: what is there in years to make a heart ache heavier? That first will be longer remembered than the last. I dare say.

SARA J. LIPPINCOTT.

(GRACE GREENWOOD.)

SARA J. CLARKE was born in Pompey, an inland town in the county of Onondaga, New York. Here, and in the neighbouring town of Fabius, she spent the greater portion of her childhood. During her early girlhood she resided with her parents, at Rochester, N. Y., but at the age of nineteen removed with them to New Brighton, Penn., which has since been her nominal home, though perhaps the larger part of her time is spent with her friends, in New England, at Washington, and Philadelphia.

Miss Clarke wrote verse at an early age, and published under her own name; but, on coming out as a prose writer, being doubtful of the experiment, she shielded herself behind a *nom de plume*. Her success has thus far greatly exceeded the expectations of her most sanguine friends. Yet, in a life of constant change and excitement, of extensive and pleasant social relations, she has not been able to concentrate her powers on any important work, but has given them at best but imperfect exercise in a series of magazine articles, brief sketches, light critiques, and lighter letters.

A selection from her prose writings, making a volume of over four hundred pages, entitled "Greenwood Leaves," was published in the fall of 1849. This work has reached a third edition. In the autumn of the following year was brought out a collection of her poems, a volume of 190 pages; also, a volume of original juvenile stories, entitled "History of My Pets," both of which publications have passed through several editions.

In the autumn of 1851, she published "Greenwood Leaves, Second Series," and another volume of juvenile stories, entitled "Recollections of my Childhood."

In the spring of 1852, Miss Clarke visited Europe, and spent about fifteen months in England, Ireland, Scotland, France, Italy, and the Tyrol. On her return, she published a volume of travels, entitled "Haps and Mishaps of a Tour in Europe." This has proved her most successful work.

In October, 1853, she was married to Mr. Leander K. Lippincott, of Philadelphia, removed to that city, and commenced with her husband the editorship and publication of a juvenile monthly journal entitled "The Little Pilgrim."

The father of Mrs. Lippincott, Doctor Thaddeus Clarke, formerly a physician of some eminence, was born in Lebanon, Connecticut, of a good old Puritan stock. He died at New Brighton, February 15th, 1854. Her mother, a native of Brooklyn, Connecticut, is of Hugenot descent. Sara, the youngest daughter, is one of eleven children, nine of whom are now living.

The following carefully written estimate of the intellectual character of Mrs. Lippincott is from the pen of that accomplished critic, the Rev. Henry Giles:

"That Grace Greenwood is a writer, ready, rapid, bold, brilliant, and most discursive, whatever she throws from her pen at once reveals. But to be ready and rapid is often to be nothing more than possessed of fatal facility; and to seem bold, brilliant, and discursive is frequently to have only the hardihood of ignorance, and to be glittering and superficial. The readiness and rapidity, however, of this writer are in themselves surprising, from the truth and force with which thought keeps pace with expression; and we wonder to find so much true beauty, so much genuine coinage of golden fancies in the prodigality with which she flings about her shining store. Yet not on these do we dwell, and not by these does she win the cordial feeling with which we regard her genius. We find in it a noble seriousness. Bounding, elastic, and sportive as her imagination is, it is not all a sparkling stream, and is not all in sunlight; it winds at times through the solemn shadows of life; and it has springs in the sources of reflective thought, to make for itself, and fill deeper and broader channels than any of those in which it has yet found outlets. As it is, the impulses of earnest purpose and the gush of generous desire, often break to pieces the delicate wreath which had been already half woven out of ingenious fancies, and cast the scattered flowers upon the boiling torrent of indignant sympathies. The workings of mere fancy, however admirable or admired, could never exhaust, could never express, could never content a nature such as hers—for she feels too much in herself, and she feels too much for others, to find only play and summer-time in the life of genius. In the gayest tale of hers, we read below it meanings from the heart; in the most laughing letter, we can often discern a pensive wisdom hidden in the smile; in the passing criticism on a work of art, we have often not only the fine enthusiasm, which flames up with the love of beauty; but when the work is devotional, we have, with phrase more happy and with spirit more profound, the subdued eloquence of inborn reverence. The seriousness of Grace Greenwood is not the less intense because it is not moody or murky; because it does not tire you with tears, nor disturb you with groans, nor disgust you with men, nor dishearten you with nature. Grace is too healthy for mumps; she is too sincere to be maudlin; she is too cheerful for lamentations; and her love is too large for creation and too kind, to tolerate the gloom of a dissatisfied spirit. But no soul is more quick to kindle at a wrong done to the lowest; and no soul more brave to rebuke unworthiness in the highest. Yet is her heart gentle, compassionate; aroused only by the very strength of its goodness; by its hatred against injustice, and by its sympathy with suffering. Even when a lofty anger moves her, there is ever sighing through its tones a sound of pity. For there is nothing that we can be rightly angry at in this world, but we must pity also. Every soul that feels much, feels this.

"We think, therefore, that in her pages, radiant as they seem, we can read, without any doubtful interpretation, meanings of sadness. If it were not so, we should be disappointed; for they manifest that genius of a loving humanity, which cannot help but oftentimes be sad. Grace Greenwood, say what persons will, is not what we should call a sprightly writer. Her productions are not mere sprightly flashes, but many-toned utterances of feelings, that lay deep down in the breast, and to which occasions gave nothing but expression.

"Genius, accompanied with strong sensibility, were it not for certain compensations, would be a penalty and not a boon. Such compensation Grace Greenwood has in considerable affluence. One of these is the relief that mental hilarity gives to mental intensity. Strong as her perception is of what is serious in life, it has its counterpoise by her equally strong feeling of what is joyous. The grave and troubled condition of man's estate we can observe that she reverently appreciates; but we can as well observe that she also detects man's absurdities and vanities, and heartily she laughs at them. Yet is there no contempt in the laughter, but an affectionate humanity. She has humour most rich and racy—that which springs from keenness of intellect, fullness of imagination, kindliness of temper, and playfulness of spirit.

"This remark has its proof and its example in the parodies contained in some of her writings. The imitation is unmistakeable; the fun resistless; and yet, we are so made to feel the beauty of the writers in the burlesque, that while we laugh we admire. And this enjoyment of beauty is another compensation for the painful sensibility of genius, and the only other we shall mention. The language, and the activity of such enjoyment in Grace Greenwood, no one can doubt, who reads her pages with any spirit like her own. Neither can we doubt the sincerity of it and its healthiness. It is no matter of artificial or factitious cultivation; it has grown with her in her native valleys and woodlands; she has listened to its music in the foamings of her native waves and torrents; she has gazed upon its majestic forms in the glory of her native mountains; and she has communed with the boundless spirit of it in that mighty azure dome of matchless purity that rests over her native land."

A DREAM OF DEATH.

How appropriate, and sadly truthful, is the expression, "The night of the grave!" How the deep shadows of impenetrable mystery hang about the dread portals of eternity; how, in approaching them, even in thought, we lose ourselves in clouds, and grope in thick darkness!

In the near and solemn contemplation of the awful change which awaits us all, how eagerly does the soul receive everything, in religion, philosophy, or personal experience, which lifts, or seems to lift, even a little way, a corner of the vast curtain which hides from our mortal view the spirit-realm to which we go; letting in gleams of its immortal joy and glory, to light and cheer our painful path through the dark valley.

During a late illness, there came a dream to me as I slept, which left a solemn and ineffaceable impress upon my mind, but to which I may seem, by relating, to attach undue importance; for, after all, it was but a dream; and I hardly know how it is, that I have so laid it away in my heart, as a treasure of exceeding worth, almost as a heavenly revelation. It was no wild, mystic, and fanciful dream, but strangely distinct and beautifully consistent throughout; and it is with the most faithful truthfulness that I now venture to relate it, hoping that to some hearts it may have, or seem to have, a meaning and a purpose.

In my vision, it seemed that my last hour of the life of earth was swiftly passing from me. The dread presence of Death filled my chamber with mourning and gloom, and awe unspeakable. My heart, like a caged bird, now struggled and fluttered wildly in my breast, now seemed sinking, faint, and panting with weariness and fear. The last mist was creeping slowly over my eyes, and I heard but imperfectly the words of prayer, sorrow, and tenderness, breathed around me. Dear forms were at my side, clasping my cold hands, and weeping upon my neck. The bosom of the best beloved pillowed my poor head; her hand wiped the death-dew from my brow; she spoke to me strong words of comfort, crushing down the great anguish of her heart the while.

It was no hour of joy or triumph; my spirit was not buoyed up by exulting faith, nor did waiting angels minister to it the peace and consolation of Heaven; but storm, and darkness, and fear, encompassed it, filling it with wild regrets, an awful expectation, a sore dismay. Its feet were already set in the river of death; but, like a timid child, it shrank from the chill, midnight waves, and clung convulsively to its earthly loves,—vain, alas! to protect, powerless to detain!

Soul and body parted, as they part who have lived and suffered, and toiled together, in bondage, but who love one another, and who, at last, are torn asunder by the inexorable will of a remorseless master.

But joy for one of these! for whom the weariness of mortal bondage was to give place to the freedom of eternity; the pain, the struggle, the fear, the sorrow of its earthly lot, to peace, rest, assurance, and joy unspeakable! for, at last, at last, that soul, breaking from this poor life, with one glad bound, leaped into immortality! Oh! the sudden comprehension of the height and depth of the fulness of being! How every thought, and aspiration, and affection, and power, seemed springing up into everlasting life!

But methought that the first feeling or sentiment, of which I was conscious, was *freedom*,—freedom, which brought with it a sense of joy, and power, and glorious exultation, utterly indescribable in words. Ah! it was beautiful, that this crowning gift of God to His creatures, which had ever been so dear to my human heart; this principle, which here I had so adored, was the first pure and perfect portion of the Divine life, whose presence I hailed with the great and voiceless rapture of a disenthralled spirit.

Methought that I witnessed no immediate visible manifestation of Deity, heard no audible revelation of the Divine existence; but that I received fullness of faith, and greatness of knowledge, in loneliness and stillness, yet instantaneously, and more like *recollections* than revelations. Cloud after cloud rolled swiftly away from the dread mysteries of eternity, till all was meridian brightness and surpassing glory. The presence of Deity was round about me everywhere—*felt*, methought, not *beheld;* it flowed to me in the air, "every undulation filled with soul;" floated about me in the rapt silence, like an all-pervading essence, diffusing itself abroad over the great immensity of being.

There was no sudden unveiling of my eyes to behold the burning splendours of the dread abode of the Sovereign of the Universe, "the city of our God," girdled about with suns, over whose "crystal battlements" float banners of light, within whose courts bow the redeemed in ceaseless adoration; there was no sudden unsealing of my ear to the triumphal psalms of the blessed, to the grand resounding march of the stars. And, methought, no fair creatures of light came to me at once, to bear me upward, nor was my soul eager to depart, on swift, impatient wing, from the dear, though darkened scenes of earth, and the strong, though transient, associations of time; but still lingered, hovering over that chamber of death, from which now arose a passionate burst of grief, the deep sobbing, and wild swell of the first storm of sorrow. Then, methought, my soul looked down upon its perishing companion in toil and suffering—the worn and resigned body; marked the rigid limbs, the parted lips, the pale and sunken cheek, the shadowed eye, and all the mortality settled on the brow; looked upon these, and felt no sorrow. But ah! the tears and groans of those dear bereaved ones, had power to grieve it still, to "disturb that soul with pity," yet not such mournful pity as it had known on earth. A serene and comprehending faith in the wisdom and loving care of the Father, reconciled it to all things; the years of this life, to the vision of its new existence, seemed shortened to brief days, and thus the time of release, for all who suffer and toil, near at hand. Yet with great yearnings it lingered there, its earthly love not destroyed, not weakened, but made stronger far, and purer, more like to the love of Heaven.

Then, methought, a form of ineffable beauty, with a countenance of peace, wherein was human love breaking through celestial glory, came to me, and said, "Oh, daughter of earth, it is now thine to go forth, with the freedom of an immortal, among the infinite worlds; to range at will through the vast domains of the wide and wondrous creation; to track the shining paths of beneficent power, leading on from beauty to beauty, and glory to glory, through the grand and measureless universe of God. Shall we visit those fair worlds, those radiant stars, thou seest shining afar in the clear depths of air?—they, who have known no fall, and on whom the

Father's approving smile rests with a perpetual warmth and serenity; whose inhabitants dwell in love, and worship, and content; where there is neither death nor oppression, suffering nor sin; no spoiler, and none 'to make afraid;' none who slay; none who starve; none who flee from their brothers, and call on God in secret places.

"There also the laws of beauty and harmony subdue and rule the elements, so that there are no harsh frosts, nor fierce heat, neither earthquake nor whelming flood; no storms, to vex the heavens, nor to desolate the earth; whose bloom is glad in the morning sun, and beautiful in the starlight. There, over hill and plain, angels have written holy music in flowers; there, summer streams chime down the mountain side, and winds play among the trees with the sound of anthems.

"Over those worlds divine beings oft walk, as once they walked in the Eden of thy earth, ere man sinned, and, covering his face, went out from the presence of God. Wilt thou go thither? Or wouldst thou ascend the steps of morning light, to the Divine courts, thence to go forth on some errand of good, or enter on some office of love, thy portion of that labour which is worship?"

Then it seemed that I made no answer, save to point downward to those beloved ones, who still sat in darkness, and would not be comforted. Then the angel smiled, and said,—"It is well; remain thou with these through their day of time; be near them, and console them always; go before them, leading their way down the dark valley; welcome them through the immortal gates, for to the holy ministration thou hast chosen wert thou appointed."

When the cold light of dawn broke the sleep which brought this heavenly vision, it was as the coming of night, and not of morning.

EXTRACT FROM A LETTER.

I AM reminded of an incident, or rather *the* incident of yesterday—an accidental meeting with the poet Longfellow.

Aside from mere curiosity, of which I suppose I have my woman's share, I have always wished to look on the flesh and blood embodiment of that rare genius, of that mind stored with the wealth of many literatures, the lore of many lands,—for in Longfellow it is the scholar as well as the poet that we reverence. The first glance satisfied me of one happy circumstance—that the life and health which throbbed and glowed through this poet's verse had their natural correspondences in the physical. He appears perfectly healthful and vigorous—is rather English in person. His head is simply full, well-rounded, and even, not severe or massive in character. The first glance of his genial eyes, which seem to have gathered up sunshine through all the summers they have known, and the first tones of his cordial voice, show one that he has not impoverished his own nature in so generously endowing the creations of his genius—has not drained his heart of the wine of life, to fill high the beaker of his song.

Mr. Longfellow does not look poetical, as Keats looked poetical, perhaps; but, as Hood says of Gray's precocious youth, who used to get up early

"To meet the sun upon the upland lawn"—

"*he* died young." But, what is better, our poet looks *well*, for, after all, health is the best, most happy and glorious thing in the world. On *my* Parnassus, there should be no half-demented, long-haired, ill-dressed bards, lean and pale, subject to sudden attacks of poetic frenzy—sitting on damp clouds, and harping to the winds; but they should be a hearty, manly, vigorous set of *inspired gentlemen*, erect and broad-chested, with features more on the robust than the romantic style—writing in snug studies, or fine, large libraries, surrounded by beauty, elegance, and comfort—receiving inspiration quietly and at regular hours, after a hot breakfast, the morning paper, and a cigar—given to hospitality and great dinners—driving their own bays, and treating their excellent wives to a box at the opera, a season at Newport, a trip to the Falls, or a winter in Rome.

The comforts of life have been long enough monopolized by thrifty tradesmen—"men in the coal and cattle line"—and good living by bishops and aldermen. It is the divine right of genius to be well kept and cared for by the world, which too often "entertains the angel unaware," on thin soups and sour wines, or, at the best, on unsubstantial *puff-paste*.

I heard yesterday that Fredrika Bremer had really arrived in New York. I hope that it is so. She has hosts of admirers all over our country, and is actually loved as few authors are loved, with a simple, cordial, *home* affection—for she is especially a writer for the fireside, the family circle, and thus addresses herself to the affections of a people whose purest joys and deepest interests centre in domestic life. America will take to her heart this child of genius and of nature—her home shall be by every hearth in our land, which has been made a dearer and a brighter place by her poetry, her romance, and her genial humour. She will be welcomed joyfully by every nature which has profited by her pure teachings, and received her revelations—by every spirit which has been borne upward by her aspirations, or softened by the spring breath, the soft warmth and light of her love.

To *woman* has the Swedish novelist spoken, and by woman must she be welcomed and honoured here; but to the *men* of America comes one whose very name should cause the blood to leap along their veins—he, the heart's brother of freemen all over the world—the patriot, prophet, and soldier, the hero of the age—Kossuth the Hungarian!

How will he be received here? How will the deep, intense, yet mournful sympathy, the soul-felt admiration, the generous homage of the country, find expression? Not in parades and dinners, and public speeches, for Heaven's sake!

Would you feast and *fête* a man on whose single heart is laid the dead, crushing weight of a nation's sorrow—about whose spirit a nation's despair makes deep, perpetual night?

I know not how my countrymen will meet this glorious exile; but were I a young man, with all the early love and fresh enthusiasm for liberty and heroism, I would bow reverently, and silently kiss his hand. Were I a pure and tried statesman, an honest patriot, I would fold him to my breast. Were I an old veteran, with the fire of freedom yet warming the veins whose young blood once flowed in her cause, I should wish to look on Kossuth and die.

Who can say this man has lived in vain? Though it was not his to strike the shackles from his beloved land, till she should stand free and mighty before Heaven, has he not struggled and suffered for her? Has he not spoken hallowed and immortal words—words which have gone forth to the nations, a power and a prophecy, which shall sound on and on, long after his troubled life is past—on and on, till their work is accomplished in great deeds—and the deeds become history, to be read by free men with quickened breath, and eyes that lighten with exultation? And it is a great thing that Europe, darkened by superstition and crushed by despotism, has known another hero—a race of heroes, I might say, for the Hungarian uprising has been a startling and terrific spectacle for kings and emperors. And "the end is not yet." There must be a sure, a terrible retribution for the oppressors—a yet more fearful *finale* to this world-witnessed tragedy. While the heavens endure, let us hold on to the faith that the right shall prevail against the wrong, when the last long struggle shall come, that the soul of freedom is imperishable, and shall triumph over all oppressions on the face of the whole earth.

ANNE C. LYNCH.

ANNE CHARLOTTE LYNCH was born in Bennington, Vermont.

Her father belonged to the gallant band of "United Irishmen," who so vainly attempted in 1798 to achieve the independence of the "Emerald Isle." At the age of sixteen, against the protests, and even commands of his father, he joined the rebels, and, with many others, was soon made prisoner. During a gloomy imprisonment of four years, he received advantageous offers of liberty and a commission in the army, if he would take the oath of allegiance. These offers he boldly spurned, and at the age of twenty, with Emmet, McNeven, and other illustrious exiles, came to the United States. He married a daughter of Colonel Gray, and finally died in Cuba, where he had gone in search of health.

On the mother's side, also, Miss Lynch has patriot blood in her veins. Her grandfather, Lieutenant-Colonel Gray, of the 6th Regiment of the Connecticut Line, received his first commission in January, 1776. He was appointed Major in 1777, and Lieutenant-Colonel in 1778, which rank he held till the close of the war. He served in the army of the Revolution during the whole period of seven years, and retired at the close of the war with a constitution so broken down by the fatigues and hardships he had undergone, that he was never able to resume the duties of his profession, and he died, after a few years, of a lingering disease, contracted in the service, leaving his family entirely destitute. The widow of Colonel Gray petitioned Congress several times ineffectually for relief. The petition was renewed by her daughter, Mrs. Lynch, in 1850, and, through the tact and persuasive eloquence of the grand-daughter, finally received a favourable hearing, even amid the exciting scenes of the Compromise Congress.

After finishing her education, which was at a female seminary of some celebrity in Albany, Miss Lynch lived for a time in Providence, Rhode Island. There she published, in 1841, a volume entitled the "Rhode

Island Book," consisting of selections of prose and verse from the writers of that State, and including several pieces of her own. She subsequently spent some time in Philadelphia, where her poetical abilities attracted much attention, and gained for her the friendship and encouragement of many persons of distinction; among others, of Fanny Kemble, then in the zenith of her popularity. Several of her poems were contributed to the "Gift" in 1845, also a long chapter in prose called "Leaves from the Diary of a Recluse."

For the last eight or nine years she has lived in the city of New York. In this period she has contributed to the current literature of the day, both in prose and verse. A collection of her poems was published in 1848, in a small quarto, elegantly illustrated with original designs by Huntington, Cheney, Darley, Durand, Rothermel, Rossiter, Cushman, Brown, and Winner.

The combination of the social element with the pursuits of literature and art, is a problem to which Miss Lynch has given a practical solution, and by which she has gained her chief celebrity. She has for many years opened her house on every Saturday evening to ladies and gentlemen of her acquaintance, connected with literature or the fine arts. Men and women of genius here meet, very much as merchants meet on 'Change, without ceremony, and for the exchange of thought. They pass together two hours in conversation, music, song, sometimes recitation, and disperse without eating or drinking, nothing in the shape of material refreshment being ever offered. At no place of concourse, it is said, is one so sure to see the leading celebrities of the town. I give two sketches of these soirées, the first from a writer—evidently a woman—in Neal's Gazette, the second from the pen of Miss Sedgwick:

"At her brilliant Saturday evening reunions one may see all who are in any way distinguished for scientific, artistic, or literary attainments, mingled with a band of fine appreciating spirits, who are content with that power of appreciation, and whose social position shows at once the high station which Miss Lynch has won by her merits as a woman and a scholar.

"One of these same reunions would be the realization of many a school-girl's dream of happiness. We can almost see the young neophyte of authorland nestled in some sheltering recess, or shrouded by benevolent drapery, and gazing with wonder and admiration on those whose words have long been the companions of her solitary hours.

"'Can that really be Mrs. Osgood?' she would exclaim, as a light figure glided before her retirement.

"'Is that truly Mrs. Oakes Smith on the sofa beside Mrs. Hewitt? Grace Greenwood! how I have longed to see her, and Darley, Willis, Bayard Taylor, ah! me,' and the sweet eyes would grow weary with watching the bright constellation, and the little hands clasp each other close—and more closely still, as she tried to realize that those whom she had long loved were in truth before her.

"Then gliding through their midst, calmly, almost proudly in her serene repose, is the hostess herself. Her wavy hair, gathered in a braided coronet, her mild, blue eyes serenely smiling, and at once thoughts of Miss Barret's Lady Geraldine come to the mind of the gazer, and these words to her parted lips—

> "For her eyes alone smiled constantly; her lips had serious sweetness,
> And her front was calm—the dimple rarely rippled on her cheek;
> But her deep blue eyes smiled constantly, as if they had by fitness
> The secret of a happy dream she did not care to speak."

"There is a warm greeting and kind word for all, and even the little trembler in the window curtain does not start as she kindly addresses her."

The next extract is from Miss Sedgwick, written in the character of a gentleman on a visit to New York.

"From Mallark's, I passed to the drawing-room of Miss Lynch. It was her reception evening. I was admitted to a rather dimly lighted hall by a little portress, some ten or twelve years old, who led me to a small apartment to deposit my hat and cloak. There was no lighted staircase, no train attendant, none of the common flourish at city parties. 'Up stairs, if you please, sir—front room for the ladies—back for the gentlemen;' no indication of an overturn or commotion in the domestic world; no cross father, worried mother, or scolded servants behind the scenes—not even a faint resemblance to the eating, worrying, and tossing of 'the house that Jack built.' The locomotive was evidently not off the track; the spheres moved harmoniously. To my surprise, when I entered, I found two fair-sized drawing-rooms filled with guests, in a high state of social enjoyment. There was music, dancing, recitation, and conversation. I met an intimate friend there, and availing myself of the common privilege of a stranger in town I inquired out the company. There were artists in every department—painting, poetry, sculpture, and music. There I saw for the first time that impersonation of genius, Ole Bull. Even the histrionic art asserted its right to social equality there in the person of one of its honourable professors. You may think that my hostess, for one so young and so very fair, opened her doors too wide. Perhaps so, for though I detest the duenna system and believe that the unguarded freedom permitted to our young ladies far safer as well as more agreeable, yet I would rather have seen the mother of Miss Lynch present. Certainly no one ever needed an ægis less than my lovely hostess. She has that quiet delicacy and dignity of manners that is as a 'glittering angel' to exorcise every evil spirit that should venture to approach her. How, without fortune or fashion, she has achieved her position in your city, where everything goes under favour of these divinities, I am sure I cannot tell. To be sure, she has that aristocracy which supersedes all others—that to which prince and peasant instinctively bow—and though unknown in the fashionable world, you would as soon confound the exquisite work of a Greek sculptor with the wax figures of an itinerant showman, as degrade her to the level of a conventional belle.

"Yet she does not open her house as a temple to worshippers of whom she is the divinity, but apparently simply to afford her acquaintances the hospitality of a place of social meeting. She retires behind her guests, and seems to desire to be the least observed of all observers.

"I had supposed that war might as well be carried on without its munitions, officers as well live without their salaries, children as well go to bed without their suppers, as a party to go off without its material entertainment. But here was the song without the supper, not even those poor shadows of refreshments, cakes and lemonade. Here was a young woman without 'position'—to use the cant phrase—without any relations to the fashionable world, filling her rooms weekly with choice spirits, who came without any extraordinary expense of dress, who enjoyed high rational pleasures for two or three hours, and retired so early as to make no drafts on the health or spirits of the next day. I communicated my perplexity to a foreign acquaintance whom I met at Mrs. Booth's.

"'Why,' said he, 'your fair friend has hit upon a favourite form of society common in the highest civilization. Miss Lynch's soirees are Parisian—only not in Paris. Not in the world, with the exception of the United States, could a beautiful young woman take the responsibility unmatronized of such a 'reception.'"

FREDRIKA BREMER.

When it was announced, a few months since, that Fredrika Bremer had landed upon our shores, the intelligence was received by the thousands who have read her works, with an interest that admiration of literary talent or genius alone could never have inspired. More than almost any other writer, Miss Bremer seems to have become a personal friend to every reader, and the cause of this is to be found in a far deeper source than mere admiration for the novelty and vividness of her narratives, her quiet pictures of domestic life, or her strong delineations of the workings of human passion. Her large and sympathetic heart is attuned to such harmony with humanity, or rather she so expresses this beautiful harmony of her own soul with God, with nature, and with humanity, that the human heart that has suffered or enjoyed, vibrates and responds like a harp-string to the master-hand. She has somewhere said, "Hereafter, when I no more belong to earth, I should love to return to it as a spirit, and impart to man the deepest of that which I have suffered and enjoyed, lived and loved. And no one need fear me;—should I come in the midnight hour to a striving and unquiet spirit, it would be only to make it more quiet, its night-lamp burn more brightly, and myself its friend and sister." Although she still belongs to earth, this aspiration has been satisfied. Even here, without having crossed the mysterious bourn, she has revealed to us great depths of suffering and joy, of life and love, and to many troubled hearts she has come in their midnight hours, a friend, a sister, a consoler. It is no wonder, then, that homes and hearts have opened to her, and that welcome and gratitude await her in every town and village of our country.

When Miss Bremer's works were first introduced to us a few years ago, the brilliant narrations of Scott had been succeeded by the passionate and romantic creations of Bulwer, and our literature was flooded with inundations from the voluptuous and sensational school of France, which deposited its *débris* and diffused its malaria wherever its impure waters subsided. At this period the writings of Fredrika Bremer came upon us, suddenly and beautiful as summer comes in her northern clime, as pure and sparkling as its mountain streams, as fresh and invigorating as its mountain air.

As works of art, or in a literary point of view, these novels have doubtless their faults. But those who have been elevated by their ennobling spirit, who have drunk at their clear, cool fountains, and felt their strengthening and life-giving influence, who have dwelt with her lovely characters in their happy homes, and participated in their joys and sorrows, would find it as impossible to turn upon them the cold eye of the critic, as to analyze the sunshine and the landscape that delight the eye, or to judge the features of a beloved friend by the strictest rules of beauty or of art. The office of the critic has come to be in literature what that of the surgeon is in the actual world. With perfect development, beauty, and harmony, he has nothing to do. He has eyes only for deformities and faults, and wherever they are to be found, he applies his merciless scalpel, with a firm hand and an unrelenting heart. But the critic who judges by rules of art alone, does not give us the highest truth any more than the chemist, who, while he shows us how to analyze the diamond and to resolve it to its original elements, forgets to place it before us flashing in the sunlight; or the botanist who, in dissecting the flower, leaves its beauty to pass unnoticed, and its perfume to escape. Mere criticism is the judgment of the intellect alone; but the highest and truest judgment is that where the heart also has a voice, and an object seen through the one or the other medium, intellect or heart, is like those transparencies which in one light represent the dreary desolation of a winter landscape, and in the other, all the luxuriance and beauty of summer.

The age in which we live is one of scepticism, of analysis, and of transition. Religion, government, society, are all in turn investigated by its indomitable spirit of inquiry. All great questions relating to humanity, its reform, its progress, and its final destiny, are agitated to a degree not known before at any period of the world's history. The conservative and destructive principles are at war, and there are moments when those of the firmest faith seem to doubt what the final issue of the contest may be. The literature, as could not fail to be the case, takes its tone from the spirit of the age, and no department of literature has more direct bearing upon the popular mind than that of fiction. He who writes the songs and romances of a people may well leave to others to make their laws. Not, indeed, those lighter romances, intended only to interest or amuse the fancy, but those which embody some deep sentiment, or some vital principle of society or of religion. Truths and principles thus inculcated or diffused, have their most direct influence upon the youthful mind, and, like the impressions made upon the rock in its transition state, they harden and remain.

As an instance of the extent of this influence of fiction, we may refer to the writings of that woman, who, possessing the most extraordinary combination of masculine and feminine qualities under the name of George Sand, for the last few years has taken the first rank among the writers of her native language, and from that eminence has exercised such incalculable influence, not only over her own but all other countries. George Sand and Fredrika Bremer stand at the head of two widely different classes of fictitious writing, each having other and higher objects than to amuse. Through the writings of both there is a deep and powerful undercurrent, to which the story is but the sparkle on the surface. Both discuss great questions of social reform, the laws of marriage, and the nature of love. Both enter the temple of humanity—but the one to overthrow its altars, and to shatter its cherished images—the other to render them more firm and steadfast—to burn incense on the shrines, and adorn them with garlands of immortal flowers. The genius of the one is the flaming torch of the incendiary, that carries destruction and desolation in its course—that of the other is the fragrant lamp, that illumines the darkness, and dispels, by its steady and benignant beams, the gathering and mysterious gloom. The course of the one has been like that of the furious tempest of the tropical regions, that uproots the old landmarks, floods the gentle streams till they overflow their channels, and sweep away banks, bridges, and barriers that oppose their course; that of the other, like the evening dews and the summer showers, that sink softly into the bosom of the earth, refreshing, gladdening, and fertilizing.

The institution of marriage, the root from which society springs, the groundwork upon which it stands, George Sand, with all the force of her genius and eloquence, seeks to degrade and to destroy; while Fredrika Bremer would ennoble, not the institution of marriage only, but she would exalt it into that deeper and holier spiritual union, of which the actual marriage is but the symbol. Love, that most divine of all our sentiments, the bloom and perfume of the tree of Life, the sun that lights and gladdens the night of existence, the one presents to us as burning with all the voluptuous ardour of the senses, the other, as glowing with the sacred fire of the impassioned soul.

It seems to be a law of Providence, that good and evil should ever co-exist, both in the outer and inner world; that wherever poisons abound, the antidotes are also to be found; and the contemporaneous appearance of the two leading minds we have been contrasting, is an instance of the verification of this law in the intellectual or moral world. Some one has truly said, that "where nothing great is to be done, the existence of great men is impossible." Goodness is only one form of greatness, and in opposing the influence of the materializing and disorganizing school of French romances, there was a great good to be attained; and by Miss Bremer, and the class of writers of which she stands at the head, it has been in a measure accomplished; for there is another law of Providence which secures the final triumph of good over evil, and renders the contest not doubtful in the end, although it may be of long duration.

Besides the French school of romance writers, there is another, to which the works of Miss Bremer offer an equally salutary antidote. We refer to those who, with contempt in their hearts, and bitterness and sarcasm on their lips, go through the world like Mephistopheles, only to sneer at the weaknesses of humanity, to magnify its errors, and to question or despise its virtues, and who, like certain birds of prey, seem to be attracted only by that which is in its nature offensive. The mischief of such works is, that they lower the standard of human excellence, they unsettle our faith in human nature, and they engender a sceptical and contemptuous spirit, that as fatally extinguishes the higher virtues and aspirations, as fire-damp extinguishes the miner's lamp. Goethe has somewhere said that if we would make men better, we must treat them as if they were better than they are; if we take them at their actual level we make them worse; much more then do we render them worse when we put them below their actual level, preserving, though caricaturing the likeness.

The characters Miss Bremer has drawn, while they are free from this charge, do not on the other hand fall into the opposite error of being too favourably depicted. They represent human nature as it often is, as it is always capable of being, refined, elevated, and noble. The home affections that she so vividly portrays, though originating in the domestic circle, radiate from that centre until they encompass all that live and suffer, genial as the sun, and embracing as the atmosphere; and, like the sun and air in the outward world, they call forth the verdure and bloom of the inner life in all those whom they thus enfold.

It may be objected that we assign too great an influence, too prominent a position, to these creations of the imagination, presented to us on the pages of fiction. But fiction, in its action on the mind, has all the effect of history; it has even an advantage over history. Since the one gives but the outward and apparent life, while the other enters the secret recesses of the heart, unveils the hidden springs of motive and of action, and lays open to our view, what no history and no confessions ever do, the secret workings of the human soul, that most mysterious and complicated of all the works of God. Into these "beings of the mind," the writer of fiction, like the sculptor of old, breathes life, thought, and immortality, and they become to us positive existences. Lear and Cordelia, Othello and Desdemona, Ivanhoe and Rebecca, are as much realities as if they had dwelt upon the earth, and their lives had come down to us beside those of the heroes and heroines of history. So it is with the characters Miss Bremer has drawn. We are as familiar with Bear and his little wife, as if we had dwelt with them at their cottage-home of Rosenvik. We shrink before the iron will and the imperious commands of *Ma chère mère*, and shudder to encounter the dark form and the lowering glance of the fierce Bruno.

If, then, fiction in its effects is to be regarded as possessing equal power with history, it becomes a more important feature, not only in literature, but in morals, and should occupy a higher place than has been assigned to it, and those who people the world with these airy yet actual beings, and present to us in them ideals to contemplate and to imitate, should be regarded as the benefactors of men. And so, indeed, it has been with her who is the subject of this brief sketch. Her works have gone abroad on their message of peace and love over the civilized world, and her fame has resounded far and wide, till its echo returned to her native land. Fame, as it is generally understood, however, is but a poor expression of the relation that exists between Miss Bremer and her world of readers; it is but the outward fact of the deep, spiritual relation she bears to them all; for each one receives from her some direct rays, as the wavelets of the lake, lying in the light of the moon, receive each some beam of her silver light.

As to Miss Bremer's future, we do not consider her course by any means as ended. We know that in her works, as in her life, she aspires to that ascending metamorphosis, without which the normal development of life is not accomplished. We know that she aspires to put the romance of individual life in closer connexion with the great romance of humanity, and that her present visit to the New World is connected with this view. We know that through the impressions here received, she hopes to realize and to give expression to ardent hopes and long-cherished visions. We know that "the light of her life's day, like that of the morning, will be an ascending one, and that whether its beam shine through mist or through clear air, that the day will increase—the life will brighten."

MARY E. HEWITT.

MRS. HEWITT'S maiden name was Mary Elizabeth Moore. She was born in Malden, Massachusetts. Her father, an independent New England farmer, a man of good education, and fine personal appearance, died when Mary was but three years of age, leaving a young wife and four children. The family removed the following year to Boston, where the subject of this sketch remained until her marriage with Mr. James L. Hewitt, an extensive publisher of music in New York city. In this latter place Mrs. Hewitt has resided ever since.

By her maternal grandfather she is descended from an old family by the name of Collins, in Kent, England. "Thomas Collins, lord of the manor,—son of John, son of Alexander, son of Alexander," was first permitted to bear a coat of arms, and to figure in heraldry with "gules," and "griffins," and "martelets azure." By her maternal grandmother, however, she had a descent still more honourable, being a lineal descendant of the good old puritan, Roger Williams.

As a writer, Mrs. Hewitt is known almost exclusively by her poetry. A volume of her poems published in Boston in 1846, called "The Songs of our Land," was very well received, both in England and America. Edgar A. Poe published three separate critiques on these poems. After a very learned show of "trochees" and "iambuses," he declares that "they are generally, rather than particularly, commendable—abounding in forcible passages," and that "many of them would do credit to any poet in the land." He pronounces the "Hercules and Omphale" to be "worthy of all praise," and "that *rara avis* in our literature, a well-constructed sonnet."

Mrs. Hewitt's prose writings, though not numerous, have been such as to justify the expectation raised by her poems. She has contributed several excellent stories to the "Memorial," the "Odd Fellows' Offering," and the "Gem of the Western World," and some sketches for the "Southern

Literary Messenger." She is at present engaged upon a prose volume, to be entitled "The Heroines of History."

The following extract is from an Irish legend, the events of which are supposed to have occurred during the times of the Druidical superstition.

A LEGEND OF IRELAND.

THE business of state was over for the day. Judgments had been awarded, the different records of the kingdom examined, and whatever material they afforded for national history had been carefully entered in the great national record called the Psalter of Tara; when a herald advanced and proclaimed to the assembly that a combat would take place on the morrow, between Conrigh, a celebrated chieftain, and Maon, a knight of the Red Branch. These warriors had each demanded the hand of the lady Brehilda, the king's ward, as the meed of their prowess in battle, and the lady was to be the reward of the successful competitor. But Brehilda had known Maon and loved him from her childhood, far away in her own home; for he was the son of a neighbouring chieftain, and years ago he had gathered flowers for her upon the hills, and walked at her bridle rein, while her rough pony scrambled with her over the rocky passes.

But her sire was dead—no son inherited his name and glory—his estate had passed away to a distant male relative; for, by the law existing among the Irish, females of every degree were precluded from the inheritance, and Brehilda was the ward of the nation's monarch.

There was feasting that night in the palace of Tara, and a noble assemblage of the brave and beautiful of the land. In the banquet hall the bards sang the praises of heroes to the harp, while the chiefs feasted at the board and quaffed meadh from the corna—the trumpet in battle, and in peace the drinking cup—and in the lighted saloon the guests of the monarch danced the *rincead-fadha*, the national dance, to the music of the harp, the tabor, and the corobasnas—an instrument formed of two circular pieces of brass, strung together by a wire of the same metal and used for marking time—but the lady Brehilda sat alone in her bower, looking out upon the moonlit scene, and thinking with a dread foreboding of the morrow, which might separate her for ever from the one she loved, and consign her to a hateful existence with Conrigh.

The walls of the apartment were hung with tapestry representing the landing of Heremon and Heber, and the contests of the Danonians with their Milesian invaders. The floor was strewn with fresh rushes, and the few articles of furniture scattered throughout the room, were as rude in design and workmanship as the age to which they belonged. An embroidery frame was placed in one corner, and near it a small harp, such as was used by ladies of the time, rested against a low table.

Without the tower lay the moonlit sward, the glittering river winding away among the woody hills, the rude castle of the chieftain, and the mud hovel of the peasant, where from the windows of each gleamed out the festal torch and the fire light.

But the sound of mirth had ceased in the palace of Tara, and the lights had gone out one by one from the distant dwellings, and still Brehilda sat at the narrow window, communing with her own sad heart. She was very beautiful as she sat there in her grief, with her fair hair, that had escaped from its fillet, falling in ripples of gold over her green, embroidered kirtle almost to the border of the white garment beneath it. Her small hands clasped, rested upon her lap, and her full blue eyes were turned tearfully upward, as if she were invoking the One great Principle of the universe, whose worship the Druids taught, to strengthen the arm of her lover and save her from the fate she would rather die than meet. The moon was now slowly descending behind the distant hills, and all nature reposed in silence, when the strings of a harp lightly touched, sounded from a grove not far off, and a full, manly voice sang the following words:

Doubt not my steed—he hath breasted the water,
  When the torrent came down from the hills in its might;
And with white, flowing mane, deeply reddened in slaughter,
  He hath borne me in battle, nor shrank from the fight.
Doubt not my lance—a young mountain scion,
  It grew 'mid the storm, rooted fast to the rock;

Its point knows the sound of a breastplate of iron,
  And gladly it springs, like my steed, to the shock.

Doubt not my arm in the combat will serve me—
  My bard sings the deeds of his chieftain, with pride;
And the strength of a legion to-morrow will nerve me
  To conquer in battle, and win thee my bride.
Doubt not my heart, in its truth, here repeating
  That thou art its life-pulse—the throb of my breast—
And never till death stops my bosom's swift beating,
  In the cold narrow house, will thy thought be at rest.

Springing to her feet at the first sound of the voice, every feature of her beautiful face lighted up with intense joy, she stood like a young pythoness filled with the oracle, and extended her arms toward a figure arrayed in the long, fringed colchal of a bard, that now emerged from the grove, and whom her heart told her truly could be no other than Maon. Casting back the hood from his face, he stood revealed in the waning moonlight, and raising his hand to his lips, then waving it upward in parting salutation to the maiden, he again entered the grove and disappeared; and Brehilda, strengthened by the words of his song, and reassured by his presence, retired to her couch, and soon in sweet slumber forgot the cares that oppressed her heart.

The morrow, like all dreaded to-morrows, dawned brightly. The combat was to take place early in the day, and the field had been prepared for the rivals and those who were to witness the contest. The thrones of the Irish monarch and the kings of the four provinces were arranged much in the same manner as in the hall of legislation, save that the King of Connaught had his place on the left of the King of Munster, while platforms or galleries were erected on either side for the accommodation of spectators.

It is not to be supposed that a trial of arms in that remote time was conducted with the order and magnificence of the more modern tournament; but still the field was not wanting in much of the material that served to make up the display of that after period. The seats around the arena were now filling to their utmost extent and capacity. There were nobles and knights, and esquires bearing the shields of their chiefs; and to the several orders of bards assembled for the convention of the states were assigned conspicuous places in the enclosure. Each king, robed in the colours appropriate to royalty, occupied the throne prepared for him, seated beneath his own banner, and in a gallery behind the throne of Ollamh sat Brehilda, arrayed like a noble Irish maiden, pale as sculptured marble, surrounded by the principal ladies of the monarch's court.

At a loud blast of the corna the combatants entered the arena from opposite sides of the field. They were noble in appearance, well matched in size, and sat their chafing steeds as firmly as the Thessalian riders whose horsemanship gave birth to the fabled Centaurs. Each warrior was arrayed in the rude and defective armour of the time—the head covered with the head-piece of iron, which at that period had neither crest nor vizor. The right hand bore a lance, the left arm a buckler, while an iron maul, powerful as the hammer of the northern Thunder God, hung pendent at each saddle-bow, for the battle-axe was then unknown in warfare. Eager for the conflict, at a signal from the herald they sprang to the encounter, and for a long time the victory seemed doubtful; but the lance of Conrigh splintered against the shield of Maon, and each unslung the ponderous maul, and poising it aloft, again spurred to the contest.

With hushed heart and dilated eyes Brehilda gazed upon the scene. A moment of intense bewilderment, and she sank in a death-like swoon upon the floor of the gallery, for Maon lay stunned upon the field, beneath his prostrate steed. The shout that hailed the victor was unheard by the maiden as they bore her from the throng, and placed her insensible form upon the couch in her tower.

But the festival was over. The solemn feast in the temple of Yiachto had been partaken of—the great fire of Samhuin had been lighted, and the Deity invoked to bless their national counsels, and Conrigh had departed to his castle on the river Fionglasse, in the county of Kerry, where he dwelt in all the barbarism of feudal magnificence, bearing with him his bride, the wretched Brehilda.

Neither the devotion of her lord, nor the splendour that surrounded her, could console, or render the new-made wife contented with her lot. She envied the peasant maidens who milked the kine beyond her window, free to love where the heart prompted and to wed where they loved—and her daily prayer to Dhia, the great Creator of all things, was that her spirit might be permitted to enter the flowery fields, and dwell in the airy halls of Flathinnis, the Druidical heaven, with those beloved who had gone before.

The winter was ended, and the festival of Beil Tinne was at hand. All nature seemed to rejoice in the season of the returning sun, and Brehilda, to whom the brightness of spring brought no joy, wandered alone on the banks of the Fionglasse. The birds sang upward to the highest heaven, and the over-hanging trees waved their fresh green leaves to the rippling water. Brehilda seated herself listlessly beside the stream, and anon the following song from her lips, in a subdued voice, sounded tunefully over the waters.

They have parted for ever
  Our hearts' rosy chain,
And bound me, all helpless,
  To a love I disdain.
They have ruthless bereft us
  Of the fond hope of years,
And given my young life
  To sorrow and tears.

Yet my heart, Oh Beloved,
  To thy memory clings,
As the bird o'er her nestling
  Folds closely her wings.
The dark clouds may gather
  Aloft in the sky,
And the tempest toss wildly
  The branches on high;

But faithful and fond,
  With her young 'neath her breast,
Still fearlessly cleaveth
  The bird to her nest.
And thus, though in peril,
  And secret it be,
Oh! Bird of my breast!
  Clings my true heart to thee.

Scarcely was the song finished when a light skiff, made of hide stretched over a frame of wicker, propelled by a single oarsman, shot out from beyond a clump of alders, and swiftly approached the river's bank. Touching the earth lightly with his oar, the boatman leaped to land almost at the feet of Brehilda. He was clad in the simple garb of a peasant, and Brehilda, alarmed at the act of the stranger, would have fled, but a motion of his hand restrained her, and the next moment she lay panting and sobbing on the bosom of Maon.

Their interview was long, and passionate their communing, and at length the lovers parted. Maon again embarked on the Fion-glasse, and Brehilda returned to the castle.

In those early days, when war and glory were the theme of song, acts of violence and bloodshed were frequent, and revenge followed fast upon wrong; for the light of revelation had not yet dawned upon the world that knew no return for injury but retribution.

It was the first of May, and the day of the festival of Beil Tinne. Fires were lighted, and sacrifices were offered on the most lofty eminences in every part of the kingdom to Beil, or the Sun. The Druids danced around their round towers the sacred dance of their profession, as was the custom of this priesthood during the religious festivals of the nation; and the martial followers of the chiefs joined in the Rinkey, or field-dance—a performance not unlike the armed dance with which the Greek youth amused themselves at the siege of Troy—to the sound of the bag-pipes, upon the green-sward.

A stranger bard feasted that night in the hall of Conrigh, with the guests and retainers of the chieftain. He wore the *truise* of weft, which covered the feet, legs, and thighs, as far as the loins, striped with various colours, and fitting so closely as to discover every motion and muscle of the limbs; and the *cotaigh*, or tunic of linen, dyed yellow, and ornamented with needle-work, reaching to the mid-thigh, and confined around the loins by an embroidered girdle. The sleeves of this garment were loose and long, and the bosom was cut round, leaving the neck and upper part of the shoulders bare. His beard was long, and his hair flowed over his neck and shoulders in wavy luxuriance. Thus arrayed in the picturesque habit allowed to that order of men whose persons were held sacred everywhere throughout the kingdom, he was one of those noble specimens of manly beauty formed to awaken the interest and admiration of all beholders.

Meadh foamed at the board—the bards sang "the days of other years," nor was the theme of love held unmeet for so joyous an occasion—the harp was passed round from hand to hand among the guests, each one contributing his portion of song to enliven the feast, and the unknown bard, in his turn taking the instrument, struck the chords loudly; and while Brehilda, who was seated near her lord, listened, trembling and pale with apprehension lest the intruder should be discovered beneath the disguise which the eyes of love had already penetrated, he sang—

The dove was the falcon's love,
  The dove with her tender breast;
Ah! weary the fate that gave
  The dove to the kite's vile nest!
The moon from yon cloud to-night
  Looks down on the feast of shells;
Oh, marked she the falcon's flight
  For the home where his own dove dwells?

There's a veil o'er my harp's true strings,
  There's a cloud o'er the fair moon's breast;
And the falcon, with outspread wings,
  Hangs o'er the kite's vile nest.
The famishing birds of prey,
  Are hurrying through the night,
But the dove with her falcon love
  Will have flown ere the morning light!

The feast flowed on, uninterrupted by aught but song; and at a late hour the revellers retired from the banquet to their apartments in the castle.

It was long after midnight, when the sleepers were aroused from their slumbers by the sound of conflict in the hall below. Hastily dressed, and half armed, they rushed forth from their apartments to meet the swords of their unknown assailants. Wildly the contest raged, and everywhere was seen the strange bard, encouraging the intruders, until at length in the affray he encountered Conrigh, and casting off the false beard that disguised him, they stood face to face amid the combat—the husband and the lover of Brehilda. They fought with all the terrible hate that animated them, and Conrigh fell, pierced with many wounds, beneath the sword of his adversary. A brief moment, and Maon, bearing the insensible form of Brehilda, passed swiftly through the hall and out at the portal. Mounting a strong steed, while the assailants continued their work of blood, and placing her for whom he had wrought the night's sacrifice, before him, he fled with all speed toward the court of Conquovar Mac Nessa, King of Ulster.

This wise and munificent king was a patron of the learned, and in his court the unfortunate and the proscribed found an asylum and a mediator. Morning dawned as Maon paused in his flight beside a running spring, and alighted with his unconscious burthen. He sprinkled her brow with the cool lymph, and filling the korn—the cup sacred to the deity of the earth and the waters, suspended from the overhanging branch of a tree—he raised the draught to her lips. Who can describe the rapture of Brehilda, on awaking from her long trance, to find herself supported by the arms of the lover of her girlhood, and to meet again his look of ardent affection.

ALICE B. NEAL.

THE banks of the Hudson seem destined to become classic ground. Not a few of our most distinguished writers, men and women, have either lent their genius to the celebration of its beauties, or have themselves drawn inspiration from its mountain breezes. The name of Alice B. Neal is now to be added to the list. Born in 1828, in the city of Hudson, she may have owed her early love for the beautiful to the romantic scenery by which her childhood was surrounded. If there be any truth in the theory of physical influences upon the mental, we may in like manner trace something of the enduring energy with which she has met her many trials to her subsequent dwelling upon the hardier soil of the granite State. Her education was finished in New Hampshire, where she gave early indications of intellectual superiority.

An apparently trivial incident of the school-room led to a most romantic issue, and fixed indeed her course in life. In a sportive hour, her schoolmates challenged her to try her success before the world with some of those compositions which had so excited the admiration of the school. The challenge was accepted, and a tale was at once despatched to Joseph C Neal, who had then just established the "Saturday Gazette." It was entitled "The Game of Checkers," and signed Alice G. Lee.

Mr. Neal was then in the prime of his days, and one of the acknowledged arbiters of taste in literature. His decision as to the rejection or the acceptance of the story was watched with eager eyes by the merry young coterie. How those eyes must have sparkled to find in a subsequent Gazette, not only the tale published in full, but on a third prose contribution, "The First Declaration," the following editorial comments:

"Taking it for granted that our literary department for the week will receive an attentive perusal, we shall be mistaken—much mistaken, ladies—for to your peculiar appreciation of the beautiful and refined we appeal, particularly in the present instance—if the reader does not agree with us in our estimate of the merits of the charming original sketch, published in our present number, from the pen of Miss Alice G. Lee.

"'No offence to the general, or any man of quality,' as Cassio has it; but though second to none in our admiration of 'Fanny Forrester,' it would be injustice not to say, that 'The First Declaration' will compare, without injury, to any other production of the kind that has adorned of late our periodical literature. How it may affect others we cannot tell; but it is to us like moonlight on the flowers when the weary day is done, or like music on the waters, to meet with a sketch so replete with playfulness, yet so delicately marked with Coleridge's 'instinct of ladyhood.' There is genius, too, and originality, in its *naiveté*—a nice and feminine perception of the beautiful, with an ability to portray it, which cannot fail of its purpose whenever it is thus executed."

The matter did not end here. The new author continued to contribute to the Gazette. A correspondence ensued, which led to the entertainment on his part of a deep and warm regard. Discovering at length, accidentally, that "Alice G. Lee" was a fiction, and that the real lady was Miss Emily Bradley, now returned to her own home on the Hudson, he immediately sought her acquaintance, and in December, 1846, received her hand in marriage, and brought her to Philadelphia, which has been her home ever since. At his request, she resumed, and she still retains, the endeared name of "Alice," by which he had first known her.

This union, so romantic in its origin, was doomed to a sad and speedy termination. In July, 1847, the hand of death left Mrs. Neal a widow, at the early age of nineteen. Experience shows, in the moral world if not in the physical, that the coarsest plants are not always the hardiest. This delicate flower, so tenderly fostered and so fragrantly blooming, beneath the genial influences that surround the parterres of city life, now that it was exposed to the blast, seemed suddenly to resume the hardihood of its mountain birth. With a courage that might do honour to an experienced matron, this widowed girl decided at once to assume the editorial duties of her deceased husband, and thus not only avoid eating the bread of dependence, but also win the dearer privilege of ministering to the comfort of her husband's now childless mother. At the death of Mr. Neal, the two ladies continued to live together, the younger gracefully acknowledging that the rich stores of experience, the varied reading, fine taste, and judicious counsels of her aged companion, have more than compensated for her own more active exertions.

Her first literary effort, after her mournful bereavement, was to superintend the publication of the third series of "Charcoal Sketches," by her late husband. She has since then, besides her weekly editorial labours in the Gazette, written several books for children, and contributed largely, both in prose and verse, to our leading Magazines. "Helen Morton," appeared in 1849 under the auspices of the Protestant Episcopal Sunday

School Union, and was well received. It has been followed by "Pictures from the Bible," and the continuations of "Helen Morton," called "Watch and Pray," and "In the World, but not of the World." She is at present engaged upon a series of juvenile books, for the Appletons. Four of them have already appeared: "No Such Word as Fail," "Patient Waiting no Loss," "Contentment Better than Wealth," "All's Not Gold that Glitters." Of her works of a different kind, the first that has assumed the book form is the "Gossips of Rivertown, or Lessons of Charity." Her other tales in Godey, Graham, and Sartain, would make, if collected, two or three volumes of the size of the "Gossips of Rivertown."

Mrs. Neal is still one of our youngest writers, and what is of most favourable omen, shows in her writings constant signs of improvement. In the language of a contemporary critic, who writes on this subject *con amore*, and whose opinion we make our own: "Her poetry has more maturity than her prose; for the gift of song comes to the bard, as to the bird, direct from Heaven. Polish and metrical correctness may be added to genuine poetry; but it is doubtful whether the fount be not as pure and sparkling at its first gush, as when quietly flowing on in a deeper stream. Mrs. Neal's prose compositions are continually improving, and the knowledge, which, with her uncommon industry, she is constantly acquiring, will enlarge her sphere of thought and illustration; and better yet, the religious tenor of her writings shows that she is guided by principles which will strengthen her intellect, and make her, we trust, in after years, an ornament and blessing to our famed land."

THE CHILD-LOVE.

"He prayeth best, who loveth best
All things both great and small;
For the dear God who loveth us—
He made and loveth all."—COLERIDGE.

"I AM sure *you* love me, little Miriam?"

"Love you?—oh, so dearly!" And, as if her childish words needed a stronger confirmation, she put her arms caressingly about his neck and laid her head upon his bosom. Her face was very lovely as she looked up to him in all the winning truthfulness of an affectionate heart. Large gray eyes, with lashes so long and deep as almost to give them a sorrowful expression at times, and a mouth now smiling, and so disclosing small pearly teeth, and then the crimson lips would meet in pouting fullness—

"As though a rose should shut,
And be a bud again."

So thought the student as he bent down to return the fond caress, and mingled his darker locks with the light floating curls that were thrown back over his shoulder.

"And will you *always* love me, Miriam?"

"Oh, always!"

"But when I am gone—for I may not be with you long; and then, when you do not see me every day, and you have other friends who love you better, and can make you more beautiful presents?"

She seemed to be pained, as if she understood the worldliness thus imputed to her, young as she was.

"But why must you go? and where will you go? Home?"

"Home! Ah, no, my child; I have not had a home these many years."

And then they were both silent for a little while; she pitying him because he had no home, and he dwelling on thoughts and recollections which the word had called up. The low brown farm-house where his boyish days were passed, with the mossy bank around the well; the little garden at the entrance of the orchard; the orchard itself, white with blossoms at this very season of the year. And then there was the brook, gurgling through the alder bushes, and reflecting the tall spires of the crimson cardinal, or the field lily, that sprung among the rich grass. He seemed once more to lie, an idle, careless boy, watching the clouds floating lazily overhead, while the summer insects sang around him, and the wind came gently to lift the hair from his sunburnt forehead.

This brought a recollection of his mother's kiss. It always seemed to him like the summer wind, so quiet, so warm, so loving. Her kiss and blessing, as she bent over his pillow, and then she would kneel and pray so earnestly for her son, her only child. How unlike his father was that gentle woman! He had wondered at that even when a boy. His stern, rigid parent, who rarely smiled, and made self-denial and never-ceasing labour his religion, as though he felt the curse of Cain ever upon his rugged fields.

They were united only in one thing, their love for him, and the zealous prayer that he might be, like Samuel, called even in childhood to the service of the Temple. So they had dedicated him; and, when he saw the grass springing upon their graves in the churchyard, and took a last look upon that humble home, now passed into other hands, he remembered this strong wish of the hearts that had loved him so, and were now mouldering to dust beneath his feet.

"But where are you going?" said the child, who had been thinking of many other things, and had now returned to this new fear of parting.

"Many, many hundred miles from this, Miriam, away from the busy city and its crowded streets. Far off to the still woods, where there are no church-bells, and even no Sabbaths. I am going to the poor Indians, to teach them where to look for the Great Spirit they worship, and to the settlers of those Western lands, ruder still, and in darker ignorance. They scarcely know there is a God."

"But they have the sky there, and the sun; and who do they think made them and the little flowers in the grass? They could not make the flowers!"

"But they do not love the flowers and the sky as you do; they are blind: 'Eyes have they, and they see not; ears, but they do not hear.' So I am going to them with God's own word, that will speak more plainly to their hearts. Do you not think it will be a beautiful life"—and his sunken eyes glanced with strange enthusiasm—"devoting every power of soul and body to those benighted people, forgetting this life and its comforts and pleasures in the thoughts of that which is to come?—reaping the broad whitening harvest?"

He forgot that he was speaking to a child. And yet she seemed to understand him, at least to feel that he was swayed by some noble emotion; for she raised her head and listened eagerly, as if a new life of thought was opened to her.

"And will you have a *home* there?"

"Nay, I shall never have a home on earth; parents, wife,

children are not for me. I go forth with neither purse nor scrip, following our Divine Master; I shall not have where to lay my head. But his love constrains me; he will not desert his servant." And his voice sank, as it were, to a thought of prayer for the strength he would need in the arduous path he had chosen.

"But you will be all alone and sick, and there will be no one to take care of you; then perhaps you will die." The look of sadness we have spoken of came into the child's earnest eyes, as she laid her soft head against his cheek, and wondered why he should choose to go away from her.

"We will not talk of this any longer, little one. I have made you so sad and grave. I do not like that look on your face; it is too womanly for such a little maiden. You are too young to understand all these things, and you must not try to; but you must love me, that is all I ask. See, there is your kitten, come to invite you away from me."

It was with a strong effort that he had shaken off the sombre mood into which he had fallen, and attempted to enter into her childish amusements once more. He was startled by the earnest, dreamy look that she still retained. As he had said, it was too womanly for that young fair face.

She smiled again; obedience to those she loved was the strong principle of her nature, for she had ever been governed by affection. No one ever spoke a harsh word to Miriam, motherless Miriam Arnold, the light of her father's lonely life, and the pet of the neighbours, who looked out to catch a glimpse of her light figure as she bounded up the dark court like a flitting ray of sunshine. It was a gloomy abode for such a bright young creature, or a stranger would have thought so. The house so old and cheerless, far away from the gay shops and the beautiful women who frequent them. There was not even a green tree or an ivy wreath to refresh the eye, nothing but Miriam's little pot of mignonette upon the window-sill, fresh and fragrant like herself, and her bird, who sang above it with a carol as light-hearted as her own. The bird, the child, and the flowers, these were the light of that lonely house, since Miriam's mother had faded in its dreariness. And it was home, too, even if the old servant, who moved with such a cautious tread among the dusty books of her master's study, was the only companionable creature, save the bird. How carefully she rubbed the dingy furniture, and mended the threadbare curtains, long since faded from their cheerful neatness! It was, perhaps, this still seclusion that had given Miriam, with all her eager childish grace, thoughts above her years; and, after her friend had gone, she put the kitten from her lap and leaned out of the window to watch for her father's return, musing, as she had never done before, how men could ever live without knowing they had a Father up in Heaven, and who else they could thank for taking care of them through the long dark night? And then her friend —Paul, he had told her to call him, when he first came to read those strange Hebrew words to her father, a daily study of the ancient language of the Bible he reverenced so much—Paul was going away to tell them to love him. How very good he was! She should miss him a great deal though. Perhaps he would take her too. Oh, she had not thought of that before! But, then, there was her father! No, Paul must go alone. Poor Paul, with no one to love him but herself! How gravely he had made her promise to love him, as if she had not always done so from that very first day when he had taken her upon his knee and talked to her as no one else could talk!

The young curate, for such he was, of a wealthy parish church, old and "lukewarm" because of its long prosperity, had gone to his daily duty of reading the evening service to a scattered congregation, half hidden in the high straight pews, that almost stifled their faint responses. He went with a heavy load upon his heart, for he was a stranger among them and to their sympathies. There was no poverty to call such as he to their homes; the rector only was bidden to the rich man's feasts. He came and went to and from the gilded chancel, with scarce a smile of recognition from those to whom his rich voice had read the "comfortable words" of their Master and his. The Bible told him they were brethren, but his heart said they were utter strangers. It was this cold supineness that had first turned his thoughts to a more earnest, active life among men "ready to perish," while his present ministry was to those who were "full and had need of nothing." And, at last, after many a struggle and many a prayer, he had steadfastly turned his face to a mission in the western wilds of his native land.

In all that wide, wide city, there was one only object his heart could cling to—the little child whose arms had circled him, whose kiss had comforted his loneliness. This was perhaps from his own reserve, for he had been solitary even from a boy. He had never attached his playmates to him, he could not seek for sympathy among strangers; opening to them the sorrows of his heart, a gentle heart like the mother who had given him life: but he checked its longing sympathies with a pride inherited from his sterner parent, and turned to fasting and lonely vigils of prayer and meditation. Miriam was the frail golden link that bound him to active human sympathies. He was attracted by her strange loveliness as she came, half pleadingly, half timidly, to prefer some request to her father, and since then she had been the prattling companion of many a lonely hour, when the task was ended, and his teacher had gone forth to impart to other pupils the stores of his great learning.

She was watching for him the next day at the entrance of the court, as he came slowly along, absorbed in one of those abstracted moods which had now become habitual to him. Her eyes brightened as she caught sight of his slender figure, and she ran to place her hand in his with the confidence of an habitual favourite. Something which pleased her very much had evidently occurred; but when she was questioned, she only smiled, and said it was a great secret; even papa was not to be told. Yet it was not naughty: Margery had said so. Every day after that, for a long time, he found the faithful little sentinel at her post; and sometimes their walk was extended, and she would go with him into the busy street, clinging closer to her dear companion, and looking up with smiles into his face, if the crowd jostled her, the embodiment of the spirit of faith.

At last the secret was revealed. It was when he came to tell her that he was going, all was ready for his departure, and he had but one farewell to make. He was later than usual, and she was watching for him with more eagerness than ever. She tripped demurely by his side, looking so beautiful in her clean white dress, and her curls in such rich profusion flowing round her delicate throat. He could not bear to pain her happy heart by the sad news of their parting, so he drew her gently to his bosom for the last time, while he waited for her father's return; and they were all alone but the kitten purring in the sun, and old Margery bustling in and out, intent on household cares. They did not talk much, but now and then she would pass her hand caressingly over his face, or he would bend down and kiss her tenderly. At last he said—

"I am going, Miriam. This is the last time I shall see you in many a day."

"Going!" she said, echoing the word sorrowfully.

"Yes, as I told you when the spring first came. To-morrow I shall be on my way to the deep woods and the boundless prairies of the western land."

He expected at least a burst of passionate sobs; but she only nestled closer to his heart, and twined her arm more tightly about his neck.

After a little time, she slid from his knee, still sorrowful, and came back to him holding a little picture. It was a miniature of herself, exceedingly lifelike, and it had the dreamy, serious gaze which he had first noticed when speaking of his mission. This was her innocent little secret. It had been painted by a poor artist, with more talent than friends, who had his home in the same dark court. He had thought her so beautiful, that he begged her to sit to him, intending a surprise to her father, who, in his unostentatious way, had once been of service to his poorer neighbour. That very day she had brought it home, so she told Paul, and laid it in a book before him.

"And he was pleased," said Paul, "and kissed you, and thought it was very like you, as I do?"

"I don't believe he liked it so very much. I don't think he

likes pictures at all," answered the child. "He never looks at my sweet mother, with the blue dress and the rose in her hair. But he smiled, and told me to give it to the person I loved best in the world."

"And you gave it to Margery, perhaps?" Paul smiled at the thought of bestowing such a gem upon Margery's dark little kitchen.

"No, I don't love her best, and that would not be right. I kept it for you, because there is no one but papa and you I ever dream about. Sometimes I have such lovely dreams, and think you are never going away. But you are, and you must take this, and keep it always. I'm sure you will, Paul."

A tear, yes, a tear, fell upon the beautiful picture—so touched was he by the earnestness and sincerity of her affection, and the thought that he was so soon to leave her.

Her father came, a mild, benevolent-looking man; but, nevertheless, with the air of one who had no strong hopes or desires. He was sorry to part with his favourite pupil, but blessed him in God's name; for he, too, had been "a minister about holy things," and knew the burning zeal which had filled the heart of the young devotee.

The morrow came, and Miriam was restless and sad as the hour for their walk drew near, and there was no friend to join her. Many and many a day did she linger at their old trysting-place, her heart beating fast, if she saw in the distance a face or figure that might be his. But one day after another came and went, and he was not there. Then she found other friends, and Time was her consoler.

Years, many years had passed, and the missionary sat at the door of his rude cabin, and leaned his weary head against the rough unhewn beams for support. He was far older, and had a dejected, sorrowful air that had deepened the lines upon his forehead, though his dark clustering hair had not silvered, and his eyes still lighted with the fire of manly thought. Yet the fresh vigour of his youth was spent, and his heart was weary and athirst for closer sympathy than he had found among the rude dwellers of the land. Their numbers had greatly increased since he first came among them, and the Indian haunts had retreated from before approaching civilization. They had prayed him to remain among them, to visit their sick and bury their dead, and they were kind to him in their own way. They had built his cabin, and furnished it with their own rude manufactures, and brought him presents of game from the forest, and fruit from their thriving farms. But, now the zeal of his first consecration was spent, he saw little fruit of all his labours; the wilderness had not yet blossomed as the rose. He longed for some one who could sympathize in his ardent desire to do good, and to encourage him to cast his "bread upon the waters." He covered his face with his hands and prayed, communing with the only intelligence that could read his heart, and then he looked around him and still sighed.

Perhaps it was that he had seen the cheerful blaze from the fire-side of some of his people, as he came homewards, and stopped to speak some playful word with the urchins before the door; but, as he sighed, he wondered if he could have been happier had he not denied to his starving heart all human, household love. "Perhaps I have wronged my nature," he thought. "It may not be required of me to lead this lonely life." And then—he never could tell what brought the recollection so vividly before him at that moment—there came a yearning thought of the little Miriam of years ago—his child-friend.

She must be a woman now, and beautiful and good. Perhaps she had already a home of her own, and her children about her. At any rate, she had forgotten him. If she had not, if she still remembered her childish promise to love him always—but no, he would not be so mad, so selfish, as to ask her to sacrifice her youth and beauty to his life of lonely privation. But he could not banish her from his mind, and he went in and unclasped the miniature he had not seen for many a day. It was a little faded now; but there were the earnest, serious look, and the soft curls, and the fond smile. How she had loved him! and he could almost feel her arms about his neck and her heart beating close to his. It was the isolation of spirit as well as outward life which had impressed these remembrances so forcibly upon him. Everything seemed as if yesterday. Again that yearning thought; and even before a resolve, he had smothered a fear, and was pouring out to her, or what he felt to be her now, all that was in his heart.

After the letter was gone, there were weeks of anxious suspense; and then he began to wonder at his own madness and folly. Sometimes he would try to calm himself with thinking that they had left their old home, and it would never reach Miriam; and then he almost wished it would be so, for she would never learn his presumption. But at last the answer came, when he had quite ceased to expect it; and he knew only by the tumult of his emotions, as he broke the seal, how much he had perilled upon what would now be revealed. He did not think to glance at the signature to see if she was still unmarried, but, as one resolved to drain to the dregs a bitter cup, he tore open the sheet, allowing himself no hope.

"Paul—*dear* Paul!"—he was so dizzy that he could scarcely see the words—"you will think me strange, unmaidenly, when I tell you that my pen trembles in my hand for very happiness. I have heard from you once more! The dream of my youth, of many, many years, has at last been fulfilled! I *knew* you had not forgotten me; and I have kept you ever in my mind, mingled with all that I counted good and noble. I have kept the promise which you recall, unconsciously, for I had forgotten it was ever required. I have 'loved you always,' Paul.

"No doubt much of this has been wild imagination, nursed in the lonely life I have ever led. I mean the seclusion; for we are still here as when you left us, except that my father is older and more feeble, and I have assumed Margery's household duties, for we are very poor. You have sought a portionless bride. But we will come to you, as you have asked, for we know you cannot leave your people, and your heart will grow strong again and be comforted by my father's gentle counsels; and *I* will be your 'home.' I can remember asking you if you were going home.

"Do not fear that I shall not be content. I am strong and well; I have never been accustomed to luxuries; and am I unwomanly in telling you how my very heart has gone out to you, at your first bidding? I have never lost trace of your labours. I have seen what you have done for those scattered people. I read of the consecration of your little church; and once I have seen one who had met you, and who told me of your fervour, and that you were wearing yourself out by your never-ceasing labour. He said your eyes were large and dark, though sunken, and that you looked too frail for so rude a life. You see it was not *all* imagination.

"Yes, we will come. My father has said so with his blessing, and he will renew his youth living among the beautiful things of nature; and I shall know you there face to face as I know you now in spirit, gentle, patient, unselfish."

The promise was kept, strange as it may seem to those who walk ever in the beaten track of cold formalities. It was again evening on those broad prairie lands, and Paul Stanbridge waited the approaching twilight, pondering on the new revelation of life, the seals of which another day would open. He wondered if it were not a blessed dream, and then he turned to look once more at the few comforts he had recently gathered in his little cabin for her who was henceforth to be its mistress. She had always loved flowers. How fortunate that he had twined the prairie rose and the clematis over the misshapen walls of his dwelling! and the smooth lawn-like slope to the river-side, how peaceful it all seemed as it slept in the sun's last rays!

Suddenly, he felt rather than saw an approach, and he turned to find two coming slowly towards him. No, no, it was a dream—they could not reach even the village before the morrow—and the strangers were alone, and coming as if they knew the foot-path.

It was no dream; one more glance, and he knew that venerable form; an instant, and that noble woman was clasped in a welcoming embrace. There was no coldness, no formality in that greeting. She was all that he had dreamed and pictured; she was much more than he had dared to hope; and she had bound him for ever by her trustful confidence, her womanly devotion. So they were united for life or death. Her father blessed them as he had done before, calling them by that holiest and dearest of titles, "man and wife,' and, for the first time in many years, the missionary had a home.

You will wonder if there was no sad awaking when the romance of youthful girlhood had passed, and Miriam knew that the step was irrevocable. You would need no other answer than a glance at the peace and happiness which sprung up in that quiet dwelling, a light that was diffused among all his little flock; for he had found the key to their hearts—his creed was no longer gloomy and morose, looking coldly on all their social joy. And every one loved Miriam, who became, young as she was, a guide and a friend to many beside her husband.

But did she truly love him?

Her father, happy in his serene old age, did not doubt it, as he saw her place their first born, Paul, in his arms, and look up to him with the trusting confidence of old, mingled with a deeper, because wifelike, tenderness.

CLARA MOORE.

Mrs. Clara Moore is a native of Westfield, Massachusetts, but has resided in Philadelphia since her marriage. Her maiden name was Jessup. She has distinguished herself as a writer both of prose and of poetry, but principally of the former. Her stories are natural in their incidents, gracefully written, and full of fine delineation of character. A vein of sentiment, which pervades most of her writings, renders them especial favourites with her sex. In describing the struggles of woman's heart, when actuated by the passion of love, she is peculiarly happy: indeed, few female authors in the United States excel her in this respect. Her story entitled "Emma Dudley's Secret" is an instance in point. This powerful tale has been republished in London with much success. "The Mother-in-Law" and "The Estranged Hearts," both prize tales, may be quoted as happy illustrations of her style.

It is a high merit with Mrs. Moore, that she seeks her subjects in every-day life, instead of dealing in the visionary regions of inflated romance. The calamities which oppress her heroines are such as might happen to any woman. Another merit in this author is, that instead of confining herself to the passion of love, as it exists in the female heart before marriage, she depicts it in the varied trials to which it is subjected after marriage; and this opens a mine which has been but little worked by novelists. Mrs. Moore understands her own sex thoroughly. It would be difficult, perhaps impossible, for a man to anatomize the female heart as she has done. Her plots are generally well managed, though she has as yet published no fiction of sufficient length to test her powers in this respect fully. As a magazinist, she enjoys an enviable reputation. Her success, indeed, is the more distinguished because authorship with her is an amusement rather than a profession. She wisely considers, that the duties of a wife and mother are paramount, and hence it is only her leisure that she surrenders to literature. Her pride is to be a woman first, an author afterwards; yet we trust that she will eventually find time for the composition of some more elaborate fiction than the short, fugitive stories with which she has hitherto graced our literature; and with her wide observation of the female heart, and her skill in managing incidents, she cannot but succeed brilliantly if she makes the attempt.

Most of her writings have been published under the *nom de plume* of "Clara Moreton."

THE YOUNG MINISTER'S CHOICE.

ALONE in her chamber, Gertrude Leslie sat, reading in bitterness of spirit the once cherished testimonials of her early love. Years had passed since those glowing words had been penned, and yet the fountains of her heart were stirred as violently as upon their first perusal. Still burned upon its altar-shrine the love which years of estrangement had not the power to destroy; and like a guilty creature she hid her face within her hands, when she remembered that her heart was now promised to another.

Too well she knew that no promise bore the power of recalling that love from the worshipped idol of her youth, and that with false hopes she had deceived herself, as well as the noble and trusting heart now resting its happiness upon hers.

For a long time Gertrude sat motionless, her white hands pressed tightly over her colourless face, and her mind far away in the dreamy past. Sweet memories of that olden time came thronging to her brain, and again she was the guileless, happy child of "long ago"—again, in fancy, her light feet crushed the grass of the valley home where her childhood had been passed—again leaning upon the arm of one most tenderly beloved, she strayed along the banks of the moonlit river, her young heart as pure as the clear depths of the stream which reflected the golden gleaming stars of the azure sky. So in her heart did the stars of love then shed round a golden glow, but years had passed, and dimmer, still dimmer had grown their lustre, until at last she had fancied that the light of that early love had died away for ever. Vain fancy, when those written words had power to waken such strong emotions!

Rising from her seat, Gertrude with a quick impatience tore

into shreds letter after letter, and one by one cast them upon the glowing grate before her.

"So perish all memory of the past," she said, "all memory of the misplaced attachment of my youth; yet not misplaced, for he would have been true to me, I know he would, had I been worthy of such love as his once was." For a long time did Gertrude thus commune with her own thoughts—then kneeling beside her couch, her bruised spirit poured itself out in broken words.

Thanks to the Author of our being, that always the prayer of the earnest heart is answered—answered by the serene happiness which ever follows aspirations after truth—by the guiding light which dawns upon the mind—by the renewed strength which gives power to trample down all obstacles, and follow without faltering that beacon light.

This light now dawned upon Gertrude's mind, showing her plainly the path of duty which led to her own happiness—the only path which could bring her peace.

Her resolution being once taken she knew no faltering, and that evening, when her affianced husband, Julien Neville, resumed his accustomed seat beside her, in the brilliantly-lighted parlours of her father's splendid mansion, she met him, nerved to carry out her firm convictions of duty.

They were alone in those large apartments, filled with every luxury. The light from the massive chandeliers flashed back from polished mirrors and costly frames of rare paintings, and from the gilded cornices of the rich curtains woven in foreign looms which shrouded the lofty windows, and fell in heavy folds to the tufted carpeting, where stainless lilies and glowing roses were blooming side by side in loving rivalry. They were alone—hope beating high in Julien's heart, although the fingers which he essayed to clasp within his own were cold and tremulous. Twice Gertrude had attempted to answer his loving words of greeting, and twice had the echo of her own thoughts died away upon her heart without leaving a vibration to the ear.

"Ah, Julien," at length she gasped, "you will cease to care for me, cease to respect me, and yet I must tell you all."

"Never, my own—my sweetest, I know all that you would say. It has been told me this day, and I have come to urge a speedy union—to offer your father a home with us. Oh! Gertrude, you wronged me by imagining for a moment, that the deep devotion of my heart could ever from such a cause know decay or change."

"My father! Julien, what do you mean? Surely he needs no other home!" she said, and her quick eyes glanced over the elegant rooms, and rested in inquiry upon those of her lover.

Julien Neville sighed heavily as he answered—

"I had hoped, my dearest, that your father's misfortunes had already been broken to you, but surely no one could do it more tenderly than myself. Trust in me, darling, and do not fear for the future. I have wealth enough for all—more than enough, thank God; and this house, Gertrude, everything herein shall remain untouched. So do not look so wildly, my own, you shall know no change; and your father shall not miss the luxuries to which he has always been accustomed."

"My father! change! misfortunes! you cannot mean, Julien, that he, that *my father* is a bankrupt!"

"You have guessed but too truly, dear Gertrude."

Overcome by the unexpectedness of the blow, Gertrude buried her head in the cushions of the lounge—refusing all the sympathy which Julien so tenderly proffered. Her heart bled at the thought of her father's disappointments, but not even for one moment did she swerve from her purpose. In days that were past she had deceived herself, but no longer was the calm affection which she had felt for Julien Neville to be mistaken for love. When she raised her face to his, it was as he had ever been wont to see it—there were mirrored there no traces of the wild torrent of emotions now deluging her bosom, and Julien gazed with pride upon her queenly beauty. The silence of that moment was broken by these words—

"Julien, you will hate me for what I have to say this night, but it must be said. You must not reproach me—you must not call me fickle until you hear the whole. Oh! Julien, my love for you is but as a sister's love, I cannot be more to you." She veiled her eyes with one hand, as if to hide the anguished expression of her companion's face, and continued—

"To you, Julien, I owe a confession which I thought should have died with me. When I was young—scarcely sixteen, my mother died. My father could not endure the mournful loneliness of our village home after she had gone, and in the bustle and excitement of business in the city he strove to forget all sad memories. It was then that I parted from Howard Beauchamp, the only child of our village minister. His mother had died in his infancy, and we had been almost constantly together from our childhood. Upon the evening of our parting we exchanged promises of eternal constancy.

"Months passed—his letters brought me the only happiness that I knew, for my father could in no way replace to me the love which in my mother's death I lost. At length the letters ceased entirely. I heard of his father's death, and of his own illness, and still I wrote, for I could not believe that he was false to me. One day a note was brought to me—the handwriting was strange. I broke the seal. It was from a cousin of his whom I had never seen, but of whom he had often spoken to me as a prodigy of beauty and talent. She wrote me that she had nursed him during his illness—that change of air had been prescribed by the physician, and that he had accompanied her to her Southern home, where it was now his intention to reside. In delicate and sympathizing words she wrote of the transferral of Howard's love from me, to her, his cousin—of their strong attachment for each other, and her earnest wish that I would not tell him that she had written. 'Not for my sake do I write this,' she said, 'but for his, whose happiness is dearer to me than life itself.' There was but one course before me. I summoned all my pride, and wrote to him what I imagined I ought to feel, not what I did. I made no allusion to his cousin. I told him that I loved him no longer; I wrote a great deal that was false, but I fully intended to make it truth. Years passed—we travelled all over the United States, and I heard no more from Howard Beauchamp. When at Newport you saved my life, and added to it the offering of your own, I felt toward you more affection than had been awakened for years; but I was deceived with regard to my true feelings; for, Julien, they can never be more than those of a sister."

Bitter, indeed, were these words to Julien Neville—doubly bitter because he knew Gertrude too well to doubt the strength of an attachment which would enable so proud a spirit to endure the mortification of such a confession. Yet with all his disappointment, he could find no heart to blame, even for an instant, the stricken form before him.

"Oh! Gertrude," he said, "nothing can change my love for you, and I will not even ask yours in return. I will strive to be satisfied with a sister's affection, only give me the blessed privilege of ever remaining near you to cherish and protect."

"It cannot be, Julien. I know how free from selfishness your love is; and I know that could you see the wild emotions which the recalled memories of those hours have this day awakened, you would never wish me to be other to you than I am. This must be our last meeting, Julien, unless you will promise not to use one persuasion to induce me to change—not that I fear my own strength, but because every effort which you make will only increase the misery which I now feel."

Hours passed before that promise was given.

Poor Julien Neville! He left Gertrude that night with the full belief that in all the world there was no balm for a heart so wounded as his own.

When Gertrude entered her father's library early the next morning, she found him sleeping lethargically in his large arm-chair. Wondering that he should be up so much sooner than his custom—or that he could thus sleep when he knew of his utter ruin, she looked in surprise upon him.

She knew not that all the weary night he had paced the room, weeping in bitter agony over the loss of his worshipped wealth.

Drawing closer to him, she said—"Father, I have something to say to you, will you listen?" There was no answering sound, save those of his heavy breathings. Alarmed, she took hold of him by the shoulder.

"Father! father!" she screamed.

The piercing tones of her voice aroused him—he started, looked around, passed one hand hurriedly over his eyes, and then with a long sigh sank back in his chair again.

Relieved from her anxiety, Gertrude drew a seat beside him.

"I have come, father, to converse with you about your misfortunes—perhaps they are not so bad as you imagine."

"All is lost! every cent!" replied Mr. Leslie, in a husky tone of voice; "but it will make no difference to you, Gertrude, for Julien is a noble fellow; but it is hard for me in my old age to be dependent upon my child."

"We will not be dependent upon Jul en, father—we will go back to our old place at Elmwood, and I can teach music and drawing in the village academy, and we shall be as happy as we have ever been here; for, father, I do not love Julien as I ought to love him, and I have told him so, and we have parted to meet only hereafter as friends."

The words which she had so dreaded to say had now escaped her lips, and her father's stern gaze was fixed steadily upon her.

"Gertrude! what have you done?—taken away my only hope! —turned us both out into the world as beggars! I tell you every cent is gone: beggars! beggars!" he repeated in a low, deep tone. He arose from his seat—his face crimsoning with excitement—stepped but one foot forward, then fell over heavily upon the floor.

Gertrude's screams brought the servants to her. Physicians were immediately summoned, and Mr. Leslie was borne in an unconscious state to his room. They pronounced him in an apoplectic fit, but the usual remedies were tried in vain. Gertrude sat constantly beside him, watching for hours for some sign of returning consciousness. At length the hand which she held moved slightly.

"Oh, father!" she cried, "speak to me once more: do not leave me alone! oh, father! father!"

The agonized tones of her voice seemed to arouse him. His

lips moved. She bent her head to listen, and caught the words, "God bless my poor child; God bless thee, Ger——," his lips still moved, but there came no audible sound.

Poor Gertrude! She was now *alone!*

At twilight, when Gertrude entered the lonely grave-yard, she met Howard Beauchamp just emerging from an avenue of cedars. He paused for a moment, and then advancing said—

"We were friends once; may I hope that we still are?"

Gertrude could not speak, but she stretched out her hand to answer his greeting.

"Time has brought many changes to both of us," he continued; "in this place of graves, your sainted mother and my revered father sleeps; but since I have become an orphan—alone and desolate in the world, I have heard but little of you, excepting of your marriage; I trust for your sake, Gertrude, that the mourning garments which you now wear are not a widow's weeds."

Gertrude Leslie looked in surprise upon him as she answered—

"I have never been married, Howard; it is for my father that I mourn."

A sudden ray of joy illuminated his fine face, then died away as he said in sad, low-tones—

"And you are an orphan, too; but oh! not so desolate an one, I trust, as myself."

"And why should I not be, Howard?—the blow which deprived me of my father left me penniless—well-nigh friendless; but you in your cousin's love have found a happiness which I can never hope."

She saw the crimson glow which spread over the marble features of her companion.

"Then you too know of her unfortunate attachment—poor Ellen! I have tried in vain to feel more than a brother's attachment to her; the memory of my youthful love, Gertrude, is too strong to bear to be replaced, even in imagination," said Howard, as he bent his dark eyes searchingly upon hers.

"And you—you, Howard—are not you married?" questioned Gertrude, almost breathless, as her eyelids drooped under the steadiness of his gaze.

"No, Gertrude; the vows which I plighted to you were too solemn ever to be broken, even though you gave them back with scornful words and bitter mockings. Do you not remember that on the evening of our parting I promised *ever* to love you, and you alone?"

As Gertrude raised her eyes to answer, she saw the figure of a graceful female gliding toward them in the dim twilight.

"It is my cousin, Ellen Beauchamp," Howard said.

They were leaning upon the marble tomb of Mrs. Leslie; and Ellen advancing stood beside them. Her cheeks were pale and transparent; and the large, brilliant eyes were sunken, yet there were many traces of exceeding beauty.

"You must neither of you curse me, for I have suffered enough," she said.

"Why should we curse *you*, dear Ellen?" said Howard, tenderly—"my poor cousin is not well, Gertrude—she was the most faithful of nurses to me when I was so ill that my life was despaired of, and she has never been well since—we are travelling now with her—her mother and myself, in hopes of restoring her health—poor Ellen!"

"Yes, poor Ellen!" echoed the hollow voice of the emaciated form beside him—"poor Ellen needs pity. Gertrude, will you promise to pity me if I tell you all?"

"No, Ellen, not pity; but my heart's warmest sympathy I will offer to you." Tears dropped like rain from Ellen's large eyes as she clasped the hand which Gertrude had extended.

"Oh, Gertrude! I wrote falsely to you, when I told you that Howard no longer loved you. I was mad with love for him—so mad that I forgot that you had a heart which could be crushed even as mine is now. Howard! I burned the letters which you penned in your first sickness—I burned all which she wrote to you. I wrote to her, and told her that you loved her not, that you waited but a release from your vows to breathe them to me; and then I told you that she was married, and I showed you the letter which I had goaded her on to write. In the relapse which followed your reading of that letter I would have told you all, but you looked so gently and tenderly upon me, I could not bear to tell you what a wretch I was. Has my repentance come too late to either of you? Have I sinned past forgiveness? Oh! believe me, I have suffered enough in the agony of my unloved life—in the memory of those false words, which I fear have perjured my soul for ever."

"No, Ellen; not for ever. Repentance never comes too late. God will forgive you, even as I know Gertrude and myself have already done—have we not, *dear* Gertrude?"

It was the first word of love, and Gertrude bent her head to conceal the warm blushes which crimsoned her face; but as she did so, she kissed the delicate hand of Ellen, which she still retained.

When they passed out of the grave-yard, Ellen and Gertrude each leaned upon an arm of Howard Beauchamp—Ellen still "sowing in tears," and Gertrude and Howard "reaping in joy."

ANN E. PORTER.

Miss Lydia Ann Emerson was born October 14, 1816, at Newburyport, Massachusetts, where was her home, except when away at school, till 1833. In that year she went to Royalton, Vermont, as an assistant teacher in the Academy of that place.

Her mother died when she was but two years old, and at four she was, with brothers and sisters, under the care of a stepmother. Between three and four years, from her thirteenth to her seventeenth year, she enjoyed a regular course of instruction at the celebrated Ipswich Female Academy.

In 1834, she went to Springfield, Vermont, and established a Select School, which met with eminent success.

In 1836, she was invited to the charge of the Southampton Academy, but was early induced to remove to Putnam, Ohio—where she became the principal of a newly opened Female Seminary. During four years' residence at this interesting place, she experienced many of those incidents of western life, so soul-stirring to the young emigrant. Those only who have enjoyed the sociality of life in a new country, or the hospitality of an earlier age, will be likely to appreciate the recollections of a lone female instructor, thus employed among strangers. It is hoped that her connexion with that seminary and community is still remembered by her pupils and their friends, as it is by herself, with interest and enjoyment.

Newark, Ohio, was the home of another year in Miss Emerson's diversified life; and the year 1841 was spent most agreeably at that place in charge of the female department of "Delaware Academy," at the Springs. Here, too, the social freedom peculiar to frontier civilization, had influences on mind and memory, often recurred to with pleasure.

In the autumn of 1841, Miss Emerson became the wife of Mr. Charles E. Porter, of Springfield, Vermont, and she has ever since been a resident of that place.

Mrs. Porter has been an occasional contributor to the periodical press since the year 1834 : of late, under her own signature. Her thoughts and sketches, though hasty, have endeared her to many friends. She has also contributed two small volumes towards the Sunday School Library. But the labours of love, and the duties of domestic life, have not as yet permitted that concentration of her powers upon any extended work, which some who know her, anticipate, when an appropriate occasion shall come.

COUSIN HELEN'S BABY.

YOUR letter, dear cousin, is before me, for I am resolved to do, what is somewhat unusual among our sex, *answer it;* that is, give a reply to all the questions contained therein, and, if possible, attend to the most important before I come to the postscript. You begin as follows :—

"How in the world am I to write this letter with my baby?"

Well, it seems from your own statement at the close, as well as from sundry other unmistakeable signs, such as a few blots, paper a little "*crumpled,*" and a few extra flourishes, that you did actually accomplish the thing, and that, too, with the baby in the room, and part of the time in your arms.

"Impossible!" said Napoleon; "let that word be struck out of my dictionary." Alas! we poor mothers often find in our pathway rugged Alps to climb, but, almost always, ingenuity and patience will work a way around the jagged rocks, or through the narrow defiles.

"Oh, this baby tending!" you next exclaim; and, from the heavy tread of the pen and the big admiration point, it seems to come from a spot deeper than the German gutturals; I conclude, even from the bottom of your heart, for you go on to say, "Oh! if these husbands, who can commence and finish their business at stated hours, and do everything by the clock, could know how tedious is the tread-mill path of one who has a troublesome, crying baby to manage, they would certainly try to initiate themselves into the mystery of baby tending, and aid us more."

Really, Ann, I had supposed you possessed of different ideas of woman's cares and man's duties; or have you become an ultra woman's rights partizan, or are you so clear-sighted as to understand

Miss Fuller's "Woman in the nineteenth century?" If so, my humble experience will be of little avail; for, as a wife and mother, I have trod a lowly path, and never dared step foot into the balloon of transcendentalism.

Again you say: "If one child is so much care, how can you manage five?"

Well might you ask, and I would answer, *if you* find that one, as you say, makes you half crazy, five will certainly send you to the insane asylum, unless upon the homœopathic principle, "that which kills will cure." But, the truth is, you lived in such a still, orderly way so long after your marriage, that the change seems more striking to you, and the care more onerous than it really is.

"But for a chapter of your experience;" and you shall have it; for, on glancing back upon what I have written, I find that it has a dictatorial air, which it ill becomes me to assume; and, to punish myself, I will give you a little sketch of my management with my first baby, that you may see I was far behind yourself in prudence and skill.

Need I tell any one who has been a mother, of the joy which one experiences at the birth of her first-born? It is like the glorious sunlight of morning after a night of storm and darkness; yea, like the rapture of heaven to the weary spirit, when she folds, for the first time, the young immortal to her bosom, and breathes from a full heart her gratitude to God. At least, such were my own feelings when my eldest, my precious child Arthur, was born.

I had read Grahame and Alcott, and a score of other writers upon the management of infants, and thought myself quite wise—certainly capable of criticising others—but now, all my wisdom forsook me, and I felt ignorant as a child. Our means were limited, and we were not able to hire just such help as we wished; but an old woman, who had had some little experience, was engaged, and so confident was she of her own abilities, that I yielded implicitly to her directions. When I remonstrated upon the use of pins, she exclaimed, "Lawful sake, ma'am! do you expect me to use these ere strings and loops? I never did afore, and you can't expect me to·begin now; besides, what kind er shape suppose your baby'll be, if I don't pin it up snug and tight now?"

Feeble as I then was, I could do little for myself or the babe, but I would sometimes quiet its cries by stealthily loosening its clothes as it lay by my side. My child was scarcely two days old before my kind neighbours began to pour in with their sympathy and congratulations. Too timid to refuse them admittance, and too weak to endure company, I suffered much, and yet the scenes were sometimes so comical I could not help laughing. Some days quite a number would call at once. Mrs. Higgins, and Aunt Lucy, and old Mrs. Gove, were in one day together.

"What a nice fat baby!" said the last, who had just entered; "for all the world the very image of its father"—(it had just been pronounced "*as like to me as two peas*")—"and not a mark about it;—why my John has an apple on his forehead, and a strawberry on his great toe. I hope you've given the little thing some physic, Mrs. Bagly."

"La, yes," said the latter, bridling up; "I always gives *caster ile* the first thing—nothing better, you know."

"And then, I suppose, you feed it some, till its mother has milk sufficient?"

"The little darling don't suffer, I can tell you," answered the nurse, proudly. "I take the top of the milk and sweeten it up well, and it has as much as it can take. Mrs. Wadsworth talked about leaving things to *nater*, but I tell her I guess *nater* would leave her if *I* didn't stick by."

"I hope, in all conscience, you won't get any of these new-fangled notions into your head," said Mrs. Higgins. "You'll sartinly kill your baby if you do. Why our minister's wife is half crazy with her book larning about babies. She washes hers all over in cold water every morning, and e'en amost starves it, too; for no matter if it cries ever so hard, she won't feed it till the time comes, as she calls it, and that's once in three hours. If she warn't the minister's wife, I believe the selectmen would take the matter up; but I eased my conscience by giving her a piece of my mind."

"I didn't say a word when she was at our house," said the

kind-hearted Aunt Lucy, "but I was a feeding it with apple pie—nothing in the world but plain apple pie, 'twouldn't hurt a flea—when she come along, and, in her pleasant way, said, 'I would rather the baby have nothing to eat, Mrs. Nutting.' I was most scared, for fear I'd done something sinful."

Arthur was now trying the use of his little lungs, and powerfully, too, much to the discomfort of the guests and myself.

"Can't you give the child something to quiet it?" said Aunt Lucy. "Some catnip tea would be good."

"Not half so good as piny root," said Mrs. Higgins, "or some camphor sling."

"Now, that reminds me," chimed in Mrs. Gove, "of one injury that these temperance societies have done. Babies didn't use to cry so when I was young; and I never thought, when I had a baby, that I could do without a decanter of gin. There's nothing like it for the cholic; and then it would strengthen you up, Mrs. Wadsworth, and set you right upon your feet again.'

"That's just what I tell her," said the nurse; "but there ain't a drop in the house, and Mr. Wadsworth says that he prefers not to use it unless the doctor prescribe."

"Well, well, every one to their notion," said Mrs. Higgins. "I'm not certain but soot tea will answer the purpose as well—that's one of my favourite remedies."

"I must go now," said Aunt Lucy, as she rose to depart, "for my old man will be wanting his supper; but between sundown and dark I'll run over with some arbs, catnip and sage, and thoroughwort. I reckon I can cure the baby."

In the mean while I had exerted all my strength to hush the little sufferer, and he now lay asleep upon my arm; but I was covered with a profuse perspiration, and, as soon as the child was removed, fell back exhausted.

The next day, about the same hour, Arthur commenced crying again, and it continued so long and loud that I became thoroughly alarmed. Poor Mrs. Bagly did her best, but all in vain. I removed the pins and loosened his dress, but it did no good, he cried without ceasing.

"There now," said Mrs. Bagly, "don't worry any more, and I'll give him something that will make him sleep sweetly."

"Not camphor sling?" I said, inquiringly.

"La, no; now don't be so scared. I'll just go into the kitchen and take my pipe and let the smoke of the tobacco go into a bowl of water, and then I'll sweeten some of that water and give it to him; it will make him so easy and still."

This was something so novel, that I hardly knew what to say; it seemed a strange medicine for a babe, and yet she assured me that she had used it a hundred times, and that it was harmless. But the screams of the child continuing, I allowed her to do as she pleased, though I said, faintly—

"I hope his father won't smell the smoke when he comes in to see the baby; he perfectly despises the weed, as he calls it."

Mrs. Bagly stopped short in the middle of the room: "Well, I'm beat now! I never heard of a lawyer before that didn't *chaw*, nor smoke, or, at least, take snuff. Why, Squire Tappan never come to see my old man, but he'd out with his box, and 'Won't you take a pinch, Mrs. Bagly?' He was a smart man, I can tell you, and I believe it was the tobacco put the grit into him. He never spoke but he had a pinch between his thumb and finger, and it was scattered as thick among his books and papers as a French stew with pepper."

"Well, well, Mrs. Bagly, my baby will cry itself to death if something isn't done."

"I know it, ma'am; it will certainly *bust itself* if it don't have the smoked water;" and she disappeared to fetch it.

"Oh, dear," I groaned within myself, "I wish Charles were here, perhaps he could aid me;" but he was gone to the next village, and would not be at home for some hours.

The nurse was not long absent, and taking the child in her lap fed it freely. Its cries ceased, and it soon fell asleep. With a feeling of relief I flung myself upon the bed, while she wrapped little Arthur in his blanket, laid him in his cradle, and left the room to attend to her duties in the kitchen.

I soon fell into a quiet sleep, and I know not how long I had lain, when a slight rustling disturbed me. I opened my eyes, and saw my dearest friend, Mary Porter, near me.

"Why have you not been to see me before?" I said, rather reproachfully.

"I have; but when you were asleep. I thought I must see you and the baby, so I stole in at that time, for I knew company would injure you, and I feared we would talk too much. There now, go to sleep again, and I will watch by the cradle—you must, or I shall leave."

Seeing her resolute, I tried to obey, but I could not refrain from opening my eyes to look at her, it seemed so pleasant to have her near me. She sat in a low rocking-chair by the side of the cradle.

She watched for a while the sleeping babe, and then I saw her stoop and place her ear as if listening to its breathing; then, rising, she knelt over it, and taking one hand, held it for a moment and let it drop, then she did the same with the other. Removing the covering, she felt its little feet, and held them awhile in her hands. I thought for the moment she was rather childish. After again covering the child, she drew the curtains of my own bed close around me, and then, as I thought, removed the cradle farther from my bed, and left the room.

I wondered what this meant, and was about to rise and go to the cradle myself, when the door gently opened, and I distinguished the voices of Mrs. Bagly and Mary, though they spoke in whispers.

"Don't make such a fuss about nothing, Miss Mary. Ha'n't I had children? and don't an old woman like me know more about nursing than such a young thing as yourself?"

"But look, Mrs. Bagly, for yourself," and she lifted the babe from the cradle.

I did not wait for a reply, but sprang to my feet and took my child. "It's certainly dead!" I exclaimed, as, with every muscle relaxed, it lay unconscious in my arms.

"Not dead, I trust," said Mary. "See, its little heart yet beats."

I tried to waken it, but in vain. It lay like one in deep stupor, and, as I believed, the stupor of death.

"We've killed it—poisoned it with that vile tobacco!" I exclaimed; and, in despair, I pressed it to my bosom and wept like a child.

"Let me take the baby," said a kind voice, and looking up I recognised Dr. Perkins.

I held it still more closely, while I begged him to tell me if there was any hope. He took the little hand in his own, and placed his ear so that he could distinguish the breathing.

"I think that we can save your babe, Helen; but," he added, in a tone of mild authority, "you are killing yourself; go and lie down, and I will see to the child."

He was our family physician; one to whom, from childhood, I had been accustomed to look up with reverence. I yielded my precious burthen, and reluctantly obeyed. My husband came in at that moment and enforced the doctor's direction, assuring me that everything in their power should be done for the child.

But what a night of anguish and suspense we passed! Morning found the doctor still there; for it was not until then that he was able to rouse the infant from that dreadful stupor, and then, for days, it hovered on the very verge of death. It was a sad lesson to a young mother.

E. W. BARNES.

Miss Barnes is a native, and has been all her life a resident, of Portsmouth, New Hampshire. Her father is by birth a Swede, the only son of an officer in the Swedish army. On his arrival in this country in early youth, he was persuaded by a clergyman of Salem to change his name from Ludwig Baärnhielm to Lewis Barnes, for greater convenience of pronunciation. Miss Barnes has published, in Annuals and Magazines, a considerable amount of prose and verse, all of a very creditable character. From a prose tale published in 1850, the following sketch has been selected as a fair specimen of her style.

THE YOUNG RECTOR.

The crash startled from his revery a pale student, who, in the same apartment by his solitary lamp, sat poring over the pages of a ponderous volume, while beside it, on his writing-desk, lay the half-written page on which, with a vigorous and rapid pen, he wrote from time to time, with an energy which told how every faculty of his mind was absorbed in the work before him. He rose from his task as the shattered glass flew even over the table at which he sat, and, still engrossed in the thoughts which had occupied him for some hours, went mechanically to the window, thrust into the aperture some old and worn-out garment, and returned again abstractedly to his work.

The hours moved on, and no sound recalled him from the intellectual world in which his spirit was far away, except the continued discord of the elements without, and the monotonous ticking of the old clock, which had grown aged with the time-worn habitation in which it had stood for nearly a century. Page after page, glowing with his own deep earnestness of spirit, and the rich imagery which the study of the Sacred Volume and of classic lore had taught him, was filled, and at length the young rector rose wearily from his desk, and pressing his hand to his aching brow, walked to the window, and, for the first time, seemed quite aware of the rude conflict amid the elements of the outward world. Shading his eyes from the light, he peered out through the shattered casement. "What a night," thought he, "for the poor and homeless! and ah! how many among my parishioners must feel this keen and cutting blast through the crevices in their wretched dwellings! Would that I could provide for each a comfortable shelter from the storm; but, alas! my miserable pittance!—what does it more than keep together 'the mortal body and the immortal soul?'"

With a sigh he turned away, and drawing his chair in front of the fire, he stirred the expiring embers, and sat gazing abstractedly into them, while his thoughts dwelt upon the different allotments of good and ill which fall to the share of human destiny. He had seen the honest and deserving poor baffled in every effort to advance, bravely buffeting the billows of misfortune, with scarce a gleam of hope to cheer them on, yet blessing God daily and hourly in their hearts for the good things they received; and he had seen the wealthy revelling in their luxury, thankless and thoughtless, closing the ear to the appeals of starving poverty, and forgetful even of Him whose bounty they enjoyed. Then came his thoughts down to a narrower sphere, and dwelt on his own personal history. Far back his memory bore him to the days of early childhood, to its poverty and its privations. Then came the labours and struggles necessary to bear him through the years of his college life, upheld by the resolution to develop by culture the powers of a naturally fine and vigorous intellect.

Re-perusing, line by line, the pages of his past existence, and suffering a tear occasionally to fall,—prompted by bitter Memory, as if to blot out the record she had made,—the young rector sat in a half-reclining position, in his well-worn arm-chair, with his feet upon the fender, and in deep revery gazed musingly into the declining fire. Ever and anon it threw up a fitful gleam, that reminded him of some of the many hopes which had arisen on his horizon, and sunk again as soon in darkness. It was Christmas Eve, the eve preceding the great festival of the Nativity. Why, then, was he gloomy and depressed at this hour of triumph to the church he loved? Fain would he have shaken off the sad fantasies which hung like an incubus upon his spirit, but his efforts were in vain. Again and again they returned to the charge, and at every onset they became an ever-increasing, darkening host, resistless in their power. He tried to picture to his imagination those happy homes, which were drawing around them at this festive season, as round a dazzling nucleus, the wanderers who had gone out from them on the voyage of life. He fancied the happy meetings and the glad welcome home; the merry fire would sparkle in the grate, and send forth its ruddiest glow; the cheerful board would be spread; merry hearts and merry voices would hail the coming of the "merry Christmas;" the aged sire, with thin, white locks, would look round with satisfaction upon his children, and his children's children, as he asked God's blessing on the festive cheer. Alas! these pictures but restored, with a deeper colouring, his own sense of loneliness; and yielding finally to its resistless sway, he suffered the hours to wax and wane, all heedless of their flight: the surging of the great and limitless ocean on the shore of time, and its rapidly advancing waves, affected him not. He was alone;—alone must he meet his doom.

Still not a sound disturbed the deepening silence, or broke in upon his gloomy revery, but the same monotonous ticking of the venerable time-piece, the hollow moaning of the storm, or the faint falling of the waning embers. He leaned his head wearily upon his hand, and watched them as they sunk and were extinguished one by one. His revery deepened; silence was becoming almost audible; a torpor was stealing over him; but now, as his gaze was fixed steadfastly upon the declining fire, a light, thin vapour seemed to rise from beneath it, and curling gently upward and over it, partially obscured it to his vision. Gradually it ascended, wreathed itself over the antiquated fire-place, stole softly up to the ceiling, and wound its enfolding arms quietly about the old clock, till its face and hands became imperceptible in the pale lamp-light. Growing denser as it proceeded, round and round the time-stained walls it noiselessly crept, and continued its quiet circuitous motion, fold within fold, filling up the whole intermediate space between them and the chair of the young rector, and shutting out every familiar object in his desolate apartment, till he was hemmed in by an impervious atmosphere. Closer and closer the walls of his prison-house were pressing upon him at each moment; his breath came thicker and heavier at every inspiration; a sense of oppression, of suffocation, was upon him; yet had he no power of motion, no ability to seek relief.

How long he thus lay bound, manacled, speechless, he knew not. He heard no sound; even the tempest seemed to have ceased its moaning; and he asked himself, "Must I thus die?—is there no hand to aid?" There was a pause, during which it seemed as if thought itself were checked in its flow, and then there was observable a slight undulation in the dense mass; it trembled, it wavered, it parted in the midst—moved slowly, almost imperceptibly, but steadily, and falling back on either side, shaped itself gradually into graceful columns. First the base appeared, then rose the shaft, and then the finished capital. Moving thence gently upward, it threw its graceful mist-wreaths into noble Gothic arches. The marble pavement noiselessly spread itself beneath his feet, and he sat before the high altar of a great cathedral. Upon it stood seven golden candlesticks, and in the midst a golden censer. Soft moonlight, tinged with the rainbow dyes of the stained glass through which it passed, rested on the surrounding objects. There was a silence, so deep, so solemn, that it pervaded his whole being; and then the strains of the organ, soft, distant, as if amid the spheres, rolled through the high arches, which, as they grew deeper and louder, trembled beneath the vibrations.

Awe-struck, he listened, and then voices, as of unseen angels, mingled in the deep swell, and the "Stabat Mater" poured its holy strains on his rapt senses; and his soul, lifted, inspired by the divine harmony, seemed borne upward, even into the presence of the Holy One. With hands clasped and unconsciously upraised, he heard the strains die away softly upon the ear, but the echoes lingered long among the lofty arches. There was a pause, and not a sound of earth disturbed that hallowed stillness; but, though he saw them not, he felt the presence of angel forms around and above him, moving silently on their silver wings. Again breathed the tones of the organ, and the grand "Te Deum" rose to the "Lord God of Sabaoth;" and that too died away upon the ear, but its heavenly music vibrated long in the listening spirit.

Now from the golden censer a soft and fragrant incense slowly ascends; and with reverential awe he watches it, till, as it higher mounts, the edges of the light and vapoury folds are touched with a silver brightness, as if a glory from on high had lightened them. And on the bosom of the cloud, gracefully reposing, he beholds a form that has no parallel amid the forms of earth. Dimly and indistinctly he sees her, cradled within those misty folds; and slowly the silvery mass descends with its heavenly burden, until it rests above the sacred altar. A holy influence steals over his senses—an unspeakable serenity—a calm like that of Gennesareth, when the voice of the Saviour spoke to the troubled waters. Whence comes the hallowed peace, the sweet repose that pervades his spirit, as, rapt and awe-stricken, he gazes on that benignant face? Ah! could it be impressed for ever on the mirror of his soul, never more would it reflect the blackening cloud,—never more would it be ruffled by the storm-winds of passion, or shadowed by the darkness of despair. Would she but speak to him!—would she but make known her angel mission!—but no, she does but gaze upon him with sweetness, with pity, with benignity. The eyes, so gentle, never for a moment turned from his; and, as bound by a resistless spell, he yielded to the repose which they inspired. He was no longer of the earth: purified by that soft smile from every trace of its corruptions, he basked in the purity of that radiance, and trembled lest a cloud should overshadow it, lest the holy spell should be broken. Oh! to be ever thus—to know such transcendent peace! This it is to be in communion with the angels.

And now the beauteous vision, with its garments of silver vapour, stood upright upon the fleecy masses of the cloud, with her eye unmoved from the face of the entranced beholder. Her left arm slowly advanced from the mists around her, and, bending gently towards him, she extended the cross, one arm of it encircled by a crown of thorns, the other draped with the purple robe, and over it this motto: "*On earth thou wilt wear these, for thy Saviour's sake.*"

Deep was the silence which followed. He moved not, spoke not, lest, like a dream, his happiness should vanish away. Soft strains of music were heard in the distance, growing fainter and fainter, till they were lost upon the ear. And now the right arm gradually rose, and a taper finger pointed upward. Following it with his eye, he descried, distant far and almost unseen, a crown, irradiated with a soft halo of golden light, and bearing these words: "*This awaits thee in Heaven.*"

One arm upraised, and one extending towards him the cross, her eye riveted upon him, she stood motionless as a statue. Again rose the soft strains of music, mingled with voices of angelic sweetness. Her voice was not heard among them, but her gaze seemed reading the secrets of that spirit, still condemned to struggle a while longer with the cares of earth. To pity and to soothe it seemed her mission; and that mission was fulfilled,—so calm, so deep was the peace which settled on his spirit, so elevated were his thoughts, and so attuned to worship. The music continued, now like the far distant sound of many waters surging upon an unseen shore, now nearer and nearer, and then floating upward and dying away in heaven. It ceased, and he fancied that the silver cloud was rising again, and that the vision was fading away. With an irresistible impulse he sprang forward, threw himself on his knees before the heavenly vision, and extended his arms to embrace the cross. Alas! in a moment all had vanished; the beautiful pageant was no more; and he awoke, to find himself prostrate, with outstretched arms, before the desolate walls of his room. There were the remains of his decayed fire, there his arm-chair, and there the old time-piece, telling the same monotonous tale. The dawn was not yet breaking, and his dim lamp was just expiring in its socket.

It was indeed the old familiar scene, which had witnessed all his struggles, all his tears, but which he had briefly exchanged for the communion and the minstrelsy of heaven. He rose, and pressed his hand to his brow. It was then indeed a dream, and he had been revelling amid the hallowed joys of "the spirit-land?" Yet, if "millions of spiritual creatures walk the earth," might not this be one, sent on a mission of mercy to his suffering, struggling spirit; to raise him from despondency; to bid him bear on unmurmuringly, and, while wearing the cross, to look ever upward and onward to the promised crown?

When the Rector awoke the next morning, the sun was brighter to his eye, the wind fell more softly on his cheek, and stirred the light clustering hair upon his brow. He was no more alone, for that ministering angel had taken up her abode within his soul, and her serene smile was fixed upon him ever. He loved the clouds, the air, the earth; he loved the glittering icicle that was melting in tears beneath the sunbeam; and he loved the snow-wreath that gracefully hung over the cottage porch. Love—love to God, and love to man—was the prevailing attribute of his soul; and those who listened that day to the voice of their rector in his village church, felt, though they knew not why, a higher, fuller sense of the "beauty of holiness." His words were fraught with a new energy; his voice rose with his choir in the full strains of the Christmas anthem; and when he entered his pulpit, a new and divine inspiration seemed to have touched his lips, as with a live coal from the altar.

That vision of the night became to the young rector the vision also of his waking hours; and when his congregation wondered at the new traits which manifested themselves in his character,—when they saw his peculiar serenity under all the ever-varying phases of his existence, they saw not the angel within the sanctuary of his spirit, and the hand that, pointing upward to the crown, pointed also to the words—"*This awaits thee in Heaven.*"

ANNE T. WILBUR.

To translate well is a rare accomplishment. So far as mere style and language are concerned, translation is more difficult than original composition. Among the few who have excelled in this line, may be mentioned the lady whose name stands at the head of this article. Her translations have, indeed, the ease and grace and the idiomatic propriety of writings of a native growth. These translations have been from the popular literature of Europe, chiefly from the French, and have consisted mostly of short tales. Some of them have been published in the form of small volumes; others have appeared in periodicals of different kinds.

Besides her translations, Miss Wilbur has written occasionally original articles for the magazines and weekly papers, under the name of "Florence Leigh," and has performed a considerable amount of editorial labour. As editor of the "Ladies' Magazine,' published in Boston, in 1848, and of the "Ladies' Casket," published the same year, in Lowell, she secured for those works many valuable contributors.

Miss Wilbur was born at Wendell, Massachusetts, in 1817. She is the daughter of the Rev. Henry Wilbur, of Newburyport, extensively known as a lecturer on astronomy, and as the originator of Bible Classes. The secluded life and leisure of a village pastor, led him to take unusual pains in the instruction of his oldest child and only daughter. This, and the possession of a mind constitutionally precocious, led to very early attempts at authorship—the first, a school-girl feat, achieved at the age of eleven, entitled "Grimalkin, a Tragedy," and ending in the destruction of an entire family of rats.

Miss Wilbur began, at the age of fifteen, to teach, and has been engaged as a teacher until within the last three or four years, which have been occupied with literary labour. Her residence is Newburyport, Massachusetts.

ALICE VERNON.

A PLEASANT company were assembled around the breakfast-table, and discussing their plans for the day. In some casual conversation, I heard a careless mention of a name very familiar and very dear—"Mrs. Vernon." I reflected a moment,—it was a name closely associated in my mind with the past, yet how, I could not immediately recall. Suddenly it came like a lightning flash—Alice Vernon, once Alice Maitland. I inquired of the individual who had spoken, and learnt that my early friend had indeed been the subject of conversation. I obtained her address, and sallied forth to find her, sure of a welcome, though we had not met for years.

A great military and civic procession was passing through the streets, and it was with some difficulty that I made my way into a retired street in a distant part of the city. There, in a modest dwelling, I found my old friend Alice. Herself and a widowed mother were the only occupants. It was scantily furnished, but bore the impress of that exquisite taste which a truly refined woman can throw over the meanest abode, giving to poverty attractions which wealth does not always bestow upon its palaces. Alice had, in our school-days, been a favourite,—not that she was beautiful, but her simplicity of character, her upright and truthful mind, her sincere and strong affections, had won friends, lasting and true, such as she well knew how to value. On leaving school we had been separated, and had since rarely met—nevertheless, with that interest which those who have been educated together often continue to feel for each other through life, we had not failed to make inquiries which kept us informed of the after-fate of those most dear to us. That of Alice had been so unlike the even and calm lot which we had planned for her, as to have excited the surprise and wonder of us all.

I found her busily at work, though the street was full of the gathering multitude, and a branch of the procession was forming immediately beneath the window. After the first cordial greetings had passed, I said to her, with the authority which, as somewhat her senior in years, I had been accustomed to exercise: "Come, Alice, put away your work for the day, and let me take you with me. I am alone, and want an escort. Your cheek is pale, and this fresh pure air will give it a little colour." "Go, Alice," said her mother, "Florence is right; it will do you good." A word from her mother was enough, and very soon we were threading our way through the crowded streets, and talking with the freedom and confidence of old times.

"Tell me your whole sad story, dearest," I said, "while we are alone, for but an allusion to it has now and then reached me, and I would know it all from yourself." An expression of sudden pain crossed the countenance of my friend, but it passed away, and her full heart was relieved by the recital, and happier, I knew, for my sympathy.

She had married young. One of whom we had often heard her speak as a dear friend and brother, but in a station so far above her, that she had never dreamed of aspiring to share it, or that he could turn from the gay and brilliant flowers which lavished their sweets around him, to cull a modest and humble violet, had found more fragrance and beauty in the latter, and passed by the gorgeous parterre, to pluck this and place it in his bosom. Her married life commenced under the happiest auspices. Ernest Vernon was proud, but his pride took the right direction;—he was proud of his own discernment in having transplanted the floweret which otherwise might have bloomed unheeded, or "wasted its sweetness on the desert air." All the luxuries which wealth could purchase were lavished upon his fair young wife;—he never seemed happy away from her, and bestowed all his love and confidence where it was gratefully appreciated and returned a thousand-fold. Ernest was, like herself, an only child, and their happiness thus centred in each other. No wonder that Alice almost worshipped him. He had always been her beau ideal of manly beauty, and now that those radiant eyes looked lovingly upon her, her heart often ached with excess of happiness, and with that fear which, in a world of change, comes like a cloud between us and perfect repose,—

> That faint sense of parting, such as clings
> To earthly love and joy in loveliest things.

Ernest, too, was happy, for his bride was a realization of the description of his favourite poet, the embodiment of his ideas of perfection in woman.

> He saw her upon nearer view
> A spirit, yet a woman too;
> Her household motions bright and free,
> And steps of virgin liberty;
> A creature not too light or good,
> For human nature's daily food;
> For transient sorrows, simple wiles,
> Praise, blame, love, kisses, tears, and smiles.

But I must pass briefly over those halcyon days, and come to the dark cloud which first and finally intercepted the sunlight. Ernest had, as I have said, the most entire confidence in his wife, and was accustomed to reveal to her every transaction in his business which could awaken her interest or command her sympathy. On one occasion he confided to her a secret in which the welfare and reputation of one of his dearest friends was concerned. Another, who had, through a different channel, got possession of a clue to this, and who supposed Mrs. Vernon must be aware of it, had, in conversation with her, designedly asked a direct question, to which she could not with truth give the denial with which she would gladly have put an end to his suspicions. He immediately made use of his information, and quoted her authority to confirm it.

Ernest returned home from an absence of a few days, to find his cherished secret, involving the honour of his friend, public, coupled with the name of his wife as the authority. He was hasty and passionate; defects which are oftener those of a truly noble and generous soul than a secret and persevering vindictiveness. In his anger he forgot that the silence and passiveness with which Alice received his reproaches might be evidences of suffering rather than of guilt, and used language which, as she thought, proved that his affections were withdrawn from her for ever.

Days passed away, and there was no relenting; Ernest was too proud to ask an explanation, and Alice scarcely knew of what she was accused. It was evident to her that her husband was alienated from her, no matter how, and in silence and in secrecy she formed her plans and executed them.

It was a bright, beautiful summer morning, when Alice Vernon stole softly down in the early twilight to bid adieu to the haunts and associations of her happiest hours. Her flowers looked lovingly upon her, and the tears that gemmed each petal and leaf were those of gratitude only, not sorrow. All was joyous, save the heart of one who was now, like Eve, to say farewell to her Paradise. But, unlike Eve, she went forth alone, with no manly arm to shield her, and no loving heart to interpose between herself and life's sorrows. The lovely cottage home she was leaving had never seemed more attractive: yet she had scarcely realized that it was her own, so far had it exceeded her wildest expectations. With a few valued relics, and simple articles of clothing, which had been a part of her own poor dowry, she sought her humble city home.

Months, years had passed away. The slight difference which had produced this alienation had been increased by professed friends,—angry words borne to the ears of the parties, and exaggerated in the repetition. Alice's only defensive weapon had been silence. It may seem strange that such a bond could thus easily be broken. One who is deeply read in the mysteries of love matters has, however, said:

Alas! how slight a cause may move
Dissension between hearts that love;—
Hearts that the world in vain has tried,
And sorrow but more closely tied;
A something light as air, a look,
  A word unkind or wrongly taken,
A love! that tempests never shook,
  A breath, a touch like this has shaken.

We had pursued our way around the common, now one sea of

heads, and glittering with military costumes and arms. The excitement was contagious, and we could not but reflect the gayety and animation which shone in every feature of the various physiognomies about us. It was nearly time, however, to begin to look for the grand event of the day—the procession—so we found a quiet spot where we could see the pageant, and sat down by an open window to breathe the cool air, and listen to the distant music.

> With thrilling fife and pealing drum,
> And clashing horn, they come! they come!

Gay banners waved, and white plumes danced in the breeze; shining arms, and glittering epaulets; regalia gorgeous in purple and gold; noble steeds and noble riders—came thronging and pouring through the narrow street, and, as they passed slowly along often pausing, as impeded by some obstacle, we could read the motto on every banner, and catch the expression of every face. As I looked at Alice I saw that she had given herself wholly to the excitement of the scene; her face was radiant with pleasure; and her cheek but now pale, crimsoned with the flush of unaccustomed interest. One must indeed have been a stoic not to have shared in the general enthusiasm and joy.

My eyes fairly ached with gazing on the brilliant array, and I had turned them for relief once more upon the face of my new found friend, when I saw her lip quiver convulsively, and the bloom which I had but now noticed, suddenly leave her cheek as colourless as before. She moved hastily from the window, and looking up to me imploringly, said: "Take me away, Florence." As I passed the window I caught a glimpse of a noble-looking horseman in the uniform of one of the principal companies, and the emotion which his fine features revealed, gave me a clue to that of my friend.

Poor Alice! Alone in the parlour, and away from the sights which had just before given her such unwonted pleasure, she threw herself on the sofa, and wept bitterly. "Dear Florence, you will think me childish," she said, when the violence of the first passionate burst of feeling had spent itself in tears; "but you must have seen him—my Ernest, my noble, my beloved husband. Oh,

Florence, you know not how many hours of bitterness and tears I have spent in my solitude for him. I ought not to have come with you to-day, for I had a presentiment of this. Go, dear Florence, and leave me alone with my heart till its wild beatings are hushed."

There are times when grief is too deep and sacred to endure the presence of a spectator, and solitude is then a luxury to the sorrowing—so I obeyed.

The bright day was drawing to its close, and the last remnant of that long and motley train was filing through the street, when the bell was rung hastily, as if by an impatient hand. The servants were not to be found on an occasion like this, so I opened the door; a face, of which I had before caught a hasty glimpse, once more met my eye, and I knew that Ernest Vernon stood before me. "Is Alice! Mrs. Vernon, here?" asked he, and on my replying in the affirmative, followed me to the room where I had left her. I opened the door, and said gently, "Shall I come, Alice?" Without waiting for her reply, Ernest stepped forward and repeated, "Alice." She hurriedly looked up, and with a cry of joy, sprang into his arms, and was clasped to his heart. There was no need of an explanation, for each read in the face of the other restored confidence, and full forgiveness of all the past.

ELIZA L. SPROAT.

Miss Sproat is known almost exclusively as a poet. All the prose that she has published, amounting at most to not more than three or four contributions to annuals and magazines, is so essentially poetical, that it seemed a matter of doubt, whether to include her name at all in the present volume. Whether prose or poetry, however, her writings are among the most original and the most beautiful that our current literature affords. The article "Love versus Cupid," which appeared in the June number of Sartain, for 1849, is alone sufficient to stamp the author as a woman of high genius.

Miss Sproat is still very young. She is a native, and has always been a resident, of Philadelphia. The extract which follows, is from the Christian Keepsake for 1847. It is the first piece she ever published.

THE ENCHANTED LUTE.

Once, in the old days of the fairy dominion, two sisters sat beneath an ancient vine-entangled tree, which overhung an old stone fountain.

They were beautiful; but why should they hide their beauty in this lonely solitude?—yet not lonely, for Mira bore in her hand a marvellous talisman—an enchanted lute, whose lightest touch had power to waken the voices of a thousand unseen spirits, and reveal to mortal eye and ear the wonderful sealed mysteries of Nature. As yet, its power had never been challenged; but the sisters had been told, that if, at the dim solemn hour between the night and morning they would venture to sit alone by the haunted fountain, they could find the key to its music; that they could then discover the master-tone which should rule their future destiny.

For a time they sat in awe; for, as the night-breeze swept over the instrument, they were oppressed with a strange sense of the surrounding invisible presence.

"Let us try the spell," at length said Mira; "a little low sound is rising in my heart, which may be the key to our music."

"Pause yet a moment," whispered Ernesta, "oh! pause, my sister, and think that of all the great world's harmony, the tone you choose this day must rule your life for ever."

"I have no fear," said Mira, touching the outer chord.

A deep harsh note arose from the instrument: the trees reared their heads towards the sky, and the night-winds raised their voices. The weak vines in their dreaming clasped the trees convulsively, and seemed striving to climb to their summits.

Mira saw gleaming eyes in the darkness, and heard the murmur of strife in the air: even the very grass-blades jostled each other, as they stood side by side.

"Ah!" said Mira, shuddering, "this is Ambition—this is not the master-tone which should rule the world."

With a trembling hand she touched the second chord. A faint indefinite sound, neither music nor discord, played around the lute. The trees swung carelessly, and the vines loosed their hold; the clear waters stagnated; the air was filled with heavy vapour; and all the while there issued from the lute the dull monotonous tone of indolent Content. "That is not music," said Mira indignantly.

"Once more, my sister," said Ernesta; and again she tried the chords.

A flash like sunlight played through the darkness;—a sweet rich strain arose from the lute, and a richer, deeper, sweeter music faintly re-echoed the notes around. The waters smiled and murmured; the little flowers laid their cheeks against each other like happy sleeping children; each created thing responded to the all-pervading music of Love.

"This is the tone," cried Mira enchanted;—"this is the one great master-key of existence: it is not to toil, nor to strive, nor to battle, that we are placed in this world of pleasure—it is only to live and to love."

"Mira," said her sister earnestly, "try them once again."

"Not again," said Mira; "I have found my life."

"But I thought, when you touched the last sweet chord, that a note still sweeter fell upon my ear; try it, Mira!"

But Mira heard her not—her heart was filled with the music of love; she had chosen her lot, and over her the untried chords had power no more.

The hour had passed, and the Night Angel was departing. As he retired, he rolled away the soft dark mists in which he had tenderly enveloped the sleeping earth. The violets opened their eyes in time to catch a glimpse of the brighter eyes which all night long had watched their slumbers; the birds waked too, and looked out from their nests;—but the Night Angel stood with his finger on his lip, and all the world was silent.

Speeding through the dim air came the Angel of the Morning. With a pencil of flame he silently streaked the eastern sky, and fringed the clouds for the reception of the monarch.

The morning breezes grew uneasy in their hiding-places; the hushed waters trembled with eagerness; the flowers held their breath; the birds seemed bursting with long-pent melody;—but still, the Night Angel stood with his finger on his lip, and all the earth waited in silence.

Silence!

The Sun! the Sun! with a warm sudden kiss he greets the earth—the spell of the night is broken; all nature rises with a shout, and from a thousand thousand tongues bursts forth the imprisoned melody. How the trees wave their arms! how the singing waters glance and sparkle! how the forest gossips nod their heads to one another, and the busy happy breezes hurry to and fro with sweet gratulations borne from flower to flower! All motion—all happiness; every nook and corner of the great earth filled with life and love.

"Ernesta," said her sister, "art thou still faithless? Does not this blessed morning teach thee that there is no one tone in earth or heaven so worthy to rule as Love?"

"Touch the lute once more," said Ernesta; "only try once more."

Again those sweet strains rose in the morning air, and again to the listening ear of Ernesta rose that faint clear echo-tone, so strange, so pure, so far surpassing music ever heard before by mortal ear, that her raptured sense could scarcely endure the excess of melody.

But Mira's ears were filled with the music of the heart, and she could not hear these higher seraph strains.

"Now, Mira," said Ernesta, "look around, and tell me truly what thou seest."

"I see a beautiful, happy world, full of rich sunlight and flowers, and thronged with good, loving fairies roaming here and there, tending the sickening plants and supporting the delicate flower-buds; helping the young birds in their flight, and teaching all created things to live and to love. And what sees my sister Ernesta?"

"I see, between heaven and earth, God's holy cherubim ascending and descending; searching out the weary fainting spirits throughout the world, and bearing to them balm from Paradise. I see them rising with the prayers of the afflicted, and returning with sweet answers fresh from Heaven. And sometimes I see a newly perfected, enfranchised soul, borne rejoicing by the angels to the Throne, to dwell for ever in the presence of the Fountain of Love transcendent. But, Mira, look *up*, and tell me what you see."

"When I look up, I see nothing, because of the dazzling sunlight."

"Ah! but through the sunlight I can see the stars! the clear stars, that ever shine and never weary. And hark! From high, above the stars, floats down the trancing echo-tone. 'Tis the voice of the angels with their harps—they answer my heaven-yearning lute! 'Tis the great master-tone which rules the universe—the music of the soul!"

SUSAN FENIMORE COOPER.

Miss Cooper is a native and resident of Cooperstown, New York, and a daughter of the great American novelist. Her first publication, "Rural Hours," a splendid octavo issued by Putnam in 1850, gave her at once a high rank among our female authors. It is in the form of a journal, running through one entire year, and giving an account of the most notable sights and sounds of country life. Miss Cooper has an observant eye, and a happy faculty of making her descriptions interesting by selecting the right objects, instead of the too common method of extravagant embellishment. She never gets into ecstacies, and sees nothing which anybody else might not see who walked through the same fields after her. Her work accordingly contains an admirable portraiture of American out-door life, just as it is, with no colouring but that which every object necessarily receives in passing through a contemplative and cultivated mind. Miss Cooper has also edited a work called "Country Rambles in England," and has in press (1854) a new volume of her own, under the title of "Fields Old and New, or the Rhyme and Reason of Country Life."

SPIDERS.

Upon one of these violets we found a handsome coloured spider, one of the kind that live on flowers and take their colour from them; but this was unusually large. Its body was of the size of a well-grown pea, and of a bright lemon colour; its legs were also yellow, and altogether it was one of the most showy-coloured spiders we have seen in a long time. Scarlet or red ones still larger, are found, however, near New York. But, in their gayest aspect, these creatures are repulsive. It gives one a chilling idea of the gloomy solitude of a prison, when we remember that spiders have actually been petted by men shut out from better companionship. They are a very common insect with us, and on that account more annoying than any other that is found here. Some of them, with great black bodies, are of a formidable size. These haunt cellars, barns, and churches, and appear occasionally in inhabited rooms. There is a black spider of this kind, with a body said to be an inch long, and legs double that length, found in the Palace of Hampton Court, in England, which, it will be remembered, belonged to Cardinal Wolsey, and these great creatures are called "Cardinals" there, being considered by some people as peculiar to that building. A huge spider, by-the-bye, with her intricate web and snares, would form no bad emblem of a courtier and diplomatist, of the stamp of Cardinal Wolsey. He certainly took "hold with his hands, in kings' palaces," and did his share of mischief there.

Few people like spiders. No doubt these insects must have their merits and their uses, since none of God's creatures are made in vain; all living things are endowed with instincts more or less admirable; but the spider's plotting, creeping ways, and a sort of wicked expression about him, lead one to dislike him as a near neighbour. In a battle between a spider and a fly, one always sides with the fly, and yet of the two, the last is certainly the most troublesome insect to man. But the fly is frank and free in all his doings; he seeks his food openly, and he pursues his pastimes openly; suspicions of others or covert designs against them are quite unknown to him, and there is something almost confiding in the way in which he sails around you, when a single stroke of your hand might destroy him. The spider, on the contrary, lives by snares and plots; he is at the same time very designing and very suspicious, both cowardly and fierce; he always moves stealthily, as though among enemies, retreating before the least appearance of danger, solitary and morose, holding no communion with his fellows. His whole appearance corresponds with this character, and it is not surprising, therefore, that while the fly is more mischievous to us than the spider, we yet look upon the first with more favour than the last; for it is a natural impulse of the human heart to prefer that which is open and confiding to that which is wily and suspicious, even in the brute creation. The cunning and designing man himself will, at times, find a feeling of respect and regard for the guileless and generous stealing over him, his heart, as it were, giving the lie to his life.

Some two or three centuries since, when people came to this continent from the Old World in search of gold, oddly enough, it was considered a good sign of success when they met with spiders! It would be difficult to say why they cherished this fancy; but according to that old worthy, Hakluyt, when Martin Frobisher and his party landed on Cumberland Island, in quest of gold, their expectations were much increased by finding there numbers of spiders, "which, as many affirm, are signs of great store of gold."

HUMMING-BIRDS.

HUMMING-BIRDS are particularly partial to the evening hours. One is sure to find them now toward sunset, fluttering about their favourite plants; often there are several together among the flowers of the same bush, betraying themselves, though unseen, by the trembling of the leaves and blossoms. They are extremely fond of the Missouri currant—of all the early flowers, it is the greatest favourite with them; they are fond of the lilacs also, but do not care much for the syringa; to the columbine they are partial, to the bee larkspur also, with the wild bergamot or Oswego tea, the speckled jewels, scarlet trumpet-flower, red clover, honeysuckle, and the lychnis tribe. There is something in the form of these tube-shape blossoms, whether small or great, which suits their long, slender bills, and possibly, for the same reason, the bees cannot find such easy access to the honey, and leave more in these than in the open flowers. To the lily the humming-bird pays only a passing compliment, and seems to prefer the great tiger-lily to the other varieties; the rose he seldom visits; he will leave these stately blossoms any day for a head of the common red clover, in which he especially delights. Often of a summer's evening have we watched the humming-birds flitting about the meadows, passing from one tuft of clover to another, then resting a moment on a tall spear of timothy grass, then off again to fresh clover, scarcely touching the other flowers, and continuing frequently in the same field until the very latest twilight.

Mr. Tupper, in his paper on "Beauty," pays a pretty compliment to the humming-bird. Personifying Beauty, he says, she

"Fluttereth into the tulip with the humming-bird."

But, although these little creatures are with us during the tulip season, it may be doubted if they feed on these gaudy blossoms. On first reading the passage, this association struck us as one with which we were not familiar; had it been the trumpet-flower, nothing would have been more natural, for these dainty birds are for ever fluttering about the noble scarlet blossoms of that plant, as we all know, but the tulip did not seem quite in place in this connexion. Anxious to know whether we had deceived ourselves, we have now watched the humming-birds for several seasons, and, as yet, have never seen one in a tulip, while we have often observed them pass these for other flowers. Possibly this may have been accidental, or other varieties of the humming-bird may have a different taste from our own, and one cannot positively assert that this little creature never feeds on the tulip, without more general examination. But there is something in the upright position of that flower which, added to its size, leads one to believe that it must be an inconvenient blossom for the humming-bird, who generally seems to prefer nodding or drooping flowers, if they are at all large, always feeding on the wing as he does, and never alighting, like butterflies and bees, on the petals. Altogether, we are inclined to believe that if the distinguished author of Proverbial Philosophy had been intimate with our little neighbour, he would have placed him in some other native plant, and not in the Asiatic tulip, to which he seems rather indifferent. The point is a very trifling one, no doubt, and it is extremely bold, to find fault with our betters; but in the first place, we are busying ourselves wholly with trifles just now, and then the great work in question has been a source of so much pleasure and advantage to half the world, that no one heeds the misplaced tulip, unless it be some rustic bird-fancier. By supposing the flower of the *tulip-tree* to be meant, the question would be entirely settled to the satisfaction of author, reader, and humming-bird also, who is very partial to those handsome blossoms of his native woods.

It is often supposed that our little friend seeks only the most fragrant flowers; the blossoms on the Western Prairies, those of Wisconsin at least, and probably others also, are said to have but little perfume, and it is observed that the humming-bird is a stranger there, albeit those wilds are a perfect sea of flowers during the spring and summer months. But the amount of honey in a plant has nothing to do with its perfume, for we daily see the humming-birds neglecting the rose and the white lily, while many of their most favourite flowers, such as the scarlet honeysuckle, the columbine, the lychnis tribe, the trumpet flower, and speckled jewels, have no perfume at all. Other pet blossoms of theirs, however, are very fragrant, as the highly-scented Missouri currant, for instance, and the red clover, but their object seems to be quite independent of this particular quality in a plant.

The fancy these little creatures have for perching on a dead twig is very marked; you seldom see them alight elsewhere, and the fact that a leafless branch projects from a bush, seems enough to invite them to rest; it was but yesterday we saw two males sitting upon the same dead branch of a honeysuckle beneath the window. And last summer, there chanced to be a little dead twig, at the highest point of a locust-tree, in sight from the house, which was a favourite perching spot of theirs for some weeks; possibly it was the same bird, or the same pair, who frequented it, but scarcely a day passed without a tiny little creature of the tribe being frequently seen there. Perhaps there may have been a nest close at hand, but they build so cunningly, making their nests look so much like a common bunch of moss or lichen, that they are seldom discovered, although they often build about gardens, and usually at no great height; we have known a nest found in a lilac-bush, and sometimes they are even satisfied with a tall coarse weed; in the woods, they are said to prefer a white oak sapling, seldom building, however, more than ten feet from the ground.

Though so diminutive, they are bold and fearless, making very good battle when necessary, and going about generally in a very careless, confident way. They fly into houses more frequently than any other bird, sometimes attracted by plants or flowers within, often apparently by accident, or for the purpose of exploring. The country people have a saying that when a humming-bird flies in at a window he brings a love message for some one in the house; a pretty fancy, certainly, for Cupid himself could not have desired a daintier *avant courier.* Unfortunately, this trick of flying in at the windows is often a very serious and fatal one to the poor little creatures themselves, whatever felicity it may bring to the Romeo and Juliet of the neighbourhood; for they usually quiver about against the ceiling until quite stunned and exhausted, and unless they are caught and set at liberty, soon destroy themselves in this way. We have repeatedly known them found dead in rooms little used, that had been opened to air, and which they had entered unperceived.

WEEDS.

THE word weed varies much with circumstances; at times, we even apply it to the beautiful flower or the useful herb. A plant may be a weed, because it is noxious, or fetid, or unsightly, or troublesome, but it is rare indeed that all these faults are united in one individual of the vegetable race. Often the unsightly, or fetid, or even the poisonous plant, is useful, or it may be interesting from some peculiarity; and on the other hand, many others, troublesome from their numbers, bear pleasing flowers, taken singly. Upon the whole, it is not so much a natural defect which marks the weed, as a certain impertinent, intrusive character in these plants; a want of modesty, a habit of showing themselves forward upon ground where they are not needed, rooting themselves in soil intended for better things, for plants more useful, more fragrant, or more beautiful. Thus the corn-cockle bears a fine flower, not unlike the mullein-pink of the garden, but then it springs up among the precious wheat, taking the place of the grain, and it is a weed; the flower of the thistle is handsome in itself, but it is useless, and it pushes forward in throngs by the wayside until we are weary of seeing it, and everybody makes war upon it; the common St. John's wort, again, has a pretty yellow blossom, and it has its uses also as a simple, but it is injurious to the cattle, and yet it is so obstinately tenacious of a place among the grasses, that it is found in every meadow, and we quarrel with it as a weed.

These noxious plants have come unbidden to us, with the grains and grasses of the Old World, the evil with the good, as usual in this world of probation—the wheat and tares together. The useful plants produce a tenfold blessing upon the labour of man, but the weed is also there, ever accompanying his steps, to teach him a lesson of humility. Certain plants of this nature—the dock, thistle, nettle, &c., &c.—are known to attach themselves especially to the path of man; in widely different soils and climates, they are still found at his door. Patient care and toil can alone keep the evil within bounds, and it seems doubtful whether it lies within the reach of human means entirely to remove from the face of the earth one single plant of this peculiar nature, much less all their varieties. Has any one, even of the most noxious sorts, ever been utterly destroyed? Agriculture, with all the pride and power of science now at her command, has apparently accomplished but little in this way. Egypt and China are said to be countries in which weeds are comparatively rare; both regions have long been in a high state of cultivation, filled to overflowing with a hungry population, which neglects scarce a rood of the soil, and yet even in those lands, even upon the banks of the Nile, where the crops succeed each other without any interval throughout the whole year, leaving no time for weeds to extend themselves; even there, these noxious plants are not unknown, and the moment the soil is abandoned, only for a season, they return with renewed vigour.

In this new country, with a fresh soil, and a thinner population, we have not only weeds innumerable, but we observe, also, that briers and brambles seem to acquire double strength in the neighbourhood of man; we meet them in the primitive forest, here and there, but they line our roads and fences, and the woods are no sooner felled to make ready for cultivation, than they spring up in profusion, the first natural produce of the soil. But in this world of mercy, the just curse is ever graciously tempered with a blessing; many a grateful fruit, and some of our most delightful flowers, grow among the thorns and briars, their fragrance and excellence reminding man of the sweets as well as the toils of his task. The sweetbriar, more especially, with its simple flower and delightful fragrance, unknown in the wilderness, but moving onward by the side of the ploughman, would seem, of all others, the husbandman's blossom.

ELIZABETH WETHERELL.

(SUSAN WARNER.)

In the year 1850, a novel in two volumes, under the title of "The Wide Wide World," was sent forth to seek its fortunes. The title-page bore upon its face a name unknown to literature, and no special pains were taken to herald the work into notoriety. But readers very soon began to multiply; every one who read the book, talked about it, and urged its reading upon his neighbours, until, within a year from the time of its publication, it had reached a circulation then considered almost unprecedented, and everybody was beginning to inquire who is "Elizabeth Wetherell?" It was one of the most signal instances in recent times of a popularity reaching almost to fame, springing up spontaneously, and entirely in advance of all the usual organs of public opinion. The tide of favour was still further swelled by the appearance in 1852 of a successor, another novel in two volumes, under the title of "Queechy." The second work had nearly all the peculiarities of the first, and reached a still higher mark of success. They were both reprinted and very widely circulated in England, and they appear to have been more generally read and to have made a deeper impression, both at home and abroad, than any recent American works of fiction, except Uncle Tom's Cabin.

These volumes are without doubt open to criticism. The "North British Review" objects vehemently to carelessness in the diction and to "the vulgarity" of some of the characters, and the "Westminster" dislikes of course the pervading religious tone of the books. Not assenting to all the criticisms of the "North British," we subscribe most fully to the opinion with which the article closes. "The heartiness and sincerity with which she dwells upon and describes, in its minutest details, the farm-life in America are very delightful, and quite new in their way, which is wholly unsentimental and truly national. But the richest qualities of this lady's mind, as shown in her works, are, *first*, the heartiness of her religion, notwithstanding the mistakes we have noticed; and, *secondly*, the clear understanding, which, having once apprehended Christianity, not as a mere logical conclusion, but as a fact of experience and a living presence, is not for an instant to be puzzled by any seeming contradiction. This clear-sightedness and the power of expressing it so as to impress others, is a very remarkable and unspeakably valuable quality of the American mind in matters of religion. Of all religious writers, the Americans are those who have the firmest footing upon this unassailable ground of personal experience and the actual facts of nature; and what our great Christian philosopher Butler felt so powerfully, and expressed with so much difficulty and obscurity in his immortal 'Analogy,' seems to be an ordinary inheritance of the religious mind in America."

The religious character of the writings of "Elizabeth Wetherell" is certainly that which is stamped upon them most deeply. We know no work of fiction in which real religion, as it is understood by Evangelical Christians, is exhibited with so much truth and force. The story of "Little Ellen Montgomery" may in all seriousness be commended as a book to make the heart wiser and better. Next to the religious tone of the books, we would name their tenderness and pathos. No living writer, not even Mrs. Stowe, knows better how to open the fountain of tears, or goes more directly to the heart of the reader. Her descriptions and narrations have the particularity and the life-like verisimilitude of Defoe, while her delineations of character are so eminently individual as to have created the general impression that they are taken from real life. Her descriptions of country life and character, too, are eminently national.

The North American Review, in a very genial article on the subject, is disposed to place this merit above all others, in estimating the value of the Wide-Wide-World books. "As a matter of pure judgment, we must place their pictures of American country life and character above all their other merits, since we know not where, in any language, we shall find their graphic truth excelled. When after times would seek a specimen of our Doric of this date, Aunt Fortune will stand them in stead; and no Theocritus of our time will draw a bucolical swain more true to the life than Mr. Van Brunt. Even the shadow of Didenhover is a portrait; we see him, though he never appears in the flesh, and we feel him, too, though we have never let out a farm 'on shares.' Captain Montgomery is another of those invisible persons with whom we are perfectly well acquainted, although not a line is given to describing him; and the 'hateful' clerk who wreaks his petty spite upon Ellen's horse, is a character whose truth to nature little girls bear witness to, by the hearty indignation with which they read the scene. Nancy Vawse is a white Topsy; Barby a perfect type of the American serving-girl, at once selfish and tender, coarse and delicate; and we might swell our list of life-like characters a good deal further, if their very number did not warn us against being too particular."

After the publication of "Queechy," the author engaged with "Amy Lothrop," who is generally understood to be a younger sister, in preparing a series of children's books, under the general title of "Ellen Montgomery's Book Shelf."

The reader of Elizabeth Wetherell's novels cannot fail to be struck with the extraordinary aptness and pertinency of her Scripture quotations. Her intimate acquaintance with the sacred volume, as here indicated, and her evident partiality for the study, fitted her in an especial manner for the work in which she next engaged, which was evidently a "labour of love." This was "The Law and the Testimony," a huge octavo volume of 840 pages, in which the proof-texts on the great doctrines of Christianity are brought together under their separate heads. In hunting up these passages, as we learn from the preface, the author had the assistance of her "young sister," as in sketching the outline of subjects she had that of her father. It is a work of stupendous labour, and of utility commensurate with the pains bestowed upon it. One sincerely desirous of learning what the Scriptures teach on any particular topic, can hardly fail to be benefited by consulting this work, no matter how familiar with the Scriptures he may be already, or how many other helps he may have at hand.

The real name of "Elizabeth Wetherell" is Susan Warner. But as she continues to use her *nom de plume* in all her publications, it has seemed but meet to do the same in writing of her.

LITTLE ELLEN AND THE SHOPMAN.

"MAMMA!" exclaimed Ellen, suddenly starting up, "a bright thought has just come into my head! I'll do it for you, mamma!"

"Do what?"

"I'll get the merino and things for you, mamma. You needn't smile,—I will, indeed, if you will let me."

"My dear Ellen," said her mother, "I don't doubt you would, if good will only were wanting; but a great deal of skill and experience is necessary for a shopper, and what would you do without either?"

"But see, mamma," pursued Ellen eagerly, "I'll tell you how I'll manage, and I know I can manage very well. You tell me exactly what coloured merino you want, and give me a little piece to show me how fine it should be, and tell me what price you wish to give, and then I'll go to the store and ask them to show me different pieces, you know, and if I see any I think you would like, I'll ask them to give me a little bit of it to show you; and then I'll bring it home, and if you like it, you can give me the money, and tell me how many yards you want, and I can go back to the store and get it. Why can't I, mamma?"

"Perhaps you could; but, my dear child, I am afraid you wouldn't like the business."

"Yes, I should; indeed, mamma, I should like it dearly if I could help you so. Will you let me try, mamma?"

"I don't like, my child, to venture you alone on such an errand, among crowds of people; I should be uneasy about you."

"Dear mamma, what would the crowds of people do to me? I am not a bit afraid. You know, mamma, I have often taken walks alone,—that's nothing new; and what harm should come to me while I am in the store? You needn't be the least uneasy about me; —may I go?"

Mrs. Montgomery smiled, but was silent.

"May I go, mamma?" repeated Ellen. "Let me go at least and try what I can do. What do you say, mamma?"

"I don't know what to say, my daughter, but I am in difficulty on either hand. I will let you go and see what you can do. It would be a great relief to me to get this merino by any means."

"Then shall I go right away, mamma?"

"As well now as ever. You are not afraid of the wind?"

"I should think not," said Ellen; and away she scampered up stairs to get ready. With eager haste she dressed herself; then with great care and particularity took her mother's instructions as to the article wanted; and finally set out, sensible that a great trust was reposed in her, and feeling busy and important accordingly. But at the very bottom of Ellen's heart there was a little secret doubtfulness respecting her undertaking. She hardly knew it was there, but then she couldn't tell what it was that made her fingers so inclined to be tremulous while she was dressing, and that made her heart beat quicker than it ought, or than was pleasant, and one of her cheeks so much hotter than the other. However, she set forth upon her errand with a very brisk step, which she kept up till on turning a corner she came in sight of the place she was going to. Without thinking much about it, Ellen had directed her steps to St. Clair & Fleury's. It was one of the largest and best stores in the city, and the one where she knew her mother generally made her purchases; and it did not occur to her that it might not be the best for her purpose on this occasion. But her steps slackened as soon as she came in sight of it, and continued to slacken as she drew nearer, and she went up the broad flight of marble steps in front of the store very slowly indeed, though they were exceedingly low and easy. Pleasure was not certainly the uppermost feeling in her mind now; yet she never thought of turning back. She knew that if she could succeed in the object of her mission her mother would be relieved from some anxiety; that was enough; she was bent on accomplishing it.

Timidly she entered the large hall of entrance. It was full of people, and the buzz of business was heard on all sides. Ellen had for some time past seldom gone a shopping with her mother, and had never been in this store but once or twice before. She had not the remotest idea where, or in what apartment of the building, the merino counter was situated, and she could see no one to speak to. She stood irresolute in the middle of the floor. Everybody seemed to be busily engaged with somebody else; and whenever an opening on one side or another appeared to promise her an opportunity, it was sure to be filled up before she could reach it, and, disappointed and abashed, she would return to her old station in the middle of the floor. Clerks frequently passed her, crossing the store in all directions, but they were always bustling along in a great hurry of business; but they did not seem to notice her at all, and were gone before poor Ellen could get her mouth open to speak to them. She knew well enough now, poor child, what it was that made her cheeks burn as they did, and her heart beat as if it would burst its bounds. She felt confused, and almost confounded, by the incessant hum of voices, and moving crowd of strange people all around her, while her little figure stood alone and unnoticed in the midst of them; and there seemed no prospect that she would be able to gain the ear or the eye of a single person. Once she determined to accost a man she saw advancing toward her from a distance, and actually made up to him for the purpose, but with a hurried bow, and "I beg your pardon, Miss!" he brushed past. Ellen almost burst into tears. She longed to turn and run out of the store, but a faint hope remaining, and an unwillingness to give up her undertaking, kept her fast. At length one of the clerks in the desk observed her, and remarked to Mr. St. Clair, who stood by, "There is a little girl, sir, who seems to be looking for something, or waiting for somebody; she has been standing there a good while." Mr. St. Clair, upon this, advanced to poor Ellen's relief.

"What do you wish, Miss?" he said.

But Ellen had been so long preparing sentences, trying to utter them and failing in the attempt, that now, when an opportunity to speak and be heard was given her, the power of speech seemed to be gone.

"Do you wish anything, Miss?" inquired Mr. St. Clair again.

"Mother sent me," stammered Ellen,—"I wish, if you please, sir,—mamma wished me to look at merinoes, sir, if you please."

"Is your mamma in the store?"

"No, sir," said Ellen, "she is ill and cannot come out, and she sent me to look at merinoes for her, if you please, sir."

"Here, Saunders," said Mr. St. Clair, "show this young lady the merinoes."

Mr. Saunders made his appearance from among a little group of clerks, with whom he had been indulging in a few jokes by way of relief from the tedium of business. "Come this way," he said to Ellen; and sauntering before her with a rather dissatisfied air, led the way out of the entrance hall into another and much larger apartment. There were plenty of people here, too, and just as busy as those they had quitted. Mr. Saunders having brought Ellen to the merino counter, placed himself behind it; and leaning over it and fixing his eyes carelessly upon her, asked what she wanted to look at. His tone and manner struck Ellen most unpleasantly, and made her again wish herself out of the store. He was a tall, lank young man, with a quantity of fair hair combed down on each side of his face, a slovenly exterior, and the most disagreeable pair of eyes, Ellen thought, she had ever beheld. She could not bear to meet them, and cast down her own. Their look was bold, ill-bred, and ill-humoured; and Ellen felt, though she couldn't have told why, that she need not expect either kindness or politeness from him.

"What do you want to see, little one?" inquired this gentleman, as if he had a business in hand he would like to be rid of. Ellen heartily wished he was rid of it, and she, too. "Merinoes, if you please," she answered without looking up.

"Well, what kind of merinoes? Here are all sorts and descriptions of merinoes, and I can't pull them all down, you know, for you to look at. What kind do you want?"

"I don't know without looking," said Ellen, "won't you please to show me some?"

He tossed down several pieces upon the counter. and tumbled them about before her.

"There," said he, "is that anything like what you want? There's a pink one,—and there's a blue one,—and there's a green one. Is that the kind?"

"This is the kind," said Ellen; "but this isn't the colour I want."

"What colour do you want?"

"Something dark, if you please."

"Well, there, that green's dark; won't that do? See, that would make up very pretty for you."

"No," said Ellen, "mamma don't like green."

"Why don't she come and choose her stuffs herself, then? What colour does she like?"

"Dark blue, or dark brown, or a nice gray, would do," said Ellen, "if it's fine enough."

"'Dark blue,' or 'dark brown,' or 'a nice gray,' eh! Well, she's pretty easy to suit. A dark blue I've showed you already,—what's the matter with that?"

"It isn't dark enough," said Ellen.

"Well," said he, discontentedly, pulling down another piece, "how'll that do? That's dark enough."

It was a fine and beautiful piece, very different from those he had showed her at first. Even Ellen could see that, and fumbling for her little pattern of merino, she compared it with the piece. They agreed perfectly as to fineness.

"What is the price of this?" she asked, with trembling hope that she was going to be rewarded by success for all the trouble of her enterprise.

"Two dollars a yard."

Her hopes and her countenance fell together. "That's too high," she said with a sigh.

"Then take this other blue; come,—it's a great deal prettier than that dark one, and not so dear; and I know your mother will like it better."

Ellen's cheeks were tingling and her heart throbbing, but she couldn't bear to give up.

"Would you be so good as to show me some gray?"

He slowly and ill-humouredly complied, and took down an excellent piece of dark gray, which Ellen fell in love with at once; but she was again disappointed; it was fourteen shillings.

"Well, if you won't take that, take something else," said the man; "you can't have everything at once; if you will have cheap goods, of course you can't have the same quality that you like; but now, here's this other blue, only twelve shillings, and I'll let you have it for ten if you'll take it."

"No, it is too light and too coarse," said Ellen, "mamma wouldn't like it."

"Let me see," said he, seizing her pattern and pretending to compare it; "it's quite as fine as this, if that's all you want."

"Could you," said Ellen timidly, "give me a little bit of this gray to show to mamma?"

"O no!" said he impatiently, tossing over the cloths and throwing Ellen's pattern on the floor; "we can't cut up our goods; if people don't choose to buy of us they may go somewhere else, and if you cannot decide upon anything I must go and attend to those that can. I can't wait here all day."

"What's the matter, Saunders?" said one of his brother clerks, passing him.

"Why I've been here this half hour showing cloths to a child that doesn't know merino from a sheep's back," said he, laughing. And some other customers coming up at the moment, he was as good as his word, and left Ellen, to attend to them.

Ellen stood a moment stock still, just where he had left her, struggling with her feelings of mortification; she could not endure to let them be seen. Her face was on fire; her head was dizzy. She could not stir at first, and in spite of her utmost efforts she *could* not command back one or two rebel tears that forced their way; she lifted her hand to her face to remove them as quietly as possible.

"What is all this about, my little girl?" said a strange voice at her side.

Ellen started, and turned her face, with the tears but half wiped away, toward the speaker. It was an old gentleman, an odd old gentleman, too, she thought; one she certainly would have been rather shy of, if she had seen him under other circumstances. But though his face was odd, it looked kindly upon her, and it was a kind tone of voice in which his question had been put; so he seemed to her like a friend. "What is all this?" repeated the old gentleman. Ellen began to tell what it was, but the pride which had forbidden her to weep before strangers gave way at one touch of sympathy, and she poured out tears much faster than words as she related her story, so that it was some little time before the old gentleman could get a clear notion of her case. He waited very patiently till she had finished; but then he set himself in good earnest about righting the wrong. "Hallo! you, sir!" he shouted, in a voice that made everybody look round; "you merino man! come and show your goods: why aren't you at your post, sir?"—as Mr. Saunders came up with an altered countenance—"here's a young lady you've left standing unattended to I don't know how long; are these your manners?"

"The young lady did not wish anything, I believe, sir," returned Mr. Saunders, softly.

"You know better, you scoundrel," retorted the old gentleman, who was in a great passion; "I saw the whole matter with my own eyes. You are a disgrace to the store, sir, and deserve to be sent out of it, which you are like enough to be."

"I really thought, sir," said Mr. Saunders, smoothly,—for he knew the old gentleman, and knew very well he was a person that must not be offended,—"I really thought—I was not aware, sir, that the young lady had any occasion for my services."

"Well, show your wares, sir, and hold your tongue. Now, my dear, what did you want?"

"I wanted a little bit of this gray merino, sir, to show to mamma;—I couldn't buy it, you know, sir, until I found out whether she would like it."

"Cut a piece, sir, without any words," said the old gentleman. Mr. Saunders obeyed.

"Did you like this best?" pursued the old gentleman.

"I liked this dark blue very much, sir, and I thought mamma would; but it's too high."

"How much is it?" inquired he.

"Fourteen shillings," replied Mr. Saunders.

"He said it was two dollars," exclaimed Ellen.

"I beg pardon," said the crest-fallen Mr. Saunders, "the young lady mistook me; I was speaking of another piece when I said two dollars."

"He said this was two dollars, and the gray fourteen shillings," said Ellen.

"Is the gray fourteen shillings?" inquired the old gentleman.

"I think not, sir," answered Mr. Saunders—"I believe not, sir, —I think it's only twelve,—I'll inquire, if you please, sir."

"No, no," said the old gentleman, "I know it was only twelve —I know your tricks, sir. Cut a piece off the blue. Now, my dear, are there any more pieces of which you would like to take patterns, to show your mother?"

"No, sir," said the overjoyed Ellen; "I am sure she will like one of these."

"Now, shall we go, then?"

"If you please, sir," said Ellen, "I should like to have my bit of merino that I brought from home; mamma wanted me to bring it back again."

"Where is it?"

"That gentleman threw it on the floor."

"Do you hear, sir?" said the old gentleman; "find it directly."

Mr. Saunders found and delivered it, after stooping in search of it till he was very red in the face; and he was left, wishing heartily that he had some safe means of revenge, and obliged to come to the conclusion that none was within his reach, and that he must stomach his indignity in the best manner he could. But Ellen and her protector went forth most joyously together from the store.

AMY LOTHROP.

"AMY LOTHROP," according to uncontradicted tradition, is a younger sister of "Elizabeth Wetherell." She is the author of a novel in two volumes, called by the very unromantic name of "Dollars and Cents," and of a sprightly and entertaining series of child's books, under the general title of "Ellen Montgomery's Book Shelf." In the preparation of this series, some little assistance is understood to have been received from the older sister, but the main part of the authorship has devolved upon "Amy."

"Dollars and Cents" appeared in 1852. It was immediately and universally recognised as having some relationship to the "Wide-Wide-World" books, though the precise connexion was not known for some time. The work was by many attributed to "Elizabeth Wetherell" herself, thus showing striking points of similarity. At the same time, the differences in style were too great to admit of such a supposition being long entertained.

If Amy Lothrop's novel has not the absorbing interest of those with which it is associated, it yet has high merit and many beauties of its own. The author has a peculiarly graceful and delicate play of the fancy, not unlike, and certainly not unequal to that of the lamented Fanny Forrester. She is moreover a nice observer of character, an intense admirer of the beauties of external nature, and altogether highly poetical in her temperament, notwithstanding the prosaic title which she has chosen for her first performance.

Our first quotation is from "Carl Krinken," one of the books from "Ellen Montgomery's Book Shelf." The other is from "Dollars and Cents."

THE STORY OF THE PINE CONE.

"Whew!" said the North wind.—"Whew—r—r—r—r—!"

The fir trees heard him coming, and bowed their tall heads very gracefully, as if to tell the wind he could not do much with them. Only some of the little cones who had never blown about a great deal, felt frightened, and said the wind made their teeth chatter.

"Do you think we can stay on?" asked one little cone; and the others would have said they did'nt know, but the wind gave the tree such another shake that their words were lost.

"Whew—r—r—r—r!" said the wind.

And again the fir trees bowed to let him pass, and swayed from side to side, and the great branches creaked and moaned and flung themselves about in a desperate kind of way; but the leaves played sweet music. It was their fashion whenever the wind blew.

"I think we shall have snow," said the tallest of the fir trees, looking over the heads of his companions.

"The sky is very clear," remarked a very small and inexperienced fir, who was so short he could not see much of anything.

"Yes," said the tall one, "so you think; but there is a great deal of sky besides that which is over our heads; and I can see the wind gathering handfuls of snow-clouds which he will fling about us presently."

"Yes," repeated the tall fir, with another graceful bend, "I see them—they are coming."

The evergreens were all sorry to hear this, for nothing depressed them so much as snow; the rain they could generally shake off,—at least if it didn't freeze too hard.

As for the beeches, they said, if that was the case, they must put off their summer clothes directly. And one little beech, with a great effort, did succeed in shaking off half a dozen green leaves the next time the wind came that way.

"You need not hurry yourselves," said the tall fir,—"this is only an early storm—the winter will not come yet. I can still see the sun for a few minutes every day."

And that was true. For a few minutes the sun showed himself above the horizon, and then after making a very small arch in the sky down he went again. Then came the long afternoon of clear twilight; and the longer night, when the stars threw soft shadows like a young moon, and looked down to see their bright eyes in the deep fiord that lay at the foot of the fir trees. * * * *

"How cold you must be up there!" said a little pine who was nearly as high as the tall fir's lower branches. But the fir did not hear him, or perhaps did not take notice, for he was looking off at the fine prospect.

"Yes, it is cold up here," answered one of the fir cones,—"and windy—and there's a great deal of sameness about it. It's just snow and rain, and wind and sunshine, and then snow again."

"That's what it is, everywhere," said the wind as he swept by.

"I can't help it," said the cone, "I'm tired of it. I want to travel, and see the world, and be of some use to society. What can one do in the top of a fir tree?"

"Why what can a pine cone do anywhere?" said some of the beech mast.

"The end of a pine cone's existence is not to be eaten up, however," retorted the cone sharply. "Neither am I a pine cone—though people will call me so. We firs hold our heads pretty high, I can tell you. But I will throw myself into the fiord some day, and go to sea. I have no doubt I could sail as well as a boat. It would be a fine thing to discover new islands, and take possession."

"It would be very lonely," said a squirrel who was gathering beech mast.

"Royally so," said the pine cone. "There one would be king of all the trees."

"The trees never had but one king, and that was a bramble," said a reed at the water's edge, who was well versed in history.

"What nonsense you are all talking!" said the tall fir tree, at length. "My top leaf is at this moment loaded with a snow flake; there is something sensible for you to think of."

SPRING WEATHER.

What is there in some exquisitely fine weather to make one feel sad? It was one of those days of which March has a few, that seem to embody the very quintescence of spring; the sky of the fairest and calmest, the grass in the yellow-green transition, the trees softened with the swelling buds as with the lightest veil of clothing, and showing green or red as flowers or leaves were to come first. In sheltered fence-corners or bank-protected hollows, there were tufts of grass that might have come from the emerald isle itself; now and then a tuft of tiny white flowers—quiet, insignificant little things—that the eye sought and rested upon because it was March and not June. And even one or two bright-faced dandelions, that had been waked up by some extraordinary sunbeam, looked at us smilingly from the wayside. The birds were in a twitter of delight and consultation; robins and song-sparrows excited each other, and the phœbe's gentle note of reproof, and the crow's loud "caw" of disdain as he sat on a cedar and bowed his head mockingly, neither calmed the spirits nor roused the ire of the warblers—their dignity was safe bound up in enthusiasm. On one bush sat a committee of fifty robins; in another, where two sparrows made mysterious darts through the evergreen foliage, there might be the nucleus of a nest. The scarce stirring air was as soft and delicious as if it had been laid up all winter in sachets of satin and sweetness—but bouquet nor patchouli can approach the unspeakable aroma of early flowers and leaves—that indefinable perfume which spring compounds for itself. And yet as we breathed it in—and breaths seemed all too short in such an atmosphere—the exceeding beauty of everything brought no exhilaration, but rather sadness. It might be the association with other spring days when our hearts were lighter—a mind somewhat out of tone with the season—it might be that the beauty was too perfect. Perfection of any kind is too near the contrast.

CAROLINE ORNE.

Mrs. Orne has published chiefly through the magazines, in which, during the last twenty years, more than a hundred of her tales have appeared. These would make, if collected, several large volumes. Her writings are generally of a practical cast, on subjects of every-day life, and have been deservedly popular.

Her early childhood was passed in the most retired part of, at that time, a retired country town, Georgetown, Mass.

Early impressions are seldom effaced, and the first six years of her life spent amid rural scenes gave a permanent tone and colouring to her mind. She was educated to love birds and flowers, and the children of the family were always called to look at a rainbow as an object worthy of peculiar admiration. One of her dearest pleasures was to watch, with her sister, the early garden-plants, when they first broke through the dark, rich soil. But the wild flowers which grew in profusion near the paternal dwelling, yielded, if possible, a delight still more vivid. Among these, the violets which gemmed the green and sunny slopes, held pre-eminence. Birds were still more fondly cherished than flowers, the love bestowed on them, like themselves, having more vitality. A number of orioles, or, as they were generally called in that vicinity, golden robins, glancing in and out of the cloud of snowy or rose-tinted blooms, which covered some old apple-tree, was a treat that must have been enjoyed with a similar zest, to be truly appreciated.

Nor were the winter evenings without their pleasures, though books were scarce, and newspapers almost unknown. Her maternal grandmother, who was a member of the family, was an accomplished story-teller, and she used to listen, spell-bound, to the wild legends, tales of Indian warfare, or the trials and hardships of the pioneer's domestic life, which were related in a clear, emphatic manner, that gave to them a charm and a raciness, which could never have been imparted to a written story.

At a very early age she commenced attempting to write her thoughts. She recollects a manuscript "Picture Book" which was the joint production of her sister, her brother, and herself. It was her part of the task to compose the stories; her sister's, who, for one so young, could very neatly execute imitation print, to transfer them to the book; and her brother's, who, only a short time previous, had attained to the dignity of jacket and trowsers, to illustrate them with appropriate pen-and-ink devices.

These stories were simple and unpretending, though she was often ambitious to press into her service, long, sonorous words. The way she managed this was unique. When in a writing mood, she used to select a number of words which she considered uncommonly splendid, and each of these she made a kind of nucleus round which to weave her thoughts, such as they were. Being always written on a slate, they were speedily effaced to make room for more.

The reading of Pope's poetical works formed a new and never-to-be-forgotten era of her life. While reading the "Rape of the Lock," the aerial sylphs, and the lovely, mischievous sprites, which form its light and graceful machinery, seemed constantly hovering round her, while passages of other poems, such as the three opening lines of "Eloisa to Abelard,"

> "In these deep solitudes and awful cells,
> Where heavenly, pensive contemplation dwells,
> And ever-musing melancholy reigns,"

haunted her with their plaintive melody, as if chanted by spirit-voices close to her ear.

At the early age of fifteen, necessity compelled her to enter upon the practical duties of life. In connexion with her sister, she opened a private school in Salem, Mass., in the mean time devoting what intervals of leisure she could obtain in pursuing such studies as would better qualify her for her task. Among their pupils was the late Mrs. Judson, whom, for a while, they subsequently employed as an assistant.

The second tale Mrs. Orne ever attempted to write, appeared anonymously in the "Ladies' Magazine," published in Boston, and edited by Mrs. Hale. Subsequently other stories from her pen were published in different periodicals, all of them anonymously. A very encouraging letter received from Isaac C. Pray, in consequence of a story which she sent to the "Pearl and Galaxy," a paper of which he was one of the editors, stimulated her to devote what leisure she could command to writing, and from that time her stories were published in her name.

Mrs. Orne's maiden name was Chaplin. She has no middle name, though it is often printed with the initial "F." This mistake arises from there being a Miss Caroline F. Orne, a resident of Cambridgeport, who has many years written for publication, though most of her articles have been in verse.

She was mostly educated by her mother, and when, for one term, as a kind of finishing, she, with fear and trembling, on account of her supposed deficiencies, entered a justly celebrated school, she, to her surprise, found no difficulty in ranking with the first.

The late Jeremiah Chaplin, D. D. (a cousin to both of her parents), who was, for several years, President of Waterville College, corrected the first compositions which she ever wrote, which she thought worthy of being seen, and the manner in which he pointed out their beauties, as well as defects, had a lasting and salutary influence.

When about six years old, her father removed from Rowley to Salem, Mass., where she resided, with a few temporary exceptions, till she was married. Since her marriage, except the first four years at Meredith-Bridge, she has resided at Wolfboro', New Hampshire.

DOCTOR PLUMLEY.

The boy who had been sent for Dr. Plumley now returned, and with a giggle, which his most strenuous efforts could not suppress, told us that the Doctor was close at hand. He then retreated to a part of the room where his mistress could not have an eye on him, and evidently made a violent effort to compose the muscles of his face. When the Doctor's footsteps were heard in the entry, he braced his whole person and tightly compressed his lips.

Dr. Plumley, it seems, had recently invented an oil for the hair, which he imagined would prove exceedingly efficacious in strengthening the roots, and prevent it from falling off. As time had begun to thin his own locks, he was desirous of personally testing its wonderful qualities. Having previously settled in his mind the improbability of being called to exert his medical skill, he made so copious an application of the unguent as completely to saturate his hair, and then drew on a flannel cap of a pyramidal form to prevent the too speedy escape of the volatile aromatics, which he imagined would strengthen, while the oleaginous part mollified. In his haste, all this escaped his memory, and when, on entering the room, he removed his hat in his usual quick and smart manner, thereby revealing his singular headgear, and made a brisk bow to each of us, the point of his cap nodding in unison, his appearance was so exquisitely ludicrous that my risibility got the better of my gravity, and I was obliged hastily to retreat behind Agnes. In the mean time I stole a glance at the poor boy, who stood convulsed with suppressed laughter, the tears streaming down his cheeks.

"Oh, dear doctor, how glad I am that you've come!" said my aunt; "though I am sorry you've got the headache," glancing at his flannel cap.

"I understand," said he, without noticing her remark, "that you have elongated the ligaments of your ankle joint—that is, sprained your ankle."

"Yes, and it pains me so, that I am afraid that the *information* will get into it afore morning."

"As it never got into your head, ma'am, there is no great danger of its getting into your ankle," he replied, winking at Agnes and me. "Be pleased," continued he, seeing my aunt about to speak, while he at the same time waved his hand in what he considered a very graceful and dignified manner, "be pleased, ma'am, to listen to a few observations which I propose to make. I shall proceed as systematically with your ankle, ma'am, as if I were treating a fever. I shall, however, omit the emetic."

"Well, I am master glad o' that, for I took some *tatramatic* once, and"——

"If you please, ma'am, permit me to proceed without interruption with my observations,—I was speaking of a fever. Now, in my estimation, to speak metaphorically, a fever is the very pink of diseases, and I had rather treat it than any other. However, a sprained ankle will do to brighten a man's science in lieu of a better case. In the first place, ma'am, in accordance with the invariable rules of my practice in all similar cases, I shall apply to the part injured, a plaster, the several ingredients of which are all eminently calorific, and which in more simple language may be called a heater."

"La, doctor, my ankle is as hot as fire coals now, and that is what makes me afraid of the *information*."

"But, ma'am, though it were ten times hotter than fire coals, I assure you, there is a great deal of latent cold, which will be brought to the surface by means of this calorific plaster, which will evaporate in the form of perspiration."

"Well, doctor, I suppose what you say is all right, but you do talk so *figurey*, that I don't understand more than half you say.

Now, as you don't pretend to doctor according to the rules of the reg'lar faculty, as they call 'em, I don't see the need of your being so high flown."

"I tell you, ma'am, there is a certain dignity in the profession, which ought to be supported by a suitable selection of long, sonorous words. But your interruption, ma'am, has broken the concatenation of my ideas. Pray, Miss Agnes, do you recollect what I was speaking of?"

"Perspiration, I believe, sir."

"Ay, ay—that word has restored the concatenation. When a copious perspiration has ensued, a reaction will be necessary. To effect this reaction, I shall apply what I call a refrigeratory plaster—in other words, a cooler. I shall, in the next place, in order to impart a proper pliancy to the cords, envelop the diseased part of the limb in a cloth completely saturated in a limpid salve, which I call a grand mollification salve, but which you may, if you please, term a laxer—the invention of which caused me to grow pale by the midnight lamp. The laxer must be succeeded by a double compound astrictory, which you will better understand by the appellation of bracer, the application of which will complete the cure, and make your ankle as much stronger than it was before the accident as it was then stronger than a baby's."

CAROLINE MAY.

Miss May, one of the sweetest of our female poets, has written also some excellent prose, entitled to consideration, besides a goodly amount of editorial labour. Her largest publication, "The American Female Poets," in 1848, contains, in the biographical and critical notices prefixed to the several extracts, an amount of original matter, sufficient to fill a considerable volume. These notices are written with much ability, and, together with the selections, they show a sound judgment, a highly cultivated literary taste, and great freedom and command of language. Miss May has also edited one or two annuals, and a volume of elegant extracts, called "Treasured Thoughts," which has been quite a favourite. An essay on "Handel," which we have had the pleasure of reading in manuscript, deserves to rank among the very best specimens of biographical criticism. A single introductory paragraph is quoted. The other extract is from the "Female Poets."

Miss May is the daughter of the Rev. Edward Harrison May, who was for many years pastor of one of the Dutch Reformed Churches of New York, and who is at present Secretary of the American Seamen's Friend Society. Her brother, a young artist of fine promise, was one of the chief designers and painters of the panorama of Pilgrim's Progress, which has been so deservedly popular. Miss May is a resident of New York.

HANDEL.

Carlyle truly observes, that "great men, taken up in any way, are profitable company. We cannot look, however imperfectly, upon a great man, without gaining something from him. He is the living light-fountain which it is so good and pleasant to be near." Carlyle was thinking of his heroes,—Odin, Mahommed, Dante, Shakspeare, Cromwell,—when he said this. Whether he would place Handel among his worshipped great men, matters not; but that he would, we have little doubt, for has he not in his own strange eloquence said, "Who is there, that in logical words can express the effect music has on us? A kind of inarticulate unfathomable speech, which leads us to the edge of the Infinite, and lets us for a moment gaze into that?" Surely, they who can silently understand, if they cannot audibly interpret, this unfathomable speech,—who have been led with wonder and admiration to gaze into Infinity, will look on Handel as on a hero, and rank his genius side by side with that of Shakspeare and Milton. But whatever the opinion of others may be, we have always found his company profitable. Whether listening to his expressive airs, or reading over his rich full choruses (lamenting, as we read, that a choir of voices could not spring at once from our grateful and delighted heart), we have always felt that, to approach Handel was to approach a living fountain of heaven-born harmony. And to be near such, is both good and pleasant.

LUCRETIA AND MARGARET DAVIDSON.

It would be wrong, merely for the sake of chronological order, to separate these sweet sisters, who, though not twins by birth, were twins in thought, feeling, loveliness, and purity. We will sketch them together, therefore, while their devoted mother and excellent father shall stand at their head.

Mrs. Davidson was a daughter of Dr. Burnet Miller, a respectable physician in the city of New York, where she was born on the 27th of June, 1787. Her mother was early left a widow, and removed to Dutchess county, where, at the age of sixteen, this daughter was married to Dr. Davidson. The greater part of her married life was spent at Plattsburg (on Lake Champlain), where all her children were born, ten in number—eight of whom passed before her into heaven. She resided in Plattsburg at the time of the battle, August, 1814. The fearful events of that season, and her own escapes and adventures, have been narrated by both Mrs. Davidson and Margaret, in a fictitious garb. She never could speak of them without great excitement; and invariably wept at the sound of martial music. An intimate friend writing of her, says—"Mrs. Davidson's appearance and manner when talking enthusiastically, as she always did on a favourite subject, could never be forgotten. The traces of early beauty were still evident in her large dark eyes and her exquisite complexion; but the great charm of her countenance was in its mingled expression of intelligence and sensibility, varying not unfrequently from deep sadness to a playful vivacity of which you would not at first suppose her capable." She possessed great elasticity of spirit and vigour of mind, which were not at all impaired by the constant pain and suffering she endured. During the last few years of her life, she resided alternately at New York, Ballston, and Saratoga Springs. At the latter place she died, on the 27th of June, 1844. She had long been thought a victim to consumption, but the fearful and agonizing disease which terminated her life was a cancer in the face. A year before her death, a volume, entitled "Selections from the Writings of Mrs. Margaret M. Davidson," was published, with a short preface from her distinguished friend, Miss Sedgwick. Her poems, however, although they display that tenderness of feeling and romantic disposition which characterized her so strongly, are too inferior to her daughter's to be quoted with any advantage.

Dr. Davidson was a man of extensive reading, and possessed a taste for natural science. His moral character, however, more than his intellectual, renders him worthy of notice. "He was one of the most guileless and pure-minded men I ever knew," writes the friend we have before quoted. "He was entirely unpretending in his manners, and always exhibited a degree of affectionate devotedness to his wife, unusual and touching. His piety was simple, confiding, and unobtrusive; and his conduct in every situation unreproachable." He died about a year ago.

Such were the parents of the inspired poet-children, Lucretia and Margaret Davidson.

Lucretia Maria was born on the 27th of September, 1808, and was distinguished almost from her birth by an extraordinary development of the imaginative and sensitive faculties. When she was four years old she went to the Plattsburg Academy, and was taught to read, and form letters in sand, after the Lancasterian method. She began to turn her infant thoughts into measured strains before she had learned to write; and devoting herself with tireless attention to her studies both at home and at school, she soon attained a wonderful amount of knowledge. It was only in her intellectual character that she was thus premature. In her innocence, simplicity, playfulness, and modesty, she was a perfect child. Her conscientiousness and dutifulness were remarkably prominent; as they were also with Margaret. Her health, always very feeble, began to decline in 1823, when she was taken from school, and accompanied her mother on a visit to some relatives in Canada. While there she finished "Amir Khan," her longest poem, and began a prose tale, called "The Recluse of the Saranac." It was about this time that the Hon. Moss Kent, an early friend of her mother, became acquainted with Lucretia, and so deeply interested in her genius, that he resolved, if he could persuade her parents to resign her to his care, to afford her every advantage for improvement that the country could afford. At his suggestion, in November, 1824, she was placed under the care of Mrs. Willard; in whose seminary at Troy she remained during the winter. The following spring, she was transferred to a boarding school at Albany; but while there her health gave way, and she was obliged to return home to Plattsburg. The strength of affection, and the skill of physicians, failed, however, to restore her. The hand of death alone gave her ease; and she gently fell asleep one morning in August, 1825; exactly one month before her seventeenth birthday. President Morse, of the American Society of Arts, first published her biography; and soon after, a delightful memoir from the able pen of Miss Sedgwick spread the name of Lucretia Davidson far and wide.

Margaret Miller was born on the 26th of March, 1823. She was therefore but two years and a half old when Lucretia died; an event which made a deep impression on her. Although so young, she seemed not only to feel her loss, but to understand and appreciate her sister's character and talents; and from the first dawning of intellect gave evidence that she possessed the same. "By the time she was six years old," says her mother, "her language assumed an elevated tone; and her mind seemed filled with poetic imagery, blended with veins of religious thought." The sacred writings were her daily study. Devotional feelings seemed interwoven with her very existence. A longing after heaven, that her spirit might be free from the thraldom of earth, was as natural to her, as a longing for a holiday to be let loose from school is to other children. Yet she enjoyed most fully the quiet pleasures that surrounded her, and her heart was always swelling with love and gratitude. Sometimes, too, the consciousness of genius,—the inward assurance that she was a poet,—would make her think on what *might* be, were she to live; but the restless thoughts of fame were soon lost again, in happier, calmer hopes of an abiding heaven.

Dear child! she little knew that so soon both were to be hers—"an honoured name" on earth, and "a glorious crown" in heaven. Like all true poets, she had a keen relish for the beauties of nature, and fed upon them from her infancy. Her earliest home was upon the banks of the Saranac, commanding a fine view of Lake Champlain, and surrounded by the most romantic and picturesque scenery; but wherever she resided, she found something to admire and love, upon the earth or in the sky.

Margaret was always instructed by her mother, whose poetical tastes and affectionate disposition made her capable of appreciating and sympathizing with the warm impulses and aspiring thoughts of her sweet pupil. The love between this mother and daughter is a poem of itself. No one can read the memoir of Margaret, by Washington Irving, without feeling the heart, if not the eyes, overflow. But the links that bound them to each other on earth were soon severed;—for when she was but fifteen years and eight months old, this gentle girl died at Ballston, Saratoga county, in

November, 1838. We could not wish that she should have stayed longer on earth, an exile from her native heaven; yet, as we listen to the soaring strains of her young genius, and are borne upward by their energy, we cannot help wondering what would have been its thrilling tones and lofty flights, had life unfolded its mysteries year after year to her poet's eye. But we thank God she was spared the sight of them; for though we have lost the songs, she has missed the sorrow!

JULIA C. R. DORR.

Mrs. Julia Caroline Ripley Dorr was born at Charleston, South Carolina, February 13th, 1825. Before she was two years old, her mother died, and her father shortly after removed to New York city, where he was engaged in mercantile business until 1830, about which time he relinquished his business there, and removed to the state of Vermont. She was married, February 22d, 1847, to Seneca M. Dorr, Esq., of Chatham Four Corners, Columbia county, New York, at which place she has continued to reside ever since.

She is the only child of William Y. Ripley, and Zulma Caroline Thomas. Mr. Ripley is a native of Middlebury, Vermont, and has been extensively engaged as commission merchant, both in Charleston and New York. Miss Thomas was the daughter of Jean Jacques Thomas and Susanna De Lacy. They were natives of France, and resided, after their marriage, in the island of St. Domingo, from which place they fled to Charleston, South Carolina, at the time of the insurrection of the slaves in that island.

Mrs. Dorr commenced writing at an early age, and has written much, both in poetry and prose. Her publications, however, did not commence until 1848. Since that time, a large number of her poems has appeared in the different magazines and annuals. Her first attempt at prose, the story of "Isabel Leslie," had the singular success of gaining one of the hundred dollar prizes proposed by Sartain.

This success, brilliant certainly for a first attempt, has given a new direction, as well as a new impetus to her talents, and she already takes a higher position as a prose writer, than that previously won as a poet. The extract which follows is from "Hillside Cottage," a beautiful story published in one of the annuals for the present year.

HILLSIDE COTTAGE.

THERE was no spot in all Elmwood that we children so dearly loved to visit as Hillside Cottage. No matter where our wanderings began—whether we started for the meadow, in pursuit of the rich strawberry—for the thick woods, where the wild flowers bloomed so luxuriantly, and the bright scarlet clusters of the partridge-berry, contrasting beautifully with its dark green leaves, sprang up at our feet—for the brook, to gather the shining pebbles, or to watch the speckled trout, as they darted swiftly through the water—no matter where our wanderings began, it was a strange thing if they did not terminate somewhere about the sweet wild place where Aunt Mary lived.

Now, prythee, gentle reader, do not picture to your "mind's eye" a stately mansion with an unpretending name, when you read of Hillside Cottage. Neither was it a cottage *ornée*, with piazzas, and columns, and Venetian blinds. It was a low-roofed dwelling, and its walls had never been visited by a single touch of the painter's brush: but the wild vines had sprung up around it, until their interlacing tendrils formed a beautiful network nearly all over the little building; and the moss upon the roof had been gathering there for many years, growing thicker and greener after the snows of each succeeding winter had rested upon it. It stood, as the name given it by the villagers indicated, upon the hillside, just in the edge of the woods that nearly covered the rounded summit of the hill; a little rivulet danced along, almost beneath the very windows, and at a short distance below fell over a ledge of rocks, forming a small but beautiful cascade, then, tired of its gambols, it flowed onwards as demurely as if it had never leaped gayly in the sunlight, or frolicked, like a child at play, with every flower that bent to kiss its bright waters. We thought there was no place where the birds sang half so sweetly, or where the air was so laden with fragrance; and sure am I there was no place where we were more cordially welcomed than in Aunt Mary's cottage.

I well remember Aunt Mary's first arrival in Elmwood. For two or three weeks it had been rumoured that the cottage on the hill was to receive a new tenant. Some slight repairs were going on, and some one had seen a wagon, loaded with furniture, unladen at the door. This was enough to excite village curiosity; and when we assembled in the church, the next Sabbath, I fear that more than one eye wandered from the pulpit to the door, to catch the first glimpse of our new neighbour. Just as our old pastor was commencing the morning service, a lady, entirely unattended, came slowly up the aisle, and entered the pew designated by the sexton. Her tall and graceful figure was robed in deepest black, and it was evident that grief, rather than years, had dimmed the brightness of her eye, and driven the rich colouring of youth and health from her cheek. But there was something in the quiet, subdued glance of those large, thoughtful eyes, in the intellect that seemed throned upon her lofty forehead, and in the sweet and tender expression that played around her small and delicately formed mouth, that more than compensated for the absence of youthful bloom and freshness. I did not think of these things then; but, child that I was, after one glance I shrank back in my seat, awe-struck and abashed by the dignity of her bearing. Yet when she rose from her knees, and I caught another glimpse of her pale face, my little heart seemed drawn towards her by some powerful spell; and after service was concluded, as we passed down the aisle side by side, I timidly placed in her hand a wild rose I had gathered on my way to church. She took it with a smile, and in a sweet low voice thanked me for the simple gift. Our homes lay in the same direction, and ere we reached my father's gate I imagined myself well acquainted with Miss Atherton.

From that hour my visits to Hillside Cottage were neither "few" nor "far between." My parents laughed at my enthusiastic praises of my new friend; but they soon became assured that they were well grounded: and it was not long before the answer, "Oh, she has only gone to see Aunt Mary," was the most satisfactory one that could be given to the oft-repeated query, "Where in the world *has* Jessie gone now?"

She lived almost the life of a recluse; seldom mingling with the villagers, save in the services of the sanctuary, or when, like a ministering angel, she hovered around the couch of the dying. Formed to be an ornament to any circle, and to attract admiration and attention wherever she moved, she yet shrank from public notice, and was rarely seen, except by those who sought her society in her own little cottage. To those few it was evident that her love of seclusion was rather the effect of some deep grief, that had in early life cast its shadow over her pathway, than the constitutional tendency of her mind. Hers was a character singularly lovely and symmetrical. With a mind strong, clear, and discriminating, she yet possessed all those finer shades of fancy and feeling, all that confiding tenderness, all those womanly sympathies, and all that delicacy and refinement of thought and manner which, in the opinion of many, can rarely be found *in woman*, combined with a high degree of talent. Love of the beautiful and sublime was with her almost a passion, and conversing with her, when animated by her favourite theme, was like reading a page of rare poetry, or gazing upon a series of paintings, the work of a well-skilled hand.

Years passed on. The little village of Elmwood had increased in size, if not in comeliness: the old church had given place to one of statelier mien and prouder vestments, and the winding lane, with its primroses and violets, had become a busy street, with tall rows of brick bordering it on either side. But still the cottage on the hill remained quiet and peaceful as ever, undisturbed by the changes that were at work beneath it. A silver thread might now and then be traced amid the abundant raven tresses that were parted on Aunt Mary's forehead; and my childish curls had grown darker, and were arranged with more precision than of yore. Yet still the friendship of earlier years remained unbroken, and a week seldom passed without finding me at Hillside Cottage. My visits had of late been more frequent than ever, for the time was drawing near when our intimacy must be interrupted. I was soon to leave my father's roof, for a new home in a far-off clime, and to exchange the love and tenderness that had ever been lavished upon me there for a nearer and more engrossing attachment.

It was the evening before my bridal. I had stolen away unperceived, for I could not resist the temptation of one more quiet chat with Aunt Mary.

"I scarcely expected you to-night, my dear Jessie," said she, as I entered, "but you are none the less welcome. Do you know I am very selfish to-night? When I ought to be rejoicing in your happiness, my heart is heavy, because I feel that I can no longer be to you what I have been, chief friend and confidant. Oh! I shall indeed miss my little Jessie."

"You will always be to me just what you have been, Aunt Mary," I replied, and tears filled my eyes, as I threw myself upon a low seat at her feet. "You must not think that because I am a wife, I shall love my old friends any the less: and you of all others, you who have been to me as a dear, dear elder sister,—you who have instructed and counselled me, and have shared all my thoughts and feelings since I was a little child; oh! do you think any one can come between our hearts? We may not meet as frequently as we have done, but you will ever find me just the same, and I shall tell you all my thoughts, and all my cares and sorrows, and all my joys too, just as I always have done."

"No, no, Jessie, say not so. That may not be. You may love me just as well, but you will love another more. Your heart *cannot* be open to me as it has been, for it will belong to another. Its hopes, its fears, its joys, its sorrows, its cares, its love, will all be so intimately blended with those of another, that they cannot be separated. No wife, provided the relations existing between her husband and herself are what they should be, can be to *any* other friend exactly what she was before her marriage."

"Why, Aunt Mary!—you surely do not mean to say that a wife should never have any confidential friends?"

"The history of woman, dear Jessie, is generally simply a record of the workings of her own heart; in ordinary cases, she has little else to consider. 'The world of affections is her world,' and there finds she her appropriate sphere of action. What I mean to say is,—not that a wife should have no friend save her husband,—but that, if the hearts of the twain are as closely linked together as they should be, if they always beat in perfect unison, and if their thoughts and feelings harmonize as they ought to do, it will be difficult for her to draw aside the veil from her own heart, and lay it open to the gaze of any other being, without, in some degree, betraying the confidence reposed in her by him who should be nearer and dearer than all the world beside. The heart is like a temple, Jessie. It has its outer and its inner court, and it has also its holy of holies. The outer court is full. Common acquaintances,—those that we call friends, merely because they are not enemies,—are gathered there. The inner court but few may enter,—the few who we feel love us, and to whom we are united by the strong bonds of sympathy; but the sanctum sanctorum, the holy of holies, that must never be profaned by alien footsteps, or by the tread of any, save him to whom the wife hath said, 'Whither thou goest I will go, thy people shall be my people, and thy God my God.'"

MARY ELIZABETH MORAGNE.

MARY ELIZABETH MORAGNE was born in the year 1815, at Oakwood, in Abbeville District, South Carolina. At this retired spot she spent the earlier years of a quiet and uniform life, the deep seclusion of which served to foster and increase a naturally contemplative and romantic turn of mind.

Her childhood and youth were characterized by an ardent devotion to books; and, though she received the benefit of some competent instruction, she may be said in this way to have become self-educated—having acquired a knowledge of some of the sciences and of the French language mainly by her own efforts. Had her reading been less varied, or had she come more in contact with the world, perhaps very different would have been her future career; but the balance of her mind was preserved by an inquisitive search after truth, and her habits and modes of thinking were kept free from the conventional rules of the so-called fashionable life.

In 1839, soon after the publication of her first effort in novel-writing, she attached herself to the Presbyterian church at Willington, in which she had been brought up, under the care of the Rev. Dr. Waddel. She experienced at the same time a change of views in regard to the propriety of that branch of literature which she had adopted; and finally, after a few more efforts, some of which were never suffered to come before the world, she yielded to her particular scruples of conscience, and has ever since resolutely denied herself this favourite pursuit.

In 1842, Dr. Waddel having been removed by infirmity, she was married to his successor, the Rev. W. H. Davis, and removed with him the following year to Mount Carmel, a situation in the vicinity of the same church, where she has since resided.

Miss Moragne is descended, on the paternal side, from the French Huguenots who sought religious freedom in this country in 1764. That portion of the colony which did not remain in Charleston found refuge on the banks of Little River, in that district, where they formed a township after the manner of the country which they had left. Her connexion with, and proximity to this settlement, gave much colouring to the feelings and pursuits of Miss Moragne, and in the introduction to an unfinished tale once contemplated on this subject, she gives a brief but beautiful history of this settlement, from the unpublished manuscript of which an extract is made, at the end of the present notice.

Among these settlers was Pierre Moragne, the grandfather of the subject of the present notice, who, having lost his wife on the passage round by Plymouth, returned to Charleston from New Bordeaux, and married Cecille Bayle, a beautiful "compagnon-du-voyage." As his letters and journals testify, he was from his youth addicted to literary pursuits, and though the wants of a primitive settlement could not have been very favourable to such inclinations, he is remembered and spoken of as a character of great eccentricity, on account of having devoted the latter years of his life to the entire companionship of his pen. His writings were not appreciated by his immediate descendants; and of the many manuscripts which he left, prepared for publication, only a few remain. These evince considerable elegance of diction, great orthodoxy of sentiment, and much fervent piety. The youngest of his four sons, who inherited much of his philosophic and eccentric temperament, was the father of Miss Moragne. On the other side, the parentage is respectable, her maternal grandmother claiming descent from the Randolphs of Roanoke.

"The British Partisan," her first publication, appeared, as a prize tale, in the "Augusta Mirror," in 1838. It was well received, adding greatly to the extension of the periodical, besides being reprinted in book form.

In 1841, appeared the "Rencontre," a short tale, embracing revolutionary incidents. Of this story, Mr. Thompson, the editor of the "Augusta Mirror," remarked as follows:—"The 'Rencontre' is of that class of literary productions which we prize above all other orders of fiction. Illustrative as it is of our own history, descriptive of our own peculiar scenery, and abounding in sound reflections and truly elevated sentiment, we hold it worth volumes of the mawkish romance and sickly sentimentality which has of late become a merchantable commodity with a great portion of the literary world."

About this time appeared also some smaller pieces, both in prose and verse. One of the latter was called "Joseph, a Scripture sketch, in three parts," comprising more than a thousand lines of blank verse.

Near the close of the year 1841, the editor of the "Augusta Mirror" says:—"We have received the first part of a tale, entitled "The Walsingham Family, or, A Mother's Ambition," by a favourite lady correspondent. We are much pleased with it, and judging from past efforts of the same pen, do not hesitate to promise our readers a rich treat."

This was a domestic tale of some length, apparently designed to illustrate the folly and vanity of a worldly and ambitious mother; but although the first six chapters were in the hands of the publisher, and the remainder nearly ready for publication, it was, for the reasons before-mentioned, entirely withdrawn, notwithstanding the earnest solicitation of the editors into whose hands it had passed.

THE HUGUENOT TOWN.

Constructed for purposes of personal convenience, by a simple community, thrown without protection among strangers, in a country yet almost savage, without money, and with few facilities for building, this town was not distinguished from the other primitive settlements except by the love of association which it evinced, and the strong marks of national character which it assumed. The common interest of safety, not less than old prejudices in favour of this mode of life, seemed to warrant the propriety of combining that strength, which, when divided, might not be sufficient to protect their lives from the Indian's scalping knife, or their customs and property from the invasions of the roving, unsettled, and shifting tide of white population. It would hardly be supposed that a people who had forsaken their own country for the sake of these hallowed customs, could easily merge them into the rude and reckless mass of provincial habits,—every feeling of national love, every principle of their sacred religion forbade it; and the formidable barrier of a foreign tongue, whilst it shut them in from the new world, guarded the treasure they had so much desired to keep inviolate. An ignorance of the common methods of agriculture practised here, as well as strong prejudices in favour of their former habits of living, prevented them from seizing with avidity on large bodies of land by individual possession; but the site of a town being selected, a lot of four acres was apportioned to every citizen. In a short time a hundred houses had risen, in a regularly compact body, in the square of which stood a building superior in size and construction to the rest, which served the threefold purpose of hotel, café house, and "bureau des affaires" for the little self-incorporated body.

The situation was not chosen with much regard to beauty or health; it was in a rich level valley, a few rods from the river, which they vainly supposed would furnish an easy access by navigation to remote places, particularly to Charleston, where many of their number remained. The simplicity of this idea is much in character with the many impracticable views which a new country suggests, and is not more strange than the belief that a small township, holding its own regulations and manners, could flourish in the midst of a wild country, independent of commercial relations; yet time alone proved the futility of both. The town was soon busy with the industry of its tradesmen; silk and flax were manufactured, whilst the cultivators of the soil were taxed with the supply of corn and wine. The hum of cheerful voices arose during the week, mingled with the interdicted songs of praise; and on the sabbath the quiet worshippers, assembled in their rustic church, listened with fervent response to that faithful pastor, who had been their spiritual leader through perils by sea and land, and who now directed their free, unrestrained devotion to the Lord of the forest.

Did I say there was no beauty there?—none but the clear glancing of the rippling stream, and the high arching of the solemn woods above, wreathing their limbs in fantastic forms against the deep blue sky, and forming a natural temple, in which each tree stood up tall and distinct as a polished shaft in the midst. The solemn Elm, and deep green river Oak were there, sustaining the slender Larch, and twining their branches through the light-green foliage of the Maple, which beautifully contrasted the glittering notched leaves of the fragrant Gum. The woods still wave on in melancholy grandeur, with the added glory of near a hundred years; but they who once lived and worshipped beneath them—where are they? Shades of my ancestors—where? No crumbling wreck, no mossy ruin, points the antiquarian research to the place of their sojourn, or to their last resting-places! The traces of a narrow trench, surrounding a square plat of ground, now covered with the interlacing arms of hawthorn and wild honeysuckle, arrest the attention as we are proceeding along a strongly beaten track in the deep woods, and we are assured that this is the site of the "old French town," which has given its name to the portion of country around. After some years, but not till the country was established in peace, it was gradually abandoned, on account of the unhealthiness of the situation, and because the narrowness of its limits obliged the citizens, as they grew rich enough, to move out upon the hills, to which their familiarity with the usages of the country had now rendered them less opposed; and it must be confessed, also, that in the course of the Indian wars, and the scenes of the revolution which followed, attrition with the more enterprising and crafty had worn off so much of their native simplicity as to admit the passion of avarice, which, by calling them to a more enlarged sphere, greatly tended to the oblivion of their town, though more than half a century had passed away before they had forfeited any of their national characteristics, or admitted any corruption of their native tongue.

MARY ELIZABETH LEE.

Mary Elizabeth Lee was born on the 23d of March, 1813, at Charleston, which her own writings have contributed something to render classic ground. Her parents were William and Elizabeth Lee. Her father practised the profession of the law in early life, and sat for a period as member of the State Legislature. Her uncle, Judge Thomas Lee, was, for many years and in several respects, one of the most distinguished citizens of South Carolina. Several others of her connexions were ardently devoted to intellectual cultivation, and thus Mary's lot fell in a family where every literary tendency was sure to be kindly encouraged and happily developed.

The extreme susceptibility of her feelings prevented her parents from placing her at school until after her tenth year. She was then consigned to the tuition of A. Bolles, Esq., a distinguished teacher of young ladies in Charleston. Here she availed herself with much diligence of her advantages, and laid the foundation of a solid and accurate education.

Genius is seldom destitute of some channel through which to communicate its inspirations to the world. It so happened, that when about twenty years had matured the mind of Mary Lee, and had stored it with a wide range of suggestive acquisitions, a little periodical for youth, edited by Mrs. Caroline Gilman, had been recently started in Charleston, under the title of "The Rose Bud," which soon after changed its name to "The Southern Rose," and aspired to some rank of literary pretension. To the pages of this publication Miss Lee contributed her earliest productions, prompted alike by the dictates of generous friendship and of tremulous ambition.

For a considerable time, the signature attached to her pieces was the modest and general one, "A Friend." As they increased in merit, inquiries as to the authorship began to be multiplied, and at last her personal relationship to them became so well and favourably known, that she discarded the timid disguise, and adopted ever after as a signature in the Rose, the initials "M. E. L." In all other publications, I believe, it was expanded into her full name.

Several brilliant and beautiful effusions now continued to increase her reputation. Among others, "The Lone Star" was admired by every one, so that for a long time the authoress herself, when she was mentioned in her native city, received generally the name of "The Lone Star." "The Blind Negro Communicant" gave her something of a national fame, and was copied into religious and other newspapers in every part of the country.

Miss Lee's incessant aspirations after perfection in every accomplishment, were in nothing more signal than in her studied efforts to acquire a correct style of writing. For many years she published no poem before exhibiting it to the literary friend of her early youth. His criticisms were always unsparing; each questionable phrase, or halting line, or ambiguous rhyme, was faithfully pointed out, and surprising often were the patience, talent, and ingenuity, with which, in availing herself of his suggestions, she surmounted every difficulty and remedied every defect.

To prose composition she devoted as much attention as to poetical. Many prefer her writings in the former department, and an edition of them would no doubt prove alike acceptable to the public and honourable to her name. Her style is characterized by graceful ease and well chosen expressions.

About this time she prepared a volume for the Massachusetts School Library, entitled "Social Evenings, or Historical Tales for Youth." The publishers have declared it to be one of the most popular and useful on their list. The style is at once chaste and vivacious, the topics are selected from a wide range of national histories, indicating a great amount of reading, the poetical illustrations, chiefly by the writer herself, are numerous and beautiful, the pathos is genuine, the characters are marked, and the whole structure of the work exhibits talents of a high order. Eight evenings are supposed to be occupied by a little youthful circle in listening to an experienced friend, who reads to them the successive tales. Each "Evening" is preceded by some animated, descriptive scene, involving throughout the book a separate narrative thread of affecting interest, thus serving to vary the attention, to make the necessary transitions from subject to subject, and to combine the different parts into one harmonious whole.

In the mean time, her literary labours and successes were advancing in every direction. As she was desirous of maintaining for herself an honourable independence, she supplied continual contributions to several widely circulated magazines. The journals and annuals for which she wrote were Graham's Magazine, Godey's Lady's Book, New Orleans Miscellany,

Philadelphia Courier, Token, Gem, Gift, Mr. Whitaker's Journal, Southern Literary Messenger, and Orion Magazine.

This gifted young lady died at Charleston, September 23, 1849. In 1851 a volume of her poems was published, with an interesting biographical memoir by the Rev. Dr. Gilman, from which this brief notice has been compiled. Her prose writings have never been collected.

EXTRACT FROM A LETTER.

You ask how I have been occupied, and why I have written so little for the pages of the "Rose." Well, I must tell you. I have forsworn poetry, and excepting a "Farewell" to it, which I wanted to make very pathetic, have not written a verse for a long while. As I tell you, this "Farewell to Poesy" was a thing I designed should be the last and best, and accordingly one dark wintry afternoon, I wrapped myself closely in cloak and boa, and slipping away from the children, who are always in readiness for a walk, I proceeded to a very lonely and romantic spot at some distance from Homestead, hoping that in this deep solitude I might strike the 'harp of solemn sound,' so that it should give out music worthy of so high a theme. But in vain the wind moaned in most doleful cadence, in vain the waterfall sang its tireless song, in vain the owl in an adjacent wood croaked ever and anon; *I* could not attune *my spirit* aright. My rhymes jingled readily enough, but I could not win "the spark of heaven to tremble down the wire," and after being seated for a full hour over a wet log, which produced, as you may suppose, a most uncommon rheumatism, I was startled by * * * * *, who came to inquire of my poetical success. With great animation I read my several verses, each ending with these emphatic lines,

I vow that I no more will be
A captive to sweet poesy;

which lines, to my surprise, produced at each repetition a most unrestrained burst of laughter, and were at last set to a most ridiculous tune, which was sung during our long walk homeward, with the most provoking perseverance, till I too was compelled to laugh at my own hard-earned composition. Now you see I have let you into one of the trials of the scribbling class, and perhaps it may take away any disposition which you may sometimes feel towards courting the gentle Muse. I wanted so much to produce that Farewell, before I "furled my sail, to try no more the unsteady breath of favour;" and now I am resolved not to give up the ship, but to hold on, so long as the storm of public opinion does not beat too hard. Don't you think I had better continue, confining myself to such innocent, simple subjects, as "Lines to the Owner of an Album," "Stanzas to E. C.," "Sonnet to the Evening Star," and so on? Such lines can do no mischief, you know, to the cause of poetry.

But I promised to tell what I was doing, and you will be alarmed to hear, that I am drinking, with great *gout*, at the fount of philosophy. To be sure, as yet my progress has been but slow, and the draught not very deep, for I have taken in but parts of Doctor Adams's Moral Philosophy, and fear to think when I shall be possessed of the whole. Have you read the work? Cousin S. thinks very well of it. If you want a treat in natural philosophy, I can recommend to your perusal "Euler's Letters," which form two volumes of that excellent publication, "The Family Library." The subjects are handled with a clearness and conciseness which pleased me greatly; and perhaps like me, and I suspect women in general, you do not like those huge tomes, that always seem to smell of poppies, whenever I venture so far as to open them. I like roast pig when stuffed with raisins and currants, for so I remember eating it some years ago at a friend's house; and though a homely simile, I would compare philosophy with this heavy, substantial dish, and can truly say I never enjoy it unless well stocked with some apropos anecdote; some short flight of fancy; some occasionally wild conjecture.

With the word conjecture, Dick's Works are brought to my mind, and I want you to read them also. I am now busy with his "Philosophy of Religion," a work which, on account of its being a little startling, interests me exceedingly. What do you think of him when I tell you that he says, "it is a pleasing fancy to suppose that a city lit with *gas lights* would present the same appearance to the inhabitants of the moon, which that satellite's luminous spots display to us." Don't you think this is but a pleasing fancy, with no reality? Cousin S. has a first-rate microscope; also an excellent telescope, through which we have been for several evenings holding pleasant intercourse with Venus and Jupiter. The queen of beauty smiled on us with a most beaming smile, but Jupiter, vexed at being spied at, would only show three moons, and although we put on one power after another, would not show the fourth, much as we desired it. However, we will take another peep to-night, and hope to find him better disposed. Don't you love to look at the stars? I do. What an idea of happiness a star conveys! With such a boundless space to move in; such an unmeasured distance before it, and such a long existence to live through! A star, with proper study, will furnish abundant food to the mind, and the heart also. Do you make the evening star your heart-study as you promised, and does it bring me any nearer to you every evening? I hope so, or you have proved a forgetful friend.

MARY J. WINDLE.

Although distinguished for her statesmen and warriors, the "diamond State" of Delaware has produced but few sons or daughters who have attained to eminence or achieved fame in the literary arena. This is an anomaly by no means easy of explanation, since there are few portions of our Union better educated, and no one which appreciates more highly literary distinction than the upper portion of Delaware.

The young lady, however, whose name stands at the head of this slight memoir, bids fair to introduce her native State to worthy companionship in the world of letters with some of her hitherto more highly favoured sisters.

Mary Jane Windle was born at Wilmington, February 16th, 1825, of respectable parents, but had the misfortune to lose her father when in early infancy. Being thus deprived of an affectionate husband, the mother of Miss Windle, with an interesting and helpless family, was thrown upon the world, dependent entirely upon her individual exertions for support. The subject of our sketch early evinced a fondness for letters, and in spite of ill health and the difficulties of her position, made herself well acquainted with modern polite literature. Of a romantic, confiding disposition, great sweetness of temper, and refinement of manner, Miss Windle has attached to herself "troops of friends," who have watched with interest her progress in public favour.

Miss Windle's literary career was commenced, as is usually the case in this country, by contributions to the public press. Her communications, both prose and poetical, attracted attention at once, and indicated the author to be one of no common or ordinary mind. As her powers expanded and became more developed, her writings likewise increased in variety and beauty of incident, until at length she drew to herself the favourable notice of a generous publisher, who transferred her talents to the pages of one of those splendid monthly periodicals which so peculiarly distinguish the present literature of the country.

Here, among the very élite of our writers, Miss Windle took a prominent stand, and proved herself capable of competing with the best of them. So marked was the public approbation—so great the desire to possess the interesting stories which monthly flowed from her graceful pen, that she was prevailed upon to reprint in book form a selection of her longer sketches.

The volume appeared during the year 1850, and an edition of several thousand copies was so soon disposed of, that another and larger edition is now in press.

Miss Windle's merits as a writer are great and varied. Purity of taste, much command of language, and fascinating descriptive powers, characterize her productions.

Feminine grace and modesty are likewise leading features; and no one can lay down even the slightest of her sketches without the full conviction that it could only proceed from the pen of a refined and accomplished lady.

Though naturally of feeble constitution, and almost a martyr to ill health, Miss Windle, in attending to literary pursuits, by no means neglects her duties to that society of which she is at once a member and an ornament.

Possessed, in addition to her other accomplishments, of fine conversational ability, she renders her associations not only agreeable, but most useful; and it is to be strongly desired, that she may be spared to her friends long enough to fulfil the promise of a career so brilliantly commenced.

ALICE HEATH'S INTERVIEW WITH CROMWELL.

At a late hour of the night, two persons were winding their way to the palace of Whitehall. One was an individual of the male sex, in whom might have been seen, even through the gloom, a polished and dignified bearing, which, together with his dress—though of the Puritanic order—declared him a gentleman of more than ordinary rank. His companion was a delicate woman, evidently like himself of the most genteel class, but attired in the simplest and plainest walking costume of the times. She leaned on his arm with much appearance of womanly trust, although there was an air of self-confidence in her step, suggesting the idea of one capable of acting alone on occasion of emergency, and a striking yet perfectly feminine dignity presiding over her whole aspect.

"I have counselled your visiting him at this late hour," said the gentleman, "because, as the only hope lies in striking terror into his conscience, the purpose may be best answered in the solitude and silence of a season like this. Conscience is a coward in the daylight, but darkness and night generally give her courage to assert her power."

"True, William," replied Alice Heath (for she it was, and her companion, as the reader is aware by this time, was her husband), "true—but alas! I fear for the success of my visit; the individual of whom we are speaking deceives himself no less than others, and therefore to him she is a coward at all times. Hast thou not read what my poor dead grandfather's old acquaintance has written about a man's 'making such a sinner of his conscience as to believe his own lies?'"

"I have not forgotten the passage, my Alice, and, ever correct in your judgment, you have penetrated rightly into the singular character we are alluding to. I wot it were hard for himself to say how far he has been actuated by pure, and how far by ambitious motives, in the hand he has had in the sentence of the king. Nevertheless, you would believe his conscience to be not altogether dead, had you seen him tremble and grow pale yesterday in the Court, during the reading of the warrant (which, by the way, he had worded and written with his own hands), when Charles Stuart raised his eyes and looked upon him as if to imply that he knew him for the instigator, and no unselfish one, either, of his doom. The emotion he then testified, it was, which led me to hope he may yet be operated upon to prevent the fatal judgment from taking effect. It is true, Charles is a traitor, and I cannot regret that, in being arraigned and tried, an example has been made of him. But having from the first anticipated this result, except for your father, Alice, I would have had no part in the matter, being entirely opposed to the shedding of his blood. All ends which his death can accomplish have already been answered; and I devoutly pray that the effort your gentle heart is now about to make for the saving of his life, may be blessed in procuring that merciful result."

At this moment they paused before the magnificent structure, known as the Palace of Whitehall, and applied for admission.

30

Vacated some time since by the king, it was now occupied by his rival in power, the aspiring Cromwell; and although the hour was so late, the vast pile was still illuminated. Having gained speedy access to the main building, the visiters were admitted by a servant in the gorgeous livery of the fallen monarch. Heath requested to be shown to an ante-room, while Alice solicited to be conducted without previous announcement to the presence of his master. After a moment's hesitation on the part of the servant, which, however, was quickly overcome by her persuasive manner, he conducted her through various spacious halls, and up numerous flights of stairs, till, pausing suddenly before the door of a chamber, he knocked gently. As they waited for an answer, the accents of prayer were distinctly audible. They were desired to enter; the servant threw open the door, simply announcing a lady. Alice entered, and found herself alone with Cromwell.

The apartment was an ante-room attached to the spacious bed-chamber formerly belonging to the king. It was luxuriously furnished with all the appliances of ease and elegance suitable to a royal withdrawing room. Tables and chairs of rose-wood, richly inlaid with ivory and mother-of-pearl, were arranged in order around the room; magnificent vases of porcelain decorated the mantel-piece; statues from the chisel of Michael Angelo stood in the niches; and pictures in gorgeous frames hung upon the walls.

There, near a table, on which burned a single-shaded lamp, standing upright, in the attitude of prayer, from which he had just been interrupted, stood the occupant. For an instant, as she lingered near the door, and looked upon his figure, which bore so strongly the impress of power, and felt that on his word hung the fate of him for whom she had come to plead, she already feared for the success of her mission, and would fain almost have retracted her visit. But remembering the accents of prayer she had heard while waiting without, she considered that her purposed appeal was to the conscience of one whom she had just surprised, as it were, in the presence of his Maker, and took courage to advance.

"May I pray thee to approach and be seated, madam, and unfold the object of this visit?" said Cromwell, in a thick, rapid utterance, the result of his surprise, as he waved his visiter to a chair. "At that distance, and by this light, I can hardly distinguish the features of the lady who so inopportunely and unceremoniously honours me with her presence."

Immediately advancing, she threw back her hood, and offering him her hand, said, "It is Alice Heath, the daughter of your friend, General Lisle."

Cromwell's rugged countenance expressed the utmost surprise, as he awkwardly strove to assume a courtesy foreign to his manner, and exchange his first ungracious greeting for something of a more cordial welcome.

With exceeding tact, Alice hastened to relieve his embarrassment, by falling back into the chair he had offered, and at once declaring the purpose of her visit.

"General Cromwell," she began, in a voice sweetly distinct, "you stand high in the eyes of man, not only as a patriot, but a strict and conscientious servant of the Most High. As such, you have been the main instrument in procuring the doom now hanging in awful expectation over the head of him who once tenanted, in the same splendour that now surrounds yourself, the building in which I find you. Methinks his vacation of these princely premises, and your succession thereunto, renders you scarcely capable of being a disinterested advocate for his death—since, by it, you become successor to all the pomp and power formerly his. Have you asked yourself the question whether no motives of self-aggrandizement have tainted this deed of patriotism, or sullied this act of religion?"

"Your language is unwarrantable and unbecoming, madam," said Cromwell, deadly pale and trembling violently; "it is written—"

"Excuse me," said Alice, interrupting him; "you think it uncourteous and even impertinent that I should intrude upon you with a question such as I but now addressed to you. But, General Cromwell, a human life is at stake, and that the life of no ordinary being, but the descendant of a race of kings. Nay, hear me out, sir, I beg of you. Charles Stuart is about to die an awful and a violent death; your voice has condemned him—your voice can yet save him. If it be your country's weal that you desire, that object has been already sufficiently answered by the example of his trial; or, if it is to further the cause of the Lord of Hosts that you place yourself at the head of Britain in his place, be assured that he who would assert his power by surrounding himself with a pomp like this, is no delegate of One who commissioned Moses to lead his people through the wilderness, a sharer in the common lot, and a houseless wanderer like themselves. Bethink you, therefore, what must be the doom of him, who—for the sake of ambition and pride—in order that he might for the brief space of his life enjoy luxury and power—under the borrowed name, too, of that God who views the act with horror and detestation—stains his hands with parricidal blood. Yes, General Cromwell, for thy own soul's, if not for mercy's sake, I entreat thee, in whom alone lies the power, to cause Charles Stuart's sentence to be remitted."

After a few moments' hesitation, during which Alice looked in his face with the deepest anxiety, and awaited his answer, he said, "Go to, young woman, who presumest to interfere between a judge raised up for the redemption of England, and a traitor king, whom the Lord hath permitted to be condemned to the axe. As my soul liveth, and as He liveth, who will one day make me a ruler in Israel, thou hast more than the vanity of thy sex, in hoping by thy foolish speech to move me to lift up my hand against the decree of the Almighty. Truly—"

"Nay, General Cromwell," said Alice, interrupting him, as soon as she perceived he was about to enter into one of his lengthy and pointless harangues, "nay, you evade the matter both with me and with the conscience whose workings I have for the last few moments beheld in the disorder of your frame. Have its pleadings—for to them I look and not to any eloquence of mine own—been of no avail? Will it please you to do aught for the king?"

"Young lady," replied Cromwell, bursting into tears, which he was occasionally wont to do, "a man like me, who is called to perform great acts in Israel, had need to be immovable to feelings of human charities Think you not it is painful to our mortal sympathies to be called upon to execute the righteous judgments of Heaven, while we are yet in the body! And think you when we must remove some prime tyrant that the instruments of his removal can at all times view their part in his punishment with unshaken nerves? Must they not even at times doubt the inspiration under which they have felt and acted? Must they not occasionally question the origin of that strong impulse which appears the inward answer to prayer for direction under heavenly difficulties, and, in their disturbed apprehensions, confuse even the responses of truth with the strong delusions of Satan? Would that the Lord would harden my heart even as he hardened that of—"

"Stop, sir," said Alice, again interrupting him ere his softened mood should have passed away, "utter not such a sacrilegious wish. Why are the kindly sympathies which you describe implanted in your bosom, unless it be to prevent your ambition from stifling your humanity? The rather encourage them, and save Charles Stuart. Let your mind dwell upon the many traits of nobleness in his character which might be mentioned with enthusiasm, ay, and with sorrow, too, that they should be thus sacrificed."

"The Most High, young woman, will have no fainters in spirit in his service—none who turn back from Mount Gilead for fear of the Amalekites. To be brief—it waxes late; to discuss this topic longer is but to distress us both. Charles Stuart must die—the mouth of the Lord hath spoken it."

As he spoke, he bowed with a determined but respectful reverence, and when he lifted up his head, the expression of his features told Alice that the doom of the king was irrevocably fixed.

"I see there is no hope," said she, with a deep sigh, as Cromwell spoke these words in a tone of decision which left her no further encouragement, and with a brevity so unusual to him. Nor was his hint to close the interview lost upon her. "No hope!" she repeated, drawing back. "I leave you, then, inexorable man of iron, and may you not thus plead in vain for mercy at the bar of God!"

So saying, she turned and rejoined her husband, who remained in waiting for her: they returned together to Lisle's house.

FANNY FERN.

WE would be glad to give the true name of this authoress. But she prefers still to maintain her *incognita*, and a proper deference to the obligations of courtesy (which are as binding in literary as in social life) forbids our doing what would otherwise be an equal gratification to our readers and ourselves. With regard to the personal history of FANNY FERN, we feel a similar restraint. We shall, therefore, only touch, and that lightly, upon such points as, under the circumstances, may be referred to without the slightest violation of propriety.

Not many years since, FANNY FERN was living—no matter where—in affluence. No home need be more lovely, no family more happy, than was hers. Ample wealth, devoted love, cultivated intellect, refined taste, and a fervid religious spirit, combined to make that home whatever could be desired on earth, and excited the respect and admiration of all admitted to the happy circle. But suddenly a bolt fell. Death came. The husband and father was smitten down. The widowed mother and the half-orphan children were left to fight the battle of life alone. Adversity succeeded adversity. Poverty followed in the dismal train, and illness and want had the afflicted family at their mercy. The mother struggled on as best she could; but we all know how hard it is for a lady to find employment which will enable her to obtain a livelihood even for herself, much less for a family of children. The female teacher generally receives only a meagre salary; the copyist pursues an uncertain calling; the seamstress can at best earn but a miserable pittance. And so, at last, after bitter years, the widowed mother, from sheer desperation, took to her pen; and another and a bright star was added to our literary galaxy.

FANNY FERN's first article was written and published in July, 1851. It was immediately copied far and wide. Each succeeding piece met with similar favour; until most of the newspapers of this country, and many British periodicals, were regularly enriched with her articles. But while she was thus furnishing amusement and instruction to the public, she was not receiving an adequate reward. Whenever a woman is obliged to go out into the world and earn her own living, she has to undergo trials and difficulties of which a man can perhaps form no just idea. A delicate, sensitive lady cannot, for instance, call at newspaper offices to solicit employment, or to offer an article for sale, without being exposed to annoyances which to her are painful, but which a man might not observe. A refined lady can ill brook the inquiring gaze and impertinent stare of hangers-on; nor can she bargain for a proper remuneration, nor "call again," and again, and again, if need be, in foul as well as fair weather. And then, it is often assumed that a woman should be paid less for her labour than a man for his, though hers be equally valuable; and it is only after she has acquired a commanding reputation that she can ordinarily obtain a just equivalent for her productions. And thus, for many months, the compensation which FANNY FERN received for her writings was not at all commensurate with their value. For articles which were worth fifty dollars, and which would have commanded that sum, had she known better how to sell them, she often received but a tenth of that amount; and during this time, her income was far from being sufficient to maintain herself and children comfortably. But with unyielding perseverance, and with her trust in God unshaken, she worked on, until she triumphed over all obstacles, earned a name of which she may well be proud, secured an ample fortune, and won the increased respect and love of those who know her best. It is, perhaps, needless to remark, that she now commands the highest prices paid to writers in this country.

In examining FANNY FERN'S writings, even the earliest of them, one is struck with the evidence they exhibit that the writer understands her own powers perfectly; or rather, that she knows positively that she can do certain things better than they have ever been done before. Though this is unquestionably the case, still, she doubtless often achieves more brilliant triumphs than she anticipated; in other words, she is probably often surprised at the excellence of her own articles. She never makes a mistake, because she never attempts what she cannot successfully achieve. This fact has been manifested throughout her literary career. At first, her articles were mere paragraphs, and contained generally only one clearly-pronounced and admirably-developed idea. No words were wasted. The idea, or fact, or principle, sought to be presented, was distinctly stated, and clearly worked up in every attractive and telling phrase possible (as Beethoven worked up the theme of a symphony); and then the article was brought to an immediate but artistic conclusion. With practice, her confidence seemed to increase, and she struck out into bolder paths. Having tried and proved the strength of her pinions, she took loftier flights and continued longer on the wing. Relieved of pecuniary embarrassments, and surrounded once more with the comforts of life, she wrote with greater freedom, and certainly gave to her articles a polish which some of her earlier pieces did not possess. Her latest productions are models of style and composition.

FANNY FERN's first volume, "*Fern Leaves,*" First Series, was published June 4th, 1853; the second, "*Little Ferns for Fanny's Little Friends,*" was issued December 5th, 1853, and the third, the "*Second Series of Fern Leaves,*" May 25th, 1854. The sales of these works, up to June 1st, 1854, were, in this country, as follows:

First Series Fern Leaves, . . .	70,000	
Little Ferns for Fanny's Little Friends,	32,000	
Second Series Fern Leaves, . . .	30,000	
Total sale in this country, . . .		132,000
Sales in Great Britain:		
First Series Fern Leaves, . . .	29,000	
Little Ferns for Fanny's Little Friends,	19,000	
Total sale in Great Britain, . .		48,000
Total sale in Great Britain and America,		180,000

This, we think, is one of the most extraordinary instances of literary success on record; and, we believe, it is thus generally considered. Various attempts have been made to account for such unprecedented popularity. In a recent review of the *Second Series of Fern Leaves,* the Boston *Post,* in referring to this subject, says: "FANNY FERN's success has not been owing to any extraneous or adventitious helps. No influence in high places has been exerted in her favour. Nor has her success been owing to any unusual amount of advertising or newspaper commendation. Her books would have sold largely had there never been a line written in their praise; and her writings will continue to be read and admired, should all the critics open their batteries against them."

The same writer, in an article written with great ability and discrimination, gives the following as his idea of the reasons of her success. He says: "FANNY FERN is not a legitimate author. She is a literary accident—a most happy one, certainly; but still an accident. She never intended to make authorship the business of her life; she underwent no preparatory training for the profession. She was simply an accomplished lady, of indisputable genius, possessing a mind of that subtle, acute, active, observing character, which penetrates and apprehends all things, and an imagination and graphic power that 'give to airy nothing a local habitation and a name.' Superadded to these qualities of mind, she had a warm, sympathetic, loving heart, a brilliant wit, a deeply religious nature, an irrepressible love of fun, and a most thoroughly independent, democratic, and '76-y spirit. Such a being, her mind enriched with varied life-experience, and her spirit deepened and chastened by affliction, suddenly finds it necessary to do something to earn bread for herself and her children. She takes to her pen. Her mind and heart are full—overflowing. She has no lack of strong emotions, of brilliant, glowing thoughts, of exquisite fancies; and she lets them flow and sparkle as they will. She writes from the very depths of her being, not caring *how* she writes. And this she can safely do. It is not necessary for her *to plan.* Her constructiveness is so large and active that her articles, as they grow, take form naturally, like a flower. Then she is always true to nature. She is real. There is nothing artificial about her. Her writings are based on fact—experience; it is a true woman's life, finding expression in literature. They abound in pungent, healthful satire, sparkling wit, and irresistible humour; but they also display varied knowledge of common every-day life and homely affairs, strong common sense, and an unwavering adhesion to the right and true. Her sympathies are broad and generous. She always takes the weak side—by instinct she takes it. She is severe on bullies and stands up for the oppressed. She wakes people up; she sets them in a rage; she electrifies them with her wit; she subdues them with her pathos. She exhibits the courage, independence, and manliness of a man, and, at the same time, she is so gentle and feminine, she exhibits such perfect refinement and delicacy, such maternal benignity, such an appreciation of the sorrows and 'little ways' of children, whom she evidently loves with an intimate and winning tenderness, that she draws all hearts after her. Her English is often splendid, and she sometimes exhibits a felicity of adjectives truly Homeric. Her observation is so keen, her memory so tenacious, and her imagination so vivid, that she seems to have her eye on the things she describes, and makes them flash on the reader's mind like a vision; and her illustrative and illuminating powers are so great, her sentences are rendered as clear as sunlight. Her diction flows murmuringly on, like a crystal stream; her ideas shining out, like pearls, from its transparent depths. These are some of the reasons of FANNY FERN'S success."

The literary critic of the *New York Tribune*—also very high authority—comments as follows upon this extraordinary success: "The secret of FANNY FERN'S literary triumph, we take to be her fidelity to nature, and her sympathy with the most universal tastes. She has none of the airs of professional authorship—does not become starched and prim at the sight of pen and ink—and has hit on one great art of good writing, to make it as much like the free talk of the writer, as the nature of the subject allows. Her style is free from all bookishness—all hard traces of weary study—and flows on as easily and blithely as the song of vernal birds. At the same time, it shows an alert and observing spirit, a flexile fancy, and a love of fun, which she could not curb if she would, and would not if she could. Her taste for satire is indeed tempered by warm womanly sympathies—otherwise it might be mischievous—but now, though she cuts and thrusts with nimble alacrity, she leaves no venom in the wound, which she has made less in malice than in sport. With her perennial mirth, she blends a genuine sense of the pathetic, and often relieves her brilliant flashes of humour with a sudden burst of sympathy. Her tendencies are progressive, and truly democratic. Her heart is with the people, and warms to homely joys and sorrows. A generous scorn of baseness and injustice often gives point to her sarcasm; while her love of truth and beauty leads her to detect all the elements of goodness in common, every-day life. She always takes the side of the weak and oppressed, as by an unerring instinct. Her fancy, it is true, often runs riot,—she overlays her pictures with blood-red tints—and seldom resists the temptation to an audacious extravagance; but she never forgets the heavenly 'quality of mercy,' nor lays aside her tenderness toward the weak, or her sympathy with every form of suffering. Such traits give FANNY FERN her popularity with the great mass of readers. They seek for what is natural, and warm, and impulsive, and humane, and of this they never fail in her writings."

Harper's Magazine—that leviathan of literature—also has the following on the same subject: "The temple of fame is not to be taken by storm, but must be approached by steep and winding ways. A desperate rush is apt to defeat itself. But FANNY FERN doubtless forms an exception to this rule. The favour with which her writings have been received—almost unprecedented both in this country and in England—has a legitimate cause. She dips her pen in her heart, and writes out her own feelings and fancies. She is no imitator, no dealer in second-hand wares. Her inspiration comes from nature, not from books. She dares to be original. She has no fear of critics or of the public before her eyes. She conquers a peace with them by sheer force of audacity. Often verging on the bounds of wholesome conventionalities, she still shows a true and kindly nature—she has always the sympathy with suffering which marks the genuine woman—and her most petulent and frolicsome moods are softened by a perennial vein of tender humaneness. Fanny Fern is a poetess, though she avoids the use of rhyme. With all her sense of the ludicrous, she knows how to seize the poetical aspects of life, and these are rendered in picturesque and melodious phrase, which lacks nothing but rhythm to be true poetry. Her rapid transitions from fun to pathos are very effective. Her pictures of domestic life, in its multiform relations, are so faithful to nature, as to excite alternate smiles and tears. We regard her extraordinary success as a good omen. She has won her way unmistakably to the hearts of the people; and this we interpret as a triumph of natural feeling. It shows that the day for stilted rhetoric, scholastic refinements, and big dictionary words, the parade, pomp, and pageantry of literature, is declining; and that the writer who is brave enough to build on universal human sympathies, is sure of the most grateful reward in unaffected popular appreciation."

FANNY FERN'S past success, and her constant, natural, and healthy improvement up to the present time, warrant us in predicting for her a still more brilliant future. We think she possesses all the necessary elements of a great novelist. Her narrative and descriptive powers are of the highest order; her wit and humor are of the most brilliant and irresistible quality; her religious faith, her sympathy with the poor and weak, her intuitive insight into human character, and her subtle perceptions of the inmost workings of the soul, are certainly greater than those of most of the successful novelists of the age; while her constructiveness, as the *Boston Post* says, "is so large and active that her articles, as they grow, take form naturally, like a flower." Now, should these qualities be brought to bear upon the writing of a continuous story, we think the result would be the production of a book, which in artistic merit would far surpass anything this author has yet written, and exceed in popularity all her other works. What direction FANNY FERN'S genius will hereafter take, is probably only known to herself; but the public await the developments of her future literary career with deep interest and hopeful anticipations.

THE AGED MINISTER VOTED A DISMISSION.

YOUR minister is "superannuated," is he? Well, call a parish meeting, and vote him a dismission; hint that his usefulness is gone; that he is given to repetition; that he puts his hearers to sleep. Turn him adrift, like a blind horse, or a lame house-dog. Never mind that he has grown gray in your thankless service—that he has smiled upon your infants at the baptismal font, given them lovingly away in marriage to their heart's chosen, and wept with you when Death's shadow darkened your door. Never mind that he has laid aside his pen, and listened many a time, and oft, with courteous grace to your tedious, prosy conversations, when his moments were like gold dust; never mind that he has patiently and uncomplainingly accepted at your hands, the smallest pittance that would sustain life, because "the Master" whispered in his ear, "Tarry here till I come." Never mind that the wife of his youth, whom he won from a home of luxury, is broken down with privation and fatigue, and *your* thousand unnecessary demands upon her strength, patience, and time. Never mind that his children, at an early age, were exiled from the parsonage roof, because there was not "bread enough and to spare," in their father's house. Never mind that his library consists only of a Bible, a Concordance, and a Dictionary; and that to the luxury of a religious newspaper, he has been long years a stranger. Never mind that his wardrobe would be spurned by many a mechanic in our cities; never mind that he has "risen early and sat up late," and tilled the ground with weary limbs, for earthly "manna," while his glorious intellect lay in fetters—*for you.* Never mind all *that;* call a parish meeting, and vote him "superannuated." Don't spare him the starting tear of sensibility, or the flush of wounded pride, by delicately offering to settle a colleague, that your aged pastor may rest on his staff in grateful, gray-haired independence. No! *turn the old patriarch out;* give him time to go to the moss-grown churchyard, and say farewell to his unconscious dead, and then give "the right hand of fellowship" to some beardless, pedantic, noisy college boy, who will save your sexton the trouble of pounding the pulpit cushions; and who will tell you and the Almighty, in his prayers, all the political news of the week.

THE FASHIONABLE PREACHER.

Do you call *this* a church? Well, I heard a prima-donna here a few nights ago: and bright eyes sparkled, and waving ringlets kept time to moving fans; and opera glasses and ogling, and fashion and folly reigned for the nonce triumphant. *I* can't forget it; I can't get up any devotion *here*, under these latticed balconies, with their fashionable freight. If it were a good old country church, with a cracked bell and unhewn rafters, a pine pulpit, with the honest sun staring in through the windows, a pitch-pipe in the gallery, and a few hob-nailed rustics scattered round in the uncushioned seats, I should feel all right; but my soul is in fetters here; it won't soar—its wings are earth-clipped. Things are all too fine! Nobody can come in at that door, whose hat and coat and bonnet are not fashionably cut. The poor man (minus a Sunday suit) might lean on his staff, in the porch, a long while, before he'd dare venture in, to pick up *his* crumb of the Bread of Life. But, thank God, the unspoken prayer of penitence may wing its way to the Eternal Throne, though our mocking church spires point only with *aristocratic fingers* to the *rich man's heaven.*

—That hymn was beautifully read; there's poetry in the preacher's soul. Now he takes his seat by the reading-desk; now he crosses the platform, and offers his hymn-book to a female who has just entered. What right has *he* to know there is a woman in the house? 'Tis n't clerical! Let the bonnets find their own hymns.

Well, I take a listening attitude, and try to believe I am in church. I hear a great many original, a great many *startling* things said. I see the gauntlet thrown at the dear old orthodox sentiments which I nursed in with my mother's milk, and which (please God) I'll cling to till I die. I see the polished blade of satire glittering in the air, followed by curious, eager, youthful eyes, which gladly see the searching "Sword of the Spirit" parried Meaning glances, smothered smiles and approving nods follow the witty clerical sally. The orator pauses to mark the effect, and his face says, That stroke *tells!* and so it did, for "the Athenians" are not all dead, who "love to see and hear some new thing." But he has another arrow in his quiver. Now his features soften—his voice is low and thrilling, his imagery beautiful and touching. He speaks of human love; he touches skilfully a chord to which every heart vibrates; and stern manhood is struggling with his tears, ere his smiles are chased away.

Oh, there's intellect there—there's poetry there—there's genius there; but I remember Gethsemane—I forget not Calvary! I know the "rocks were rent," and the "heavens darkened," and "the stone rolled away;" and a cold chill strikes to my heart when I hear "Jesus of Nazareth" lightly mentioned.

Oh, what are intellect, and poetry, and genius, when with Jewish voice they cry, "*Away with* HIM!"

With "Mary," let me "bathe his feet with my tears, and wipe them with the hairs of my head."

And so, I "went away sorrowful," that this human preacher, with such great intellectual possessions, should yet "lack the *one thing needful.*"

FATHER TAYLOR, THE SAILOR'S PREACHER.

YOU have never heard FATHER TAYLOR, the Boston Seaman's preacher? Well—you should go down to his church some Sunday. It is not at the court end of the town. The urchins in the neighbourhood are guiltless of shoes or bonnets. You will see quite a sprinkling of "Police" at the corners. Green Erin, too, is well represented: with a dash of Africa—checked off with "dough faces."

Let us go into the church: there are no stained-glass windows—

no richly draperied pulpit—no luxurious seats to suggest a nap to your sleepy conscience. No odour of patchouli, or *nonpareil*, or *bouquet de violet* will be wafted across your patrician nose. Your satin and broadcloth will fail to procure you the highest seat in the synagogue,—they being properly reserved for the "old salts."

Here they come! one after another, with horny palms and bronzed faces. It stirs my blood, like the sound of a trumpet, to see them. The seas they have crossed! the surging billows they have breasted! the lonely, dismal, weary nights they have kept watch!—the harpies in port who have assailed their generous sympathies! the sullen plash of the sheeted dead, in its vast ocean sepulchre!—what stirring thoughts and emotions do their weather-beaten faces call into play! God bless the sailor!—Here they come; sure of a welcome—conscious that they are no intruders on aristocratic landsmen's soil—sure that each added face will send a thrill of pleasure to the heart of the good old man, who folds them all, as one family, to his patriarchal bosom.

There he is! How reverently he drops on his knee, and utters that silent prayer. Now he is on his feet. With a quick motion he adjusts his spectacles, and says to the tardy tar doubtful of a berth, "Room here, brother!" pointing to a seat *in the pulpit.* Jack don't know about *that!* He can climb the rigging when Boreas whistles his fiercest blast; he can swing into the long boat with a stout heart, when creaking timbers are parting beneath him: but to mount the *pulpit!*—Jack doubts his qualifications, and blushes through his mask of bronze. "Room enough, brother!" again reässures him; and, with a little extra fumbling at his tarpaulin, and hitching at his waistband, he is soon as much at home as though he were on his vessel's deck.

The hymn is read with a *heart-tone.* There is no mistaking either the poet's meaning or the reader's devotion. And now, if you have a "scientific musical ear," (which, thank heaven, I have not,) you may criticise the singing, while I am not ashamed of the tears that steal down my face, as I mark the effect of good *Old Hundred* (minus trills and flourishes) on Neptune's honest, hearty, whole-souled sons.

The text is announced. There follows no arrangement of dickeys, or bracelets, or eye-glasses. You forget your ledger and the fashions, the last prima donna, and that your neighbour is not one of the "upper ten," as you fix your eye on that good old man, and are swept away from worldly moorings by the flowing tide of his simple, earnest eloquence. You marvel that these uttered truths of his, never struck your thoughtless mind before. My pen fails to convey to you the play of expression on that earnest face—those emphatic gestures—the starting tear or the thrilling voice; but they all *tell* on "Jack."

And now an infant is presented for baptism. The pastor takes it on one arm. O, surely he is himself a father, else it would not be poised so gently. Now he holds it up, that all may view its dimpled beauty, and says: "Is there one here who doubts, should this child die to-day, its right among the blessed?" One murmured, spontaneous *No!* bursts from Jack's lips, as the baptismal drops lave its sinless temples. Lovingly the little lamb is folded, with a kiss and a blessing, to the heart of the earthly shepherd, ere the maternal arms receive it.

Jack looks on and weeps! And how can he help weeping? *He* was once as pure as that blessed innocent! His *mother*—the sod now covers her—often invoked heaven's blessing on *her* son; and well he remembers the touch of her gentle hand and the sound of her loving voice, as she murmured the imploring prayer for him: and how has her sailor boy redeemed his youthful promise? He dashes away his scalding tears with his horny palm; but, please God, that Sabbath, that scene, shall be a talisman upon which memory shall ineffaceably inscribe,

"Go, and sin no more."

THE BABY'S COMPLAINT.

Now, I suppose you think, because you never see me do anything but feed and sleep, that I have a very nice time of it. Let me tell you that you are mistaken, and that I am tormented half to death, although I never say anything about it. How should you like every morning to have your nose washed *up*, instead of *down?* How should you like to have a pin put through your dress into your skin, and have to bear it all day till your clothes were taken off at night? How should you like to be held so near the fire that your eyes were half scorched out of your head, while your nurse was reading a novel? How should you like to have a great fly light on your nose, and not know how to take aim at him, with your little, fat, useless fingers? How should you like to be left alone in the room to take a nap, and have a great pussy jump into your cradle, and sit staring at you with her great green eyes, till you were all of a tremble? How should you like to reach out your hand for the pretty bright candle, and find out that it was away across the room, instead of close by? How should you like to tire yourself out crawling way across the carpet, to pick up a pretty button or pin, and have it snatched away as soon as you begin to enjoy it? I tell you it is enough to ruin any baby's temper. How should you like to have your mamma stay at a party till you were as hungry as a little cub, and be left to the mercy of a nurse, who trotted you up and down till every bone in your body ached? How should you like, when your mamma dressed you up all pretty to take the nice, fresh air, to spend the afternoon with your nurse in some smoky kitchen, while she gossipped with one of her cronies? How should you like to submit to have your toes tickled by all the little children who insisted upon "seeing the baby's feet?" How should you like to have a dreadful pain under your apron, and have everybody call you "a little cross thing," when you couldn't speak to tell what was the matter with you? How should you like to crawl to the top stair (just to look about a little), and pitch heels over head from the top to the bottom?

Oh, I can tell you it is no joke to be a baby! Such a thinking as we keep up; and if we try to find out anything, we are sure to get our brains knocked out in the attempt. It is very trying to a sensible baby, who is in a hurry to know everything, and can't wait to grow up.

"MILK FOR BABES."

ONCE in a while I have a way of thinking!—and to-day it struck me that children should have a minister of their own. Yes, a child's minister! For amid the "strong meat" for older disciples, the "milk for babes" spoken of by the infant, loving Saviour, seems to be, strangely enough, forgotten.

Yes, I remember the "Sabbath Schools;" and God bless and prosper them—as far as they go. But—there's your little Charles—he says to you on Saturday night, "Mother, what day is it to-morrow?" "Sunday, my pet." "Oh, I'm so sorry, I'm so *tired* Sundays."

Poor Charley! he goes to church because he is bid—and often when he gets there, has the most uncomfortable seat in the pew—used as a sort of human drudge, to fill up some triangular corner. From one year's end to another, he hears nothing from that pulpit he can understand. It is all Greek and Latin to him, those big words, and rhetorical flourishes, and theological nuts, thrown out for "wisdom-teeth" to crack. So he counts the buttons on his jacket, and the bows on his mother's bonnet, and he wonders how the feathers in that lady's hat before him can be higher than the pulpit or the minister (for he can't see either.) And then he wonders, if the chandelier should fall, if he couldn't have one of those sparkling glass drops—and then he wonders if Betty will give the baby his humming top to play with before he gets home—and whether his mother will have apple dumplings for dinner? And then he explores his Sunday pocket for the absent string and marble, and then his little toes get so fidgety that he can't stand it, and he says out loud, "hi—ho—hum!" and then he gets a very red ear from his father, for disturbing *his* comfortable nap in particular, and the rest of the congregation generally.

Yes, I'd have a church for children, if I could only find a minister who *knew enough* to preach to them! You needn't smile! It needs a very long head to talk to a child. It is much easier to talk to older people whose brains are so *cobwebbed* with "isms" and "ologies," that you can make them lose themselves when they get troublesome; but that straight-forward, childish, far-reaching question! and the next—and the next! That clear, penetrating, searching, yet innocent and trusting eye! How will you meet them? You'll be astonished to find how often you'll be cornered by that little child—how many difficulties he will raise, that will require all your keenest wits to clear away. Oh, you must get off your clerical stilts, and drop your metaphors and musty folios, and call everything by its right name when you talk to children.

Yes, I repeat it. Children should have a minister. Not a gentleman in a stiff neck-cloth and black coat, who says solemnly, in a sepulchral voice (once a year on his parochial visit,)—"S-a-m-u-e-l—my—boy—how—do—you—do?" but a genial, warm-hearted, loving, spiritual father, who is neither wiser, nor greater, nor better than he who took little children in his arms and said, "Of such is the kingdom of heaven."

UNCLE JOLLY.

"Well, I declare! here it is New Year's morning again, and cold as Greenland, too," said Uncle Jolly, as he poked his cotton night-cap out of bed; "frost an inch thick on the windows, water all frozen in the pitcher, and I an old bachelor. Heigho! nobody to give any presents to—no little feet to come patting up to my bed to wish me 'A happy New Year.' Miserable piece of business! Wonder what ever became of that sister of mine who ran off with that poor artist? Wish she'd turn up somewhere with two or three children for me to love and pet. Heigh-ho! It's a miserable piece of business to be an old bachelor."

And Uncle Jolly broke the ice in the basin with his frost-nipped fingers, and buttoned his dressing-gown tightly to his chin; then he went down stairs, swallowed a cup of coffee, an egg, and a slice of toast. Then he buttoned his surtout snugly up over them, and went out the front door into the street.

Such a crowd as there was buying New Year's presents. The toy-shops were filled with grandpas and grandmas, and aunts and uncles, and cousins. As to the shopkeepers, what with telling prices, answering forty questions in a minute, and doing up parcels, they were as crazy as a bachelor tending a crying baby.

Uncle Jolly slipped along over the icy pavements, and finally halted in front of Tim Nonesuch's toy shop. You should have seen *his* show windows! Beautiful English dolls at five dollars a-piece, dressed like Queen Vic's babies, with such plump little shoulders and arms that one longed to pinch 'em; and tea sets, and dinner sets, cunning enough for a fairy to keep house with. Then, there were dancing Jacks, and jumping Jenny's, and "Topsys," and "Uncle Toms" as black as the chimney back, with wool made of a ravelled black stocking. Then, there were little work-boxes with gold thimbles and bodkins, and scissors in crimson velvet cases, and snakes that squirmed so naturally as to make you hop up on the table to get out of the way, and little innocent-looking boxes containing a little spry mouse, that jumped into your face as soon as you raised the lid, and music boxes to place under your pillows when you had drank too strong a cup of green tea, and vinaigrettes that you could hold to your nose to keep you from fainting when you saw a dandy. Oh! I can tell you that Mr. Nonesuch understood keeping a toy shop; there were plenty of carriages always in front of it, plenty of taper fingers pulling over his wares, and plenty of husbands and fathers who returned thanks that New Year's didn't come *every* day!

"Don't stay here, dear Susy, if it makes you cry," said the elder of two little girls; "I thought you said it would make you happy to come out and *look* at the New Year's presents, though we couln't *have* any."

"I did think so," said Susy; "but it makes me think of last New Year's, when you and I lay cuddled together in our little bed, and papa came creeping up in his slippers, thinking we were asleep, and laid our presents on the table, and then kissed us both, and said, 'God bless the little darlings!' Oh! Katy—all the little girls in that shop have their papa's with them. I want MY papa," and little Susy laid her head on Katy's shoulder, and sobbed as if her heart was breaking.

"Don't, dear Susy," said Katy, wiping away her own tears with her little pinafore; "don't cry—mamma will see how red your eyes are,—poor, sick, tired mamma,—don't cry, Susy."

"Oh, Katy, I can't help it. See that tall man with the black whiskers (don't he look like papa?) kissing that little girl. Oh! Katy," and Susy's tears flowed afresh.

Uncle Jolly couldn't stand it any longer;—he rushed into the toy shop, bought an armful of playthings helter-skelter, and ran after the two little girls.

"Here, Susy! here, Katy!" said he, "here are some New Year's presents from Uncle Jolly."

"Who is Uncle Jolly?"

"Well, he's uncle to all the poor little children who have no kind papa.

"Now, where do you live, little pigeons?—got far to go?—toes all out your shoes here in January? Don't like it,—*my* toes ain't out my shoes;—come in here, and let's see if we can find anything to cover them. There, now (fitting them both to a pair), that's something like; it will puzzle Jack Frost to find your toes now. Cotton clothes on? *I* don't wear cotton clothes;—come in here and get some woollen shawls. Which do you like best, red, green, or blue?—plaids or stripes, hey?

"'Mother won't like it?' Don't talk to me;—mothers don't generally scratch people's eyes out for being kind to their little ones. I'll take care of that, little puss. Uncle Jolly's going home with you. 'How do *I* know whether you have got any dinner or not?' *I've* got a dinner—*you* shall have a dinner, too. Pity if I can't have my own way—New Year's day, too.

"*That* your home? p-h-e-w! I don't know about trusting my old bones up those rickety stairs,—old bones are hard to mend; did you know that?"

Little Susy opened the door, and Uncle Jolly walked in,—their mamma turned her head, then with one wild cry of joy threw her arms about his neck, while Susy and Katy stood in the doorway, uncertain whether to laugh or cry.

"Come here, come here," said Uncle Jolly; "I didn't know I was so near the truth this morning when I called myself your *Uncle* Jolly; I didn't know what made my heart leap so when I saw you there in the street. Come here, I say; don't you ever shed another tear;—you see I don't,"—and Jolly tried to smile, as he drew his coat sleeve across his eyes.

Was'nt that a merry New Year's night in Uncle Jolly's little parlour? Wasn't the fire warm and bright? Were not the tea cakes nice? Didn't Uncle Jolly make them eat till he had tightened their apron strings? Were their toes ever out of their shoes again? Did they wear cotton shawls in January? Did cruel landlords ever again make their mamma tremble and cry?

In the midst of all this plenty, did they forget "papa?" No, no! Whenever little Susy met in the street a tall, princely man with large black whiskers, she'd look at Katy and nod her little curly head sorrowfully, as much as to say—"Oh, Katy, I never—never can forget *my own dear papa*."

THANKSGIVING STORY.

"MARY!" said the younger of two little girls, as they nestled under a coarse coverlid, one cold night in December, "tell me about Thanksgiving-day before papa went to heaven. I'm cold and hungry, and I can't go to sleep;—I want something nice to think about."

"Hush!" said the elder child, "don't let dear mamma hear you;' come nearer to me;"—and they laid their cheeks together.

"I fancy papa was rich. We lived in a very nice house. I know there were pretty pictures on the wall; and there were nice velvet chairs, and the carpet was thick and soft, like the green moss-patches in the wood;—and we had pretty gold-fish on the side-table, and Tony, my black nurse, used to feed them. And papa!—you can't remember papa, Letty,—he was tall and grand, like a prince, and when he smiled he made me think of angels. He brought me toys and sweetmeats, and carried me out to the stable, and set me on Romeo's live back, and laughed because I was afraid! And I used to watch to see him come up the street, and then run to the door to jump in his arms;—he was a dear kind papa," said the child, in a faltering voice.

"Don't cry," said the little one; "please tell me some more."

"Well, Thanksgiving-day we were so happy; we sat around such a large table, with so many people,—aunts and uncles and cousins, —I can't think why they never come to see us now, Letty,—and Betty made such sweet pies, and we had a big—big turkey; and papa would have me sit next to him, and gave me the wish-bone, and all the plums out of his pudding; and after dinner he would take me in his lap, and tell me 'Red Riding Hood,' and call me 'pet,' and 'bird,' and 'fairy.' O, Letty, I can't tell any more; I believe I'm going to cry."

"I'm very cold," said Letty. "Does papa know, up in heaven, that we are poor and hungry now?"

"Yes—no—I can't tell," answered Mary, wiping away her tears;

unable to reconcile her ideas of heaven with such a thought. "Hush! —mamma will hear!"

Mamma had "heard." The coarse garment, upon which she had toiled since sunrise, dropped from her hands, and tears were forcing themselves, thick and fast, through her closed eyelids. The simple recital found but too sad an echo in that widowed heart.

ALICE CAREY.

Miss Alice Carey is a native of Mt. Healthy, Hamilton county, Ohio, and is descended from a New England family, her father having emigrated from Vermont at the period of the first settlement of the country near Cincinnati. Her first appearance in print was as the writer of occasional poems in the neighbouring journals; and one of her earliest effusions was the song commencing

"Among the beautiful pictures
Which hang in Memory's hall,"

which Edgar A. Poe pronounced the finest from the genius of any American woman. Miss Carey subsequently wrote a series of prose sketches and essays in the National Era, under the signature of "Patty Lee," and having previously (in 1848), in connexion with her sister, Miss Phœbe Carey, published in Philadelphia a volume of "Poems," she brought out her first prose work in New York, in 1851, under the title of "Clovernook, or Recollections of our Neighbourhood in the West." The success of this was immediate and very great, both in this country, and in England, where several editions appeared in rapid succession, and in Germany and France, where it was published in translations. J. G. Whittier, in a review of the book said, "These sketches bear the true stamp of genius—simple, natural, truthful—and evince a keen sense of the humour and pathos of the comedy and tragedy of life in the country. No one who has ever read it can forget the sad and beautiful story of Mary Wildermings; its weird fancy, tenderness, and beauty; its touching description of the emotions of a sick and suffering human spirit, and its exquisite rural pictures. The moral tone of Alice Carey's writings is unobjectionable always." Similar opinions were expressed by Fitz Greene Halleck, and many other distinguished critics; and the Westminster Review declared the author superior to any other female writer in America.

Miss Carey's next work, published a few months afterward, was "Hagar, a Story of To-Day." It was written to counteract what the author supposed to be the sceptical tendencies of several recent novels, for the most part by women, and its ethical purpose prevented the freedom in the dramatic management of the story which might have made it more popular and effective as a work of art; yet it unquestionably possessed great merits in the delineation of character, the exhibition of manners, and moral analysis. In 1852 she published "Lyra, and other Poems;" in 1853 a second series of "Clovernook," which has been even more popular than the first; and in 1854, at Boston, a new collection of "Poems," including one of several thousand lines, entitled "The Tlascalan Maiden, a Romance of the Golden Age of Tezcuco." She has also published a new novel in the National Era, under the title of "Hollywood."

In "Clovernook," her principal and best known work, Miss Carey attempted to describe the frequent American phenomenon of a village suddenly growing up in the wilderness, and the advance of its humble society until the scene becomes to some degree one of intelligence, refinement, and fashion. Her characters are remarkable, considering their variety, for fidelity to nature, and her sentiments are marked by womanly delicacy, humanity, and reverence for religion, while over all is the charm of a powerful imagination, with frequent manifestations of the most quiet and delicious humour.

MRS. HILL AND MRS. TROOST.

It was just two o'clock of one of the warmest of the July afternoons. Mrs. Hill had her dinner all over, had put on her clean cap and apron, and was sitting on the north porch, making an unbleached cotton shirt for Mr. Peter Hill, who always wore unbleached shirts at harvest time. Mrs. Hill was a thrifty housewife. She had been pursuing this economical avocation for some little time, interrupting herself only at times to "*shu!*" away the flocks of half-grown chickens that came noisily about the door for the crumbs from the table-cloth, when the sudden shutting down of a great blue cotton umbrella caused her to drop her work, and exclaim—

"Well, now, Mrs. Troost! who would have thought you ever *would* come to see me!"

"Why, I have thought a great many times I would come," said the visiter, stamping her little feet—for she was a little woman—briskly on the blue flag stones, and then dusting them nicely with her white cambric handkerchief, before venturing on the snowy floor of Mrs. Hill. And, shaking hands, she added, "It *has* been a good while, for I remember when I was here last I had my Jane with me—quite a baby then, if you mind—and she is three years old now."

"Is it possible?" said Mrs. Hill, untying the bonnet strings of her neighbour, who sighed, as she continued, "Yes, she was three along in February;" and she sighed again, more heavily than before, though there was no earthly reason that I know of why she should sigh, unless perhaps the flight of time, thus brought to mind, suggested the transitory nature of human things.

Mrs. Hill laid the bonnet of Mrs. Troost on her "spare bed," and covered it with a little, pale-blue crape shawl, kept especially for like occasions; and, taking from the drawer of the bureau a large fan of turkey feathers, she presented it to her guest, saying, "A very warm day, isn't it?"

"Oh, dreadful, dreadful; it seems as hot as a bake oven; and I suffer with the heat all summer, more or less. But it's a world of suffering;" and Mrs. Troost half closed her eyes, as if to shut out the terrible reality.

"Hay-making requires sunshiny weather, you know; so we must put up with it," said Mrs. Hill; "besides, I can mostly find some cool place about the house; I keep my sewing here on the porch, and, as I bake my bread or cook my dinner, manage to catch it up sometimes, and so keep from getting overheated; and then, too, I get a good many stitches taken in the course of the day."

"This *is* a nice, cool place—completely curtained with vines," said Mrs. Troost; and she sighed again; "they must have cost you a great deal of pains."

"Oh, no—no trouble at all; morning-glories grow themselves; they only require to be planted. I will save seed for you this fall, and next summer you can have your porch as shady as mine."

"And if I do, it would not signify," said Mrs. Troost; "I never get time to sit down from one week's end to another; besides, I never had any luck with vines; some folks haven't, you know."

Mrs. Hill was a woman of a short, plethoric habit; one that might be supposed to move about with little agility, and to find excessive warmth rather inconvenient; but she was of a happy, cheerful temperament; and when it rained she tucked up her skirts, put on thick shoes, and waddled about the same as ever, saying to herself, "This will make the grass grow," or "it will bring on the radishes," or something else equally consolatory.

Mrs. Troost, on the contrary, was a little thin woman, who looked as though she might move about nimbly at any season; but, as she herself often said, she was a poor unfortunate creature, and pitied herself a great deal, as she was in justice bound to do, for nobody else cared, she said, how much she had to bear.

They were near neighbours—these good women—but their social interchanges of tea-drinking were not of very frequent occurrence, for sometimes Mrs. Troost had nothing to wear like other folks;

sometimes it was too hot, and sometimes it was too cold; and then again, nobody wanted to see her, and she was sure she didn't want to go where she wasn't wanted. Moreover, she had such a great barn of a house as no other woman ever had to take care of. But in all the neighbourhood it was called the big house, so Mrs. Troost was in some measure compensated for the pains it cost her. It was, however, as she said, a barn of a place, with half the rooms unfurnished, partly because they had no use for them, and partly because they were unable to get furniture. So it stood right in the sun, with no shutters, and no trees about it, and Mrs. Troost said she didn't suppose it ever would have. She was always opposed to building it, but she never had her way about anything. Nevertheless, some people said Mr. Troost had taken the dimensions of his house with his wife's apron strings—but that may have been slander.

While Mrs. Troost sat sighing over things in general, Mrs. Hill sewed on the last button, and shaking the loose threads from the completed garment, held it up a moment to take a satisfactory view, as it were, and folded it away.

"Well, did you ever!" said Mrs. Troost; "you have made half a shirt, and I have got nothing at all done. My hands sweat so I can't use the needle, and it's no use to try."

"Lay down your work for a little while, and we will walk in the garden."

So Mrs. Hill threw a towel over her head, and taking a little tin basin in her hand, the two went to the garden—Mrs. Troost under the shelter of the blue umbrella, which she said was so heavy that it was worse than nothing. Beans, radishes, raspberries, and currants, besides many other things, were there in profusion, and Mrs. Troost said everything flourished for Mrs. Hill, while her garden was all choked up with weeds. "And you have bees, too—don't they sting the children, and give you a great deal of trouble? Along in May, I guess it was, Troost (Mrs. Troost always called her husband so) bought a hive, or rather he traded a calf for one—

a nice, likely calf, too, it was—and they never did us one bit of good"—and the unhappy woman sighed.

"They *do* say," said Mrs. Hill, sympathizingly, "that bees won't work for some folks; in case their king dies they are very likely to quarrel, and not do well; but we have never had any ill luck with ours; and we last year sold forty dollars worth of honey, besides having all we wanted for our own use. Did yours die off, or what, Mrs. Troost?"

"Why," said the ill-natured visiter, "my oldest boy got stung one day, and, being angry, upset the hive, and I never found it out for two or three days; and, sending Troost to put it up in its place, there was not a bee to be found high or low."

"You don't tell! the obstinate little creatures! but they must be treated kindly, and I have heard of their going off for less things."

The basin was by this time filled with currants, and they returned to the house. Mrs. Hill, seating herself on the sill of the kitchen door, began to prepare her fruit for tea, while Mrs. Troost drew her chair near, saying, "Did you ever hear about William M'Micken's bees?"

Mrs. Hill had never heard, and expressing an anxiety to do so, was told the following story:

"His wife, you know, was she that was Sally May, and it's an old saying—

'To change the name and not the letter,
You marry for worse, and not for better.'

"Sally was a dressy, extravagant girl; she had her bonnet 'done up' twice a year always, and there was no end to her frocks and ribbons and fine things. Her mother indulged her in everything; she used to say Sally deserved all she got; that she was worth her weight in gold. She used to go everywhere, Sally did. There was no big meeting that she was not at, and no quilting that she didn't help to get up. All the girls went to her for the fashions, for she was a good deal in town at her Aunt Hanner's, and always brought out the new patterns. She used to have her sleeves a little bigger than anybody else, you remember, and then she wore great stiffners in them—la, me! there was no end to her extravagance.

"She had a changeable silk, yellow and blue, made with a surplus front; and when she wore that, the ground wasn't good enough for her to walk on, so some folks used to say; but I never thought Sally was a bit proud or lifted up; and if anybody was sick, there was no better-hearted creature than she; and then, she was always good-natured as the day was long, and would sing all the time at her work. I remember, along before she was married, she used to sing one song a great deal, beginning

'I've got a sweetheart with bright black eyes;'

and they said she meant William M'Micken by that, and that she might not get him after all—for a good many thought they would never make a match, their dispositions were so contrary. William was of a dreadful quiet turn, and a great home body; and as for being rich, he had nothing to brag of, though he was high larnt, and followed the river as clark sometimes."

Mrs. Hill had by this time prepared her currants, and Mrs. Troost paused from her story while she filled the kettle, and attached the towel to the end of the well-sweep, where it waved as a signal for Peter to come to supper.

"Now, just move your chair a leetle nearer the kitchen door, if you please," said Mrs. Hill, "and I can make up my biscuit, and hear you, too."

Meantime, coming to the door with some bread-crumbs in her hand, she began scattering them on the ground, and calling, "Biddy, biddy, biddy—chicky, chicky, chicky"—hearing which, a whole flock of poultry was about her in a minute; and stooping down, she secured one of the fattest, which, an hour afterwards, was broiled for supper.

"Dear me, how easily you do get along!" said Mrs. Troost.

And it was some time before she could compose herself sufficiently to take up the thread of her story. At length, however, she began with—

"Well, as I was saying, nobody thought William M'Micken would marry Sally May. Poor man, they say he is not like himself any more. He may get a dozen wives, but he'll never get another Sally. A good wife she made him, for all she was such a wild girl.

"The old man May was opposed to the marriage, and threatened to turn Sally, his own daughter, out of house and home; but she was headstrong, and would marry whom she pleased; and so she did, though she never got a stitch of new clothes, nor one thing to keep house with. No; not one single thing did her father give her, when she went away, but a hive of bees. He was right down ugly, and called her Mrs. M'Micken whenever he spoke to her after she was married; but Sally didn't seem to mind it, and took just as good care of the bees as though they were worth a thousand dollars. Every day in winter she used to feed them—maple-sugar, if she had it; and if not, a little Muscovade in a saucer or some old broken dish.

"But it happened one day that a bee stung her on the hand—the right one, I think it was,—and Sally said right away that it was a bad sign; and that very night she dreamed that she went out to feed her bees, and a piece of black crape was tied on the hive. She felt that it was a token of death, and told her husband so, and she told me and Mrs. Hanks. No, I won't be sure she told Mrs. Hanks, but Mrs. Hanks got to hear it some way."

"Well," said Mrs. Hill, wiping the tears away with her apron, "I really didn't know, till now, that poor Mrs. M'Micken was dead."

"Oh, she is not dead," answered Mrs. Troost, "but as well as she ever was, only she feels that she is not long for this world." The painful interest of her story, however, had kept her from work, so the afternoon passed without her having accomplished much—she never could work when she went visiting.

Meantime Mrs. Hill had prepared a delightful supper, without seeming to give herself the least trouble. Peter came precisely at the right moment, and, as he drew a pail of water, removed the towel from the well-sweep, easily and naturally, thus saving his wife the trouble.

"Troost would never have thought of it," said his wife; and she finished with an "Ah, well!" as though her tribulations would be over before long.

As she partook of the delicious honey, she was reminded of her own upset hive, and the crisp-red radishes brought thoughts of the weedy garden at home; so that, on the whole, her visit, she said, made her perfectly wretched, and she should have no heart for a week; nor did the little basket of extra nice fruit, which Mrs. Hill presented her as she was about to take leave, heighten her spirits in the least. Her great heavy umbrella, she said, was burden enough for her.

"But Peter will take you in the carriage," insisted Mrs. Hill.

"No," said Mrs. Troost, as though charity were offered her; "it will be more trouble to get in and out than to walk"—and so she trudged home, saying, "Some folks are born to be lucky."

FRANCES MIRIAM BERRY.

(THE "WIDOW BEDOTT.")

FRANCES MIRIAM BERRY was born Nov. 1, 1812, at Whitesboro, a village of central New York lying near the banks of the Mohawk, and there spent the greater portion of her life. In her veins flowed the mingled blood of the English and Scotch races. Perhaps from the first, which was on the maternal side, she inherited the wonderful humorous talent—from the other, the rectitude of purpose and strong veneration—that marked her character.

One of the first indications of her remarkable intellect was a strong memory, which was displayed, to the delighted admiration of her family circle, in remembering poetry. When only two years old—yet ignorant of A B C—she is said to have repeated accurately Wordsworth's exquisite ballad of "We are Seven;" and, when a little older, that equally touching poem of Montgomery's, "The Vigil of St. Mark."

A few years later, she began making rhymes herself; seizing upon some trifling domestic scenes, whether serious or amusing, as subjects; dictating, before learning to use a pen, to some older member of the family. Some of these childish productions are still preserved. She also showed a decided taste for drawing, was intensely interested in fine pictures, and seemed to have an intuitive perception of what was correct in the art. Her sense of the ridiculous was so strong as to prompt her to indulge in caricature, a propensity that afterwards exposed her to the censures of unappreciating and dull-minded people. Her first attempt to draw, when she was about five years old, was inspired by the strikingly ugly visage of a neighbour, a man of excessively polished exterior, a gentleman of the old school, whose efforts to win the confidence of the interesting child only served to terrify and repel her.

Seeing him one day absorbed in a newspaper, she mounted a chair, at a high writing-desk, and "drew his likeness." In the midst of her artistic labours he laid aside his paper, and observing her occupation walked to the desk, inquiring, with a profound bow, "What are you doing, my little dear? Writing a letter to your sweetheart?" Such a question completed her disgust and alarm; she caught up her unfinished production, and ran to another apartment.

In a letter written towards the close of her life, she thus alludes to this feature of her childhood.

"You possess the happy faculty of drawing all hearts at once to you; but I, unfortunately, do not. And I will tell you what I believe to be the secret of it: I received, at my birth, the undesirable gift of a remarkably strong sense of the ridiculous. I can scarcely remember the time when the neighbours were not afraid that I would 'make fun of them.' For indulging in this propensity, I was scolded at home, and wept over and prayed with, by certain well-meaning old maids in the neighbourhood; but all to no purpose. The only reward of their labours was frequently their likenesses drawn in charcoal and pinned to the corners of their shawls, with, perhaps, a descriptive verse below. Of course I had not many friends, even among my own playmates. And yet, at the bottom of all this deviltry, there was a warm, affectionate heart. If any were really kind to me, how I loved them!"

Her school education was more varied than beneficial. Her first teacher was a sour-faced woman, who knocked the alphabet with her thimble into the heads of a little group of unruly children, at so much "a quarter," with small love, and no just appreciation of the dawning minds under her care.

Her experience under the sway of this woman was thoroughly delightful compared with the ordeal which she next underwent. Being transferred, after a few months, to the village academy, placed under a man's tuition and the care of older playmates, it was thought that she would learn faster and be more safe than among children of her own age.

Woe worth the day to the little creature! The pedagogue was a stern, cruel, vindictive man, who literally whipped knowledge into his pupils' noddles, and in his hands the rod and ferule were never idle. In this school, before she had completed her sixth year, Miriam passed some miserable months. The little ones, indeed, were whipped with less severity than fell to the lot of young misses and half-grown boys, who felt the full measure of his ungovernable rage. But light as may have been her punishments, they were doubtless too heavy for her misdeeds, which were nothing worse than indulging a childish desire for fun or play, while made to sit three hours together on a backless bench.

It was a happy day for Miriam when the term closed, and the cruel A—— was discharged. He has gone to his account. May he receive more mercy from Heaven than he meted out to Christ's little ones here!

A second time little Miriam was introduced within the walls of the Academy, but under a new and quite different dynasty. The principal was the kindest-hearted and most indulgent of pedagogues, well skilled in mathematics and learned in all classic lore; greatly successful, moreover, in "fitting young men for college," as the phrase goes. But the younger fry were left to take care of themselves, or, at most, received a kind of desultory instruction from some older pupil, while their misbehaviour was kindly overlooked by the classical master.

Her slate did not always present the sums in addition duly set, which it ought to have done. The stiff, tallowed locks and long-nosed visages of the serious, matter-of-fact young men, intently poring over their Virgils and Latin grammars, on the opposite side of the room, were oftener transferred by her pencil to its surface. She could no more keep from drawing a striking or peculiar set of features than she could stop her heart's beating; but she had no thought of giving pain, and was unwilling to have her pictures seen.

Her copybook presented an appearance very unlike those of her schoolmates. She followed no formally set copy, but wrote little poems which had struck her fancy in reading, interspersed with an occasional verse of her own, the margins being adorned with heads and various devices, something after the ancient fashion, modernly revived, of embellishing books.

Two or three years' attendance at school under the nominal instruction of this indulgent master and his successors, with an occasional winter passed in studying at home, where she was taught by an older relative, brought Miriam to her teens.

An association, partly social and partly literary in its design, was formed in Miriam's native village, the members of which met semi-monthly for reading, music, and conversation. Their gatherings took place at the residences of the members, were agreeable, informal, and not without benefit particularly in the way of encouraging literary tastes and promoting refinement of manners. The reading matter, in accordance with the rules of the society, being mostly furnished by the pens of the members themselves, this unambitious association was the means of eliciting much latent ability.

Being induced to join them, Miriam wrote occasionally a little poem or a light essay, the latter always in a mirthful or slightly satirical strain, and well received by the listeners. Afterwards, for the entertainment of several successive gatherings, she produced a humorous tale in chapters. Taking for her text the absurdities of the "Children of the Abbey," and kindred works, she led her heroine, a vain, ignorant girl, with a head full of the notions which such fictions would create in a weak mind, through many ludicrous scenes and adventures, and having chosen her own vicinity as the theatre and country life as the illustrating link of the tale, it was made vastly amusing and popular in the opinion of her friends. A chapter of "Widow Spriggins' Recollections" was ever sure of a welcome, and an evening without a production from Miriam's easy and versatile pen was pronounced dull.

In the summer of 1846, a warm personal friend of Miriam's, himself a contributor to "Neal's Gazette," prevailed upon her to forward a few of her little poems to Mr. Neal. The poems were speedily published with laudatory notices, and such a reply given as to determine Miriam on beginning a series of prose articles for the Gazette, under the title of "Widow Bedott's Table-Talk." She chose the style in which those pieces were written as being one in which she had already, in a small sphere, been successful in pleasing. It is needless to dwell upon the applause with which the first chapters were received by the public. They were universally regarded as the best Yankee papers then written, and indeed they have not yet been excelled.

Yet nothing was sufficient to prevent her constitutional timidity and self-distrust from suggesting the thought of failure, and a wish to lay aside the pen. So she wrote to Mr. Neal, expressing her doubts as to proceeding.

Mr. Neal's well-timed approbation, joined to other considerations, induced her to proceed with the "Table-Talk," of which in the following spring she began a new series.

On the 6th of January, 1847, she was married to the Rev. B. W. Whitcher, of the Episcopal Church, and removed to the western part of the State. Yet amid the cares of housekeeping and the difficult duties of her station as a clergyman's wife, she found time, while never neglecting any occupation that devolved upon her, to write for the press.

Miriam's rare and mirth-moving articles having attracted the notice of Mr. Godey, she complied with his request to enrich the pages of the "Lady's Book" with productions of a like nature, and under the name of "Aunt Maguire," began a series for that Magazine.

Besides those pieces under the caption of "Aunt Maguire," she furnished a few in a different style for the "Lady's Book," entitled "Letters from Timberville," which were exceedingly popular.

"Mrs. Mudlaw's Recipe for Potato Pudding," which appeared in the "Philadelphia Saturday Gazette," about the close of the year 1850, was the last of her productions published in her lifetime. It is a most amusing sketch, showing striking marks of the vigour of her pen in the delineation of character in various spheres.

In the autumn of 1850, the symptoms of the fatal malady, which finally carried her off, began to develop themselves. She sank gradually and serenely to her close, which took place on the 4th of January, 1852.

Her writings have never been published in a collected form. They lie scattered chiefly through the pages of Godey, and of Neal's Gazette. A judicious selection from them, and from her unpublished manuscripts, of which it is understood her friends have quite a large number, would be a valuable addition to our literature, and would be likely to hold a permanent place there.

MRS. MUDLAW'S RECIPE FOR POTATO PUDDING.

Mrs. Mudlaw was a short, fat woman, with a broad, red face—such a person as a stranger would call the very personification of good nature; though I have never found fat people to be any more amiable than lean ones. Certainly, Mrs. Mudlaw was not a very sweet-tempered woman. On this occasion, she felt rather more cross than usual, forced, as she was, to give one of her receipts to a nobody. She, however, knew the necessity of assuming a pleasant demeanour at that time, and accordingly entered the nursery with an encouraging grin on her blazing countenance. Mrs. Philpot, fearing lest her cook's familiarity might belittle her mistress in the eyes of Mrs. Darling, and asking to be excused for a short time, went into the library, a nondescript apartment, dignified by that name, which communicated with the nursery. The moment she left her seat, a large rocking-chair, Mudlaw dumped herself down in it, exclaiming—

"Miss Philpot says you want to get my receipt for potater puddin'?"

"Yes," replied Mrs. Darling. "I would be obliged to you for the directions." And she took out of her pocket a pencil and paper to write it down.

"Well, 'tis an excellent puddin'," said Mudlaw, complacently; "for my part, I like it about as well as any puddin' I make, and that's sayin' a good deal, I can tell you, for I understand makin' a great variety. 'Tain't so awful rich as some, to be sure. Now, there's the Cardinelle puddin', and the Washington puddin', and the Lay Fayette puddin', and the—"

"Yes. Mr. Darling liked it very much—how do you make it?"

"Wal, I peel my potaters and bile 'em in fair water. I always let the water bile before I put 'em in. Some folks let their potaters lie and sog in the water ever so long, before it biles; but I think it spiles 'em. I always make it a pint to have the water bile—"

"How many potatoes?"

"Wal, I always take about as many potaters as I think I shall want. I'm generally governed by the size of the puddin' I want to make. If it's a large puddin', why I take quite a number, but if it's a small one, why, then I don't take as many. As quick as they're done, I take 'em up and mash 'em as fine as I can get 'em. I'm always very partic'lar about *that*—some folks ain't; they'll let their potaters be full o' lumps. *I* never do; if there's anything I hate, it's lumps in potaters. I *won't* have 'em. Whether I'm mashin' potaters for puddin's or for vegetable use, I mash it till there ain't the size of a lump in it. If I can't git it fine without sifting, why, I *sift* it. Once in a while, when I'm otherways engaged, I set the girl to mashin' on't. Wal, she'll give it three or four jams, and come along, 'Miss Mudlaw, is the potater fine enough?' Jubiter Rammin! that's the time I come as near gittin' mad as I ever allow myself to come, for I make it a pint never to have lumps—"

"Yes, I know it is very important. What next?"

"Wal, then I put in my butter; in winter time I melt it a little, not enough to make it ily, but jest so's to soften it."

"How much butter does it require?"

"Wal, I always take butter accordin' to the size of the puddin'; a large puddin' needs a good sized lump o' butter, but not *too* much. And I'm always partic'lar to have my butter fresh and sweet. Some folks think it's no matter what sort o' butter they use for cookin', but I don't. Of all things, I do despise strong, frowy, rancid butter. For pity's sake, have your butter fresh."

"How much butter did you say?"

"Wal, that depends, as I said before, on what sized puddin' you want to make. And another thing that regulates the quantity of butter I use is the 'mount o' cream I take. I always put in more or less cream; when I have abundance o' cream, I put in considerable, and when it's scarce, why, I use more butter than I otherways should. But you must be partic'lar not to get in too much cream. There's a great deal in havin' jest the right quantity; and so 'tis with all the ingrejiences. There ain't a better puddin' in the world than a potater puddin', when it's made *right*, but 'tain't everybody that makes 'em right. I remember when I lived in

Tuckertown, I was a visitin' to Squire Humprey's one time—I went in the first company in Tuckertown—dear me! this is a changeable world. Wal, they had what they called a potater puddin' for dinner. Good laud! Of all the puddin's! I've often occurred to that puddin' since, and wondered what the Squire's wife was a thinkin' of when she made it. I wa'n't obleeged to do no such things in them days, and didn't know how to do anything as well as I do now. Necessity's the mother of invention. Experience is the best teacher after all—"

"Do you sweeten it?"

"Oh, yes, to be sure it needs sugar, the best o' sugar, too; not this wet, soggy, brown sugar. Some folks never think o' usin' good sugar to cook with, but for my part I won't have no other."

"How much sugar do you take?"

"Wal, that depends altogether on whether you calculate to have sass for it—some like sass, you know, and then some, agin don't. So, when I calculate for sass, I don't take so much sugar; and when I don't calculate for sass, I make it sweet enough to eat without sass. Poor Mr. Mudlaw was a great hand for puddin'-sass. I always made it for him—good, rich sass, too. I could afford to have things rich before he was unfortinate in bisness." (Mudlaw went to State's prison for horse-stealing.) "I like sass myself, too; and the curnel and the children are all great sass hands; and so I generally calculate for sass, though Miss Philpot prefers the puddin' without sass, and perhaps *you'd* prefer it without. If so, you must put in sugar accordingly. I always make it a pint to have 'em sweet enough when they're to be eat without sass."

"And don't you use eggs?"

"Certainly, eggs is one o' the principal ingrejiences."

"How many does it require?"

"Wal, when eggs is plenty, I always use plenty; and when they're scarce, why I can do with less, though I'd ruther have enough; and be sure to beat 'em well. It does distress me, the way some folks beat eggs. I always want to have 'em thoroughly beat for everything I use 'em in. It tries my patience most awfully to have anybody round me that won't beat eggs enough. A spell ago we had a darkey to help in the kitchen. One day I was a makin' sponge cake, and havin' occasion to go up stairs after something, I sot her to beatin' the eggs. Wal, what do you think the critter done? Why, she whisked 'em round a few times, and turned 'em right onto the other ingrejiences that I'd got weighed out. When I come back and saw what she'd done, my gracious! I came as nigh to losin' my temper as I ever allow myself to come. 'Twas awful provokin'! I always want the kitchen help to do things as I want to have 'em done. But I never saw a darkey yet that ever done anything right. They're a lazy, slaughterin' set. To think o' her spilin' that cake so, when I'd told her over and over agin that I always made it a pint to have my eggs thoroughly beat!"

"Yes, it was too bad. Do you use fruit in the pudding?"

"Wal, that's jest as you please. You'd better be governed by your own judgment as to *that*. Some like currants and some like raisins, and then agin some don't like nary one. If you use raisins, for pity's sake pick out the stuns. It's awful to have a body's teeth come grindin' onto a raisin stun. I'd rather have my ears boxt any time."

"How many raisins must I take?"

"Wal, not *too* many—it's apt to make the puddin' heavy, you know; and when it's heavy, it ain't so light and good. I'm a great hand—"

"Yes. What do you use for flavouring?"

"There agin you'll have to exercise your own judgment. Some likes one thing, and some another, you know. If you go the hull figger on temperance, why some other kind o' flavourin' 'll do as well as wine or brandy, I s'pose. But whatever you make up your mind to use, be partic'lar to git in a sufficiency, or else your puddin' 'll be flat. I always make it a pint—"

"How long must it bake?"

"There's the great thing after all. The bakin' 's the main pint. A potater puddin', of all puddin's, has got to be baked jest right. For if it bakes a leetle too much, it 's apt to dry it up; and then agin if it don't bake quite enough, it's sure to taste potatory—and that spiles it, you know."

"How long should you think?"

"Wal, that depends a good deal on the heat o' your oven. If you have a very hot oven, 'twon't do to leave it in too long; and if your oven ain't so very hot, why, you'll be necessiated to leave it in longer."

"Well, how can I tell anything about it?"

"Why, I always let 'em bake till I think they're done—that's the safest way. I make it a pint to have 'em baked exactly right. It's very important in all kinds o' bakin'—cake, pies, bread, puddin's, and everything—to have 'em baked *pre*cisely long enough, and jest right. Some folks don't seem to have no system at all about their bakin'. One time they'll burn their bread to a crisp, and then agin it'll be so slack 'tain't fit to eat. Nothing hurts my feelin's so much as to see things overdone or slack-baked. Here only t'other day, Lorry, the girl that Miss Philpot dismissed yesterday, come within an ace o' letting my bread burn up. My back was turned a minnit, and what should she do but go to stuffin' wood into the stove at the awfullest rate. If I hadn't a found it out jest when I did, my bread would a ben spilt as sure as I'm a live woman. Jubiter Rammin! I was about as much decomposed as I ever allow myself to git! I told Miss Philpot I wouldn't stan' it no longer—one of us must quit—either Lorry or me must walk."

"So you've no rule about baking this pudding?"

"No rule!" said Mudlaw, with a look of intense surprise.

"Yes," said Mrs. Darling, "you seem to have no rule for any thing about it."

"No rule!" screamed the indignant cook, starting up, while her red face grew ten times redder, and her little black eyes snapped with rage. "No rules! do *you* tell *me* I've no rule! Me! that's cooked in the first families for fifteen years, and always gin satisfaction, to be told by such as *you* that I hain't no rules!'

ESTELLE ANNA LEWIS.

This well-known and elegant writer is a native of the city of Baltimore Her father, a gentleman of much cultivation, and of liberal fortune, was from the island of Cuba, and was of mixed English and Spanish parentage. At an early age she was sent to the admirable seminary of Mrs. Willard, at Troy, where for several years she was an ambitious and most successful student in all the higher branches of learning; so that she has frequently been pronounced the most thoroughly educated of all the female writers of this country. The late Edgar A. Poe, struck with the classical finish displayed in some of her works which had fallen under his observation, sought her acquaintance, and has left, in his "Literati," an estimate of her acquired abilities equally decided and just.

"She is not only cultivated, as respects the usual acquirements of her sex," he says, "but excels as a modern linguist, and very especially as a classical scholar; while her scientific acquisitions are of no common order. Her occasional translations, from the more difficult portions of Virgil, have been pronounced by our first professors, the best of the kind yet accomplished—a commendation which only a thorough classicist can appreciate in its full extent."

She is mistress of several modern as well as ancient languages, and speaks and writes fluently in French, Spanish, and Italian.

It is as a poetess that Mrs. Lewis is best known; since it is only in poetry that she has published largely under her proper signature. The volumes entitled "Records of the Heart," "The Child of the Sea," "Myths of the Minstrel," attest her fine taste, vigorous imagination, and singular control of all the harmonies of our language.

But in prose she has also written with force, precision, and elegance. Beginning while a school-girl, as a contributor to the "Family Magazine," edited by Solomon Southwick, of Albany, and continuing (after her marriage to S. D. Lewis, Esq., a lawyer of Brooklyn) in the Democratic Review, and other leading journals, she has produced a number and variety of essays, memoirs, and novelettes, altogether surprising. Among her latest productions in this form is a series of sketches of the leading artists of the United States, published in Graham's Magazine, and widely copied. They are models of narration and critical exposition in its most difficult department.

Mrs. Lewis is not less highly esteemed for her personal graces than for her literary eminence; and her hospitable home in Brooklyn is the frequent resort of men and women of genius and accomplishments in letters and the arts, as well as of an enviable circle of friends known only in private society.

IMAGINATION.

Imagination is a complex power. It includes conception or simple apprehension, abstraction, judgment or taste, and fancy. When Milton created his garden of Eden, association suggested to him a vast variety of natural objects; conception placed each of them before him in its rude state; abstraction separated them, while taste made a selection, out of which, by a skilful combination, imagination created a more perfect and beautiful landscape than was ever realized in nature.

Taste and imagination are inseparable. An union of these two powers in the same mind is necessary for the production of every work of genius. Without taste imagination could produce only a random analysis and combination of our conceptions, and without imagination taste would be destitute of the faculty of invention. The one supports the other.

Of all our faculties imagination is the most subservient to mortal happiness. It is the great source of human activity and of human progress. It dwells not on the past. It fills the future with eternal beacons of hope, love, beauty, compensation; and lends to the pilgrim courage to overcome all intervening obstacles to reach the illusive goal of unattainable bliss. Persuasion and illusion are its cardinal virtues—its matchless powers. It closes the eyes of reason, and leads all the other faculties captive. It is the lightning that illumes the sunless paths in the great desert of life,—the master artist of the mind, who hangs the picture galleries of the soul with worlds of its own creation, and dreams that were never realized save in heaven.

Imagination is unlimited. It can create and annihilate, and dispose at pleasure. It seizes upon all materials. It knows no obstacles. It acknowledges no bounds. It plunges into the fiery heart of man—drinks the liquæ vitæ of its arteries, sips at its crystal springs, gathers diamonds from its deserts; fruits, flowers, and sweet music from its oasis, and celestial fires from the bosom of its simoom. It looks not into the eyes—it lists not the voice—it takes no cognisance of the outward features; yet it talks with the soul, with hope, love, sorrow, bliss—lays its finger on the pulse of life, and counts its finest vibrations. It peoples the dark bosoms of mountains with ghouls, goblins, and witches; the trackless forests with tribes of nymphs, sylphs, and fairies; the ocean with sea-gods, green-haired water-nymphs, mermaids, naiads, and leviathans: and amid the thunders of Jove sits on the stars, gathering the fires of heaven. In fine, it peoples every atom of earth, sea, air, with the beings of its own boundless brain, and then fuses them down into its own white fire.

ART.

What is the chief end of high poetry, of high painting, and of high sculpture? Those who argue that information and entertainment constitute their highest aim, deprive them of their divinity. Entertainment and information are not all that the mind requires at the hands of the artist. We wish to be elevated by the contemplation of what is noble; to be warmed by the presence of the heroic, and charmed and made happy by the sight of purity and loveliness. We desire to share in the lofty movements of great minds—to have communion with all their images of what is godlike—and to take a part in the raptures of their love, and in the ecstasies of their innermost beings.

The real value and immortality of the productions of all art, lies in their truth, as embodying the spirit of a particular age, and a faith that lived in men's souls, and worked in their acts—a faith, whose expression and impress time cannot obliterate, but leaves standing, the eternal Mecca of thought, love, imagination—grand, awful, soul-lifting, heart-speaking as the pyramids of Egypt.

We do not propose to consider, in this essay, art with reference to any creed, religious or classic, nor with reference to taste, whether it leans to piety or poetry, to the real or ideal; but simply as art—art the interpreter between nature and man—art evolving to us nature's forms with the utmost truth of imitation, and, at the same time, clothing them with a high significance derived from the human purpose and the human intellect. Art is only perfect when it fills us with the idea of perfection; when it presents to our minds a perfect structure of life, form, action, beauty, heart, soul; when it calls not upon our judgments to supply deficiencies, or to set limits to the bounds of fancy and imagination. This lifting up of the heart and soul, this fulness of satisfaction, this brimming of the bowl of delight, we have never found, save in a few of the old masters.

CAROLINE CHESEBRO'.

MISS CHESEBRO' has been before the public as an author for four or five years, at first by means of short stories in the Magazines and other periodicals, and afterwards by larger publications. Her first volume was a collection of these Magazine stories, under the title of "Dreamland by Daylight," which appeared in 1851. In March, 1852, "Isa, a Pilgrimage," was published. It was a novel of a highly original character, and one which gave rise to the greatest contrariety of opinions, both respecting its merits as a composition, and the revelations it was supposed to make of the social and religious views of its author. The most considerate and impartial judgment of the merits of "Isa" with which we have met, was given by the accomplished critic of Harper's Magazine. We quote the greater part of it, as also the same critic's opinion of her former work.

"In 'Dreamland,'" says this writer, "we find the unmistakeable evidences of originality of mind, an almost superfluous depth of reflection for the department of composition to which it is devoted, a rare facility in seizing the multiform aspects of nature, and a still rarer power of giving them the form and hue of imagination, without destroying their identity. The writer has not yet attained the mastery of expression, corresponding to the liveliness of her fancy and the intensity of her thought. Her style suffers from the want of proportion, of harmony, of artistic modulation, and though frequently showing an almost masculine energy, is destitute of the sweet and graceful fluency which would finely attemper her bold and striking conceptions. We do not allude to this in any spirit of carping censure; but to account for the want of popular effect which, we apprehend, will not be so decided in this volume as in future productions of the author. She has not yet exhausted the golden placers of her genius; but the products will obtain a more active currency when they come refined and brilliant from the mint, with a familiar legible stamp, which can be read by all without an effort."

"Isa," the same reviewer says, "is a more ambitious effort than the former productions of the authoress, displaying a deeper power of reflection, a greater intensity of passion, and a more complete mastery of terse and pointed expression. On the whole, we regard it as a successful specimen of a quite difficult species of composition. Without the aid of a variety of incident or character, with scarcely a sufficient number of events to give a fluent movement to the plot, and with very inconsiderable reference to external nature, the story turns on the development of an abnormal spiritual experience, showing the perils of entire freedom of thought in a powerful, original mind, during the state of intellectual transition between attachment to tradition and the supremacy of individual conviction. The scene is laid in the interior world—the world of consciousness, of reflection, of passion. In this twilight region, so often peopled with monstrous shapes, and spectral phantasms, the author treads with great firmness of step. With rare subtlety of discrimination, she brings hidden springs of action to light, untwisting the tangled webs of experience, and revealing with painful minuteness, some of the darkest and most fearful depths of the human heart. The characters of Isa and Stuart, the leading personages of the story, certainly display uncommon insight and originality. They stand out from the canvass in gloomy, portentous distinctness, with barely light enough thrown upon them to enable us to recognise their weird, mysterious features. For our own part, we should prefer to meet this writer, whose rare gifts we cordially acknowledge, in a more sunny atmosphere; but we are bound to do justice to the depth and vigour of the present too sombre creation."

Miss Chesebro's other publications have been "The Children of Light," in 1852; a book for children in 1853, called "The Little Cross-Bearers;" besides almost continual contributions to the first-class Magazines. She is a native of Canandaigua, New York, at which place she has always resided.

The extract which follows is from the introductory chapter of "Isa."

THE PAUPER CHILD AND THE DEAD WOMAN.

A WOMAN had died in the poor-house; and her funeral was to take place that day. Before her last illness, or rather before its increase unto death, and during all its continuance, till the very night of her death, I had slept in her room, in a state of hushed and terrified, but then to me, unexplainable awe; I lived with her, and helped to attend her during her last days. She had long existed a mere miserable wreck of humanity, hideous to look upon. But she had always been kind to me, and I entertained such a sort of regard, and respect, and feeling for her, as made it very dreadful for me to witness her increased sufferings.

What death really meant I could not clearly understand. They came out from her room that last night, and said, "She is gone!" they said it in such a way as made me shudder. DEAD! I kept thinking the word over and over. GONE—where? She was lying there on the bed. I saw that through a crack in the door to which I crept, when none were by. She certainly was there;—what had gone? She was "dead." Could anything awaken her—could she hear—could she speak still? It was a mystery. I heard some of the other old women talking together—they seemed glad, for some reason, that she was DEAD; that she would never want for anything again, that her sufferings were over, they said. The silence about the house oppressed me; I could hardly breathe in it; it frightened me; and I went off, to get rid of my thoughts, with the other children, to a playhouse in a corner of the yard. But, before noon, I got tired of them; I could think of nothing but the DEAD old woman. It seemed wrong in me to think of anything else. She used to call me child, and dear, sometimes, and I loved her for that, if for no other reason. They were at dinner; I did not want to eat, so I went and hung around the door of the chamber where she still was sleeping. Wondering yet, and continually, what Death meant, and if she were happy, and if *I* should ever be happy, and, if so, would I be happy before I died, and if people could die whenever they wished to do so. Suddenly an uncontrollable desire seized me. I would find it all out at once. I would ask mammy! she could tell me what I wanted to know; she was dead—she must know all about it!

I went softly into the room, and shut the door after me. Then I paused a moment, in doubt, for she was not lying on that bed in the corner of the room, where she had lain ever since I could recollect; but near the bed there was a high table, and a board upon it, and that was covered with a cloth. Something told me she must be there; I had often seen her sleeping with the bed-clothes drawn over her head. I went up to the table carrying a chair with me, for I was bent on knowing all about it now. I placed the chair close beside the table, and then stood upon it, and uncovered her face. The sight that met my eyes took away my breath for a moment; I had never seen anything like it before, and her appearance startled me beyond measure. It was a horrid spectacle. The recollection makes me tremble to this day. If I had never seen another corpse, that remembrance would tempt me to say, how horrible, as well as how wonderful, is death! Her face was always pale, but not of that hue—and it was always wrinkled, and had an ugly look, yet she was not ugly; there was now a fixedness, a rigidity, in the wrinkles and the colourless face, that made it awful beyond imagination. It struck such a chill, such a horror through me, that for many minutes, in my astonishment and terror, I forgot to ask what I intended. Then again I recollected the object with which I went there, and said:—

"Mammy, are you happy? Do you sleep good?"

No answer. I would have one. I had broken the awful silence, and was not to be quieted again. That silence, at least, could not chill me to quiet; it the rather hurried me on in my questioning. They would be coming back, and I must hear from her lips what I longed to know.

"Mammy," I said, "do you have hateful dreams? Do you know what's going on here? Can you tell me what they're going to do with you? Mammy! wont you look at me? Are you sorry they moved you from the other bed? Oh, do say something!"

I stooped over her; I had at first spoken in a whisper, but the last query was made in a loud voice. I bent further down—my face touched hers! God! what an embrace was that! The chair on which I stood, slipped, in my impetuous movement; I fell, and —fainted!

When my consciousness returned, the corpse had been removed, but the broken board, and overturned chair, and table, told me what a sight must have been presented to the people when they came into that room.

ELIZA FARRAR.

THIS estimable writer is the wife of Professor John Farrar, of Harvard University. Her writings have been prompted evidently by the aim to be useful, rather than by love of notoriety or fame. They have been directed chiefly to the improvement of her own sex and of the young. The titles of some of these useful volumes are, "The Children's Robinson Crusoe," "The Life of Lafayette," "The Life of Howard," "Youth's Letter Writer." But the work, beyond all others, by which she is most extensively and most favourably known, is "The Young Lady's Friend." It was first published in 1837, and it has gone through a very large number of editions, both here and in England. It is a manual of practical advice to young ladies on their entering upon the active duties of life, after leaving school. It contains no flights of fancy, or attempts at fine writing, but for sound, practical sense, expressed in good English, and in a style perfectly adapted to the subject, it is a work worthy of Hannah More or Maria Edgeworth.

BROTHERS AND SISTERS.

If your brothers are younger than you are, encourage them to be perfectly confidential with you; win their friendship by your sympathy in all their concerns, and let them see that their interests and their pleasures are liberally provided for in the family arrangements. Never disclose their little secrets, however unimportant they seem to you; never pain them by an ill-timed joke; never repress their feelings by ridicule; but be their tenderest friend, and then you may become their ablest adviser. If separated from them by the course of school or college education, make a point of keeping up your intimacy by full, free, and affectionate correspondence; and when they return home, at that awkward age between youth and manhood, when reserve creeps over the mind like an impenetrable veil, suffer it not to interpose between you and your brothers. Cultivate their friendship and intimacy with all the address and tenderness you possess; for it is of unspeakable importance to them that their sisters should be their confidential friends. Consider the loss of a ball or party, for the sake of making the evening pass pleasantly to your brothers at home, as a small sacrifice,—as one you should unhesitatingly make. If they go into company with you, see that they are introduced to the most desirable acquaintances, and show them that you are interested in their enjoying themselves.

If you are so happy as to have elder brothers, you should be equally assiduous in cultivating their friendship, though the advances must of course be differently made. As they have long been accustomed to treat you as a child, you may meet with some repulses when you aspire to become a companion and friend; but do not be discouraged by this. The earlier maturity of girls will soon render you their equal in sentiment, if not in knowledge, and your ready sympathy will soon convince them of it. They will be agreeably surprised when they find their former plaything and messenger become their quick-sighted and intelligent companion, understanding at a glance what is passing in their heart; and love and confidence on your part will soon be repaid in kind. Young men often feel the want of a confidential friend of the softer sex, to sympathize with them in their little affairs of sentiment, and happy are those who find one in a sister.

Once possessed of an elder brother's confidence, spare no pains to preserve it; convince him, by the little sacrifices of personal convenience and pleasure which you are willing to make for him, that when you do oppose his wishes, it is on principle, and for conscience' sake; then you will be a blessing to him, and even when differing from you, he will love and respect you the more for your adherence to a high standard.

So many temptations beset young men, of which young women know nothing, that it is of the utmost importance that your brothers' evenings should be happily passed at home, that their friends should be your friends, that their engagements should be the same as yours, and that various innocent amusements should be provided for them in the family circle. Music is an accomplishment chiefly valuable as a home enjoyment, as rallying round the piano the various members of a family, and harmonizing their hearts as well as voices, particularly in devotional strains. I know no more agreeable and interesting spectacle, than that of brothers and sisters playing and singing together those elevated compositions in music and poetry, which gratify the taste and purify the heart, while their fond parents sit delighted by.

Sisters should be always willing to walk, ride, visit with their brothers, and esteem it a privilege to be their companions. It is worth while to learn innocent games for the sake of furnishing brothers with amusement, and making home the most agreeable place to them.

If your brothers take an interest in your personal appearance and dress, you should encourage the feeling by consulting their taste, and sacrificing any little fancy of your own to a decided dislike of theirs. Brothers will generally be found strongly opposed to the slightest indecorum in sisters; even those who look with indifference upon freedom of manners in other girls, have very strict notions with regard to their own sisters. Their intercourse with all sorts of men enables them to judge of the constructions put upon certain actions, and modes of dress and speech, much better than women can; and you will do well to take their advice on all such points.

Sisters should as scrupulously regard each other's rights of property as they would those of a guest staying in the house; they should never help themselves without leave to the working materials, writing implements, drawing apparatus, books, or clothing of each other. It is a mistake to suppose that the nearness of the relationship makes it allowable; the more intimate our connexion with any one, the more necessary it is to guard ourselves against taking unwarrantable liberties. For the very reason that you are obliged to be so much together, you should take care to do nothing disagreeable to each other.

Love is a plant of delicate growth, and though it sometimes springs up spontaneously, it will never flourish long and well without careful culture. When I see how it is treated in some families, my wonder is, not that it does not spread so as to overshadow the whole circle, but that any sprig of it should survive the rude treatment it meets with.

Genuine politeness is a great fosterer of family love; it allays accidental irritation, by preventing harsh retorts and rude contradictions; it softens the boisterous, stimulates the indolent, suppresses selfishness, and, by forming a habit of consideration for others, harmonizes the whole. Politeness begets politeness, and brothers may easily be won by it to leave off the rude ways they bring home from school or college. Never receive any little attention without thanking them for it, never ask a favour of them but in cautious terms, never reply to their questions in monosyllables, and they will soon be ashamed to do such things themselves. You should labour, by precept and example, to convince them that no one can have really good manners abroad, who is not habitually polite at home.

HANNAH F. LEE.

THE work of Mrs. Lee which has been the most extensively and permanently popular, is the "Three Experiments of Living." It was published in 1838, and it has gone through about thirty editions in this country, besides numerous editions in England. Besides this, she has published a novel, called "Grace Seymour," and a large number of juvenile books, to none of which, however, she has put her name.

Mrs. Lee's writings are pervaded throughout with a tone of good sense, and a desire to be useful. She is a keen observer of the follies of social life, and in pruning its excrescences she does not hesitate to apply the knife freely. She is animated, however, by a spirit of true Christian benevolence; and her writings have been as useful as they have been popular.

Mrs. Lee is a native of Newburyport, Massachusetts, and she resides at present in Boston.

The extracts are from the "Three Experiments of Living."

BEGINNING LIFE.

Most young physicians begin life with some degree of patronage, but Frank Fulton had none; he came to the city a stranger, from the wilds of Vermont, fell in love with Jane Churchwood,— uncle Joshua's niece,—a man whom nobody knew, and whose independence consisted in limiting his wants to his means. What little he could do for Jane, he cheerfully did. But after all necessary expenses were paid, the young people had but just enough between them to secure their first quarter's board, and place a sign on the corner of the house, by special permission, with *Doctor Fulton* handsomely inscribed upon it. The sign seemed to excite but little attention,— as nobody called to see the owner of it,—though he was at home every hour in the day.

After a week of patient expectation, which could not be said to pass heavily,—for they worked, read, and talked together,—Frank thought it best to add to the sign, *Practises for the poor gratis*. At the end of a few days another clause was added, *Furnishes medicines to those who cannot afford to pay for them.* In a very short time, the passers by stopped to spell out the words, and Frank soon began to reap the benefit of this addition. Various applications were made, and though they did not as yet promise any increase of revenue, he was willing to pay for the first stepping-stone. What had begun, however, from true New England *calculation*, was continued from benevolence. He was introduced to scenes of misery, that made him forget all but the desire of relieving the wretchedness he witnessed; and when he related to his young and tender-hearted wife, the situation in which he found a mother confined to her bed, with two or three helpless children crying around her for bread, Jane would put on her straw bonnet, and follow him with a light step to the dreary abode. The first quarter's board came round; it was paid, and left them nearly penniless. There is something in benevolent purpose, as well as in industry, that cheers and supports the mind. Never was Jane's step lighter, nor her smile gayer, than at present. But this could not last; the next quarter's board must be provided,—and how? Still the work of mercy went on, and did not grow slack.

LIVING BEYOND THE MEANS.

JANE was not behind Mrs. Bradish, in costume or figure. Every morning, at the hour for calls, she was elegantly attired for visiters. Many came from curiosity. Mrs. Hart congratulated her dear friend, on seeing her moving in a sphere for which it was evident nature intended her. Mrs. Reed cautioned her against any *mauvaise honte*, that might remind one of former times. Others admired her furniture and arrangements, without any sly allusions. On one of these gala mornings, uncle Joshua was ushered into the room. Jane was fortunately alone, and she went forward and offered two fingers with a cordial air, but whispered to the servant, "if any one else called while he was there, to say she was engaged." She had scrupulously observed her promise, of never sending word she was not at home. There was a mock kind of deference in his air and manner that embarrassed Jane.

"So," said he, looking round him, "we have a palace here!"

"The house we were in was quite too small, now that our children are growing so large," replied Jane.

"They must be greatly beyond the common size," said uncle Joshua, "if that house could not hold them."

"It was a very inconvenient one; and we thought, as it was a monstrous rent, it would do better to take another. Then, after we had bought this, it certainly was best to furnish it comfortably, as it was for life."

"Is it paid for?" asked uncle Joshua, dryly.

Jane hesitated.

"Paid for? O certainly; that is,—yes, sir."

"I am glad to hear it; otherwise, I much doubt if it is taken for life."

Jane was silent.

"Very comfortable," said uncle Joshua; "that is a comfortable glass for your husband to shave by; and those are comfortable curtains, to keep out the sun and cold." Both of these articles were strikingly elegant. "That is a comfortable lamp that hangs in the middle of the room; it almost puts out my eyes with its glass danglers. Times are strangely altered, Jane, since you and I thought such comforts necessary.

"Frank has been very successful in his speculations, uncle; he does not now depend on his profession for a living; indeed, he thinks it his duty to live as other people do, and place his wife and children upon an equality with others."

"And what do you call an equality,—living as luxuriously, and wasting as much time, as they do? Dwelling in as costly apartments, and forgetting there is any other world than this? When you were left to my care, and your dear mother was gone from us, how often I lamented that I could not supply her place,—that I could not better talk to you of another world, to which she had gone; but then, Jane, I comforted myself that I knew something of the duties that belonged to this, and that if I faithfully instructed you in these, I should be preparing you for another. When I saw you growing up, dutiful and humble, charitable, self-denying, sincere, and a conscientious disciple of truth, then I felt satisfied that all was well. But I begin now to fear that it was a shortsighted kind of instruction,—that it had not power enough to enable us to hold fast to what is right. I begin now to see that we must have motives that do not depend on the praise or censure of this world,—motives that must have nothing to do with it."

CAROLINE THOMAS.

MISS THOMAS (if indeed that be a real name—which has been publicly doubted) is known to the world only as the author of "Farmingdale," a novel, in two volumes, published in 1854. The work has not as yet created what is called a sensation. It is quiet in its tone, and it has not been ushered upon the public with any of that "pomp and circumstance" now so common. But the impression, so far as we have heard, of every one who has read the work, is, that it must, sooner or later, win its way into general notice, and that the author, whoever she be, is one who will certainly make her mark.

"Farmingdale" is thoroughly indigenous, every page and paragraph being redolent of its native soil. It is a tale of New England domestic life, in its incidents and manners so true to nature and so free from exaggeration, and in its impulses and motives throughout so throbbing with the real American heart, that we seem ourselves to have seen, twenty times over, just such woods and skies, and to have known by scores just such men and women, and children, too, as those described by the author of "Farmingdale."

The story is very simple in plot, and rather bare of incident. The author evidently relies for her effects more upon the direct force of truth and nature, than upon that artificial interest which grows out of complexity of plan, and multiplicity of actors. This is subjecting her work to a severe test. But it can bear the ordeal. The story abounds in scenes of absorbing interest. The narrative is everywhere delightfully clear and straight-forward, flowing forth towards its conclusion, like a gentle and limpid stream, between graceful hillsides and verdant meadows. In the conception and delineation of character, Miss Thomas is bold and clear, always individualizing perfectly. In the delicate appreciation of what is beautiful, whether in human character or in circumstances and events, in the skilful grouping of incidents, and in all those numberless graces of style and diction which give finish and tone to a work of fiction, the author of "Farmingdale" has shown herself a true artist.

To understand the extract which follows, it is necessary to say, that Mary and Tommy Lester were two orphan children, living at a farm house, with their only surviving relation, a hard-hearted old aunt. It is a fair specimen of the author's style of description and narration.

TRIALS.

The garret of a country farm-house has been so often and so ably described—its time-stained, weather-beaten walls, its dark rafters, dim recesses, and shadowy corners, have figured upon so many a page of story and romance, that it is not necessary to paint them here. Suffice it to say, that this was a large, low room, lighted at either end by a semicircular window, and containing its full share of old clothes and empty barrels. Strings of seed-corn, dried apples, and red peppers hung upon the walls, together with huge bunches of dried herbs, and paper bags filled with sage and summer-savory. A large rope was securely fastened across one corner, and upon it were arranged the feather-beds, for which the family found no use during the summer. There was a broken reel, a pair of swifts that looked as if they had seen hard service, and a spinning-wheel.

But what more immediately concerned Tommy, was a large blue and white blanket filled with wool, and fastened together by long, sharp thorns, in lieu of pins. It lay on the floor in one corner, but Mrs. Graham hauled it into the middle of the room, directly in the range of the two windows, pulled out the thorns, and straightened the blanket. Then she spread a clean sheet at a little distance, and looked about her, seemingly in search of something else. Presently she spied a small box, turned up against the wall, and bringing that, she placed it bottom side up between the two.

"There, Tommy, you set down on that box, and go to picking this wool. Put what you pick in this sheet."

"I don't know how to pick it," said Tommy, looking dubiously at the immense (so it appeared to his eyes) pile before him.

"You don't? Well, it won't take me long to show you. You must take a handful—so—and pull each lock apart in this way; and when you find any burs, or any ticks, or anything, you must be sure to get them all out."

"What are *ticks?*" asked Tommy.

"There's one; that little brown thing."

"Is it alive?"

"'Twon't bite, if 'tis. Come, don't take hold so carefully, as if you was afraid of dirtying your fingers. Be spry."

She stood watching Tommy for a while, as he pursued his task, rather awkwardly at first, but more adroitly as he became familiar with the *modus operandi*, and then left him to go on with it alone.

Tommy did not like his new business remarkably. It was dull and lonesome up there in the old garret, with nothing but the rats, that occasionally made him start as they scampered about in the walls, to keep him company. Still, for two or three days he bore it very well. It was a change, and all children like that. Once in a while Mary would steal away from her own work, and pay him a flying visit, just long enough to speak a few cheering words, or to give him a kiss, and sometimes more substantial aliment in the shape of an apple or a doughnut. But this was not often.

One morning she noticed that he did not eat much breakfast, and that his eyes looked dull and heavy. He hung about while the table was being cleared, as if reluctant to go to his task, but said nothing. Pretty soon Mrs. Graham came in from the garden, with vegetables for dinner.

"Mercy, Tommy! ain't you to work yet? Go right straight along up stairs—quick!"

Tommy hesitated for a minute, "I've got a headache, aunt Betsy—a hard one."

"Nonsense! You always have a headache when a body wants to get any work out of you. Go along; you'll be just as well off up there as down here, if it does ache."

The child obeyed in silence; but Mary caught a glimpse of his face as he turned to go up stairs, and its expression made her heart ache all the forenoon. She tried to find a spare moment in which she might run up and see how he was. It was an unusually busy day with her, however, and she did not succeed.

When the horn was blown for dinner, he came down, looking pale and sad; but as he made no complaint, Mary said nothing to him about his head. She had long ago learned that it is seldom worth while to remind a child that it does not feel well. He came to the table with the rest, ate a few mouthfuls, and then pushed his plate back with an air of disgust.

"What's the matter with your victuals, Tom?" asked Mrs. Graham.

"Nothing; only I don't like pork and beans, nor beets either. They make me sick. I wish I could have some bread and milk."

"Well, you ain't a-going to: if you can't eat what's on the table, you can go without your dinner. You needn't be so mighty particular."

Tommy swallowed a few mouthfuls of dry bread, and left the table. He walked about in the yard until the men were done eating, and then Mrs. Graham called him, and sent him up stairs again.

"And you must hurry with that wool, Tommy," she said; "I want it out of the way just as quick as ever it can be."

The garret was intensely hot. The fervid August sun beat directly down upon the roof; one window was partly open, but it seemed to give admission to scarce a breath of air. Tommy climbed up on an inverted barrel, and tried to unfasten the window opposite. It resisted all his efforts, and he returned wearily to his little seat again, and his fingers resumed their monotonous employment. He glanced at the open window. He could see the tops of the cherry-trees waving in the light breeze that might not reach his burning brow. On the loftiest branch a little bird swayed to and fro, chirruping merrily. Occasionally, as the breeze freshened, he could hear the rustling of the leaves; and when it died away, the faint murmur of the creek would reach his ear, filling his little heart with a feverish longing to bathe in its cool waters. But that was only when he listened intently. For the most part of the time he heard nothing but the creaking of an old window-shutter, that swung lazily on its rusty hinges. The sound became inexpressibly annoying to him. He was exceedingly afraid of thunder: yet the wildest war of the elements would have been a relief to him.

His seat was hard, and there was nothing to support his back. He wondered if he couldn't fix it somehow, and that diverted his thoughts for a few moments. There was an old cushion peeping out from beneath some rubbish in one corner. With a good deal of effort he succeeded in pulling it out and carrying it to his seat; he laid it on the box, and sat down to try the effect.

"There, that's nice," he said: "now if I only had something to lean against, I should be fixed. Oh, there's a bigger box: that will do, if I can only get it here."

He dragged the box from its place, and set it up in the required position. But when he attempted to lean against it, it was not sufficiently heavy, and his weight pushed it back. What should he do now? Not give it up; he was in no mood for that. Looking about him, he spied some billets of wood that had been carried there, doubtless for some wise purpose; and, one by one, he brought them and put them in the box.

"This goes better, a great deal," said Tommy. "Now I can lean my head against it, and I guess it won't ache so hard."

It did not; but his comparatively easy position, and the dull drowsy nature of his work, were too much for him. Slowly his head drooped upon one side, his fingers grew still, and then, with a sudden start, he straightened himself up, and put them in motion again.

Of course, all this was not accomplished without some noise. The shoving of the large box across the floor was distinctly heard in the kitchen.

"Hark!" exclaimed Mrs. Graham, "what is all that racket? I am sure it comes from the garret. I'll bet a shilling that boy plays half his time."

She wanted very much to go immediately and learn the cause of the disturbance. But she was working butter, and could not conveniently leave it. As soon, however, as she had packed it down, and put away her various utensils, she washed her hands and went up the first pair of stairs. Softly opening the door at the foot of those that led to the garret, she listened for a minute. If Tommy was in any mischief, he was very still about it; but she thought she would go on and see what he had been doing.

She mounted the stairs, and it was a moment or two before her eyes became accustomed to the dim light of the garret—dim, at least, when compared with that of the lower parts of the house—so as to admit of her seeing anything. Gradually one object after another became visible, and she saw Tommy lying, half upon his seat, half on the pile of wool, fast asleep!

Angrily she strode across the floor, grasped the little fellow by one arm, and raising him from his impromptu couch, shook him violently.

Frightened and bewildered, the child did not speak nor cry, but stared about as if his senses were forsaking him.

"What are you doing there, you lazy little imp?—going to sleep on the wool, instead of picking it—eh? I've caught you finely this time. There, take that, and that, and that," and she brought her broad hand heavily against one side of his head and then the other, several times in succession. "How did you dare go to sleep when I sent you up here to work—eh?"

Tommy was fairly stunned by the heavy blows. His sudden awakening, too, had caused his old headache to return, with redoubled strength, and every nerve in his body thrilled with pain. He did not utter a word.

"Answer me, when I speak to you, Tom Lester, if you know what's good for yourself. What made you go to sleep?"

Tommy did not answer. It seemed to him that he could not.

"Answer me!" and Mrs. Graham's hand was again raised.

He shrank from the threatened blow.

"Don't strike me again, aunt Betsy. I couldn't help it!"

His aunt's eye was roving about the room.

"No wonder you couldn't. What's this cushion doing here?"

"I got it to sit on," said Tommy. "The box was so hard."

"So hard! And what's this for?"

"For me to lean against. My head ached, and my back. I feel sick, aunt Betsy; and it's so hot!"

"I think it's very likely," said Mrs. Graham, mockingly; "being woke up don't agree with you. But I guess you'll get over it. Now, put these things back where they belong, and then see if you can sit up straight, and attend to your work. And don't you let me catch you asleep again. If you do, it will be the worse for you."

She remained in the garret while the cushion, billets of wood, and box were being restored to their respective places, and until Tommy was again seated on *his* box. Then, with an admonitive warning, she descended the stairs.

Half an hour afterwards, Mary went up to her own room after a clean apron, and while taking it from the closet shelf, she thought she heard a low, suppressed sobbing from the garret. Up she flew, to see what was the matter.

Tommy was at work, picking his wool with busy fingers; but tears were chasing each other down his cheeks, and he did not stop to wipe them away. As he raised his eyes and saw Mary, he dropped the wool, and sprang eagerly into her arms.

"Oh, Mary, Mary!" he sobbed, "you haven't been to see me once in all this long day!"

"I know it, Tommy darling; but I have been just as busy as I could be, every single minute. What makes you cry so, dear?" and she tenderly smoothed back his brown curls, and kissed his little tear-stained face.

But he only cried the more.

"Oh, my head aches so badly, Mary, and I am so tired! I did not mean to go to sleep, but aunt Betsy boxed my ears very hard."

Mary did not know what he meant, but by a little skilful questioning she drew the whole story from him. An indignant flush mounted to her brow, and she clasped him closer to her breast.

ELLEN LOUISE CHANDLER.

It is something of an achievement for a young woman, at the age of only nineteen, to have written a book of nearly five hundred pages, of which a second edition was called for and printed, in less than three months from the date of the first. Such has been Miss Chandler's first experience of literary adventure.

She was born at Pomfret, Connecticut, in the year 1835, at which place she has always continued to reside. The influences that have been at work in moulding her mind and character, can best be judged from a sketch of her early years communicated by herself to the Editor, from which he is permitted to make the following extract.

"I commenced my school education," says Miss Chandler, "at the age of two years, and, during the period that followed, I was in no wise distinguished from other fun-loving, school-disturbing little girls. My amusements, it is true, were of a different character, but this fact arose from the circumstance of my being an only child. Casting my eyes outward from my window, I can see where the morning sunshine kisses the grave of my baby brother. Long before his feet had learned to tread the steep paths of earth, God gave him wings, wherewith to climb the stairs of Heaven. After that, I was alone. Had I been of a less imaginative temperament, this early loneliness might have soured my temper, and embittered my life. As it was, I found plenty of ideal companions. Before I could guide a pen, I used to weave romances. I remember, when I was four years old, to have carried in my head for weeks an embryo epic, entitled "The Spanish Knight," to which I was daily making additions. I used to gather pale, blue-eyed flowers, and tend them carefully, fancying they were young girls, fading with consumption. A feather, or even a sprig from the northern pine-tree, would suffice for a hero, and I was never lonely when surrounded by the creations of my fancy.

"I formed friendships with the patient stars, or the black storm-clouds, sweeping the sky like contending armies; but of all the voices of my childhood, none spoke to me so lovingly as the winds. I believed, in those days, that they blew right out of Heaven, from under the very foot-stool of Alla's throne; and listening to them, with my ear at the key-hole of an outside door opening to the north, I believed that I was hearing the secrets of the stars, that

"It was the Spirit of the Flood that spoke,
And he called on the Spirit of the Fell."

"It was (or rather, it is, for I reside here still) a beautiful home, where I lived with my parents. I cannot conceive a more delightful dwelling-place for a child, whose worship for the beautiful amounted to a passion, whose very soul thrilled a response to all the voices of nature. I raise my eyes—a landscape lies spread before me, so fair, description could not realize half its charms. A low murmur steals to my ear, from subterranean fountains, and, to the eastward, lies the valley of the Quinebaug, distinguished for an appearance I have never seen elsewhere. It is a kind of phantom-sea. A mist rises from the valley, so heavy that strangers always mistake it for a large pond; but to *me* it is a mighty sea, whereon spectral ships are sailing, and the skeleton at the helm talks to the skeleton at the prow.

"I have grown up among the sights and sounds of nature, and my soul leans lovingly toward them. There is something in the very atmosphere of a city which seems to stifle me. My heart *needs* the blue sky, the green fields, and the free breath of the country breezes. My life has been passed for the most part in my quiet home, though I have had no small share of boarding-school experience. But the teacher to whom, most of all, my gratitude is due, is the Rev. Dr. Park, now President of Racine College, and formerly, for some years, Professor in the University of Pennsylvania. For five years I was his pupil, and his kind hands opened for me the gates of classic antiquity.

"From him, I learned to love all that was grand and beautiful in the folios of the past, and the ancient and modern languages which I acquired under his tuition are daily opening to my eager gaze new mines of richness. I have in a great degree, however, been my own instructor. That is, I have been allowed for the most part, in my whole course of education, to follow the bent of my erratic and poetical fancy. If I learned geography, it was always with a map and a pencil, tracing out the mountain sources of mysterious rivers, or building huts for South-sea Islanders, in imaginary groves of banyans. I studied mathematics, with an undefined sense of companionship with grim old Egyptian sages, and faces like the model for a Sphinx. I worshipped the stars, over my astronomy, with the devotion of a Chaldean, and rendered the Latin hexameters of my Virgil into English heroics.

"I commenced writing for publication nearly four years since, at the age of fifteen, and my efforts were confined to the poetical corner of my favourite papers. A year later, I commenced to furnish prose contributions to the periodicals, over the signature of "Ellen Louise." I have not written for fame or fortune, but because I love to write, and cannot help it, any more than the free thrush in the cherry-tree at my window can help his singing."

Miss Chandler's first volume was issued in May, 1854, and had such immediate success that a new edition was called for in August. It is a collection of stories, essays, reveries, and poems, under the odd but appropriate title of "This, That, and the Other." These pieces give evidence of an extraordinary compass of thought and of reading, for one so young, a command of expression ordinarily attained only after long years of apprenticeship at the trade of authorship, a wild and frolicsome play of fancy that soberer years will probably tame, and occasional touches of pathos and tragedy that the stern realities of life all too soon will deepen. Miss Chandler is yet in the heyday of life, and the offering she brings is redolent of spring and flowers. The mellowed fruits of autumn will come in their season.

"I CANNOT MAKE HIM DEAD."

HUSH! tread very lightly! The long shadows stretch across the floor, the canary is silent in the window, the air seems heavy with the perfume of the violets you hold in your hand.

There he lies,—your little Charlie! Yes, yours, for Charlie's mother has gone to sleep. They put her down in the cold, dark earth, in the gray of a winter's morning; daisies grow over her grave now, and wild birds, southern birds, with gay, brilliant wings, sing over her. Charley is yours.

Watch him as he sleeps. The eye is like yours when it opens, but the blue-veined lid that closes over it is his mother's. Those lips are hers! Do you remember how they trembled when you first told her your love, and how in long years they only parted to breathe for you words of gentle kindness? Sometimes you were impatient, petulant. O, how you repented it when it was too late! But nothing had power to dim the love-light in those clear blue eyes—nothing! not even death itself, for her last words were a blessing, when she died, and—gave you Charlie. O, how you have loved that boy! You have watched the breath of heaven, lest it fall too roughly on his cheek. You have buttoned your coat around you, as you turned homeward, after a profitable speculation, saying to yourself, "Yes, he shall be rich, my Charlie."

But there came days when there was no little foot to meet you on the stair, no childish voice to whisper welcome.

The room, your room and Charlie's, was hushed and still; the nurse stepped softly; the whip you bought him hung upon the wall, and Charlie could only whisper faint words of thanks for the flowers or fruit you brought him as you hurried homeward. Now you have come once more to look upon him, as he slumbers. It is fearful, all this stillness. "Charlie," you say, "Charlie!" Slowly the blue-veined lids uprise; the dark eyes—your eyes—look up to your other eyes.

Strange how bright they are! You put the violets in that tiny hand. He clasps them closely, but he whispers, "Papa, mamma has been singing me to sleep, and now she's calling me. Kiss me, papa!" and with that last, fond kiss your little boy's eyes close, and the white dimpled hands tighten over the fresh flowers.

No need to step softly, lest you waken him. His mother guards her boy! No, no—you need not sob, or groan. Bear a brave heart, man!

Do you hear that carriage in the street? Do you hear the town-clock strike, and the church-bells peal? The world is going onward, brisk, lively, smiling as ever, with the joy-pulse beating at its great heart; and you, what are you, that you should make your moan, sitting there in the silence, holding your dead boy to your breast?

"You cannot make him dead," you say, and small need! The earth was a cold soil for your fair flower to grow in.

The great Gardener has transplanted it to the ever-blooming gardens of Paradise. He is yours still! You have but nursed an angel for heaven! You have held him on your lap, cradled him in your arms, and when you have hushed him to rest laid him down on the bosom of Jesus. No, to you, Charlie "is not dead, but sleepeth!"

THE END.

E. B. MEARS, STEREOTYPER. C. SHERMAN, PRINTER.

www.ingramcontent.com/pod-product-compliance
Lightning Source LLC
LaVergne TN
LVHW021257110826
845150LV00003B/414

* 9 7 8 1 4 2 5 5 6 0 9 9 7 *